Work for Giants

CIVIL WAR SOLDIERS AND STRATEGIES

BRIAN S. WILLS, SERIES EDITOR

Richmond Must Fall: The Richmond-Petersburg Campaign, October 1864

HAMPTON NEWSOME

Work for Giants: The Campaign and Battle of Tupelo/Harrisburg, Mississippi,
June–July 1864

THOMAS E. PARSON

Work for Giants

The Campaign and Battle of Tupelo/Harrisburg,

Mississippi, June–July 1864

Thomas E. Parson

Foreword by Timothy B. Smith

The Kent State University Press

Kent, Ohio

First paperback edition, 2024

Library of Congress Catalog Card Number 2014015057
ISBN 978-1-60635-476-6 (paper)
ISBN 978-1-60635-222-9 (cloth)
Manufactured in the United States of America

Library of Congress Cataloging-in-Publication Data
Parson, Thomas E., 1960–
Work for giants : the Campaign and Battle of Tupelo/Harrisburg, Mississippi,
June–July, 1864 / Thomas E. Parson ; foreword by Timothy B. Smith.
pages cm. — (Civil War soldiers and strategies)
Includes bibliographical references.
ISBN 978-1-60635-222-9 (hardcover) ∞
1. Tupelo, Battle of, Tupelo, Miss., 1864. I. Title.
E476.84.P37 2014
973.7'37—dc23
2014015057

28 27 26 25 24   5 4 3

To Charlie, my mother and friend
1934–2012

What does a soldier know about war?

I went into the army a light-hearted boy, with a face as smooth as a girl's and hair as brown as my beautiful mother's. I fought through more than a score of battles and romped through more than a hundred frolics. I had the rollicking time of my life and came home stronger than an athlete, with robust health builded to last the rest of my life. And my mother, her brown hair silvered with the days of my soldiering, held me in her arms and counted the years of her longing and watching with kisses. When she lifted her dear face I saw the story of my marches and battles written there in lines of anguish. If a mother should write her story of war, she would pluck a white hair from her temple, and dip the living stylus into the chalice of her tears, to write the diary of the days upon her heart.

What does a soldier know about war?

   —Pvt. Robert J. Burdette, *The Drums of the 47th*

Contents

Foreword

I first met Tom Parson fifteen years ago, when he and I both arrived at Shiloh National Military Park about the same time. Since then I have come to know him as a jack of all trades. He is probably one of only a few people—and certainly the only person I know—who can run the engine room of a mighty warship, maintain a national cemetery, and write good history.

Indeed, Tom is one of our unsung national heroes, having served in and retired as a chief petty officer from the United States Navy, where he manned the engine rooms in the bowels of many a ship. His performance of duty in a changing world at the end of the Cold War as well as in more recent conflicts, including his wartime service in the Gulf War, deserves our thanks. But Tom is also mindful of other veterans who came before him, particularly those who gave the "last full measure of devotion" for our nation. The manner in which he oversaw and groomed the Shiloh National Cemetery in his many years of service there is evidence of this and is similarly commendable.

It is through Tom's love and study of history, however, that I have come to know him best. As an avid Civil War historian who wrote his first book on the California Hundred of the 2nd Massachusetts Cavalry while still aboard ship, Tom and I have spent many hours studying, debating, and discussing the war, particularly Shiloh and Corinth. As next-door neighbors for many years, living in park housing behind the visitor center at Shiloh, we've had many opportunities to tramp the battlefield and learn together. And in his new interpretive work at the Corinth Civil War Interpretive Center (still under the Shiloh National Military Park), he has similarly immersed himself in the history of that town and campaign. Tom has put his historical skills to work in other writings, including this book as well as numerous articles for such publications as *Blue and Gray*. The National Park Service is fortunate to have Tom in its stable of historians.

Similarly, my association with the Tupelo campaign has had a trajectory comparable to my friendship with Tom, mostly emanating from my association with its history. Growing up in Mississippi, and for a time living near Tupelo itself, I often passed the marked battlefield and urbanized actual sites and wondered what it must have been like then. As I developed into a historian and came to have more than an inquisitive interest in Mississippi's Civil War heritage, I came to appreciate the importance of the summer 1864 raids into the state. And when I learned that I had a great-great-great-grandfather as a first lieutenant in the 6th Mississippi Cavalry at Tupelo, my interest became even more acute.

Yet, I learned little of the battle or campaign, simply because there was pitifully little written on it. The standard source then, and indeed until now, was Ed Bearss's *Forrest at Brice's Cross Roads*, which was very well done. Still, that book was written in the 1970s, and Tupelo was included among other raids, such as the more famous Brice's Cross Roads effort. Tupelo has long deserved a solid, modern, academic treatment in and of itself.

Thus, my excitement grew when I learned my good friend Tom Parson had decided to work on a book on the battle that had so long intrigued me. The result has been worth the wait, and this book definitely meets all expectations. Putting the summer 1864 Union raids into north Mississippi in the correct military context while describing the action in a gripping narrative, Tom has produced what will become the standard work on the battle. I have thoroughly enjoyed learning about a battle and campaign that so little is known about but that held so much importance at the time, and I am positive that readers of *Work for Giants* will come away with the same feeling.

Timothy B. Smith
University of Tennessee at Martin

Preface

This book started as a simple research project that I hoped would someday evolve into a magazine article. It turned into something more and is actually at the very heart of my study of the war. I have lived in Corinth for most of the last decade and have developed a passion for studying that part of the war that extends for about a hundred miles in every direction from my home. It began with my work at Shiloh and later extended to Corinth and then to the battlefields of Iuka, Holly Springs, Brice's Crossroads, Memphis, Britton Lane, Davis Bridge, Davis Mills, and Parker's Crossroads, as well as a couple dozen lesser sites.

I suppose it started a long time ago when a wise historian, George Reaves, reminded me that "Shiloh was not fought in a vacuum." I had become so intent on my studies of a single battle I had lost sight of the bigger picture. He encouraged me to broaden my horizons, and I did. Eventually I realized just what it was he was trying to tell an excited young fanatic with tunnel vision. I began to see how far-flung events in one theater of the war could decide outcomes in another. Like how a campaign in Georgia could lead to a pair of battles in north Mississippi.

When the battles of Brice's Crossroads and Tupelo/Harrisburg are broken down to the fundamentals of strategy, they are nearly identical in design. Neither had the specific goal of killing Nathan B. Forrest, nor was it in the plan of either to capture territory or even destroy the rich agricultural heartland known as the Black Prairie. The ultimate goal of each campaign was simply to keep Forrest's cavalry away from the Tennessee railroad supplying William T. Sherman's armies in north Georgia.

The first attempt to keep Forrest in Mississippi was made by Samuel Sturgis, a raid that resulted in the disastrous Union defeat at Brice's Crossroads. Despite a series of bad decisions on his own part, as well as being out-generalled by Forrest, Sturgis still managed to achieve his primary goal. There were few people at the time who would voice the opinion that Sturgis's campaign had been a success, but, in the larger scope of the war, it had been: Forrest remained in Mississippi.

By the spring of 1864, the war in the West was not going to be won or lost in Mississippi, not with the major armies fighting north of Atlanta. But the success or failure of the primary armies could be affected by the lesser activities in outlying districts. Forrest's spectacular victory over Sturgis did nothing to add to the Confederate war effort, but the very fact that it kept Forrest in Mississippi ensured that Sherman's tenuous supply line remained undisturbed, at least in the short term.

Sherman realized that his supply system remained threatened as long as Forrest was free to move through the area at will. Forrest's superior officer, Stephen D. Lee, was under enormous pressure to send the famed cavalry leader on the very type of expedition Sherman feared. Unknown to the Union general, he had an ally of sorts in Confederate president Jefferson Davis. In the face of all military logic, Davis steadfastly refused to allow Forrest to leave Mississippi. His decision was based less on military priorities and more on stubbornness and the intense disregard he harbored against political rivals and anyone who questioned his authority. Had Sherman known of Davis's insistence on keeping Forrest in Mississippi, it is possible he would have never bothered to send another raid into the state.

It was more fate than planning that placed A. J. Smith and two veteran divisions in Memphis on the eve of Sturgis's defeat. They had arrived fresh from the Red River campaign and were truly in the right place at the right time. Yet, it was Smith's careful planning that paved the way for his eventual victory at the small town of Harrisburg. He asked questions and learned from the mistakes of his predecessors, and there was certainly no shortage of lessons to be learned. No Union officer had ever gone up against Forrest and come out the victor. But for all of Smith's careful planning, he made several serious logistical mistakes, simple staff work, actually, that could have resulted in disaster rather than victory. The failure to adequately inspect ammunition and rations was nearly his undoing.

Tupelo/Harrisburg was a Union victory. It achieved the intended results of keeping the Confederate cavalry away from Sherman's supply lines, as well as the secondary goal of handing a defeat to the man who had never been bested. The defeat had long-term effects; Forrest's corps was devastated and never again was able to toe the line against Union infantry, as it had done so often in the past.

The story of Tupelo/Harrisburg is, however, more than the explanation of strategy and tactics. It is a human story that explores the experiences of civilians whose lives were forever altered by the march of the armies and the stories of veteran soldiers, tired men who had campaigned for three years and were showing signs of exhaustion, though their morale and resolve remained high, and also novices, men like Elijah Edwards, a young chaplain who had never seen battle and whose first exposure brought him face to face with the cruelty of war and death.

It is also a tale of the price paid by the three principal leaders of the campaign: Forrest, whose legendary strength and tenacity was weakened by physical ailments that clouded his judgment; Stephen Lee, who, at only thirty years of age, was forced to make life-or-death decisions across a vast department he had no real hope of protecting; and A. J. Smith, whose star was ascending, though he was called on to exercise a cruelty that was not in his nature.

The narrative continues well past the fighting itself, when the participants wrote their individual accounts of the campaign and the facts of the battle became blurred. Indeed, there was a second battle, waged on the printed page, which came close to proclaiming a victory for the southerners, something they did not achieve on the field. It began with the official reports, followed by the books and articles by the men who fought and a host of writers up to the present time.

I once sat through a two-hour program in which the lecturer went to great lengths to prove this revisionist history of the battle. It was amusing as well as frustrating, but it was a defining moment in my decision to write this book. The final chapter of this book is devoted to the history of the history of the battle and the efforts to soften a harsh defeat.

Acknowledgments

How do you thank all the people that were part of the voyage? (All the land-lubber authors call it "a journey," but there is still too much of the old salt from the Goat Locker in me—it was a voyage.) There is no way I could have done this without assistance, and the people who have helped me have done so graciously and selflessly.

Timothy Smith, University of Tennessee, read the manuscript, wrote the foreword, and gave me invaluable guidance and advice. He is one of the foremost scholars of the Civil War in the Western Theater, and I am lucky to have such a friend.

Brian S. Wills, the director of the Civil War Center and professor of History at Kennesaw State University, encouraged me to give Kent State University Press the first look at my book. His suggestions on the manuscript were priceless.

The staff at the Kent State University Press has made the process of publishing an enjoyable task, and, if it must be considered work, it was definitely like working with friends. My special thanks go to Joyce Harrison, who guided me every step of the way, as well as to Will Underwood, Carol Heller, Mary Young, Christine Brooks, and Susan Cash.

My copy editor, Joanna Craig, cannot be given enough thanks for her contributions.

My cartographer, Dave Roth, surpassed himself with his excellent maps. Dave is the publisher of *Blue and Gray Magazine*, and his first-rate maps are known throughout the Civil War community.

Thomas E. Buffenbarger, Library Technician, Research and User Division, U. S. Army Heritage and Education Center, sent me countless letters, journals, and diaries from the army's priceless collections. His invaluable knowledge of the collections put the right materials in my hands.

My good friend Mark Detgen was of particular help copying materials at the Abraham Lincoln Presidential Library and Museum in Springfield, Illinois. Also, Cheryl Schnirring, the curator of manuscripts, provided Mark with the resources I needed.

Historian David Powell unselfishly shared a number of primary sources he acquired for a project of his own.

My old friend Bjorn Skaptason of the Abraham Lincoln Bookshop sent me some fascinating primary material. A longtime friend of Shiloh National Military Park, Bjorn is an exceptional Civil War scholar, and it was a black day for the park when he was allowed to slip away.

Park Ranger Jim Minor, my friend and co-worker at the Corinth Civil War Interpretive Center, has been an immeasurable help over the years, serving as a sounding board for my thoughts and theories. A leading expert on Brice's Crossroads, he is a storehouse of knowledge.

Historian Jeff Giambrone sent me some wonderful material on the 38th Mississippi Mounted Infantry.

And who could think of completing such a project without the assistance of H. Grady Howell Jr. of the Mississippi Department of Archives and History?

Others who helped me in my research include Duane Swanson, curator of manuscripts at the Minnesota Historical Society; Jacob Laurence, curator of exhibits at the Museum of Mobile; Suzanne Hahn, director of reference services, Indiana Historical Society; Susie Dent, Northeast Mississippi Historical and Genealogical Society; Linda Sebree, DePauw University; and Dennis Belcher, Dean Burchfield, Terry Gerdes, John Gunter, Garth Hagerman, Dick Hill, Kathy Kroeger, George Martin, Dave Paul, Jill Smith, Joel T. Smith, Charles Sullivan, Forrest and Janis Tutor, and Frank Wood.

I could not have completed this project without the assistance and patience of the staff at the Northeast Regional Library in Corinth, particularly Ann Coker, Brandon Lowrey, and Rita Millsaps.

Edwina Carpenter, the director of the Mississippi's Final Stands Interpretive Center in Baldwyn, deserves special thanks not just for the assistance she gave in providing me with materials and maps, but for the work she does every day in maintaining a wonderful museum dedicated to preserving the history of the Battles of Tupelo/Harrisburg and Brice's Crossroads.

Last on the list but first in my heart is my wonderful wife, Nita. She is the wisest woman I know, and she always knew just when to inspire me when I was down, kick me when I was lazy, leave me be when I was in The Zone, or bring me a hot cup of coffee when I really needed it. Her support, patience, guidance, understanding, and love have seen me through the project from beginning to end. Thank you, Daisy.

ONE

The Gorillas

Brig. Gen. Andrew Jackson Smith stood at the rail of the transport *Leviathan* and looked across the brown waters of the Mississippi River toward the city of Memphis. The *Leviathan*, a brand-new side-wheel packet, had made its way upriver to the port city. A long line of twenty transports followed in its wake, ships that bore two divisions of the Sixteenth Corps returning from Louisiana and the debacle of the Red River campaign. The men were seasoned campaigners, veterans of nearly every western battle and campaign from Fort Donelson through the recent action at Lake Chicot, Arkansas. They had a well-deserved reputation as tough fighters, and they were currently very much in demand throughout the Western Theater.[1]

The flotilla had left the mouth of the Red River on May 22, 1864, with plans to put in for fuel at Vicksburg, Mississippi, before pushing upriver to Memphis. Its arrival in Tennessee was much anticipated and long past due. Back in March, Smith's two divisions had been assigned to Maj. Gen. Nathanial P. Banks's expedition with the clear understanding that the right wing of the Sixteenth Corps would be returned to Maj. Gen. William T. Sherman no later than mid-April. Sherman intended on using Smith's men in his upcoming campaign to take Atlanta. But as it turned out, he launched his campaign during the first week of May with three armies but without the corps' First and Third divisions. Banks's failed expedition to take Shreveport had taken longer than intended, and Smith's missing men were already six weeks overdue. The two divisions were loaded aboard the transports with an immediate destination of Memphis. Their destination beyond this was a matter of conjecture among the generals of the Union armies.[2]

On May 24, just two days after the transports steamed out of the Red River, Maj. Gen. Edward Canby, commander of the Military Division of West Mississippi, stated his intention to use Smith's men in operations in Arkansas. Technically, the two divisions were within Canby's jurisdiction, and he could use them as he saw fit; but Canby's command was still within the dominion of Sherman's department, and the attempt to divert the veterans was short-lived. Sherman quickly reasserted his ownership of the two divisions and amended orders from Canby's headquarters directed Smith to continue on to Memphis and then to secure the supply line of Sherman's advance. Sherman was trying to keep at least two moves ahead of the enemy and had new plans for Smith, which he laid out in a letter to Canby on June 4. Smith would take his troops, along with reinforcements from Vicksburg, and make a feint against Mobile by way of Pascagoula. If conditions warranted, he could even make an attack on the city. This movement would create yet another threat to an already overextended Confederate defensive line and would hopefully draw troops away from Gen. Joseph E. Johnston's Army of Tennessee.

Another attempt to claim Smith's two divisions came from Adm. David D. Porter, who wanted Smith to stay in Vicksburg and operate against Confederate troops crossing the Mississippi River from Arkansas, an idea that was quickly squashed if given any consideration at all. A fourth and final call for Smith's force originated from a desk in the War Department. While Sherman was making his plans, Maj. Gen. Henry W. Halleck, the army's chief of staff, was working out his own. Halleck informed Sherman he had sent orders for Smith to make a move into north Mississippi to deal with the cavalry under Confederate Maj. Gen. Nathan B. Forrest. The presence of Forrest's cavalry in northern Mississippi and Alabama was a threat to Sherman's supply line stretching across Tennessee from Chattanooga to Nashville. These were essentially the same orders handed down from Canby, but with one major difference: rather than reacting to an expected raid by Forrest into Tennessee, Smith would take the initiative and confront the cavalry commander in Mississippi.[3]

The First and Third divisions steaming upriver with Smith were known as "the Gorillas," a nickname they had picked up in the early days of the Red River campaign. The two divisions were composed of men typical of the Union's Western Theater: tough fighters but ill-disciplined and not overly concerned with the trappings of military bearing or appearance. Their uniforms were faded and patched and not always very clean, and they favored the shapeless, wide-brimmed slouch hats. In general, they appeared sloppy, even slovenly and were described as "gorillas, course, uncouth ill-dressed braggarts and chicken thieves." One account has the nickname coming from General Banks, who, when he first saw the westerners, reportedly said, "What in the name of Heaven did Sherman send me these ragged guerillas for?" Indeed, they were in marked contrast to the spit-and-polish eastern soldiers of Banks's army, men from New York, Massachusetts, and Maine who took great pride in their appearance, conduct, and efficiency on the parade ground—but men who were untested on the battlefield and were therefore scorned by the seasoned veterans of the Midwest as being "undependable holiday soldiers, paper collar and white glove gents, who could neither shoot nor forage."[4]

Unknown to Smith or his men, events were unfolding that would determine the nature of their future operations. It was June 10, 1864, and as the line of transports began to tie up at the Memphis city docks to unload their human cargo, a battle was raging 100 miles to the southeast at a nondescript intersection in Mississippi known as Brice's Crossroads. Union Brig. Gen. Samuel Sturgis and his small army were in the process of being routed by a significantly smaller Confederate force under the command of General Forrest. Sturgis's fiasco would prove reason enough to divert Smith and his Gorillas to north Mississippi. The initial reports of the battle indicated that Sturgis's entire army had been wiped out and with it the only force available to defend Memphis. Smith would stay, for the time being, to protect the city from Forrest, but the underlying reasons for his halt in Memphis were to be found an additional 250 miles to the east in Dalton, Georgia.

The first week of May 1864 found the Confederate Army of Tennessee under General Johnston waiting, watching, and looking to the north. A massive army group was poised some twenty-five miles to the north. Johnston had 53,000 men in Dalton, barely half as many as his opponent, Sherman, who was about to strike south from Chattanooga. Sherman led not one but three armies under three very competent major generals: the Army of the Cumberland under George H. Thomas, James B. McPherson's Army of the Tennessee, and John Schofield's Army of the Ohio. Four divisions of cavalry and 254 cannon swelled Sherman's ranks to nearly 100,000 men. Johnson was well aware he could not overcome Sherman in a bloody stand-up fight. His plan, as it was inevitably throughout the war, was to fall back and maneuver, watch for an opening, and then capitalize on the error and strike when and where the opportunity presented. The coming weeks would show flaws in the tactics and the man.

A story about Johnston sums up his dilemma. A friend, Hamilton Boykin, invited Johnston and future Confederate general Wade Hampton to his estate for a duck hunt. "He was a capital shot, better than Wade or I, and we were not so bad, that you'll allow. But to Colonel Johnston—I think he was colonel then—the bird flew too high or too low—the dogs were too far or too near—things never did suit exactly. He was too fussy, too hard to please, too cautious, too much afraid to miss and risk his fine reputation for a crack shot. Wade and I bulged through the mud and water briars and bushes and came home with a heavy bag. We shot right and left—happy-go-lucky. Joe Johnston did not shoot at all. The exact right time and place never came." Johnston's campaign above Atlanta in the summer of 1864 was much like that duck hunt. Neither Johnston nor his opponent, Sherman, was ever in quite the right place at the right time for the Confederate commander to take advantage of an opportunity. The weakness in Sherman's plan was the length of his supply line. A single track line, the Nashville & Chattanooga Railroad, supplied the entire army and could be easily broken in a raid. Johnston was well aware of the weakness but, for want of an effective cavalry force, was unable to capitalize on this Achilles' heel. He watched and waited while Sherman's army moved ever closer to Atlanta.[5]

Back in Memphis, Smith watched his troops debark and then rode into town to his Poplar Street headquarters. A casual observer on the street might have been fooled by his outward appearance, that of a tall, thin, balding, gray-haired, gray-bearded man. A second glance, however, saw a forty-nine-year-old man deceptively aged in appearance. Smith had a piercing eye and a rigid military frame, and he could cuss like a mule skinner when the occasion demanded it. His presence exuded confidence in himself and his men; he was a career soldier from the "old school."

The name "Smith" had been a mainstay in the American military since 1607, when Capt. John Smith arrived in the Virginia colony. During the four years of the Civil War, no fewer than nineteen men with the surname Smith were promoted to the rank of general in the Union or Confederate armies, and another seventeen Federals were breveted to the rank. Some of these Smiths won fame on the battlefield, though just as many were as obscure and unheralded as the name might imply. There were so many Smiths at West Point that most of them received nicknames, which made the sobriquets Seminole, Baldy, Gus, Sooy, and Extra Billy an easier way to identify the cadets in question. Andrew Jackson Smith was occasionally called Whiskey or Whiskey Smith during the war, but this nickname seems to be more of a postwar label than an accepted nom de guerre. From West Point through retirement, he was known simply as A. J. or Andrew.[6]

Andrew Jackson Smith was born on the family farm in Bucks County, Pennsylvania, on April 28, 1815. His father served in the Revolution and the War of 1812 and named his youngest son after his commander at the Battle of

Maj. Gen. Andrew
J. Smith (Library
of Congress)

New Orleans. Little is known about A. J.'s childhood, and his story really begins with his acceptance into West Point in 1834. His older brother, Samuel,
had been elected to the U.S. House of Representatives in 1832; and through
his brother's influence, A. J. was admitted to the class of 1838. In his class
of forty-five, Smith was ranked thirty-sixth, behind a host of future generals, including Pierre G. T. Beauregard, Irvin McDowell, William J. Hardee,
Henry Hopkins Sibley, and Edward Johnson. His low class ranking should
have consigned him to the ranks of the infantry, but somehow he was awarded
a commission as second lieutenant in the more prestigious 1st Dragoons.[7]

Promotions in the prewar army came slowly. In 1845 A. J. was at last ad-
vanced to first lieutenant, and two years later he was promoted to captain.
While he was stationed at Jefferson Barracks, Missouri, A. J. met and married
Ann Mason Simpson, the daughter of Dr. Robert Simpson, the postmaster of
St. Louis. It was a lonely marriage, as Ann stayed behind in St. Louis during

A. J.'s frequent postings to the western plains and Oregon. Over the years she bore six children, but only one of them reached adulthood. A. J.'s record of postings was impressive and included duty on the "Trail of Tears," relocating the Cherokee Indians from the Carolinas to the Indian Territories. He next served as the temporary commander of the Mormon Battalion in their march west during the Mexican War. The battalion was composed of some 550 Latter Days Saints and was led by Mormon company officers who were commanded by U.S. Army officers. Smith was far from popular with the Mormons, who resented his regular army discipline and standards. After the Mexican War he alternately protected and pursued different Indian tribes in Oregon and also saw duty in Los Angeles, San Francisco, Santa Fe, and St. Louis. In 1853 he and two companies of the Dragoons established Fort Lane in Oregon's Rogue Valley.

At the outbreak of the Civil War, Smith was serving in San Francisco, a major in what had been the Dragoons but was subsequently redesignated the 1st U.S. Cavalry. By October 2, 1861, he was wearing the eagles of a colonel and was in command of a volunteer regiment, the 2nd California Cavalry. His stint in California was short-lived, however, and less than six weeks later he accepted a commission of brigadier general of volunteers with the title "chief of cavalry" in Maj. Gen. Henry W. Halleck's Department of Missouri. Chief of cavalry was an administrative job, and there was little chance for A. J. to distinguish himself, though this changed shortly after the Battle of Shiloh when Smith took to the field. He was active during the Siege of Corinth, Mississippi, in May 1862, and when the city fell he remained in the field with his men rather than taking a comfortable headquarters in town. A few months later he was sent to Cincinnati to prepare for a possible attack by Confederate major generals Braxton Bragg and Kirby Smith during the fall Kentucky campaign. In December he was back in the field and led a division in Sherman's unsuccessful attack on Chickasaw Bluffs, Mississippi, and again during the subsequent victory at Arkansas Post.

Though A. J. Smith probably was not called "Whiskey" during the war, this doesn't mean he wasn't fond of the stuff. Cpl. Charles Haseltine of the Chicago Mercantile Battery thought the world of General Smith and recalled, "There was a soldier for you; a commander after our own hearts. How he could fight—and swear—and drink whiskey. We called him *our* general." Quartermaster Will Brown of the same battery had a similar high opinion of the hard-drinking commander and described him in a letter home to his father: "By the way, what a worker Smith is. I mean Gen. A.J. Smith, our old division commander during the Vicksburg Campaign. He is nearly always in the field and never so happy as when filled with whiskey and at the head of his command." His heavy drinking would continue into his postwar years, when he commanded the 7th U.S. Cavalry, when Sherman confided to Grant in 1867, "I fear A. J. Smith takes too many toddies & sees more than double." Noteworthy is the fact that though several people observed him drinking heavily during the war, no one ever claims to have seen him drunk.[8]

In the course of the Vicksburg campaign, A. J. came under the watchful eye of Ulysses S. Grant, who developed a high regard for Smith and included him in the party that met with General Pemberton to discuss the surrender of the Confederate Army. It was also during this time that the men under his command began to grow a strong attachment to their crusty leader. They liked him so much they began to tease him, a sure sign of their respect: a soldier may abuse an unpopular commander and talk about his lack of qualities in the confines of the mess, but good-natured mocking is always an indication of high esteem. Pvt. William Wiley of the 77th Illinois wrote,

> Our boys got to calling themselves Gen Smith's greyhounds on account of being run about so much and on this march when ever Gen Smith would come in sight they would set up the most unearthly howling like a pack of hounds. At one time the Gen rode up to our Col and asked him what the H_ll his men meant by howling that way when he came near. The Col told him he guessed the boys thought he was trying to make hounds of them by running them so hard. Huh says the Gen d__n them I give them enough to do without howling that way and he put us through all the faster from that to Vicksburg and the harder he marched us the harder we yelled.

Later in the war, during the Red River campaign, "Smith's Greyhounds" spotted their old division commander riding with General Banks and "received him with cheers long and loud."[9]

Smith led the Third Division of the Sixteenth Corps in Sherman's Meridian campaign through Central Mississippi and was then immediately dispatched to join the ill-fated Red River campaign under Banks. Smith's two divisions had captured Fort DeRussey, saved Banks's army from defeat at the Battle of Pleasant Hill, and served as the infantry protection for Admiral Porter's flotilla when it was stranded by the falling waters of the Red River. For this act Smith earned the undying support of Porter, who told Sherman, "The more I see of that old gentleman the more I like him." His assignment to Banks had been a short-term loan, and Sherman was anxious to have Smith's men return to Tennessee for the upcoming campaign to take Atlanta.[10]

While assigned to Banks's expedition, Smith exhibited his matchless characteristics as a soldier and his irascible temper. Smith's troops were not present during the Union defeat at Mansfield of April 8 but were enduring a forced march of twenty-one miles. The following morning the victorious Confederates attacked Banks at Pleasant Hill; Smith and his men marched an additional fourteen miles and arrived in time to turn certain defeat into a stunning victory. Banks was so overcome he took Smith by the hand and said, "God bless you General, you have saved the army." At midnight Smith received orders from Banks to withdraw at once from the field, a move that infuriated Smith. His wounded were still being brought in for treatment, and his dead were yet to be buried. He pleaded with Banks to remain long enough to care for his casualties, but Banks was adamant. Smith stormed over to the headquarters of Maj. Gen. William B. Franklin and, in his anger, asked Franklin to place Banks under arrest and take over command of the army. Franklin replied, "Smith, don't you know this is mutiny?" Smith backed down, but his low regard for Banks remained.[11]

West Point historian Leslie J. Perry, who knew Smith and observed him during the war, succinctly described A. J.'s contribution to the war: "It was one of the queer things in Smith's career that he never seemed permanently attached anywhere, but was constantly tossed about from pillar to post, at the will and necessity of his chiefs, on important detached service." This was echoed by the newly commissioned Chaplain Elijah Edwards of the 7th Minnesota Infantry, who, before he had even reached his regiment in the summer of 1864, wrote, "This corps is famous as being almost continually on the march." Later in the war an amused A. J. referred to his command as "the Lost Tribe of Israel" for all of its wanderings.[12]

Smith's regiments arrived on their transports throughout the day on June 10. A heavy rainstorm had forced several of the steamboats to seek shelter near the shore, and, as a consequence, they were pulling into Memphis well into the afternoon and evening. Most of the regiments stayed on the boats one last night, though a few lucky units were allowed to disembark and sleep in the city. The 117th Illinois marched to the terminus of the Memphis & Charleston Railroad and slept on the covered plankway at the Charleston Depot. By midmorning the bulk of Smith's two divisions had marched off the boats and was headed for camps southeast of Memphis, expecting a well-earned rest. "As we marched through the streets of the city," wrote Ben Thomas of the 14th Iowa, "the weather being very warm, many of the citizens came out with pails of cool, fresh water for us to drink. They were very kind to us and we fully appreciated their kindness." The men rigged tents and sought shelter from the intense heat of the sun, and the camps were soon white with wall tents, shelter halves, and conical Sibley tents. Camp guards and pickets were assigned, but the general mood was one of ease and relaxation. "We are not annoyed daily with the boom of cannon, and shriek of shells and still more disagreeable rattle of Musketry." Some of the men tried to make their way into town to take in the sights but were turned back if they didn't carry a pass. Proper pass or not, many of the men snuck into town, prompting Albert Underwood of the 9th Indiana Battery to observe, "I went through the city this evening quite lively time since Smith's command has come in." The streets of Memphis were patrolled by the 8th Iowa Infantry under Col. James L. Geddes, which was quick to quell any boisterous behavior. The contrast between the tattered uniforms of Smith's Gorillas and the well-turned-out provost guard was remarkable. One observer noted, "These patrols were exquisitely dressed in new and clean uniforms wearing in addition to their blue uniforms polished shoes and white gloves." In his journal, Chaplain Edwards of the 7th Minnesota described a run-in with the city guards.

Squads of these holiday soldiers patrol the various parts of the city enforcing elaborate military rules and regulations, that seem to savor too much of useless red tape. None of our soldiers was allowed to walk the streets without the regulation pass. I was myself arrested for appearing without one. It was one of my duties to visit the Hospitals and this I did every day. I had passed without notice a few times, and supposed myself a privileged character, when to-day, as I attempted to pass the guard the clear voice of the dandified officer in charge rang out "Halt!" There was a clang of arms. The officer approached, extended as I innocently supposed to extend to me the courtesy of a hand-shake, so ignorant was I of military usages. I was about to grasp it in a true western manner when he further remarked "Your pass if you please." When he heard my answer to the effect that I had none, he asked me to give my Regiment and rank which I did, adding that I was on duty and was visiting the Hospitals, he responded, "Chaplain; consider yourself under arrest, and report immediately to Head Quarters." I considered myself immediately under arrest and reported at once to my Regimental Head Quarters, and was duly laughed at.[13]

For most of the soldiers in occupied Memphis, the city was a great place to rest from the wearisome campaigning in Louisiana. One of them was Cpl. William Ibbetson of the 122nd Illinois, who described the port city as "a shady & cool place. Memphis is one of the nicest places we were ever in, that is in the south. The streets have rows of trees planted along the sides, splendid gardens

& nice houses, but yet the same carelessness marks everything. Southerns are all lazy. Memphis has been an aristocratic place, but has been humbled. Terribly humbled. Woe be unto the transgressor. Hard is his path."[14]

June 10 was marred by an ugly incident, an event that stuck out in the minds of the soldiers even beyond the horrors of war. It was not unusual to see men drummed out of the service for their crimes, but, as Pvt. Robert Burdette of the 47th Illinois recalled, "What we were to witness this beautiful June morning in the suburbs of the busy city of Memphis was something entirely different." Three soldiers of the 2nd New Jersey Cavalry had been found guilty by a general court martial on the charges of rape and were ordered to be executed in front of the garrison of Memphis. The event troubled young Burdette, and he left a gripping account of the crime.

According to Burdette, "The three condemned men had occupied one of the most responsible positions in which a soldier is ever placed. Just outside the city a few miles they were on picket duty. They had the keeping of the city's garrison and the surrounding camp in their care." He went on to describe how a local farmer, along with his wife and adult daughter, were making their way from Memphis to their home and passed by the picket post after showing the proper pass. A short way down the road their wagon broke down. The father set out on foot and passed the soldiers again as he made his way back to Memphis to engage a wheelwright. The women, resting nearby with the wagon, were placed under the protection of the pickets. "Then the devil got into the hearts of these men. They took the first false step. They abandoned their duty and hurried along the road where the disabled wagon was waiting the return of its owner. There upon the persons of these helpless women, confided absolutely to the protecting care and honor of these soldiers, whose wards they temporarily were, they committed a crime, to a woman worse than death, doubly horrible from the fact that the victims of the lust of these soldiers were mother and daughter." When he learned of the outrage, the husband/father reported the transgressors to the military authorities in Memphis, and the men were soon shackled in the guardhouse.[15]

Sgt. William Tucker of the 14th Wisconsin was unsure of the crimes and assumed the men guilty of "violating some general orders. Whether the sentence was just or not, we could not tell, but the impression held was the execution was wrong." Pvt. James Newton, of the same regiment, knew the men were guilty "of an outrage upon the person of a defenseless female" and had no issue with the punishment. The soldiers of the 47th Illinois, familiar with the facts of the crime, consoled themselves with the knowledge that the offense had been committed by an eastern regiment, "for we insisted that the native chivalry common to the western men would have held back from the commission of such a crime." Even still, they said, "we felt that in their crime somehow they had besmirched the rest of us."

As the hour of the execution approached, 4,000–6,000 men formed three sides of a square, with the east face of Fort Pickering, just south of the city, forming the fourth side. The men stood in formation for hours in the hot morning sun until a band entered the square playing a funeral dirge, followed by the mounted troopers of the 2nd New Jersey with their sabers drawn. At the rear of the procession were three ambulances, their white canvas covers removed, bearing the condemned men, who were sitting on their coffins, their hands tied behind their backs. Accompanied by clergymen, the men were led to the center of the square, their backs to Fort Pickering, were blindfolded and directed to sit on their open, waiting coffins. The officer in charge dropped a handkerchief, a detachment of the 8th Iowa Infantry fired at the prisoners, and the deed was done. The harsh lesson was summed up by Private Burdette, "It was the moral of the true fable we had just witnessed—the inevitable 'Haec fibula docet'; 'This fable teaches.'"

A. J.'s men had engaged in burning and looting during the Red River campaign, a precursor to the heavy-handed "total war" advocated by Sherman and grudgingly practiced by Smith. Under Smith's direction, they burned public buildings as well as any infrastructure that supported the Confederate war effort. Warehouses, depots, factories, mills, and plantations went up in smoke. Smith, however, did not condone wanton violence against civilians who were merely trying to eke out a living during the hard times. The execution made it abundantly clear that though soldiers may engage in burning as part of their duties, personal crimes such as rape and murder would be dealt with in the swiftest and harshest terms.[16]

General Smith went to bed the night of June 11 believing he was about to outfit an expedition to make a demonstration against Pascagoula, Florida, and possibly, if events dictated, against Mobile. From his headquarters in the field at Altoona Creek, Georgia, Sherman had finally decided on a course of action and ordered Smith to put together a force of 6,000–10,000 men. The men of the expedition were to come from his own troops as well as those who could be had from Memphis and Vicksburg. The movement on Mobile, as envisioned by Sherman, would prove to be such a threat it would force the Confederates to draw troops away from Joe Johnston's army in Georgia. Although Grant approved of the Mobile expedition, he doubted it would have the impact Sherman was banking on: "The object of sending troops to Mobile now would not be so much to assist General Sherman against Johnston as to secure for him a base of supplies after his work is done." For whatever reason, Smith was to outfit an expedition against Mobile and do it quickly. "What is done should be done at once," ordered Sherman.[17]

When news of Smith's orders reached Halleck's desk in Washington, "Old Brains" put an end to the plan before it could get fairly started. He wired Sherman that the plan to take Mobile had already been suggested to General Canby at Vicksburg, who could take care of the expedition on his own. Halleck had been the general in chief of the Union armies before being superseded by Grant and demoted to chief of staff. Grant, whose headquarters were in the field with the Army of the Potomac in Virginia, gave Halleck plenty of leeway, and as such Halleck still carried the authority to make things happen.

Instead, Halleck told Sherman, Smith was on his way to "break up Forrest's operations on your line of supplies." In the course of the message Halleck didn't bother to mention Samuel Sturgis, who was already on a similar mission for Sherman, one he likely doubted Sturgis could pull off. If Halleck held reservations about Sturgis's abilities, they were confirmed shortly after midnight on the morning of June 12. Whatever plans existed for the active operations against Mobile were scrapped when news of Sturgis's defeat reached Memphis.[18]

TWO

A Pair of Raids

There had been two raids into the interior of north Mississippi during the first half of 1864. They had set out with different purposes but ended with similar results.

The first began in February as a pet project of Sherman's, to march a force eastward from Vicksburg into the Mississippi interior destroying as much as he could of the railroad and rolling stock. He hoped to make the state militarily untenable for the enemy, thus reducing the number of garrison troops required to maintain the security of the Mississippi River. He thought he could free up to 20,000 troops that could be used later in the year in his anticipated campaign against Atlanta. He wanted to start out right after Vicksburg fell, but the hot summer of 1863 delayed his plans, and the subsequent campaigning around Chattanooga forced him to postpone the expedition once again. By New Year's Day 1864, Sherman was at last ready to make his march across the Magnolia State, and with Grant's blessing he traveled to Memphis to set things in motion.[1]

Sherman's plan called for a two-pronged thrust into the heart of Mississippi commencing on February 1. Four divisions of infantry (one led by Gen. A. J. Smith) would head east from Vicksburg, destroying the tracks of the Southern Railroad of Mississippi to the junction with the Mobile & Ohio at Meridian. And out of Memphis would come the second part of the assault: 7,000 cavalry under his chief of cavalry, Brig. Gen. William Sooy Smith. The two forces would rendezvous at Meridian on February 11, complete the destruction around Meridian, and then return to Vicksburg.[2]

In his memoirs Sherman expanded on the orders he gave Sooy Smith, explaining that "a chief part of the enterprise was to destroy the rebel cavalry commanded by General Forrest, who were a constant threat to our railway communications in Middle Tennessee." As for Sooy Smith's opponent, he said, "I explained to him personally the nature of Forrest as a man, and of his peculiar force; told him that in his route he was sure to encounter Forrest, who always attacked with a vehemence for which he must be prepared, and that, after he repelled the first attack, he must in turn assume the most determined offensive, overwhelm him and utterly destroy his whole force." In his written orders to Sooy Smith at the end of January, Sherman stressed:

> I wish you to attack any force of cavalry you meet and follow them southward, but in no event be drawn into the forks of the streams that make up the Yazoo nor over into Alabama. Do not let the enemy draw you into minor affairs, but look solely to the greater object, to destroy his communications from Okolona to Meridian and thence eastward to Selma. From Okolona south you will find abundance of forage collected along the railroad, and the farms have standing corn in the fields. Take liberally of all these, as well as horses, mules, cattle, &c. As a rule respect dwellings and families as something too sacred to be disturbed by soldiers, but mills, barns, sheds, stables, and such like things use for the benefit and convenience of your command.[3]

Under any other circumstances Sooy Smith should have done well; he was a competent commander with plenty of battlefield experience. Thirty-four years old, he came from a line that had eschewed its Quaker roots to serve in the military when their country called. Sooy Smith's grandfather had served in the Revolution and had severed his connections to the Society of Friends, as did his son, who was a captain during the War of 1812. Sooy Smith was a West Pointer, class of 1853, who chose to resign his commission in the 2nd U.S. Artillery for a job designing and building bridges. Sooy Smith returned to the army as a volunteer at the outset of the war. He fought at Shiloh as colonel of the 13th Ohio Infantry and won his promotion to brigadier for his performance. He led divisions in both the Army of the Ohio and the Army of the Tennessee, and at the end of the Vicksburg campaign he was made Grant's chief of cavalry. He was at the zenith of his military career when he had the misfortune to come up against Forrest.[4]

Nathan Bedford Forrest—the name had become a scourge for Union soldiers in the Western Theater. He was born July 13, 1821, in Bedford County, Tennessee, the first of eleven children to blacksmith William Forrest and his wife, Marian. The Forrest family roots were planted in western Virginia and

Maj. Gen. Nathan B. Forrest (Library of Congress)

North Carolina, and most of its men made a living in agriculture and livestock. The oldest Forrest child was named for the county of his birth.[5]

When Bedford was thirteen, the family moved to Tippah County, Mississippi. A few years later William died, leaving his teenage son to provide for his mother and siblings. There was little time for formal education, less than six months all told, and Bedford entered adulthood nearly illiterate. It never seemed a hindrance, though, and over the next fifteen years he amassed a fortune in slave trading and real estate and, eventually a member of the planter class, as the owner of a sizable cotton plantation. At the outbreak of the war he was one of the wealthiest men in Memphis, and his marriage to Miss Mary Ann Montgomery had produced two children, though their daughter Fanny had died at the age of five.[6]

Forrest's military experience was limited; his only service was a short stint as lieutenant of the DeSoto Dragoons, a prewar militia unit. When Tennessee seceded, he, along with his brother Jeffery and fifteen-year-old son Willie, enlisted as a private in Capt. Josiah White's Tennessee Mounted Rifles. Within days the governor learned of his enlistment and realized it was a waste to leave a wealthy man of influence in such a lowly position. Forrest was given a commission as lieutenant colonel and was authorized to raise his own battalion of cavalry.[7]

Over the next few years Forrest built a reputation for fearlessness in battle and for having the ability to read an engagement and react with lightning speed. He was never really defeated in battle, though there were a few close calls. He cut an imposing figure—tall, straight-backed, wavy brown hair, thick goatee, piercing gray eyes. He was also a strict disciplinarian with a volatile temper. On one occasion one of his men, unable to swim and frightened out of his wits, refused to cross the Hatchie River. Unwilling to have his orders disobeyed no matter the reason, Forrest physically picked up the man and flung him into the current. In another altercation, this time with one of his officers who questioned his motives, he was shot in the hip before fatally stabbing his subordinate to death with a knife.[8]

One of Forrest's most distinguishing but unfortunate characteristics was his inability to serve in a subordinate role, particularly under West Pointers, for whom he held particular contempt. If orders were not to his liking, he protested in a most vocal manner or simply ignored them, as he did at Fort Donelson and Shiloh. As for his commanders, he refused to serve under Generals Earl Van Dorn and Joe Wheeler and threatened the life of Braxton Bragg. His own friend Col. David C. Kelly wrote, "The truth may as well be told—he was unfit to serve under a superior; he was like a caged lion on the field of battle where he was not himself commanding." Despite flaws as a commander and a subordinate, there was no denying that he was an extremely talented man when it came to making war. And he had no equal in either army when it came to raiding behind enemy lines with mounted infantry.[9]

It was the altercation with Bragg that had resulted in his transfer to west Tennessee and Mississippi at the head of a new command. After being stripped of nearly all of his cavalry, Forrest was sent west with a single battalion and a battery of artillery, less than 300 men, and given authority to ride into Tennessee and recruit-up his force. Despite the fact Tennessee was well occupied with Union troops, Forrest managed to recruit 2,000 men and was well on his way to creating a new cavalry corps. A drawback to his new duties was that he was once again placed under the direct command of a West Point–trained officer; Maj. Gen. Stephen D. Lee.[10]

The first child of Dr. Thomas Lee Jr. and his wife, Caroline, was born in Charleston, South Carolina, on September 22, 1833. Stephen Dill Lee was named for his uncle and was a distant relation to the Lees of Virginia, though the family was not aware of it at the time. Stephen was two when his mother died, and though Thomas remarried and fathered several more children, he was in poor health and unable to adequately provide for the large family. And so he shipped Stephen off to the boarding school run by his Uncle Stephen, a man who had attended West Point for two years but dropped out for unknown reasons. It was probably due to his uncle's influence that he applied for and received an appointment to the U.S. Military Academy.[11]

The class of 1854 produced nine cadets who would eventually rise to the rank of general during the Civil War, among them James "Jeb" Stuart, Oliver O. Howard, and Stephen's friend Dorsey Pender.[12] Another good friend was Custis Lee, the son of Superintendent Robert E. Lee, who took the helm of the Academy in 1852. At the end of his four years, Stephen ranked seventeenth in a class of forty-six graduates and was posted to Company D, 4th Artillery.[13]

His first active service was against the Seminole Indians in Florida, and then he served as the regimental quartermaster in Fort Leavenworth, Kansas. His last months in the uniform of the United States were spent at Fort Randall in the Dakota Territory, where he performed a number of administrative chores, including quartermaster, commissary, and ordnance officer. The threat of war and the secession of South Carolina prompted him to resign his commission and return to his home state.[14]

Stephen arrived in Charleston to find a city embroiled in the conflict with the Union garrison at Fort Sumter. He was appointed captain in the South Carolina Regular Artillery Service and was assigned to the staff of Gen. Pierre G. T. Beauregard. He was in the small party that twice tried to convince the Federal commander to yield the fort without resorting to bloodshed, but the attempts failed, and hours later the first shots of the war were fired. He and a small party rowed out a third time after the bombardment and accepted Maj. Robert Anderson's surrender.[15]

By July 1861 he was in Virginia commanding the artillery battery in the famed Hampton Legion. It was here his natural gifts as a leader were first realized. When Brig. Gen. Wade Hampton secured a second battery for his legion, he promoted Lee to major and battalion commander.[16]

During the Seven Days' campaign he served as chief of artillery under Maj. Gen. John Magruder and won great praise for his abilities and a promotion to full colonel. At Second Manassas and Sharpsburg he led a six-battery battalion in Lt. Gen. James Longstreet's corps. His performance in both battles was nothing short of magnificent and earned him another promotion, to brigadier general.[17]

Along with the brigadier's star came a transfer to Mississippi to assist in the defense of Vicksburg. Confederate president Jefferson Davis was looking for a capable artillery officer and requested Robert E. Lee to "select the most efficient and accomplished artillery officer for duty on the Mississippi." Stephen

Lt. Gen. Stephen D. Lee (Library of Congress)

Lee played a major role in the defeat of Sherman at Chickasaw Bayou and for a time led an infantry brigade. He was captured when Vicksburg fell, and, unlike many officers and men, he spent a mere nine days in captivity before he was exchanged and released. Less than a month later, and still shy of his thirtieth birthday, he was made a major general and assigned to command the cavalry in Lt. Gen. Leonidas Polk's department.[18]

Luckily, and significantly, the young Lee differed from other Academy alumni. The first thing Lee did was assure his difficult subordinate that there would be no problems from his quarter: he told Forrest, "Whether you are under my command or not, we shall not disagree, and you shall have all the assistance and support I can render you."[19]

Another difference was that Lee was not at all cowed by his older subordinate, despite Forrest's fearsome reputation. Physically they were very similar. A friend once claimed that "by nature's endowments, [Stephen] stands like Saul of Kish, higher than the masses." Indeed, he was six feet tall, a full half foot taller than the average man of his day. He was fond of wearing a thick brown beard, sometimes neatly trimmed and other times in a long fall nearly halfway down his chest.[20]

It was a cordial friendship but a strange chain of command. Polk commanded the Department of Alabama, Mississippi and East Louisiana, and Lee served as the commander of his cavalry. Forrest headed up the new Forrest's Cavalry Department, a semi-autonomous command within Polk's jurisdiction. By the first week in February, Forrest's force had increased to nearly 2,500 men. The new unit was still forming when Sherman's two-pronged Union offense began to converge on Meridian.[21]

Sherman's part of the expedition proceeded methodically and stayed true to the planned schedule. The Sixteenth Corps under Maj. Gen. Stephen Hurlbut and the Seventeenth Corps under Maj. Gen. James McPherson marched to Meridian, burning and destroying nearly everything in their path. Every foot of track between Jackson and Meridian, 100 miles, was destroyed, along with dozens of bridges, culverts, and trestles.[22]

Sherman's main opposition was the two infantry divisions under Polk's command, and they did little to interfere with the Union juggernaut. There was little real fighting along the way, and Polk's outmatched troops retreated into Alabama and out of the path of Sherman's columns. Sherman was in Meridian by February 14 and spent five days destroying the southern rail network. For five days he waited for Sooy Smith to arrive, and on the 20th, out of time and out of patience, he set his men back on the path to Vicksburg.[23]

Sooy Smith never came close to making the planned rendezvous in Meridian. In fact, he did not even leave Memphis until February 11, the day he was supposed to meet up with Sherman. Sooy Smith had readied two brigades for the expedition and awaited a third under Col. George Waring, who was en route from Columbus, Kentucky. Waring was slowed by bad roads and worse weather and did not drag his column into Memphis until February 8. Already a week behind schedule, Smith allowed Waring's men to recuperate for three days before setting out for Mississippi. Smith's decision to wait until he had his full complement was contrary to his orders, though later he claimed Sherman had given him verbal permission to wait for Waring, a claim Sherman strongly denied.[24]

Once finally on the road to Meridian, the column pressed on in a timely manner, passing through New Albany, Pontotoc, and Houston and then veering east to Okolona on the Mobile & Ohio Railroad. Sooy Smith ordered a detachment to destroy the Confederate arsenal at Columbus as the main column moved south to West Point. Forrest had kept tabs on Sooy Smith's movements and moved his own scattered forces in the direction of Aberdeen and West Point to confront the Union column. To assist him, Stephen D. Lee dispatched three cavalry brigades he no longer needed to fight Sherman.[25]

With the original plan to rendezvous with Sherman in ruins, Sooy Smith paused near West Point, and there he lost his nerve. Many of his men had been detailed to assist the nearly 3,000 runaway slaves who had joined his column leaving only 5,000 effectives to face what he convinced himself was a superior force. He informed the commander of his cavalry division, Brig. Gen. Benjamin Grierson, of his intention to return to Memphis, and his senior cavalryman immediately asked permission to take a single brigade and set out on his own to rendezvous with Sherman's force. Initially, Smith gave him permission, but he quickly withdrew it; he needed all of his men for the retreat to Tennessee.[26]

On the morning of February 21, Smith began to pull back, and his rear guard got into a vicious fight near Okolona. In the heat of the fighting, Forrest's younger brother, Jeffery, was killed. A short time later Forrest arrived on the scene and took command. He approached Brig. Gen. James Chalmers for a quick briefing. "It was the first time I had been with him in a fight," wrote Chalmers.

> I watched him closely. His manner was nervous, impatient and imperious. He asked me what the enemy were doing, and when I gave him the report I had just received from Colonel [William] Duff, in command of the pickets, he said, sharply, "I will go and see myself," and started across the bridge, which was about thirty yards long, and then being raked by the enemy's fire. This struck me at the time as a needless and somewhat braggadocio exposure of himself, and I followed him to see what he would do. When we reached the other bank, the fire of the enemy was very heavy, and our men were falling back—one running without hat or gun. In an instant Forrest seized and threw him on the ground, and while the bullets were whistling thick about him, administered a severe thrashing with a brush of wood.

With the beating over, Forrest gathered his forces to attack the superior force, but Sooy Smith struck first.[27]

Sooy Smith ordered his cavalry into three lines. The mounted troopers drew their sabers and charged the Confederates. "I am proud to say my men did not disappoint me," bragged Forrest. "Standing firm, they repulsed the grandest cavalry charge I ever witnessed." Three times the Federals charged, and each time Forrest's men drove them back; and then the Confederates counterattacked. Only the falling darkness saved Sooy Smith's command from being completely destroyed.

When the tally of the day's killed, wounded, and missing was complete, Forrest, who had been outnumbered nearly three to one, suffered 144 casualties to Sooy Smith's 388. The Federals were able to return to Memphis without too much more difficulty, but Sooy Smith's expedition and career were both in shambles.[28]

In the weeks following the Meridian campaign, the military activity in north Mississippi slackened, ushering in a short period of relative quiet. Forrest reorganized his department into two divisions, and his command was thereafter known as Forrest's Corps. Sherman had returned to Nashville to prepare for his spring campaign against Atlanta. The eighteen-month Federal occupation of Corinth had ended, and nearly all of the Union soldiers in and around the crossroads had left the region. Aside from a scattering of garrison troops south of Memphis and the Union enclave at Eastport, on the Tennessee River, the Federal presence in the state was confined to Vicksburg and the Mississippi River.

The absence of enemy troops in the region allowed Forrest to move his operations into west Tennessee and even conduct raids as far as Paducah, Kentucky. For the time being Sherman seemed unconcerned and was content to allow Forrest to "cavort" around the western countryside rather than move into middle Tennessee and disturb the plans for his upcoming campaign. After the fall of Fort Pillow, however, and the resulting furor over alleged atrocities committed by the Confederates, Sherman ordered Maj. Gen. Cadwallader C. Washburn in Memphis to drive Forrest back into Mississippi. Washburn cobbled together a mixed command of infantry and cavalry and sent the newly arrived Brig. Gen. Samuel D. Sturgis to rid Tennessee of Forrest's Corps.[29]

Sam Sturgis was another West Pointer from the class of 1846, the same class that produced the likes of George McClellan, Thomas "Stonewall" Jackson, A. P. Hill, and John Gibbon. Sturgis's only distinction during his Mexican War service was being captured during a reconnaissance and spending eight days as a prisoner. A cavalry captain when the Civil War commenced, he accepted a promotion to brigadier general after his strong performance during the Union defeat at Wilson's Creek, Missouri. He was then sent east and commanded the Reserve Corps in the Army of Virginia during the disastrous Second Bull Run campaign, where he was heard to utter the infamous line about his commander, "I don't care for John Pope one pinch of owl dung." In the Army of the Potomac he led a division at Antietam and again at Fredericksburg. He went west with the Ninth Corps into east Tennessee, where he returned to his first calling, the cavalry. It was his success with the mounted branch that led to his new assignment.[30]

Sturgis did well enough in moving Forrest out of west Tennessee but only because Forrest seemed in no mood to resist. There were a few clashes of

Brig. Gen. Samuel
Sturgis (Library of
Congress)

arms, nothing too serious, and Sturgis was content to call off his pursuit, which
had led him as far as Ripley, Mississippi.[31] The easy march left Sturgis feeling cocky and overconfident. He reported to Sherman, "My little campaign
is over, and I regret to say, Forrest is still at large. He did not come to West
Tennessee for the purpose of fighting, unless it might so happen that he could
fall upon some little party or defenseless place. I regret very much that I could
not have the pleasure of bringing you his hair, but he is too great a plunderer
to fight anything like an equal force, and we have to be satisfied with driving
him from the State. He may turn on your communications and I rather think
he will, but see no way to prevent it from this point and with this force."[32]

Stephen D. Lee was having similar thoughts about Sherman's line of communications. Sherman's army group began to move the first week of May, and

by the 13th Johnston's Army of Tennessee had been flanked out of its position near Dalton. The necessity of breaking Sherman's supply and communication lines became paramount, and Forrest's was the only mobile command with a chance of succeeding. Accordingly, Lee gave orders for Forrest to set out with 3,000 men, cross the Tennessee River, and destroy as much of the rail line south of Nashville as he could. Forrest set out on his raid on June 1 but did not get far. A messenger caught up with him two days later in Russellville, Alabama, with news of a Federal column moving out of Memphis into Mississippi. Lee ordered an immediate return to Tupelo.[33]

Lee had not been the only one to observe the vulnerability of Sherman's supply and communication network. Sherman himself was well aware of the weakness and ordered General McPherson to divert Confederate attention away from Tennessee. "Keep the enemy occupied in your district," McPherson wrote to Washburn, "and press him at all points as far as your force will allow." Washburn responded by putting together a force for Sturgis to lead south into Mississippi. Sherman felt that 6,000 soldiers should be sufficient, but Washburn bumped up the number of men to over 8,000. There would be 3,300 cavalry, 5,000 infantry, and 16 pieces of artillery. Sturgis's orders were to engage Forrest "and if possible to whip and disperse his force."[34]

The cavalry, divided into two brigades, was under the direct command of Grierson, who had done well enough in Sturgis's first encounter with Forrest but had not done as well at Okolona under Sooy Smith. Col. William McMillen led the three infantry brigades, one of which consisted of a pair of black regiments of the U.S. Colored Troops (USCT).[35]

Forrest could not hope to muster anything close to the numbers of troops with Sturgis. His overall command had grown to nearly 9,000 men, but they were spread across north Mississippi and Alabama, and he could not draw them all in quick enough. To respond to the immediate threat, he had three brigades from the division of Brig. Gen. Abraham Buford and a fourth brigade sent to help him from Roddey's Division in Alabama. Along with eight pieces of artillery, Forrest was able to pull together some 4,900 men and ordered them to rendezvous near Tupelo on the Mobile & Ohio Railroad.[36]

Late in the afternoon of June 2, the Union column set out from Lafayette, Tennessee. Sturgis's orders called for him to proceed east to Corinth and then travel south along the route of the Mobile & Ohio, destroying as much of the tracks as they could southward to Meridian. Once they had defeated Forrest they were to return to Memphis by way of Grenada. Sturgis was directed to avoid the more direct route to the railroad, via Ripley, "on account of want of forage for animals." The foray into Mississippi the previous month had shown the region to be stripped of hay and grain vital to the subsistence of the horses and mules. There was an abundance of corn stored in Corinth, however, enough to see to the needs of the animals, and his first goal of the raid was to capture the grain. But as the column began to march east, the skies, which had been raining intermittently through the day, opened up and drenched the marching men. The rain continued for seven days.[37]

By June 8 Sturgis's expedition had proceeded no further than Ripley, a mere eighty miles from its starting point. Sturgis had received information that Corinth had been abandoned and the grain had been removed or destroyed, so he altered his course and took the Ripley Road. He had been warned against taking this route, and, indeed, the results were disastrous. From Ripley he wrote to General Washburn to explain his predicament. "I regret exceedingly to record our position here, after being out eight days, but it has rained incessantly from the first hour, and our train has scarcely been able to get along at all. This was especially unfortunate, as it compels us to move at a snail's pace over a desert region where there is absolutely nothing for the animals." He indicated that the weather had cleared that morning and expressed optimism that they would soon arrive in Tupelo. He did not tell Washburn that he was fearful of his predicament and that he had nearly decided to return to Memphis but had been persuaded to continue on by Colonel McMillen.[38]

The slow pace of the Union force had given Forrest time to draw in his forces and place them in the path of the enemy. On the morning of June 10, his scouts reported the enemy moving east on the Guntown Road. He knew that if Sturgis continued on this route, he would cross over the bridge spanning Tishomingo Creek and then through the small community of Brice's Crossroads. He sensed an opportunity and immediately set out with the brigade of Col. Edmund Rucker and ordered General Buford to follow with the balance of the troops. As they rode along he explained his plan to Rucker:

> I know they greatly outnumber [us] . . . but the road along which they will march is narrow and muddy, they will make slow progress. The country is densely wooded and the undergrowth so heavy that when we strike them they will not know how few we have. Their cavalry will move out ahead of the infantry, and should reach the crossroads three hours in advance. We can whip the cavalry in that time. As soon as the fight opens they will send back to have the infantry hurried up. It is going to be hot as hell, and coming on a run for five or six miles over such roads, their infantry will be so tired we will ride right over them.[39]

And so it played out. Sturgis ordered his cavalry far out in advance of his infantry column, and soon the horsemen were engaged with the enemy. Grierson's cavalry held its own against greater numbers when the exhausted infantry arrived on the field. Rather than use the infantry to bolster his line, Sturgis ordered the cavalry to withdraw and allow the infantry to form its own line. Grierson protested the bizarre tactics, but to no avail. When Sturgis ordered the cavalry out of line, the infantry could not contain the surging Confederates, and the fight quickly evolved into a rout.[40]

There was a bottleneck at the bridge over Tishomingo Creek, and panicked troops abandoned wagons and artillery. What was not lost here was later left along the muddy roads leading back to Memphis. Annihilation was prevented by the stalwart action of the black troops under Col. Ed Bouton and Grierson's cavalry. These units withdrew slowly under fire, buying time for the panicked troops to flee northward. Sturgis himself, completely demoralized and unfit to command, left his troops in the field and was one of the first to make it back to Tennessee.

Forrest reported a loss of 96 killed and 396 wounded to Sturgis's 223 killed, 503 wounded, and 1,800 taken prisoner. In addition, the Confederates captured 16 pieces of artillery, 186 wagons, 16 ambulances, hundreds of rounds of artillery ammunition, and 300,000 rounds for small arms. By any measure, it was one of the most complete victories of the war and nearly the undoing of Sturgis's career.[41]

THREE

A Third Raid

After learning of Sturgis's rout at Brice's Crossroads, Washburn hastened to notify Generals Sherman and Canby as well as Secretary of War Edwin Stanton.
In the telegram to Stanton, Washburn attempted to divert blame from himself
by pointing out that the expedition was ordered by General McPherson and
led by "an officer sent me by General Sherman." To General Canby he stressed
how he had felt the expedition "too weak" and had actually encouraged delay
before sending Sturgis into Mississippi. He also pointed out that Sherman and
McPherson had underestimated the size of the enemy force but that he, Washburn, had added an extra 2,000 to the number of men Sherman felt sufficient
for the expedition. In his telegram to Sherman Washburn left out the critical
remarks but did ask a pertinent question: "Under existing circumstances shall
General Smith make the contemplated demonstration on Mobile?"[1]

With light-blue eyes, piercing gaze, well-trimmed beard, and sweptback
hair, Cadwallader Washburn looked every inch the military man. Though he
had experienced some success on the battlefield, he was more at home in the
halls of Congress. He was a born politician who, before the war, had served
three terms as a congressman from Wisconsin and, after the war, went on to
serve two more and eventually moved into the governor's mansion. Washburn
amassed a fortune in land speculation, lumber, milling, railroads, and banking. After being selected as a member of the short-lived Washington Peace
Conference of 1861, he went on to raise the 2nd Wisconsin Cavalry, serving
as the regiment's first colonel. His older brother, Elihu Washburne, was an
Illinois congressman, a close friend of President Lincoln, and one of General
Grant's political benefactors.[2] Cadwallader's political connections, coupled

with his competence in the field, prompted his meteoric rise to major general in just thirteen months. During the Vicksburg campaign he rose to command three divisions of the Sixteenth Corps but thereafter was relegated to administrative postings in areas far from the active campaigns. Washburn's downfall may or may not have come as a result of letters he wrote to his brother from Vicksburg in which he was very critical of Elihu's friend Ulysses Grant. "He is frittering away time and strength to no purpose. The truth must be told even if it hurts. You cannot make a silk purse out of a sow's ear." It may have only been a coincidence, but the "sow's ear" became the commanding general of all of the armies of the United States, and General Washburn never held another command in the field.[3]

To give the devil his due, Washburn was a competent administrator but was never an inspirational leader, nor was he able to hold the trust of men in the field. Sgt. William Tucker of the 14th Wisconsin Infantry stated simply, "General Washburn, one of the greatest failures of the war, was in command of the department at Memphis. However the rebel General Forrest held him strictly to his headquarters." These words were echoed by Capt. William Burns of Smith's staff, who noted how Washburn "was nominally in command of the large Union department of which Forrest had the real control (excepting the headquarters at Memphis)."[4]

A. J. Smith was actually the first person Washburn notified of Sturgis's defeat, and a courier was sent at 1:00 A.M. with the message, "I have this moment received bad news from General Sturgis." Smith was ordered to immediately turn out two thousand troops with three days' rations and a hundred rounds of ammunition. These men were to report to the railroad depot without delay, for, as Washburn told him, "the case is urgent." Washburn had two initial concerns: first, he believed Sturgis needed immediate assistance at Collierville from the pursuing enemy, and, second, he wanted soldiers up and moving for a possible defense of Memphis itself. Sturgis's communication had not fostered any reassurances. The enemy had pursued his column "with great vigor" all the way to Collierville, twenty-five miles east of Memphis. His ammunition was almost gone; only a few troops had any at all, and because of this he was unable to fend off the frequent attacks against his rear guard. "Had our ammunition not been exhausted our loss would not have been so severe, except in material of war, and that could not be avoided in the present execrable condition of the roads." He stressed that he had not actually lost any artillery in battle but had been forced to spike and abandon all of his cannon and destroy the remainder of his supplies when the wagons and carriages, mired in mud, could not be pulled free by the starving draft animals. A short time later, following the arrival of a relief train loaded with ammunition and forage, a rattled Sturgis asked, "Do you wish me to hold this place or withdraw when I get my debris away?"[5]

While Sturgis foundered and Washburn hastened to inform his superiors of the debacle, A. J. Smith acted with promptness. Col. David Moore, commander of the Third Division, was ordered to send his Third Brigade under Col. Edward Wolfe to Sturgis's aid. Unfortunately, the Third Brigade was unable to place 2,000 men in the field as Washburn requested. The bulk of the 49th Illinois Infantry had reenlisted prior to the Red River campaign and was happily making preparations for their thirty-day veteran furloughs. Another regiment from the division replaced the 49th, and the men of the relief column loaded their cartridge boxes and gnawed on hardtack while waiting for a train to take them to Collierville.

Wolfe's men had been expecting at least another day of rest and grumbled in the predawn as they prepared for the move. "Before daylight we rec'd orders to report to the Charleston depot *immediately*," complained Pvt. Benjamin Hieronymous, "not giving us time even to make our coffee." Moore must have been anticipating further orders from above and ordered Col. John Gilbert's Second Brigade to be roused and readied as well. Gilbert was to see that his men had haversacks filled with three days' rations as well as forty rounds in each cartridge box and another sixty rounds of ammunition per man in the charge of the ordnance officer. They were to be held in readiness "to move at a moment's notice."[6]

Eventually, the train loaded with Wolf's men made the trip out to Collierville, but there was little for them to do but watch Sturgis's men stagger into camp. Private Hieronymous, still bitter over being deprived of his morning coffee, watched with irritation as the demoralized column straggled in. "Numbers of the men were wounded & all had thrown away everything that would in the least retard their progress. The trains that took us out returned—loaded with the panic stricken mass." Gilbert's brigade spent the day quietly in camp, never receiving orders to leave the city.[7]

Smith spent the day in his headquarters on Poplar Street and at the end of the day allowed himself a rare night out. It had been four months since he had been at his leisure in a city of any size, and on the night of June 13 he chose to attend the theater and a showing of *Satan in Paris*. The outing was not only a diversion but a celebration; on his coat were new shoulder straps, each bearing the twin stars of a major general. The promotion was his reward for the Red River campaign, and his commission to the rank was backdated to May 12.[8]

It soon became apparent that Forrest's cavalry was no longer threatening Sturgis or Memphis, and Sturgis began moving his exhausted soldiers into the city. Additional details of the battle were forthcoming, and on June 14 Washburn reassured Sherman that "the affair of Sturgis' not as bad as first reported by him." Stragglers continued to return to their regiments, and Washburn estimated the loss of men at 1,500–2,000, a high enough number but still lower than the 3,000 initially reported. "That our troops were badly handled from the moment they left here I have no doubt," he conceded. "They were nine days in going out and thirty-six hours in returning." Colonel Wolfe and his Third Brigade returned from Collierville to their Memphis camp after helping Sturgis withdraw to the safety of the city. "Not a man was lost, not a gun was fired," reported Wolfe.[9]

In his telegram to Sherman on the 14th, Washburn maintained his focus on the purpose of the Sturgis raid and the ongoing need to keep Forrest occupied and away from Sherman's supply lines. He suggested to his boss that he could send A. J. Smith's force out for thirty or forty miles, "which will tend to keep the force that whipped Sturgis away from you." Though he had suffered a humiliating defeat and was destined to be shipped off to fight Indians on the western frontier, Sturgis had, in fact, accomplished his primary mission and prevented Forrest from harassing Sherman's supply lines in Georgia and Tennessee. As for Washburn's suggestion, Sherman had already made up his mind, and he responded, "Your dispatch [of June 12] is received. Under the circumstances, the expedition to Mobile should not be attempted. If General Canby can spare Smith's command, it should go out and meet Forrest, and check him."[10]

With the removal of Sturgis's command from the field, there was nothing to stop Forrest from resuming his raid into Tennessee and harassing Sherman's supply lines. Something would have to be done quickly. With that thought in mind, Washburn sent orders to Smith to ready his command to march out of Memphis on June 16. The two divisions would move twenty-eight miles to the east on the Memphis & Charleston Railroad to Grissom's Bridge, a burned-out span on the Wolf River that marked the terminus of travel on the line. Their presence alone was believed to be adequate to hold Forrest in Mississippi. There were insufficient locomotives and cars to move the entire force at once, so the first 3,000 men would entrain at 6:00 A.M., with the balance following at 2:00 P.M. Officers were ordered to ensure that the men had the standard three days of cooked rations in their haversacks and forty rounds of ammunition in their cartridge boxes, and quartermasters were instructed to have their wagons ready to be loaded at a moment's notice, and the artillery prepared to move out on the morning of the 16th with a full supply of ammunition. But, inevitably, nothing happened.[11]

Soldiers then, as ever, complained of the army's never-ending habit of "hurry up and wait." All preparations were made and everyone down to the last drummer boy awaited the order to move out. The orders never came. For forty-eight hours the army had been reacting to Sturgis's defeat, but a calm eventually descended when it was determined Forrest was in fact not moving on Memphis as believed. In a letter to General Canby the following day, Washburn revealed that the orders and troop movements had been merely a ruse, "as though I was again sending out to attack the enemy."[12]

Truth be told, A. J. Smith's divisions were simply not prepared for another major expedition so close on the heels of the recent Red River campaign. Not only did his men need a new supply of uniforms and equipment, most had not been paid for over four months. Most importantly, the right wing of the Sixteenth Corps was in desperate need of reorganization. Regimental, brigade, and even division commanders needed reassignment to duties equal to their abilities. During the course of the campaign, some officers had been forced—through death, wounds, or sickness—to take on responsibilities they were simply unprepared or unsuited for. There were captains commanding regiments and colonels who had no idea how to effectively lead a brigade. Not only was a reshuffling of commanders needed, regiments had to be shifted to other brigades as well in order to ensure that each brigade was fairly equal in size. In addition, many of the regiments in the Memphis camps were reduced to battalion strength, not because of the rigors of the Louisiana campaign but due to the departure of men on promised veteran furloughs.

Most Union regiments enlisted in the early days of the war for a period of three years. Few believed the war would last so long; in fact, most repeated the old soldier's litany about the war being over by Christmas. Yet, three Christmases had come and gone and the war was still in full swing, and the enlistments of the "three years men" were about to expire. This potential shortage was affecting all of the Union armies, east and west. And with the prospect of tens of thousands of men taking their discharges and going home, the War Department was becoming very anxious. How could the war effort be maintained with so many veteran soldiers going home? It boiled down to two alternatives: mass reenlistments of men in ranks or drafting them back into service. The latter was not a choice; the legal ramifications of conscripting men who had fulfilled their obligations and the resulting effects on troop morale were too distressing to contemplate. Reenlistment was the answer. But how could a man be persuaded to reenlist when he had already seen the horrors of three years of war?

The answer came from some bright soul in the War Department who hit on the brilliant idea of forgoing the individual and pushing for the reenlistment of the entire regiment. A regiment that reenlisted would be given "veteran volunteer" status—for example, the old 14th Wisconsin Volunteer Infantry would become the 14th Wisconsin Veteran Volunteer Infantry—and the regimental flag would be altered to proclaim it. In addition, men who reenlisted in veteran regiments would be granted a thirty-day furlough in their home state, with transportation provided. And just to sweeten the deal, the War Department paid each reenlisting soldier a cash bonus of $400, with many of the states kicking in additional cash. If a man chose not to reenlist with the regiment, as was his right; he simply stayed in the field until his time was up and took his discharge.

The plan was a huge success. Regiment after regiment reenlisted, and the soldiers sewed veteran braids onto the left sleeve of their uniforms. Stories of veterans returning home on furlough with pockets full of money, marching in parades, and being lauded as heroes enticed more than 200,000 men to reenlist. The manpower disaster was averted. Recruits were enlisted to replace those who declined to re-up, and the replacements revered these men who had taken three years of war and asked for more.[13]

Smith's dilemma with his veteran volunteers was caused by their promised furloughs. The men of the 47th and 49th Illinois infantries, the 5th Minnesota Infantry, and the 3rd Indiana Battery had all reenlisted prior to the Red River expedition and were authorized to travel home on leave. Each of these happy units was paid off and sent up the Mississippi on steamboats, leaving the detachments of nonvolunteers behind. The loss of these veterans—the equivalent of an entire brigade—left a big hole in Smith's expeditionary force. On June 16 he began to cast about for more men to fill the ranks. He did not have far to look.

When the Sixteenth Corps had set out for Louisiana back in March, a brigade had been left behind to serve garrison duty in Memphis. The First Brigade in Mower's division, under Col. William L. McMillen, consisting of four regiments and an artillery battery, had stayed behind and wound up being pressed into service during the Brice's Crossroads expedition, where it was beaten up pretty badly in the battle. Reduced to a thousand officers and men, it was snatched from the Memphis defenses and returned to Mower's division. The 9th Minnesota of Alexander Wilkin's Second Brigade had likewise been left behind and fought at Brice's, and its numbers swelled the ranks of the Second Brigade with an additional 401 rifles.[14] These veterans of Brice's Crossroads were delighted to be back under Smith and had the utmost confidence in his abilities as a soldier. Sgt. Harrison Chandler of the 114th Illinois confidently wrote in his diary, "I can hardly make myself believe that only 2 weeks ago tomorrow the enemy captured us, but we have not Gen'l Sturgis with us this time but our own Andy Smith who will handle his troops as a Gen'l should."[15]

The Memphis garrison also lost the 12th Iowa Infantry as well as the 2nd Iowa and 7th Kansas cavalries. Adding to the growing force were Brig. Gen.

Brig. Gen. Benjamin Grierson (Library of Congress)

Ben Grierson's three cavalry brigades of the Sixteenth Corps, which had not accompanied the corps to Louisiana and had been roughly handled during the fight at Brice's Crossroads. These additions were good but not good enough. Smith commandeered elements of the Seventeenth Corps that had served under him during the Red River campaign and traveled north with the Gorillas while returning to their own corps in Georgia. The 33rd Wisconsin and detachments of the 41st Illinois and 14th Wisconsin formed a fourth brigade in Mower's division, under the command of Col. Lyman Ward of the 14th Wisconsin. These regiments had been Thomas Ransom's brigade of the Seventeenth Corps and had been fighting alongside Smith's divisions since the middle of March. They were not then aware that the move would become permanent and were more than willing to become temporary members of the Sixteenth Corps. As June 16 drew to a close, Smith's expeditionary force had increased dramatically, yet he and Washburn continued to look for troops to add to the small army.[16]

Sherman, in the field near Big Shanty, Georgia, was almost out of the communication loop concerning the upcoming expedition into Mississippi. His telegrams, coming and going, generally took an additional two days longer in transit than the communications between Washington and Memphis. From his headquarters tent he commanded the Military Division of the Mississippi, and his orders were passed down to General McPherson commanding the Department of Tennessee and then on to Washburn at the head of the District of West Tennessee. Although the delay in communications slowed down the planning process, Sherman took an active role in planning and promoting the raid against Forrest.

On June 15 Sherman wrote Secretary of War Stanton, assuring him that he was looking closely into Sturgis's recent defeat. He expressed his amazement that Sturgis had been beaten when his force was more than sufficient for the mission at hand, even stating that he personally would have been willing to lead the same troops in the same task, "but Forrest is the very devil, and I think he has got some of our troops under cower." He then went on to confidently endorse his two lieutenants in Memphis, Smith and Mower: "The latter is a young brigadier of fine promise, and I commend him to your notice. I will order them to make up a force and go out and follow Forrest to the death, if it costs 10,000 lives and breaks the Treasury. There will never be peace in Tennessee till Forrest is dead."[17]

Another important communiqué sent on the 15th was from Washburn to General Canby in New Orleans. Though Canby knew of Sturgis's defeat at the hands of Forrest, he was still operating under the assumption that Smith would lead the operation against Pascagoula and Mobile. Since these two locations were in his jurisdiction as commander of the Military Division of West Mississippi, Canby was actively coordinating the proposed movement with Adm. David G. Farragut. Washburn began the letter with an update on Sturgis's casualties and then briefly explained why an expedition under Smith to the Gulf would be fruitless. The Confederates, Washburn explained, had repaired the Mobile & Ohio Railroad from Tupelo (actually Corinth) to its terminus at Mobile Bay, and the large force that had whipped Sturgis could move within twenty-four hours to the Mobile defenses. Therefore, the same force could be in position to confront Smith when he arrived in force on the Gulf Coast. Washburn, unwittingly or deliberately, exaggerated the number of Confederates along the railroad to be 15,000–20,000, of which 12,000 were cavalry. Though he neglected to mention that the operation was already being coordinated, he suggested that he would send 10,000 men to the end of the rail line (twenty-five miles) east of Memphis and then push the cavalry further on to search out the enemy. Never mind that a similar plan had just ended in disaster; the expedition would "detain" Forrest from Sherman's supply line and, thus, "a point will be gained." Though Washburn's motives are unclear, it is obvious that he was being less than candid with

General Canby and continued to feed him less-than-accurate information, all the while seeking Canby's advice.[18]

Throughout the day of June 15, couriers and messengers rushed from camp to camp with letters and orders about the imminent departure of Smith's force. The flurry of activity was all part of a plan Washburn had concocted to fool the southern spies skulking about Memphis. The ruse went on for days. "On the 12th came orders to be ready at any time, and such orders came almost daily," recalled Pvt. John Scott of the 32nd Iowa Infantry. Soldiers were checking their cartridge boxes for the required forty rounds on an almost daily basis.[19]

* * *

The morning of June 16 found Sherman relaxing in his headquarters tent at Big Shanty, settled into a camp chair with a three-day-old copy of a Confederate newspaper from Atlanta. Most of the articles dealt with the war—Robert E. Lee's troops besieged by Grant at Petersburg, Johnston valiantly defending Georgia against Sherman, Forrest whipping the Federals near Guntown with only two brigades of cavalry. Furious, Sherman immediately dispatched a telegram to Washburn: "It is all nonsense about Sturgis being attacked by 15,000 or 20,000. He was whipped by a force inferior to his own. Let the matter be critically investigated."[20]

In a matter of minutes, a letter from Sherman was in the hands of a courier making his way to the nearby headquarters of General McPherson. Sturgis's conduct was to be investigated immediately, he said, including the possibility of his "being in liquor" during the recent battle. Sherman eventually cooled down and admitted that he doubted that to be true, but all the same it had to be investigated. And if there was any truth to the rumor, "then the remedy must be applied of trial and punishment." The newspaper Sherman read must have made note of the support for Forrest among the citizens of Mississippi, for in his orders to McPherson he made clear that he expected the upcoming expedition to be carried out with a heavy hand. Smith was to pursue Forrest on foot, "devastating the land over which he has passed or may pass, and make him and the people of Tennessee and Mississippi realize, that although a bold, daring and successful leader, he will bring ruin and misery on any country where he may pause or tarry. If we do not punish Forrest and the people now, the whole effect of our past conquests will be lost."[21]

McPherson sent another message to Washburn via Brig. Gen. Joseph D. Webster, Sherman's chief of staff in Nashville, reminding him of the necessity of making a great show of activity in order to hold the highest number of the enemy in the theater and "to destroy as much as you can of the growing crops." There would be little need to burn crops, Washburn confided to Canby, since "the country is a desert between here and where [Forrest] is."[22]

In the flurry of correspondence flying over the wires, Sherman suggested the advantages to be gained by a small demonstration made against Mobile in conjunction with the raid against Forrest. "Could not the Secretary of the Navy order this, and Canby spare a small force (one brigade) for this purpose?" Canby had an idea of his own and wired Washburn that he had 5,000 infantry at Vicksburg ready for a rapid movement into the interior of the state. The diversion could be coordinated to set out at the same time as Smith's column from Tennessee. If nothing else, he suggested, the diversion would create confusion with General Lee in Mobile and pin down the small Confederate cavalry force near Jackson, Mississippi.[23]

But it would take more than words and ideas to make the raid a success, so concrete steps to put the plan into action began on the morning of June 16. Washburn ordered the Memphis & Charleston Railroad tracks, which were intact for twenty-eight miles to the east of Memphis, terminating at the burned Grissom's Bridge beyond Collierville, to be repaired an additional thirty miles to the small town of Saulsbury, and a special construction train soon pulled out of the Memphis depot. Work on the tracks began that very morning. Smith assigned the 11th Missouri Infantry of Col. Alexander Wilkin's brigade as train guard, and the more mobile 7th Kansas Cavalry, under Col. Thomas Herrick, was ordered to the end of the tracks to patrol the work site and keep an eye out for the enemy. The Jayhawkers packed their saddlebags with three days of rations and a hundred rounds of ammunition.[24]

Repairs to the railroad proceeded at an acceptable pace. On June 18 Washburn wrote Sherman an encouraging letter assuring him that he was investigating the Sturgis disaster thoroughly and that he had anticipated the general's orders in regard to Smith's raid: "With his own troops and such others as I can give him he will have a force ample to whip anything this side of Georgia." Sherman was elated. Washburn was working with abandon and seeing to every detail of the raid. Sherman had no worries for the expedition with crusty old A. J. Smith at the helm, and he also had every confidence in Smith's senior lieutenant, Joe Mower, and sent him an encouraging note via Washburn: "Say to General Mower I want him advanced, and if he will whip Forrest I will pledge him my influence for a major-general, and will ask the president as a personal favor to hold a vacancy for him." Without waiting for Mower to "whip" Forrest, Sherman wrote President Lincoln a week later from near Kennesaw, Georgia: "I have ordered General A. J. Smith and General Mower from Memphis to pursue and kill Forrest, promising the latter, in case of success, my influence to promote him to Major-General. He is one of the gamest men in our service. Should accident befall me I ask you to favor Mower, if he succeeds in disposing of Forrest."[25]

Among a thousand other details, Washburn still worked to find additional sources of manpower for Smith's upcoming raid. The District of Columbus, Kentucky, which included the garrison at Paducah, had a number of Sixteenth Corps regiments that had never shipped to the front. On June 15 orders went out to the 7th and 10th Minnesota and the 122nd Illinois infantries and Battery G, 2nd Illinois Light Artillery, to report to Smith at Memphis. The men struck their tents, stuffed their knapsacks with the necessities of active campaigning, and filed onto steamboats for the trip down the Ohio and Mississippi rivers. Later in the day, back in Memphis, Col. Edward Bouton's Colored Brigade, consisting of three regiments and a battery of USCT, marched down the rails to augment the construction guard at Grissom's Bridge.[26]

Smith was ready to move his expedition out of Memphis to Moscow but delayed issuing any orders until the men had received their back pay. Cash in hand, the men were ready to blow off a little steam, and the results were predictable. The paymaster arrived in the camp of the 178th New York on June 21, and by evening there were "a great many drunken soldiers in camp." The following day Pvt. Charles Tiedman noted in his diary that the regiment had received orders to march but that "we [had] to spend our greenbacks first." When the 4th Iowa Cavalry was paid, "of course all hands wanted to go to town." Captain Abraham of Company D was kept awake until midnight the following night by the happy, boisterous drunks returning to camp. Most of the men wired at least some of the money home, through express agents brought into the camps. If it were not for the agents, "it would be impossible to keep the men in camp, for they don't believe in carrying such an amount of money with them on a tramp, if they can help it." The camp of the 47th Illinois was no different, and as Pvt. Jacob Melick noted, "Vets spend their money free, some of them got in a weaving way." A few days later he recorded how "some of the boys went to town and came back with a little too much beer aboard, was quite merry for awhile, when they got—oh how sick."[27]

Many of the soldiers were content in their camps and in no hurry to begin a new campaign. The 117th Illinois was camped in the woods along the Hernando Road leading south out of the city, a very comfortable location. "A lovely day!" wrote Pvt. Benjamin Hieronymous.

> The "Hernando" for a half mile commencing at our camp affords a splendid
> drive for the pleasure seekers of the city to exercise their fast horses upon.
> This evening from an hour by sun till dusk they were passing & repassing in

carriages & buggies & on horse-back—but the most attractive feature was the splendid horse-manship of the gaily dressed ladies—"Hats and Feathers & Flowing robes"—bringing forcibly to our minds the festive days of by-gone years, when we were happy in the presence of those we love at home![28]

One of the few complaints voiced by the soldiers in Memphis was the overall health of the men. A week of rest had gone far to bring the weary soldiers back into fighting trim, but a great many had been laid low by disease. The voyage north from Louisiana, on transports described as "pesthouses" by Rear Adm. David Porter, had resulted in more than thirty cases of smallpox. Forced to drink river water during the journey, scores of men still suffered from diarrhea and other intestinal ailments. Pvt. Hugh Bay of the 89th Indiana grumbled to his wife:

If we get our pay I will buy myself a bottle of stomach bitters and try that[.] Our doctors is not worth Powder enough to blo them up[.] I have nown Boys to ask them for medicine when they was sick and all the sadisfaction they would give them was that they might as well be in hell as to take medicine[.] hear some of them has the clap the half of the time But I hope the day is coming when we will not have to ask them for any medicine.

A much-weakened Bay was finally able to announce that he was cured on July 2.[29]

Finally, on the morning of Wednesday, June 22, the orders came for Smith's men to shoulder their packs and leave their Memphis camps. This time the orders were not a ruse, and there were no bold statements about filling cartridge boxes and cooking rations. The soldiers left their camp tents standing, and a sufficient guard of convalescents remained to keep an eye on things. One such guard was Pvt. Louis Bir of the 93rd Indiana Infantry. Bir had been captured during the retreat from Brice's Crossroads and after three days of captivity had managed to escape. With the assistance of a friendly slave, he hid out in swamps and slowly made his way back to Memphis. Exhausted and ill, he arrived in camp the night before his regiment moved out and, naturally, was determined to join his comrades—"But the doctor would not let me go[.] I even ast him to let me straddle one of the cannons but it was no good for I was just able to walk." In the morning a disappointed Bir watched his regiment march away without him.[30]

The men leaving the Memphis camps packed lightly. The convalescents kept watch over the belongings left behind—quite a bit of materiel, actually, as Smith's army was marching with as little encumbrance as possible. Pvt. Ben Thomas of the 14th Iowa described the light marching order in his journal:

Packed all our things but the clothes we wore, and wore blouses rather than coats, and sent them to the city to be stored till we returned. Carried besides our guns and accouterments a canteen, haversack, rubber blanket or a piece of canvas five by six feet square called a dog tent. We were probably in the lightest marching condition we could be and have any protection from the weather. For cooking utensils we each had a quart tin fruit can with the top melted off and a wire bale to carry it with. This to make coffee or boil meat in. We also had half a canteen, that is, a canteen with the seam melted so the disks came apart. This was the frying pan. The blanket or canvas was rolled into a roll and the two ends tied with a string and hung over one shoulder and under the other arm. This was but a slight encumbrance.[31]

Each regiment was allowed two wagons to carry essentials such as cooking gear and some extra luggage for the officers, though even the officers were required to travel light. Lt. Henry McConnell of the 10th Minnesota Infantry wrote home that he had left his dress coat and pillow behind in a friend's trunk. Being an officer with a mount had it benefits, and Henry was able to cram a few personal items in the leather valise strapped behind his saddle in addition to an extra blanket.[32]

At 7 A.M. on the 22nd, Mower's division began to board the train cars for the trip to Grissom's Bridge at Lafayette. It was a short trip, only twenty-eight miles, and the trains spent the day shuttling the men to their destination, where a temporary camp was established along the tracks. Still, it was the army, and nothing went smoothly. "A train of flat cars came in and we were ordered to get aboard," recorded Private Thomas.

After we were on the cars they still remained standing in the yards. The sun was very hot for it was now about eleven o'clock and we were in the full glare of the sun and surrounded by buildings. [Pvt. William] Leach was sitting on the edge of a car with his feet off the side when he suddenly became unconscious and fell to the ground. He was taken up and placed in an ambulance and sent to the hospital. It was sunstroke that ailed him.[33]

Among the division was the 7th Minnesota Infantry, which had been traveling three days to reach its new assignment with Col. J. J. Woods's Third Brigade of Mower's command. From Paducah the regiment had taken the steamer Belle of St. Louis to Cairo, Illinois, and the following day another steamer brought them to Memphis, arriving at the wharves at midnight. At first light the men of the 7th Minnesota disembarked and marched straight for the railroad depot, where they had the option of climbing inside or on top of the boxcars, "the men generally preferring the roof." When the cars were full, inside and on top, there was still not enough space for the entire regiment, so a number of flat cars were added to the train. Capt. Theodore Carter was certain there would be a calamity: "The weight on top of the boxcars caused the old rickety things to sway over badly, and it seemed to those on top, as well as those inside, that they would surely collapse." One of the soldiers, sitting on the edge of a boxcar, stuck his leg out and struck a post set next to the tracks. In a flash he was swept from the roof and lay sprawled on the rail bed with the train pulling away and his comrades waving and calling out his name. Just before the dazed soldier passed from their sight, the men of his company were relieved to see him rise to his feet and begin to stumble after the train. On its return trip to Memphis, the train passed him ten miles from camp, still limping along gamely to catch up with his regiment.[34]

The infantry bivouac near Lafayette was a miserable camp site. The 33rd Wisconsin camped in an open field with no cover from the hard rain that had begun to fall. Pvt. William Truman complained to his diary, "I was most sick. Got some bundles of wheat to lay on, as we camped in a wheat field that was cut and shocked up." Men of the 8th Wisconsin Infantry were not even allowed the luxury of seeking shelter from the passing thunderstorm. John Williams, the regimental historian, remembered, "We disembarked and were at once detailed as 'pioneers' to assist in rebuilding the railroad bridge across Wolf River." No enemy activity was expected along the right-of-way, and the 7th Kansas Cavalry, patrolling the tracks, had reported there were no Confederates within twenty miles. They were wrong.[35]

The next day, June 23, David Moore's Third Division embarked on the train at Memphis and began the ride out to Grissom's Bridge. Farther up the line, Mower's First Division had risen early and was marching along the right-of-way to Moscow, an additional twelve miles to the east. The trip was uneventful until the train reached Spring Hill, where, with no warning, a group of guerrillas hiding in the brush fired a volley into the open flat cars. The range was point-blank. Five men were shot and killed instantly, and another thirteen were wounded. In the confusion, six men of the 178th New York either fell or jumped from the train and were captured by the enemy. Five of them were executed, their bodies left lying along the tracks; the sixth man, though badly wounded, was able to escape through the brush. "A great mode of warfare," one Illinois soldier wrote, "a specimen of *Southern Chivalry*."[36]

Not long after the ill-fated train pulled out of the station, a sizable column left Memphis under the escort of the 2nd Iowa Cavalry; six artillery batteries, with their attendant limbers, caissons, wagons, and forges; scores of wagons loaded with the commissary supplies; and a second wagon train bearing the reserve artillery ammunition. The scene prompted Sgt. Harrison Chandler, responsible for four of the wagons, to write his wife: "This to a Yankee girl would be quite a sight—to see 200 six mule teams stretched along the road as far almost as the eye can see. Then too, ambulances and [et]c. making a great train." The long line of troops and wagons traveled nine miles without incident before halting for the night at White's Station.[37] Activity continued on the 24th as Col. James Gilbert's brigade of Moore's division entrained at the depot as more supply wagons rolled out of Memphis. Grierson sent the cavalry brigades of Colonels Edward Winslow and George Waring to the Spring Hill area to watch for guerrillas, but none were found. Another detachment of cavalry escorted a wagon train of Grierson's ammunition that set out for Moscow. All along the right-of-way of the Memphis & Charleston there was military activity, and all of it was headed east toward Moscow on the Wolf River.[38]

Moscow, however, was not the point of departure Smith desired for the start of his expedition. The bridge across the Wolf River would be repaired by Sunday, June 26, and he intended to push further east. A cavalry detachment had ridden as far as LaGrange, and it was to this destination Smith was sending his men. Washburn revealed a bit of Smith's plans in a letter to Canby: "When Smith moves it will be to draw Forrest and his force as well up toward Corinth as possible." The point of Washburn's letter was to encourage Canby to attack Mobile while all of the enemy's force was moving northward to engage Smith. Whether Washburn or Smith believed Forrest would venture forth from Tupelo is just conjecture; Forrest had a habit of doing things Federal commanders did not expect. As the morning wore on Smith left his Memphis headquarters and took the train to Moscow. He would remain in the field until the campaign was concluded.[39]

FOUR

Stretched to the Limit

Despite the pummeling of Sturgis at Brice's Crossroads, Forrest was not free to resume his aborted raid into Tennessee. General Lee was faced with potential Union advances on at least three fronts and was ordered by President Jefferson Davis to hold Forrest in Mississippi until Federal intentions within the state could be determined. The critical task of destroying Sherman's supply line was left in the hands of the overworked and overextended cavalry serving with Gen. Joseph Johnston in Georgia. The administration in Richmond perceived threats to the Mississippi heartland to be of such a high priority that it believed it would be disastrous to allow Forrest to leave the theater. Thus, in the glow of the recent victory, Lee was forced to surrender the initiative to the enemy.

The threats were real enough. Lee watched with trepidation as Federal forces in his department continued growing in numbers he could never hope to match. On May 26, sixteen days before the fight at Brice's Crossroads, he received a report of reinforcements arriving at Vicksburg and lost no time in passing the information on to Richmond: "Nineteen transports loaded with troops passed Grand Gulf, going up, on afternoon of 23d, and are now at Vicksburg, supposed to be Smith's troops from Red River, 10,000 strong." In response, Lee dispatched the 1,400 men of Brig. Gen. Samuel Gholson's brigade in Forrest's corps to bolster the Confederate forces at Canton, twenty-four miles north of Jackson.[1] Brig. Gen. Wirt Adams, commanding a division of cavalry at Canton, was ordered by Lee to watch over the ever-fluctuating Federal garrison in Vicksburg—an unenviable assignment. Gholson's brigade had hardly arrived at Canton when Col. Hinchie P. Mabry's stronger and better-armed brigade separated from Adams's division in response to Sturgis's column advancing out of

— 41 —

Memphis. Mabry's four regiments arrived too late to participate in the battle at Brice's Crossroads; but, rather than returning to Adams, Lee attached them to Buford's division and directed them to make camp in Okolona. The exchange of Gholson's brigade of questionable militia, partisans, and state guards for Mabry's four veteran regiments was a material boost to Forrest's ranks.[2]

The active campaigning in early June prevented Forrest from closely monitoring enemy troop movements around Memphis, but once Sturgis was put back in the bag, the general maintained a close eye on movements around the river city. Forrest dispatched Pvt. R. H. Bonner, a scout from the 7th Tennessee Cavalry, to Holly Springs to coordinate the efforts of the spies in Memphis and Byhalia, Mississippi. On June 13 Bonner reported a remarkably accurate assessment: Federal reinforcements had arrived by steamboat and were actively repairing the Memphis & Charleston Railroad forty miles east to Moscow. He observed working parties laying down new crossties. In addition, he reported that a brigade of cavalry was preparing for operations and that an order had been issued exempting all blacksmiths and wagonmakers from military duty in Memphis for a period of six days. He indicated that several trains had been dispatched to the east bearing men and horses. All of this pointed to one conclusion: the Federals were preparing another, larger expedition out of Memphis. Forrest forwarded the information from Bonner to General Lee, adding, "I think every preparation should be made to meet the enemy in case they should move out." Lee reported the developments to Adj. Gen. Samuel Cooper in Richmond, noting how the Federals were again "threatening" from Memphis. But Forrest and Lee came to the correct conclusion for the wrong reasons; the trains moving out of Memphis was not the start of another raid but, rather, Col. Edward Wolfe's brigade moving to Collierville to cover Sturgis's withdrawal.[3]

A second threat to Lee's department surfaced early in June in a message from General Adams at Canton. On June 2 Adams relayed to Lee that he had intelligence of an intended raid from Vicksburg in the direction of Jackson. The intelligence proved to be false, but the threat prompted Lee to enquire about what enemy troops were at Vicksburg and where they had come from. This proved to be a headache for Adams, charged with gathering the intelligence, as Federal troops were constantly arriving and departing the busy river port, particularly in the wake of the Red River campaign. To make things worse, Adams's opposite number, Maj. Gen. Henry Slocum, the Federal commander of the District of Vicksburg, was a veteran campaigner who took measures to screen his forces from the prying eyes of Adams's scouts.[4]

From his headquarters in Meridian, Lee had no sooner informed Richmond of the Memphis threat when he learned of yet another risk developing on the Gulf Coast. Maj. Gen. Dabney Maury, commander of the Confederate garrison at Mobile, reported three men-of-war and three transports arriving at the mouth of Mobile Bay. In addition, there was also suspicious military activity at the Federal enclave at Fort Pickens, Florida. Maury reported that the movements at Fort Pickens seemed to indicate an imminent raid by two regiments of cavalry.[5]

The city of Mobile was still firmly in Confederate hands, as was the expansive deepwater bay, but the mouth of the bay was nearly choked shut by the Union navy hovering off the bar. Only one channel remained open, and it was tricky to navigate under the best of conditions. During 1864 there were twenty-two attempts by steamers to break the Federal blockade at Mobile; nineteen were successful. The presence of the Federal blockaders discouraged most captains from attempting the passage. The added risk of being able to depart from the harbor after discharging a cargo was also a factor; there were few captains willing to risk being bottled up in port for the duration of the war. Even when a ship did manage to run the blockade, there was no guarantee the cargo would contain any needed military supplies, since so many captains opted to import luxury items in the expectation of a higher profit. (On June 7 the steamer *Denbeigh* arrived from Havana and was compelled to dump part of its cargo over the side to escape the pursuing Federals. Within its hold was a cargo of doubtful military value: musical instruments for the band of the 1st Louisiana Heavy Artillery.) In prewar Mobile nineteen ships pulling into port would have been an average *day*, but in 1864, for all practical purposes, the port was closed. Though ships continued to trickle through the blockade, the Confederate presence in Mobile was no longer concerned with keeping the port open as much as denying its use to the enemy.[6]

Maury's reasons for concern were valid. The six vessels arriving south of Mobile swelled the Federal presence off the bar to twenty-two ships. For the moment the Federal fleet was kept at bay by the heavy guns of Fort Morgan and Fort Gaines at the bay's narrow entrance. Maury was also counting on the presence of the ironclad CSS *Tennessee* to deter the Union ships under Admiral Farragut. The *Tennessee*, Adm. Franklin Buchanan's flagship, was a heavily armed and armored dreadnought mounting two 7-inch rifles and four 6.4-inch rifles. The tense situation was alleviated somewhat on June 20 when Maury was able to report that "Farragut's fleet has been detained for the last week. It apparently assembled for defensive purposes against the Tennessee." For the moment, Lee could turn away from the threat against Mobile and concentrate on A. J. Smith in Memphis.[7]

Lee directed Forrest to deploy his cavalry in anticipation of an enemy movement out of Memphis and to also be prepared for the possibility of supporting

Maury in Mobile. In effect, he was asking his subordinate to prepare for action on either of two fronts roughly 350 miles apart. For the time being, the Federal threat in West Mississippi would be in the hands of Wirt Adams and his cavalry. Forrest responded by directing Brig. Gen. Philip Roddey to move his division from North Alabama to Corinth. A 350-man detachment from Col. Josiah Patterson's brigade remained behind near Decatur to watch for enemy incursions. Chalmers's division took a position in Columbus, where they could move quickly north or south as conditions warranted. Between them, at Tupelo, Abraham Buford's division of Tennesseans, Mississippians, and Kentuckians rested from the recent battle.[8]

For most of Forrest's men the two weeks following the battle of Brice's Crossroads were a welcome break from campaigning. Capt. William Pirtle of the 7th Kentucky Mounted Infantry recalled, "We had nothing to do but attend our horses, cook and eat, thus we remained for two weeks." They mended uniforms, wrote letters, and caught up on sleep. Inevitably discipline suffered, and men were caught wandering the camps or performing duties without their weapons nearby. General Order No. 57 reminded each man that he was to be "armed with his gun and necessary accouterments to go into the fight." Another infraction in the cavalry camps that angered Forrest was the poor condition of the recently captured Federal wagons. Many of the vehicles had been stripped of parts rendering them useless. In General Order No. 56 he spelled out in no uncertain terms what an offender could expect:

> It is therefore the intention of the Major-General Commanding, whenever he finds a wagon, in camp or on the march, deficient in any of these needed articles, with all of which it has been supplied, or finds them damaged, or neglected, or missing, to hold the proper party to a most rigid responsibility, and without mercy, inflict the severest punishment known to the regulations, upon the head of that officer in whose department such neglect shall be found.

No one wanted to find out what Forrest meant by "without mercy"; the wagons were quickly restored to working order.[9]

The men might have been able to rest, but not the department commander. The amount of stress placed on the shoulders of the thirty-year-old was enormous. Lee had been in command of the department for six weeks; in that time a major battle had been fought and won, and now danger presented itself from three different directions. And his attention was pulled in a fourth direction by the continued requests by Gen. Johnston to dispatch Forrest's cavalry against

Sherman's line of supply and communication. Lee was on the verge of being overwhelmed when he wrote Johnston, "At this time, and as long as there is any considerable force at Memphis, it is impracticable to make any move into Middle Tennessee."[10]

In early May Lt. Gen. Leonidas Polk had turned his departmental command over to Stephen Lee and departed for Georgia with virtually all of the department's infantry. Shortly thereafter, Johnston began making requests for Lee to send a cavalry column to sever Sherman's supply lines. Johnston wanted Forrest's cavalry for the raid, and he simply refused to take no for an answer. In addition to asking Lee directly, Johnston took another tack and solicited Gen. Braxton Bragg, Johnston's predecessor as army commander, who was then serving as President Davis's chief military adviser. An unsympathetic Bragg reminded Johnston that he had cavalry of his own, in particular the small division of Brig. Gen. William H. Jackson, which had already been sent from Stephen Lee's department, and Maj. Gen. Joseph Wheeler's cavalry corps. Wheeler craved the opportunity to disrupt Sherman's communications and supplies; in fact, he told Bragg, "I have begged General Johnston to allow me to go to the enemy's rear nearly every day." The army commander believed he could not spare Wheeler's men, who served the traditional role of cavalry—guarding the army's flanks, screening troop movements, gathering intelligence, and serving as pickets. Johnston instead allowed "Red" Jackson's cavalry to attack Sherman's supply and communication lines between Dalton and Acworth, even though the beat-up troopers and horses were so worn out from continuous service they were of next to no value in such an enterprise. Sent out in detachments of 75–100 men, the cavalry's efforts were far too feeble to inflict any real damage to Sherman's supply line.[11]

Thus, Johnston was convinced he needed additional cavalry. Early in the campaign he spoke with General Polk and then later with his successor, Stephen D. Lee, about the available cavalry in the Department of Alabama, Mississippi and East Louisiana. Johnston, in his memoirs, stated that the figures supplied by both men indicated

that an adequate force to destroy the railroad communications of the Federal army could be furnished in Mississippi and Alabama, under an officer fully competent to head such an enterprise—General Forrest. I therefore suggested the measure to the President, directly on the 13th of June and 10th of July; and through Bragg on the 3rd, 12th, 13th, 16th, and 26th of June; also to Lieutenant General Lee on the 10th of May, and the 3rd, 11th, and 16th of June. That

officer promised on two occasions, to make the attempt. I made these suggestions in the strong belief that this cavalry would serve the Confederacy far
better by contributing to the defeat of a formidable invasion, than by waiting
for and repelling raids.

In this belief he was probably correct.[12]

At Johnston's urging, Polk wrote to President Davis suggesting that the cavalry commands of Chalmers, Roddey, and Brig. Gen. Gideon Pillow be sent under Forrest's guidance to "operate on the enemy's communications from this to
Chattanooga." Fellow corps commander Lt. Gen. William J. Hardee concurred.
Johnson's third corps commander, Lt. Gen. John Bell Hood, remained silent on
the matter.[13]

Davis responded through his chief of staff, Bragg:

> The within indicates the propriety of concentrating the force of General S. D.
> Lee for the defense of his department and for such operations on the enemy as
> were contemplated before detachments were made to operate on the rear of the
> enemy in front of General Johnston. The movement of General Polk's infantry
> alone was authorized, and that was done on the supposition that the enemy
> would be met at Dalton or in front of it, so as to relieve the danger to Alabama
> and Mississippi. The retreat of the Army of Tennessee has exposed the country
> for the protection of which General Polk's troops were posted. Under the facts
> as now presented, General S. D. Lee should get and keep in hand all the force he
> had left, including that of Pillow and Roddey, and General Johnston should be
> notified of the condition of things in that department so that he may not count
> on aid from General Lee, but rather perceive that the drafts upon the Depart-
> ment of Alabama, Mississippi, and East Louisiana have been already too great.[14]

As far as Davis was concerned, the matter was over. Georgia governor Joseph
E. Brown, however, soon joined the chorus of voices imploring the president
to send Forrest against Sherman's supply line. Atlanta and all of Georgia were
threatened by Sherman, he reminded Davis, saying,

> I need not call your attention to the fact that this place is to the Confederacy
> almost as important as the heart is to the human body. We must hold it. Could
> not Forrest or Morgan, or both, do more now for our cause in Sherman's rear
> than anywhere else? He brings his supplies from Nashville, over nearly 300
> miles of railroad, through a rough country, over a great number of bridges. If
> these are destroyed, it is impossible for him to subsist his large army, and he

must fall back through a broad scope of country destitute of provisions, which he could not do without great loss, if not annihilation.

The president responded to Brown with a fabrication: "I have sent all available re-enforcements, detaching troops even from points that remain exposed to the enemy. The disparity of force between the opposing armies in Northern Georgia is less as reported than at any other point. Forrest's command is now operating on one of Sherman's lines of communication, and is necessary for other purposes in his present field of service." The day Davis penned his response to Brown, June 29, Forrest was in Tupelo, attempting to divine Smith's intentions. In no way could his activity be construed as "operating on one of Sherman's lines of communication."[15]

Specifics about the "disparity of force" mentioned by Davis came in a letter to Brown from Bragg, whose creative use of arithmetic gave Johnston a badly needed boost in numbers—at least on paper. Bragg stressed that "in proportion to the enemy confronting him," Johnston was in far better shape than Stephen Lee, and, if anything, Johnston should "return a part of what he has received." It was an absurd statement given Johnston's predicament, but it was indicative of the poor relations between the general and the administration in Richmond. Brown remained unconvinced. On June 29 Brown sent Senator Benjamin H. Hill on a mission to Richmond to secure the support of Secretary of War James Seddon. Hill planned to communicate with the president and "present to him the necessity of ordering General Forrest, with certain cavalry forces, to cut the communications and destroy the supplies in General Sherman's rear." After meeting with Governor Brown in Richmond, Hill visited Johnston's headquarters, where the commander made another plea for Forrest and 5,000 men to be set loose on Sherman's supply line. A subsequent audience with the president proved to be fruitless.[16]

Another call for Forrest's presence came from Maj. Gen. Howell Cobb, former congressman, Speaker of the House, governor of Georgia, and secretary of the treasury in the Buchanan administration. Cobb, who had recently been sent to Athens, Georgia, to organize local defenses, took the time to write to Secretary Seddon.

> While I know too little of the condition of our different armies in the field to express an opinion worthy of much consideration, yet there is a conviction upon my mind so strong and overwhelming that I cannot throw it off, that the defense of Atlanta and Georgia, and the certain defeat and destruction of Sherman's army, are involved in some movement to be made by Forrest (if possible) or

some other cavalry on Sherman's line of communication. Unless it is done, I see no end to the slow process of Sherman's advance through Georgia.

Cobb's request made no more of an impression on the president than those of Johnston, Brown, and Hill.[17]

Governor Brown was unwilling to let the matter alone, especially after receiving the president's response to his original request. It was obvious to Brown that Forrest's continued presence in Mississippi was doing nothing to sever Sherman's line of communication, and he could feel the opportunity for action passing.

> I received your dispatch last night [July 4]. I regret exceedingly that you cannot grant my request, as I am satisfied Sherman's escape with his army would be impossible if 10,000 good cavalry under Forrest were thrown in his rear this side of Chattanooga, and his supplies cut off. The whole country expects this, though points of less importance should be for a time overrun. Our people believe that General Johnston is doing all in his power with the means at his command, and all expect you to send the necessary force to cut of the enemy's subsistence. We do not see how Forrest's operations in Mississippi, or Morgan's raids as conducted in Kentucky, interfere with Sherman's plans in this State, as his supplies continue to reach him. Destroy these and Atlanta is not only safe, but the destruction of the army under Sherman opens up Tennessee and Kentucky to us. Your information as to the relative strength of the two armies in North Georgia cannot be from reliable sources. If your mistake should result in the loss of Atlanta, and the occupation of other strong points in this State by the enemy, the blow may be fatal to our cause and remote posterity may have reason to mourn over the error.

Jefferson Davis was livid. His relationship with Governor Brown was strained under the best of circumstances, and he wasted no time penning his acerbic reply.

> Your telegram of [today] received. I am surprised to learn from you that the basis of comparison I made on official reports and estimates is unreliable. Until your better knowledge is communicated I shall have no means of correcting such errors, and your dicta cannot control the disposition of troops in different parts of the Confederate States. Most men in your position would not assume to decide on the value of the service to be rendered by troops in distant positions. When you give me your reliable statement of the comparative strength of the armies, I will be glad also to know the source of your information as to what the whole country expects and posterity will judge.[18]

Brown, ever persistent, gave it one last shot.

I regret the exhibition of temper with which I am met in your dispatch refusing to grant my request to send Forrest or Morgan, or both, with their commands, to cut off Sherman's supplies and relive my State. I have not pretended to dictate, but when Georgia has forty to fifty regiments defending Richmond and Atlanta is in great danger, probably no one but yourself would consider the anxiety of the efforts of her Governor to use every argument in his power to obtain re-enforcements just cause of rebuke, while defense of the Gulf States depends upon the strength of one of the armies in front of Atlanta and the Western States upon the other. If you continue to keep our forces divided and our cavalry raiding and meeting raids while enemy's line of communication, nearly 300 miles from his base, is uninterrupted, I fear the result will be similar to those which followed a like policy of dividing our forces at Murfreesborough and Chattanooga. If Atlanta is sacrificed and Georgia overrun while our cavalry are engaged in distant raids, you will have no difficulty in ascertaining, from correct sources of information, what was expected of you by the whole people, and what verdict posterity will record from your statements as to the relative strength of the two armies. I venture the hazard of further rebuke, to predict that your official estimates of Sherman's numbers are as incorrect as your official calculations at Missionary Ridge were erroneous.

President Davis declined to continue the debate and left Brown's letter unanswered.[19]

In a letter to General Johnston Davis attempted to explain his adamant refusal to release Forrest. If Forrest and his men were removed from Mississippi, he said, Federal columns from Memphis "might lay waste the stored and growing supplies of the Tombigbee Valley, and the main body, liberated from the protection of Memphis and free from flank attack, could (and probably would) move rapidly on to re-enforce Sherman." But there were several other reasons why Davis refused to allow Forrest to act against Sherman in Georgia, and none of them were logical from a military standpoint. For one, the president was unyielding in his resolve to protect every square inch of the Confederacy. There was no trading territory for a merging of forces no matter how big the potential results or how much damage could be realized by inaction. That the land would be left unguarded by Forrest's departure was Davis's home state of Mississippi was a major factor as well. In addition, the president had proven himself to be closed-minded to advice once he had made a decision and the continued requests by Johnston, Brown, and the others only succeeded in rousing his stubbornness and ire. His resolve was such that he allowed himself to be blinded to creditable proposals and considered those making such suggestions to be disloyal and therefore untrustworthy.[20]

One of the few people Davis did listen to was Braxton Bragg, a man who had a deep-seated enmity toward General Forrest. Bragg considered the uneducated Forrest to be unmanageable, hot tempered, and unpredictable. Perhaps Bragg's perception of his subordinate was biased after Forrest threatened to personally kill his commander in the fall of 1863. Davis himself later admitted that Forrest's abilities were "not understood at Richmond," and although he was considered a "bold and enterprising partisan raider and rider," his stunning victory at Brice's Crossroads was at the time considered to be nothing more than "another successful raid." So, Forrest, a man whose presence and reputation were just as much in demand as was his opponent Smith, remained in Mississippi.[21]

Stephen Lee eventually succumbed to Johnston's repeated requests and grudgingly dispatched 1,500 troopers under General Pillow from Oxford in east Alabama. He ordered Pillow to enter Georgia and destroy the railroad between Sherman's rear and the city of Dalton. When word of the raid reached a furious President Davis, his response was immediate. He sent a letter to Bragg calling for Pillow's instant recall back into Alabama and the immediate notification to Johnston that he should not expect any reinforcements from Lee's department.

At the very heart of the matter was Davis's disappointment with Johnston's performance at the head of the Army of Tennessee. Back in May, Johnston had been reinforced with Polk's corps, literally stripping Mississippi and Alabama of available infantry. In the following weeks Johnston was been unable to stop Sherman's advance into Georgia, and Davis lost confidence in Johnston's abilities as an army commander. Johnston's replacement by Gen. John B. Hood was only a few weeks away.[22]

FIVE

A Gathering Army

The weekend of June 25–26 was marked by scenes of either great activity or abject boredom. While the Union supply trains and artillery batteries began rolling into camp, the infantry took the opportunity to relax in whatever shade they could find. Summer had come to west Tennessee, and the weather changed from pleasantly mild to oppressively hot. The infantry camps at Moscow and along both sides of the Wolf River were not highly regarded. Lt. Henry McConnell of the 10th Minnesota wrote his wife that "Moscow was once a flourishing little inland town but now is nothing but a heap of ruin." Years of raids and occupation had taken its toll, "and the whole town with the exception of two buildings reduced to ashes." The historian of the 7th Minnesota recalled that it "was at this camp we had our first introduction to the 'chigger' or red tick. It is needless to say that we did not like our welcome." Several men from the regiment went out foraging, killing a number of goats belonging to a local citizen. For their crime the regimental commander ordered the perpetrators bound at the hands and feet with a rod placed under their knees and over the arms. A stick was placed sideways in the mouth and tied firmly in place. "Bucking and gagging" was not only a humiliating punishment but a painful one as well. Depending on the popularity of the offender, the sight brought great amusement or seething anger from his comrades.[1]

Sherman's orders to "devastate the land" and "bring ruin and misery" on any country that supported Forrest were off to a shaky start. There was a great inconsistency in the implementation of the order, for the degree of severity in which the duty was carried out usually rested on the shoulders of the regimental commanders. Some officers, like Col. William Marshall of the 7th

Minnesota, found such orders not only brutal but repugnant. Others felt not only justified in taking this heavy-handed approach but actually enjoyed it. A good number of the commanders believed the civilians were receiving their just rewards for supporting the enemy with food and forage. The men of the 14th Wisconsin, for example, had no qualms about helping themselves to local produce and livestock. "Here, it will be proper to say, that the boys of the Fourteenth were noted for their adaptability for forming acquaintances with the natives. They never passed through a country without becoming familiar with every sweet potato patch, every chicken roost, and every smoke house for miles around, which naturally brought the boys in close contact with the natives." No man from the 14th Wisconsin was bucked and gagged for foraging; in fact, there was no punishment whatsoever for such thievery, and the locals suffered as a result.[2]

In reality, the poor people of the region had very little to take. Washburn had been close to the truth when he described the area as a desert. For three years the towns and villages of west Tennessee and northeast Mississippi—especially those that lay along the tracks of the Memphis & Charleston Railroad—were subjected to depredations by both armies. Even worse was the continued presence of the dangerous irregular guerrillas, whose habits of theft and murder had little basis in actual military activities. A female resident of Ripley, Mississippi, Mrs. Cole, wrote of these dangers in a letter to her cousin after a visit by Maj. Gen. Earl Van Dorn's Confederate Army of West Tennessee in September 1862: "Cornfields and cribs, potato patches and gardens, meat houses and pantries suffered to the last point of endurance." And the situation only got worse when the Federals arrived: "We soon found out the difference between a tired and famished friendly army and a tired, famished, infuriated foe." Hungry soldiers shot cows and hogs, stole clothing and bedclothes, and destroyed furniture. "They completely gutted houses that had been left by families too timid to stay." Nearly two years had passed since the war began, and conditions had not gotten any better. Judge Orlando Davis of Ripley kept an accurate diary, and his entries are rife with accounts of theft, arson, and even murder. A typical entry, June 13, 1863, recalls the day 300 troops of the 9th Illinois Cavalry arrived on a raid: "They were by far the most inhuman and barbarous men and most consummate rogues that ever visited the place. They searched every house for plunder, three or four times, taking everything valuable, such as jewelry, clothing, blankets, cutlery, tools, etc." The residents of north Mississippi hid away whatever valuables remained.[3]

By early evening on June 26, crews had completed repairs to the bridge over the Wolf River, and the train rolled forward toward LaGrange. A detachment of Grierson's cavalry returned to camp after riding as far as Saulsbury, an additional nine miles east of LaGrange. It was wearisome work, even on horseback, as noted by Pvt. Erastus Bennett of the 2nd Iowa—"A very hot & dusty day & waughter very scarce along the road." The scouts returned with the welcome news that the rails would require little repair to reach the small town. Smith gave orders for the entire command to move out in the morning, and he expected to be in LaGrange by 10:00 A.M. In anticipation of the next day's march, David Moore held a review and inspection of the entire Third Division.[4]

Reveille came early to the camps on Monday the 27th. It was already hot, and the sun had yet to rise. The entire column moved out at 6:00 A.M. for the ten-mile march to LaGrange, a walk that should have been over by noon but, for many, lasted the entire day. The scorching sun beat down relentlessly on the men clad in wool pants and coats. The humidity along the Wolf River bottom, a lack of clean drinking water, and the choking dust soon took their toll. And though the men had been told to fill their canteens before leaving the Wolf, as there would be no water until reaching camp in the afternoon, Pvt. Thomas of the 14th Iowa cynically noted that "this was a mistake for just after noon we came to a large pond of water that was covered with a thick green scum. The water when the scum was pushed away was thick clouded like dirty soap suds. It was quite warm to the hand and yet some of the boys tried to drink it. But these that did drink it soon threw it up again."[5]

Men began to fall out of ranks and slump down along the roadside. It was far more than just a few men collapsing from fatigue; it was first dozens and then hundreds of cases of dangerous heat stroke. Men who had been sweating profusely suddenly stopped perspiring and turned a deep red as the body's natural ability to cool itself shut down. Shuffling along they became disoriented and delirious. Those who did not reach shade quickly collapsed into unconsciousness. "A great many men were sun struck and several died from the effects," observed Capt. Theodore Carter of the 7th Minnesota. Like so many others, Carter, who was still recovering from an earlier illness, was overcome by the heat and could not keep up with his regiment. Resting and walking in turn, he slowly made his way to LaGrange and was on the verge of passing out when he entered the town. Near the LaGrange Female College he recognized a friend among a group of cavalrymen and called out, "For God's sake, John, get some water and cool the arteries at my temples and wrists, quick!" Carter collapsed in John's arms, but his friend's quick actions restored him and quite possibly saved his life. By sundown Carter was able to stagger into the regimental camp.[6]

The heat did not respect rank; regimental commanders, junior officers, hardened sergeants, and lowly privates alike lay sprawled out in the dusty road.

Col. Edward Wehler of the 178th New York, a native of Vienna, Austria, was a Mexican War veteran and had been wounded at the Battle of Antietam. He fell to the heat and had to be replaced for the duration of the campaign by Capt. George Young. Second Lt. Nehemiah Starr of the 21st Missouri considered marching in the heat "a much faster way of killing men than in battle."[7]

Another regiment hit hard by the heat was the 32nd Iowa Infantry, which left Memphis with 416 men "reported fit for duty." A great number of these men, however, were still feeling the effects of the dysentery and malaria they had contracted while campaigning in Louisiana and were, or should have been on, the sick list. On Monday morning only 281 men answered the roll at muster. In just two days 135 men were down from the heat, and when the regiment arrived in LaGrange only twenty officers and men were still marching in the line. General Mower rode his horse near the rear of the column and, seeing the degree of suffering, gently urged the men on with kind words as well as a warning against roving bands of the enemy.[8]

It wasn't the first time Union troops had suffered on this road. Almost two years earlier Maj. Gen. William T. Sherman's Fifth Division of the Army of the Tennessee was on a march from Corinth to Memphis, repairing the tracks as they traveled west. The heat was blistering then, too. "Troops cannot march these hot days," he wrote. "You cannot count over 12 miles a day with trains." Two of Smith's regiments, the 72nd Ohio and 14th Wisconsin, had been with Sherman on that trek and undoubtedly remembered the hot, dusty road.[9]

Not all of the Federal units had arrived in west Tennessee; another regiment was still in transit to reinforce Smith's expeditionary force. Col. John Rinaker's 122nd Illinois Infantry left camp at Cairo, Illinois, on Sunday, June 26, for the journey to west Tennessee. The 122nd was made up of garrison troops, though the men considered themselves veterans. They had fought Forrest's men at Parker's Crossroads, Tennessee, and again at Paducah, Kentucky. But they had never done any hard campaigning. When the orders came to prepare for the move south, the men happily passed their guard duties to the 139th Illinois Infantry. The 139th was a "hundred-days regiment" recruited with the understanding that its men would only serve in the ranks for a hundred days and then be discharged. As such, they were scorned by the veterans of the 122nd. Cpl. William Ibbetson spoke for the regiment when he noted that the newcomers were "supposed to be a good Regt. but wholly composed of little boys; caked breasts will be rather numerous in the north. But as they are *national guards* we should not make fun of them. They cannot leave their mamas longer than 3m[onths]. Children should be under the eye of their mother."

Ironically, the 139th Illinois stayed in the ranks for over five months and later campaigned alongside the 122nd in Missouri.[10]

In a scene reminiscent of the early days of the war, the docks at Cairo bustled with crowds of people—"some good citizens, but many women of easy virtue," observed Corporal Ibbetson. The 122nd filed aboard the steamer *Magenta*, and at 9:00 P.M. the mooring lines were cast off, and the regiment was under way. The men enjoyed the boat ride and took delight in pointing out the former Confederate strongholds of Columbus, Island No. 10, and Fort Pillow. The steamer arrived in Memphis at nightfall on the 27th, and by July 3 the 122nd had settled into the LaGrange camps alongside the rest of Smith's growing army.[11]

While on the march to LaGrange, General Smith took note of the USCT on guard duty at different points along the railroad tracks. He was not particularly fond of black troops; in fact, he held a very low opinion of them. But he needed more men. He sent a note to Washburn back to Memphis, asking, "Am I to take the colored regiments now at La Fayette as part of my command?" With an affirmative answer, his column grew with the addition of the Col. Edward Bouton's brigade, made up of three infantry regiments and a four-gun battery. Two of the regiments, the 61st and 68th USCT, had seen only garrison duty, and their fighting ability was a question mark. The 59th, however, had fought with great tenacity at Brice's Crossroads and proven its mettle. Rumors swirled through the camps that the black soldiers had taken vows to avenge the atrocities of Fort Pillow and that they wouldn't take any Confederate prisoners. The rumors were true.[12]

After the fight at Brice's Crossroads, General Forrest learned of the pact and sent a messenger under a flag of truce to question Washburn about the facts. He noted, "It has been reported to me that all your negro troops stationed in Memphis took an oath on their knees, in the presence of Major-General Hurlbut and other officers of your army, to avenge Fort Pillow, and that they would show my troops no quarter." Forrest went on to claim that the high rate of casualties at Fort Pillow and Brice's Crossroads was not a result of any excesses by the Confederate forces but, instead, due to the mistaken belief that Union prisoners would be murdered on surrender. He placed the blame squarely on the shoulders of the Federal commanders who told their soldiers to expect no quarter. He finished the letter with a query: "In all my operations since the war began I have conducted the war on civilized principles, and desire still to, but it is due to my command that they should know the position they occupy and the policy you intend to pursue. I therefore respectfully ask whether my men now in your hands are treated as other Confederate prisoners."[13]

Washburn's reply did little to appease Forrest's concerns; rather, it seemed to be designed to inflame them. He began with an attempt to put Forrest in his place, suggesting that communication should be made with Stephen D. Lee, the officer in command. He confirmed that the soldiers had indeed taken such an oath, "but not in the presence of General Hurlbut. From what I can learn, this act of theirs was not influenced by any white officer, but was the result of their own sense of what was due to themselves and their fellows, who had been mercilessly slaughtered." Washburn quickly dismissed any claims of Forrest pursuing the war on "civilized principles" and warned him, "The attempt to intimidate the colored troops by indiscriminate slaughter has signally failed, and that instead of a feeling of terror you have aroused a spirit of courage and desperation that will not down at your bidding."

Forrest's concern about the status of Confederate prisoners went unanswered as Washburn attempted to turn the tables with questions about the fate of captured black soldiers.

> I am left in doubt by your letter as to the course you and the Confederate Government intend to pursue hereafter in regard to colored troops, and I beg you to advise me with as little delay as possible as to your intention. If you intend to treat such of them as fall into your hands as prisoners of war, please so state. If you do not so intend, but contemplate either their slaughter or their return to slavery, please state that, so that we may have no misunderstanding hereafter. If the former is your intention, I shall receive the announcement with pleasure, and shall explain the fact to the colored troops at once, and desire that they recall the oath that they have taken. If the latter is the case, then let the oath stand, and upon those who have aroused this spirit by their atrocities, and upon the Government and the people who sanction it, be the consequences.[14]

The communication between the two antagonists continued for several days but broke down into a matter of accusations and counteraccusations over the alleged atrocities at Fort Pillow. Washburn never did provide an answer to Forrest's query about the future of Confederates captured in battle, and as to the status of black prisoners, Forrest wrote:

> I regard captured negroes as I do other captured property and not as captured soldiers, but as to how regarded by my Government and the disposition which has been and will hereafter be made of them, I respectfully refer you through the proper channel to the authorities at Richmond. It is not the policy nor the interest of the South to destroy the negro on the contrary, to preserve

and protect him and all who have surrendered to us have received kind and humane treatment.[15]

In the exchange with Washburn, Forrest threatened to execute the prisoners taken at Brice's Crossroads if he was not satisfied that his own men would be properly cared for if captured in any future engagements. It is doubtful that Forrest, even with his volatile nature, would have resorted to retaliatory executions. He was a proven master of bluffing Union commanders, and it could not hurt to let the Federals think he might act violently when and if any of his own men were abused as prisoners. There was no need to follow through on the threat, he knew; with most Federal commanders the threat was sufficient.

The exchange continued in Forrest's correspondence with Smith at the end of June. Once again, Forrest raised the specter of retaliatory killings, this time in response to alleged atrocities perpetrated against soldiers and civilians by men of the 9th Illinois and 7th Kansas Cavalry, "whose major I learn has vowed to kill every man they find in Confederate uniform." He explained that he was holding all of the officers taken at Brice's "under the order of Lieutenant-General Lee . . . and shall certainly execute them man for man, or in any other proportion to stop it."[16]

The truth was, Forrest's accusations were baseless, and his threats were nothing more than smoke and mirrors. There is no mention of the killing of scouts and civilians in any of his correspondence or by any of the members of his command. And the only Union soldiers he could have laid his hands on for execution were the wounded men still being treated by southern surgeons, for the vast majority of Federals captured at Brice's Crossroads were either on their way to or were already being held in Confederate prisons. In all likelihood, the letter, delivered under a flag of truce by Capt. John C. Jackson, was no more than an attempt to get a look at the enemy encampments in and around LaGrange; it was a good opportunity for a trusted officer to judge the size and composition of Smith's army.

Smith was not fooled. His response was predictable: his men had not participated in any killings of civilians or scouts and had already been ordered not to engage in such heinous activities. He did point out, however, that he would have no compunction against punishing civilians who were actively aiding the Confederates. Interestingly, Smith declined to mention the murder of the soldiers of the 178th New York Infantry, who had been found executed along the tracks on June 23 after they had fallen off the train and been captured. Not taking the bait, Smith ended the correspondence between the two commanders.[17]

* * *

The Sixteenth Corps' right wing, reinforced by whatever regiments and detachments that could be pulled together, appeared more than strong enough for the task ahead. By his own count, Smith commanded 14,000 men, nearly twice the number Sturgis had led south a month before. His organization consisted of Mower's First Division, composed of four brigades; Moore's Third Division, made up of three brigades; Bouton's Colored Brigade; and the two brigades of Benjamin Grierson's Cavalry Division.[18] And interspersed among the brigades were seven batteries plus a detached section of artillery, totaling some thirty cannon. Also, the 7th Kansas Jayhawkers rode with the column in an unassigned status and took orders directly from Smith and Grierson.[19]

The men's morale was high, though they had every reason to be pessimistic. The majority had been with Smith slogging through the swamps and bayous of Louisiana or with Sturgis and tasted defeat at Brice's Crossroads. Their opponent, Forrest, had become a legend. To a great many of the Federals he seemed unbeatable. Even Sherman admitted to Stanton that Forrest's reputation was affecting the troops; he believed some of them were afraid of Forrest. But as far as the men under Smith were concerned, Sherman was wrong; their own setbacks in Louisiana and Mississippi had emboldened them. They were eager to remove any stains on their honor as well as those that had besmirched the men under Sturgis. "The brave men endured the hardships with great fortitude," wrote the historian of the 12th Iowa, "for they were to retrieve our arms in that quarter from disgrace." Or, as Sgt. Charles Ewringmann of the 27th Iowa said, "We were determined to hone out the notches again."[20] Used to winning, these men fully expected to do so again. And they looked forward to engaging the unbeatable Forrest.

Smith's goal was simple: keep Forrest away from Sherman's supply line. To achieve this goal, he intended on accomplishing two things. First, he had to destroy as large a section of the Mobile & Ohio Railroad as possible. The interruption of the rail line would hamper the Confederate ability to shift troops rapidly across the state, particularly to Mobile, which was still being eyed by Grant and Sherman for future operations. The Confederate government's ability to repair damaged rail lines had been limited at best, and by the summer of 1864 was nearly impossible. Not a single mile of new track was laid in the southern states during the course of the war, resulting in a cannibalization of lines, with rails from an irreparable line, or one less vital to be used to repair another.[21]

Second, and most important, Smith planned to pick a fight with Forrest. If Forrest could be held in Mississippi, the goal of keeping his legions away from Sherman's supply line would be achieved. Sturgis had actually attained this goal at his defeat at Brice's Crossroads, though few were prepared to admit it. For two weeks before the excursion, Smith had asked questions and studied his colleague's campaign, determined to not repeat the mistakes made by Sturgis.[22]

It is doubtful that Smith put much stock in Sherman's challenges to "follow Forrest to the death" and "pursue and kill Forrest." He likely never even saw the messages, since they were not sent to Smith. Windy rhetoric like this was intended for politicians, not soldiers. The recipients of Sherman's bold declarations were President Lincoln and Secretary of War Stanton, men who reveled in such bold proclamations. Indeed, Sherman could act the part of a politician well, telling Lincoln and Stanton exactly what they liked to hear. So while Sherman never directly ordered Smith to prepare the raid against Forrest, he used the chain of command effectively, and the order to "pursue Forrest and punish him" made its way to McPherson to Washburn to Smith. And to Sherman's order McPherson added, "Forrest should be followed until brought to bay somewhere and then whipped." In the communications between the *professional* soldiers, however, there were no references to the killing of Forrest or that the man's death was a goal of the expedition.[23]

Smith's goal was not to kill Forrest but to disrupt or damage his ability to wage war. Smith's corps was not an army of conquest. His plans did not include occupying any towns or strategic points, as Forrest supposed. He was leading a raid into enemy-held territory to cripple his opponent, disrupt rail transportation in east Mississippi, and then return with his column to Memphis. Communications among Federal leaders mention marching on Tupelo, Okolona, or Columbus, but the cities themselves were just reference points on the map; the targets were Forrest and the railroad. It was a textbook raid until Sherman sent a new element to the expedition.[24]

It was not so much a goal but rather a directive for the raid that came down the chain of command from Sherman himself and authorized the use of total war. "Pursue Forrest on foot, devastating the land over which he has passed or may pass, and make him and the people of Tennessee and Mississippi realize that, though a bold, daring and successful leader, he will bring ruin and misery on any country where he may pause or tarry. If we do not punish Forrest and the people now, the whole effect of our past conquest will be lost." Forrest biographer Robert Selph Henry claimed this added a new element to the war, "at least as an avowed policy 'to punish Forrest and his people' not as a military measure aimed against armies but a punitive measure applied to peoples."

But there was nothing new about this practice. Civilians North and South had been forced to bear a terrible burden for no other crime than living too close to warring armies or vengeful partisans. Citizens were hanged or shot for their declared or avowed loyalties, be they northern or southern, and public buildings, cotton and cotton gins, barns, warehouses, and even homes were burned. In east Tennessee Union supporters were jailed or hanged and had their homes burned. In a letter concerning civilians found guilty of support- ing Federal activities, Confederate secretary of state Judah Benjamin suggested that "it would be well to leave their bodies hanging in the vicinity of the burned bridges." There were exceptions. In Virginia, Col. Charles Lowell of the Inde- pendent Cavalry Brigade was ordered to burn the homes of men known to sup- port the Confederates but found the orders offensive and refused. Similarly, his brother-in-law, Col. Robert G. Shaw of the 54th Massachusetts, got into hot water for his unwillingness to burn the town of Darien, Georgia. And though he ordered his men to observe restraint in the upcoming expedition, defying Sherman's wishes, Smith did not always condemn the very behavior he assured Forrest would not be tolerated, as was evident when his command dealt the Louisiana countryside a heavy blow during the campaign up the Red River.[25]

There were times when Smith reacted swiftly when his soldiers crossed the line. On New Year's Eve 1863, Smith's troops were in Jackson, Tennessee, on an expedition from Union City. Smith was walking with Capt. William Burns when two ladies rushed up to them and begged for help. An officer and several soldiers of the 7th Indiana Cavalry were pillaging their house. By the time Smith arrived at the scene, the officer in question, Lt. Abram Hill, had been placed under arrest by men of the 4th Missouri Cavalry. "The appear- ance of the house aroused the ire of the General to an unwonted degree." A court-martial was held the following day, and Smith asked Burns, his assistant inspector general, to serve on the court, a request Burns vehemently refused. Smith, not used to having his orders disobeyed, asked the young officer what he meant by refusing. "I mean General, that so thoroughly am I convinced of the guilt of the Lieutenant that I shall vote to have him shot, and with that conviction, I think I am not competent to act as a member of the court." Smith agreed, and the trial proceeded without Burns's participation.[26] Yet, Smith could just as easily turn a blind eye to the activities of his men. A few days after the Jackson incident, the column was returning to its Union City camp when a local farmer came to Smith's tent and complained, "in very forcible language," that the soldiers were burning his fence rails. Captain Burns recalled:

> The General replied he had given strict orders that his soldiers should take no rail but the top ones and if he could discover any of them disobeying orders he

would have them punished, and told the man to go and see if they were taking anything but the top rail. In a few minutes he returned, saying they were taking everything on the fence. The general started with him to find the culprits, accompanied by his staff, to see the fun.

The irate farmer pointed to the culprits who were dismantling the fence, but Smith dismissed him, noting, "You can't point out one of my soldiers taking any but the top."

Burns commented on Smith's reactions to his soldiers' behavior: "There was no telling how the general would react. There would be instances of gross pillaging and burning without orders during the upcoming expedition, but the perpetrators always made sure they carried out their deeds far from the General's eye."[27]

* * *

The town of LaGrange was well known to a great many of the Union troopers; it was from there that Grierson had set out on his famous raid through Mississippi in April 1863, and it had frequently been used as a garrison post since June 1862. The infantry camp was comfortably situated about a mile south of town near the banks of the Wolf River. Nehemiah Starr of the 21st Missouri thought it a wonderful place to camp. "The evenings here are very pleasant and afford a pleasant night's rest under those large beech trees on Wolf River bottom." Another soldier described it as "a beautiful spot of ground covered with tall trees and luxuriant grass." The men settled into normal camp routines while Smith and his staff continued their preparations. For most of the men the new camp was preferable over the scorching sun and dust at Moscow. They relaxed in the shade, wrote letters home, wrote in their diaries and journals, and strolled up the road to look over the town. "LaGrange is a fine little town having a beautiful location," observed James Krafftt of the 117th Illinois. "From all appearances it was once a thriving place, but it is now almost entirely deserted by its former inhabitants. The country around seems fertile, but the farms & plantations are mostly abandoned." Of course, not every regiment was situated in a fine, shady grove. Pvt. Virgil Downing of the 114th Illinois complained, "We have a very uncomfortable camp at present camped on a sandy hill subject to the hot rays of a scorching sun and as the weather is very hot it makes our present position very disagreeable indeed." Perhaps least impressed was Harrison Chandler of the 114th Illinois, who "thought Moscow was rough, but this is *rougher*." [28]

The men of the 8th Wisconsin knew LaGrange well. They had spent the Christmas of 1862 there in a cotton bale fort, while tens of thousands of Union troops were marching across the countryside in a vain attempt to capture Confederate Maj. Gen. Earl Van Dorn's raiding party. The following Christmas the 8th Wisconsin was back, serving as a garrison force for LaGrange and nearby Saulsbury. The regimental historian fondly remembered, "Lagrange is a rather antiquated town, and in peaceful times, could boast of about 1,500 population. Most of its wealthiest citizens, however, have migrated further South, while the remaining portion of its inhabitants are seeking protection at our hands."[29]

Aurelius Bartlett, surgeon of the 33rd Missouri Infantry, recalled treating several men who wandered into camp, "soldiers who became separated from their respective commands during and after the battle of Guntown," the northern name for the Battle of Brice's Crossroads. More than two weeks after the fight, men were still wandering through the woods in search of the Union lines. "I extracted bullets and dressed wounds for some of these men and in one case in particular it seemed almost incredible, that a person could have travelled 80 or 90 miles, as he had done, with such an injury." Exhausted and near starving, most of the men were so far gone they could barely stagger into the Union camps. "It was the subject of remark however that of all those sorely tired men, not a single colored soldier approached our pickets without his musket." It was an interesting observation by Bartlett, certainly noticed by others as well, who may have been harboring doubts about the USCT troops assigned to their army.[30]

Late in the morning of the 27th, General Smith reported that his entire command had arrived at LaGrange, though heat-stricken stragglers would continue to shuffle in for hours. While most of the regiments were allowed to relax in the shade, the 14th Iowa and 21st Missouri were called to fatigue duty, to unload "eight hundred sacks of oats from the cars and built them into a huge stack." Trains pulled in and out of LaGrange at regular intervals transporting supplies necessary for the raid—rations, ammunition, forage, and the tools needed to destroy the railroad tracks.

While the men worked and the supplies rolled in, Smith attended to a hundred details including the reports of his scouts. An important piece of information came to him by way of a Confederate deserter captured by a detachment of the 7th Kansas Cavalry. The deserter talked freely and informed his captors that the previous day Forrest and his bodyguard had been at Lamar, Mississippi, twelve miles south of LaGrange and that his main force, 9,000 strong, was centered at Tupelo and Okolona. The information proved correct; Forrest was not only massing his men, he had a greater number of them than had faced Sturgis.[31]

As the infantry settled into its campsites, Winslow's and Waring's brigades of cavalry rode out of town on Tuesday, June 28, and made the short nine-mile ride to Saulsbury. Despite the heat—what Captain Abraham of the 4th Iowa considered the "hottest day yet"—the men of the 3rd Iowa found themselves in a very satisfactory camp on the lawn of the Woodland Female Institute. Observing the column from the woods, Abraham saw several of the enemy, and he believed another Confederate detachment was up ahead "destroying the R.R." Grierson's Third Brigade, under Col. Datus Coon, split up for the time being; the 9th Illinois stayed in LaGrange with the infantry while the 2nd Iowa and detachments of the 3rd and 7th Illinois moved their camp three miles east to Grand Junction.[32]

Washburn urged Smith to be patient: "I think you had better be in no hurry leaving the line of the railroad." He believed Smith's presence in LaGrange and Saulsbury was sufficient to hold Forrest in Mississippi and that "if we can bring him up toward Corinth it will be a great deal better than to go down to Tupelo after him." No one really believed Forrest would make it easy for them; Washburn said, "If he won't be decoyed up, then you must go after him."[33]

The quiet camp life of Winslow's brigade in Saulsbury was disturbed on July 3 when 100 mounted Confederates attacked the Union pickets on the Ripley Road south of camp. Companies D and E of the 3rd Iowa Cavalry, some fifty men, were on Sunday duty and were the only men involved in what was really just a minor skirmish. The 2nd and 4th Iowa heard the crash of carbines, but by the time they arrived on the scene the action was over. Col. John Noble, commander of the 3rd Iowa, reported how his men "advanced upon the aggressive party and compelled him to leave the field with a loss of 5 killed and wounded. Our loss 1 wounded. Although this skirmish was of minor importance in the presence of so large an army, yet I was highly gratified with the conduct of the officers and men, who, on a small picket post, learned the rebels from the first that on this expedition it was our intention neither to stop nor to retire, but to advance always." William Scott of the 4th Iowa agreed that the skirmish was "a good omen of the success of the campaign to come."[34]

On the morning of July 4, the bugles that blew reveille over the cavalry camps in Saulsbury were joined by "several coronet bands," to remind the soldiers of the national holiday. The country was eighty-eight years old, and at noon an artillery salute fired in celebration. "We expected a *fighting celebration* to begin early this morning," complained Capt. Lot Abraham of the 4th Iowa Cavalry, but the regiments remained in camp idling away the hot day. Later in the afternoon the 2nd New Jersey Cavalry struck camp and, along with the rest of Waring's brigade, headed west for Memphis. Before departing, however, they left a number of quality horses with the grateful troopers of the 7th

Kansas Cavalry, adding to the numbers that had arrived earlier in the day on a special train loaded with twenty boxcars of horses. If nothing else, Grierson's troopers would be well mounted.[35]

An artillery salute was fired in the infantry camps at LaGrange, as well, one soldier noting that "the officers ordered them loaded with ball or shell and pointed across the country where the rebel marauders might be." Several officers with political aspirations took the opportunity to entertain the soldiers with patriotic speeches. In the camp of the 117th Illinois Infantry, no fewer than six officers took turns addressing the regiment.[36]

Corporal Ibbetson of the 122nd Illinois Infantry was, like a great many of his fellow infantrymen, disappointed with the subdued holiday spirit. "If we were at home today we would be fixing to celebrate the 4th by going after our gal. But now, alas, it's all a dream. There is no 'knick knacks,' lemonade, big speeches or pretty gals. Bad, very bad." But later in the day Ibbetson

> concluded to go out & shoot some squirrels against orders, as the boys had been doing it all day. Also some of the officers had been at it too, so I went out, treed Mr. Squirrel & commenced firing. Had shot twice when lo Mr. Patrol came up & arrested us & took us to the officer of the day. He formed us in line & right faced us & forward marched. As luck had it I was in the rear & he did not think about putting a guard in the rear. In this way we started for Reg'tl Hd. Quarters. The timber was thick & the first tree we came to I went through with the movement known as a "side step to the right," which movement placed me behind the tree & there I remained until they were out of sight when I broke for camp, arriving there safe.[37]

Any disappointment Captain Abraham felt about not fighting on the Fourth of July was dispelled when the regiment was issued new Spencer carbines, perhaps the weapon most highly regarded by the rank and file during the war. Seven metallic rim-fire cartridges were held in a magazine in the stock and could be fired infinitely faster than the muzzle loaders carried by the infantry. Confederates referred to the Spencer as "that damn Yankee rifle they load up on Sunday and fire all week!" Many of the cavalry regiments in camp turned in their older Sharps and received the new weapons. Cpl. Simon Duck of the 4th Iowa was delighted with his new weapon—"I got new Spencer and now feel myself a match for any rebel that ever drew a bead"—while Pvt. Erastus Bennett of the 2nd Iowa had some misgivings about it: "They are a very pretty gun but they will make a big load to carry with the sabers." Adjutant William Scott of the 4th Iowa considered it an event which was of the greatest value in increasing the effectiveness of the regiment. Looking at it now, it seems clumsy and heavy, and, compared with inventions of later years, it cannot be classed very high. But to have a carbine of better range and more certain shot than any other gun they knew, from which seven shots could be fired without loss of time, and without taking the attention off the enemy, was of striking value in heightening the self confidence and improving the *morale* of the cavalry. From that time on to the end of the war [Colonel Edward] Winslow's regiments not only clearly won in every contest, but they *expected* to win, and even acquired a sort of habit of looking upon every approaching fight as "a sure thing."[38]

In the afternoon there was a flurry of activity when Smith's General Order No. 6 was distributed to the commanding officers of all the units in camp: "This command will be held in readiness to march early to-marrow morning, July 5." Adjutants and quartermasters busied themselves filling out the requisitions to draw three days' rations (five days' for the cavalry) for every man. Working parties carried boxes of hardtack, coffee, bacon, and sugar to be distributed to every regiment and battery. The General Orders indicated that "as much forage (particularly oats) should be carried as possible" for the thousands of horses and mules that came with the expedition. Some of the men in the cavalry camp took a last opportunity to forage in the neighborhood. Pvt. Jacob Gantz of the 4th Iowa Cavalry and a few comrades on picket duty made a visit to a nearby farm: "We sent out in the country and got us a lot of potatoes chickens & other things cabitch beets & c. & had a regular good dinner of which I eat very harty fo I was hungry."[39]

Earlier that day Smith dispatched Captain Burns on a ride into Mississippi under a white flag of truce. Escorted by a few troopers of the 7th Kansas Cavalry, Burns carried a copy of the congressional report of the investigation of the massacre at Fort Pillow, a copy of which Forrest had requested from Washburn. The detachment passed through the Union picket line into "Forrest's dominions" and at 4:00 P.M., while galloping along the road, was called to a halt by enemy videttes. "I can see even now the picture there presented, with a vividness that doesn't diminish with time. On the brow of a hill, just ahead of us, sat two Confederate officers, with revolvers in their hands, taking deliberate aim at us." After a few tense moments the men lowered their guns, and Burns handed over the package.

Since it was late in the day, and the prospect of returning to the Union lines in the dark was too dangerous to consider, Burns passed the evening with the two officers in a nearby plantation house. Burns noted that "from their conversation, it was apparent that Forrest knew he now had a general to fight, of whom, he must be, to say the least, very wary. The fights with Generals Sooy Smith and Sturgis were lightly spoken of, but it was admitted that in Gen. A. J. Smith, they had an antagonist worthy of their own commander." The conversation soon turned to the North enlisting and arming black regiments, and Burns asked them how they would treat colored soldiers captured in battle. "One replied, and I never forgot his answer, 'If I capture negro soldiers, strangers to me, I shall treat them as well as I would a white soldier, but if I ever capture one of my own slaves in your uniform, I shall shoot him as I would a dog.'"[40]

Back in the LaGrange camp General Order No. 9 made its way down from the brigade headquarters of Col. James Gilbert of Moore's Division; this one addressed the straggling during the march from Memphis.

> Commanding officers of regiments and companies will not permit any strag-
> gling from their respective commands on the march. The disgraceful manner
> in which our march was conducted on the day we marched to this camp must
> not be repeated. Commanding officers of companies will see that every man
> has his canteen filled with water before the hour of marching in order that the
> subterfuge of looking after water may be no excuse. Experience has proven to
> both officers and men that those who remain with their companies uniformly
> endure the march better than those who straggle. Firing of guns while on the
> march will not be permitted. Regimental and company officers will be held
> responsible for the non-fulfillment of this order, which will be published to
> each regiment before we enter upon the march.[41]

Late in the afternoon of July 4, Smith met with Brig. Gen. Edward Hatch, a brigade commander in Grierson's cavalry division, who was reporting for duty after a long sick leave after being seriously wounded in an engagement near Moscow in December. Hatch carried a letter of introduction from General Washburn which, among other things, said that if he was well enough he should take command of his old brigade, now under Col. Datus Coon. In the letter Washburn spoke highly of Hatch's abilities: "He knows the country like a book, and has had several turns with Forrest." But Hatch was not well enough to take to the saddle for a long campaign, and Smith chose to leave him in command of a small force remaining behind in LaGrange. But Smith did make use of the brigadier general's knowledge of the enemy territory to the south. Hatch, who had been down the road to Okolona several times the previous year, informed Smith that he could find plenty of forage for his animals beyond Ripley. The men talked at length about Forrest, forage, and the roads leading south.[42]

Also in the letter, Washburn restated what he believed should be Smith's direction of travel: "I think your route should be via Ripley, New Albany, Pontotoc to Okolona, thence to Columbus." He warned Smith that Tupelo was strongly held by the Confederates, and, if possible, he should draw Forrest out rather than attack him in his defenses. He also recommended that the expedition forage heavily from the countryside around Okolona and Aberdeen and save the hard bread for the return trip.[43]

The rank and file had not been officially informed about where they were headed, but nearly every corporal and mule skinner knew they were headed out after Forrest. Smith's veterans didn't seem worried; if anything, they were anxious to get on down the road for the meeting. Cpl. Adolphus Wolf of the 117th Illinois spoke for most of the enlisted men when he wrote, "From what I can understand, Gen A. J. Smith is to take the offensive against Forest. I am certain they could not have chosen a more able man than our old Guerilla Chieftain. I am confident that if he gets a chance, he will learn Forest a lesson, that he will remember to the last day of his life and one day over." Lt. Alfred Fitch of the 33rd Wisconsin wrote of how much faith the men in ranks placed in their commander: "So perfect was the confidence of his troops in their leader that they would have stuck to the tail of his old black pacer if it had led them to the mouth of the bottomless pit." The sun set over a quiet, confident camp.[44]

SIX

Watching and Waiting

By the third week of June, it had become evident to General Lee that the Federals in Memphis were continuing with their preparations for an active campaign and that this constituted the gravest of the four threats to his department. On the 20th he informed Adj. Gen. Cooper that "A. J. Smith, with considerable force, still at Memphis. Indications are for rebuilding Memphis and Charleston Railroad to Grand Junction and another raid in force." Forrest had received good intelligence about the Federal activities in the area, but the developing situation called for a larger scouting force to observe the enemy's movements. The following day, June 21, Forrest directed Gen. James Chalmers to send a regiment from Columbus to Abbeville. Chalmers selected the 2nd Missouri Cavalry under Lt. Col. Robert "Red Bob" McCulloch.[1]

Chalmers ordered Red Bob to take his regiment to Abbeville, twenty-five miles south of Holly Springs, and to set up camp where the Mississippi Central Railroad crossed the Tallahatchie River. Patrols would be sent in the direction of Memphis as far as Byhalia and northward to points along the tracks of the Memphis & Charleston, and any information they gathered was to be sent to the telegraph station at Holly Springs, where it would be forwarded first to Okolona and then on to Chalmers's headquarters in Aberdeen. If the enemy was found to be moving out in force, McCulloch was to harass the Federal column to the best of his ability before returning to the brigade in Columbus. In addition to the scouting duties, Chalmers ordered McCulloch to be on the lookout for Confederate deserters, to "arrest all officers and men who are absent from their commands without proper authority" and send the offenders to Forrest's headquarters with their horses, arms, and equipment. Desertion was on the rise in Forrest's ranks; some deserters were new recruits from Tennessee who were having second thoughts about being soldiers, and others were men of Hinchie Mabry's brigade who were not all pleased with being transferred from Canton to Columbus. Second Lt. A. D. Clifton of the 6th Mississippi wrote home about two friends who were considering deserting: "I herd from them capt Brown had 8 men runaway last sunday night we have not had but one or too runaway since we left Columbus." It was the uncertainty of their future that drove several of the men from the ranks, a worry Pvt. John Cato of the 4th Mississippi confided to his wife: "I hear a rumor in camp this evening that we are going back to Canton soon. We may go to Johnston or may make a raid into Tennessee, there is no telling where we will go, nor when we will ever get back home again."[2]

On June 9 Forrest had tried to quell the flood of soldiers abandoning their duty and heading home to work their farms or to spend time with family and friends by making an example of three soldiers found guilty of desertion. Sgt. Frank Reid of Morton's Tennessee Battery was a witness to the event.

The battery was encamped a few feet from the track, where stood a box-car, in which three deserters were confined, who were to be shot the next day. A preacher was with them, and I can still hear their loud voices in prayer and singing hymns. The next morning the clouds had passed away and the woods were jubilant with the twittering of birds. The command was all drawn up in an old sedge-field, in the center of which three newly-dug graves opened their mouths to swallow the three blindfolded victims of war who knelt at their brink. How awful it was! The clear, blue, unsympathetic sky so far away overhead, the world so full of freshness and joyous life, and before the bandaged eyes of these poor human beings doubtless the picture of their childhood's home, where sits at the open window this bright June morning the old mother with her knitting in her lap, the wife with her little children about her knee, all unconscious of the tragedy that is about to becloud their lives forever. A sharp command, a crack of musketry, and two lives snuffed out like worthless tallow-candles. One of them was spared on account of his extreme youth. Will he ever forget the moment he knelt by the open grave and heard that crack of musketry?[3]

The brutal lesson was meant to serve as a deterrent, but it made little impression on the men who were determined to go home—even if for only a few days. Pvt. A. W. Montague of the 7th Tennessee Cavalry, who had watched the execution and then fought at Brice's Crossroads, recalled how "the next morning after being Sunday [June 12], three other soldiers and myself decided to go home, as we were only about forty miles away . . . After spending about three weeks at home I heard that the Federals had started out of Memphis into Mississippi under General Smith, and I started again with some comrades to join my regiment before the two armies met." The men did not arrive back in camp until two days after the battle. They were not punished for their untimely vacation.[4]

Despite the rash of desertions among the recruits and the complaints of the new arrivals under Mabry from Canton, morale in Forrest's cavalry remained high. Those men not patrolling kept busy stockpiling forage and rations at central points on all of the roads that could be used in upcoming operations. Many of the men underwent thorough physical examinations, and those found to be unfit were sent down to Lauderdale County to recuperate. The constant campaigning had taken a toll on the men in ranks. Pvt. John Hubbard of the 7th Tennessee could not help but notice "the smallness of the companies, and when on the march the regiment did not string out as it formerly did. This was significant. Though one man could not do the work of two, preparations for another battle went forward." The horses were also examined, and those that could no longer maintain the pace of active operations were sent south to rest and fatten up. Healthy horses were brought in from wherever they could be had. "Special attention was given to the selection of strong horses for the artillery," noted Maj. John Morton, Forrest's artillery chief.[5]

On June 22, as Union troops in Joseph Mower's division were boarding trains for the thirty-seven-mile ride from Memphis to Moscow, Forrest reported to Lee, "I am satisfied the enemy are preparing to move against me in large force from Memphis." Lee had already come to the same conclusion and again shifted some of his troops to meet the myriad threats poised to assault his department. He ordered General Adams in Jackson to leave 500 of Gholson's brigade to maintain a close watch on Vicksburg while the balance of the command moved out to West Station and Brookhaven because of "a report that a heavy force, under A. J. Smith, is about to leave Memphis for the invasion of Mississippi." This redeployment placed a portion of Adams's troops in a position to move to assist Forrest while still maintaining a minimal force to look after Henry Slocum's garrison in Vicksburg itself. "You will hold yourself and staff in readiness to take the field in North Mississippi at any time it may become necessary," cautioned Lee.[6]

False rumors of enemy reinforcements arriving at Vicksburg from Morganza, Louisiana, only served to confuse Lee's situation further. Scouts along the Mississippi River informed Lee of ten transports laden with five regiments of white troops and 2,000 colored troops that had come ashore, in addition to 2,000 reenlisted soldiers returning from veteran furloughs. While there were no troops sent from Morganza, Lee was forced to spend valuable time determining if the threat was real. The report of reinforcements arriving from the North was true enough. Lee incorrectly assumed that the reinforcements in Memphis and Vicksburg were hundred-days men rather than hardened veterans. He was receiving such reports several times a day and updating the War Department just as often. The strain of defending his department was growing by the hour. On the morning of June 23, Lee received a telegram from Richmond: "You have been appointed lieutenant general, to command the Department of Alabama, Mississippi and East Louisiana." But what he needed more than the promotion was additional troops.[7]

Aside from coping with the challenges of commanding the department, there was an element of tension with his ranking subordinate, Nathan Forrest. It was no secret Forrest preferred the freedom of independent command and had no qualms about voicing his disdain for the orders of West Point–trained officers. Also, twelve years Lee's senior, Forrest felt perfectly capable of handling the department on his own. Yet, as the probability grew of another Federal incursion, Forrest understood the likelihood of Lee taking overall command in the field. To a proud man such as Forrest, it had to rankle. His note to Lee acknowledging his advancement as the youngest lieutenant general in the Confederacy was less than effusive: "Allow me to congratulate you on your promotion. I am suffering from boils. If the enemy should move out I desire you to take command of the forces. Our force is insufficient to meet this command. Can't you procure some assistance?"[8] The message is strange, if not unique. When circumstances required a senior officer to relinquish his command, he invariably appointed or suggested the most capable of his subordinates to replace him. In this case, Forrest should have been proposing one of his brigadiers—Chalmers, Buford, Lyon, or Roddey—to step up and replace him until he recovered his health. Whether intended or not, for Forrest to suggest that a serving departmental commander step down and assume duty as a corps commander was insulting to Lee as well as the four brigadiers.[9]

It was true that Forrest was tired. He rarely took time off for himself. He had been wounded three times, twice by the enemy and once by a subordinate, and in each instance he was back in command after the briefest period of recuperation. And while his boundless energy was well known throughout the corps, three years of campaigning was taking a toll. As for the boils, it's hard to imagine anyone—even a man of Forrest's caliber—being able to withstand the excruciating pain of infected abscesses and remain in the saddle. But Forrest could not be spared.

As each passing day made it increasingly clear that the enemy was massing around LaGrange, Forrest needed more eyes and ears on the scene to keep him informed of Union activity. Later in the day on June 23, Lt. Col. Jesse

A. Forrest of the 16th Tennessee Cavalry led a 400-man detachment from Buford's division to Ripley. The orders for the younger Forrest, his general brother's junior by eight years, were twofold. First, the men of his detachment were to provide pickets and videttes and follow the roads north to ascertain the location of the enemy. Second, Jesse was to open the dispatches from all of the scouts in the area destined for his brother's headquarters. In an effort to cut down on unnecessary staff work and to keep from wearing out the couriers' horses, only the most important dispatches were to be forwarded.[10]

"I was in this detale also several of my company," reminisced Lt. William Pirtle of the 7th Kentucky Mounted Infantry.

> Here we stayed two days and nights in peace until a little before day the second night when we heard gun fire by advance videt and as a matter of fact we mounted our horses quick and stood ready for the frey. Not many minutes until we heard horses feet, soon decided that it was only one horse, in a few moments more Jim Cox rode up about as much out of breath as his horse, reported he had killed a yank that was trying to slip around him through the bushes, but cracked the dry sticks so that he could be heard. And when the yank had got even with him took the best aim he could at the nois, and fired. Then listened at him kicking, so I *know* he is dead.

The next morning the Confederates rode out to inspect the deceased enemy. "[We] moved forward causously, but when we reached the place where Jim had killed his yank, there we found a surenough dead cow."

Forrest's scouts worked tirelessly, and by June 25 the general was able to report to Lee that Smith's plans were to destroy the Mobile & Ohio Railroad as far south as possible, ride west to do the same to the Mississippi Central, and finish up by returning to Memphis. He was convinced the enemy force was made up primarily of inexperienced hundred-days men, and there was little thought of them being sent to Sherman. His scouts had observed some of the Union troops marching eastward, which lead him to state, "I have no doubt but that they have and will probably move with 18,000 to 20,000 men, a portion of which will be used to garrison the points already fortified on the Memphis and Charleston Railroad, with a base secured as far east as practicable. They will then attempt the programme previously referred to."[11]

Forrest's information regarding enemy movements toward LaGrange was correct, as was his belief that Smith's force was not destined to join Sherman in Georgia. However, much of the other information in the message was wide of the mark. He overestimated the number of men who would march with

Smith by 6,000, and none of the 14,000 Federals who would participate in the campaign were left behind as garrison troops. Significantly, Forrest incorrectly identified the target of the expected raid to be the tracks of the Mobile & Ohio and the Mississippi Central railroads. These two lines (along with the Southern Mississippi connecting them at Jackson and Meridian) were vital to Lee's ability to shift troops rapidly within his department. While it is true Smith planned to destroy a section of the Mobile & Ohio somewhere between Tupelo and Columbus, the intended target was not railroad tracks, southern communications, or the rich agriculture of the Black Prairie region; the target was Forrest's cavalry corps. Neither Lee nor Forrest had yet to grasp the Federal strategy in Mississippi of diverting attention away from Sherman's campaign.

The continued Union activity in Tennessee prompted Forrest to make adjustments to his troop deployments. He ordered all but 300 men in Roddey's Division to be pulled out of north Alabama and put into camps around Corinth. He instructed Chalmers's two brigades to move "as near Okolona as nature of forage will permit." Each man was issued a hundred rounds of ammunition and five days' rations and told to "hold yourself in readiness to move at a moment's notice." A note from Forrest the following day assured Chalmers that there was no immediate danger—"Not necessary to make a forced march. Bring all men except those needed to get up forage." The extended operations in the area over the past month had cut into the available grass and grain stores, and as a consequence forage was becoming more difficult to obtain in large amounts. This shortage caused Chalmers to scatter his forces rather than concentrate them at Okolona as instructed. He dispersed regiments and brigades along the eighteen-mile corridor between Okolona and Tupelo.[12]

The 300 men who remained behind were to keep their eyes open for yet another threat to Lee's department: 3,000 Union cavalrymen were gathering in Decatur under Maj. Gen. Lovell Rousseau for a raid deep into Alabama. Rousseau's orders were to take a lightly equipped, fast-riding force and, with no wagons or other supply means, destroy the Montgomery & West Point Railroad thirty miles northwest of Columbus, Georgia. "You may give out that you are going to Selma," instructed Sherman, "but be sure to go to Opelika, and break up railroad between it and Montgomery. There is but a single road there which unites the Mississippi road with the Alabama roads."[13]

Forrest was not happy with the situation as it was on the morning of June 28. His own approach to warfare was to take the fight to the enemy, seize the initiative, strike hard where least expected, and never let up. For the time being, due to the threats against Mobile and from the Federals in LaGrange, he was forced to watch and wait. The only thing he could do was shift troops in preparation for Smith's anticipated movement. It was clear to him that either Tupelo or Okolona would be the target of the invading expedition, and with this in mind he deployed his available troops accordingly. James Chalmers's division (Rucker's and McCulloch's brigades) moved their tents to Verona, four miles south of Tupelo. Abraham Buford's division (Lyon's and Bell's brigades) waited in Tupelo. Hinchie Mabry's brigade arrived from the Yazoo country in the west of the state and was assigned to Buford. This all-Mississippi brigade moved nine miles north of Tupelo to Saltillo. And Philip Roddey's two brigades (Patterson's and Johnson's) waited in Corinth, fifty-five miles north of Tupelo, in the unlikely event that Smith headed east rather than the anticipated southeast.[14]

Six miles west of Tupelo Forrest established his dismounted camp, where all cavalrymen without a horse went to serve as an infantry reserve. Several hundred men from Gholson's all-Tennessee brigade made their way to the dismounted camp, while Gholson and the bulk of his command were with Wirt Adams near Canton.[15] In a letter to Lee, Forrest complained how "a number of General Roddey's men have run away rather than come to the dismounted camp, but once in camp and assured of the design to recruit their stock and render it serviceable they appear very well satisfied." The unsettling prospect of being sent to the dismounted camp resulted in a rash of horse thefts. Among those unhorsed by such activities was Capt. Elisha Hollis of the 7th Tennessee. Hollis made several entries in his diary noting the lovely, warm days spent in Tupelo but was sad to note that, for the first time in his military career, he was reported as "not able for duty." Physically he was fine; but the loss of his horse had rendered him unable to perform his duties. By evening his mount was found and he was once again ready to face the enemy.[16]

Another source of reinforcement came from Gen. Dabney Maury and the fortifications around Mobile. Among Maury's limited resources was Brig. Gen. Edwards Higgins's artillery brigade. By the end of June the 1st Louisiana Heavy Artillery, the 1st Mississippi Light Artillery (acting as infantry), and the 3rd Missouri Battery were the only troops in the city. Lee set up a school of heavy artillery in a building on Government Street and placed it under the command of Lt. Col. Daniel Beltzhoover. Most of the students were from the 1st Louisiana, and Lee put them on alert for possible use in the upcoming campaign.[17]

Not all of the new arrivals were happy to be part of Forrest's command. Pvt. John Cato of the 4th Mississippi wrote, "Report says we are turned over to Forrest, if this be the case we are done going home . . . I intend to try to get a transfer." And Maj. Robert McCay, commander of the 38th Mississippi Mounted Infantry, confided to his wife, "I can but hope that I am mistaken, but now feel that we are Forrest men, not temporarily, but permanently." McCay was also unhappy with the camp at Saltillo just north of Tupelo, complaining that it was "one of the very places I hoped it would never be my lot to soldier in." Nor was he content with the food and drink available to his men: "We have had miserable water and eating in proportion, still my health is fine, weigh 146 lbs. This does not look like living on poor beef and cornbread, but I assure you it is so, no vegetables or anything else." But despite his grumblings, McCay was quite confident that the Federals "will be whipped" when the fighting began.[18]

This optimism was prevalent throughout the Confederate army. Barely two weeks had passed since the victory over Sturgis, and the troopers were still euphoric over the success. It was not just the victory they were pleased with, but the spoils that came along with the victory. "We got plenty of coffee at the Battle of Brice's XRoads," gloated Lt. Samuel Rennick of the 7th Kentucky, "and, of course, are using coffee 3 times a day." In a letter to his brother, Rennick assured him, "We are encamped here and getting along finely. The boys are enjoying good health, but we are very scarce of Confederate money. Ours is getting thundering hard to find. The hospital where the boys are at is a fine one, well-ventilated, clean and nice, good doctors, good nurses, and they have plenty of everything good to eat. They have plenty of ice."[19]

In addition to the pleasant camp conditions, there was even a bit of a social scene, such as it was, in and around Tupelo. Miss Isabella "Belle" Buchannan Edmondson, a Memphis socialite who had been forced to flee her home due to her smuggling and spying activities, kept a running account of the southern society in Pontotoc and Tupelo. Her diary entries are filled with the names of officers and friends in the army who stopped at the house for visits and games of euchre. One occasion was the June 23 wedding of her sister Helen (Hal) and Maj. Browdie S. Crump of General Chalmers's staff, which was well attended by officers in their best uniforms. The officers of Colonel Edmund Rucker's brigade were especially frequent guests of Belle's, and on one memorable night there was even a party.

Jake Anderson & Ebb Titus came by this morning. Col. Polk came out in Gen. Forrest's ambulance for us to go in and spend the day with Maj. Leverson & Maj. Rambeaut. We had a beautiful day, the Miss Skurlarks and Miss Bills, of Jackson, Tenn. were there, we played Cards, talked, and had a gay time. All of our friends nearly, we saw, ate dinner at three o'clock, and a more sumptuous fare I never saw grace a table. We all talked a while on the Porch after dinner, when our crowd came home to fix a little dance, which we enjoyed very much, danced until two o'clock, and only got through six sets. Gen. Forrest was opposed to the dance, so none of his crowd was there.

Belle was particularly impressed on July 8 while visiting General Forrest's head-quarters. "Met with Gen. Lee who had just arrived on the cars. I am perfectly delighted with him, if I had a heart to lose, I think it would be in danger."[20]

Belle's entries in late June and early July 1862 are filled with the enthusi-asm and confidence that was felt throughout the ranks of Forrest's army. Sgt. Maj. William Elder, Forrest's assistant chief quartermaster, also expressed this optimism:

> This day one year ago Vicksburg fell, causing a gloomy and despondent feel-ing throughout the entire Confederacy, causing many of our best men to have dark forebodings of the future. What a contrast between the present and this time last year, all are now hopeful and confident of success, our brave sol-diers being victorious on every battlefield, and are eager at every point in the Confederacy to meet the enemy and convince him the South cannot be subjugated. Gen'l Forrest's Head Quarters are at this place, how long he will remain here depends entirely upon the movements of the enemy. It is reported the Yankees are now at LaGrange, Tenn., with a force estimated at 20,000, whether it is their object to reinforce Sherman or "hunt" up Forrest has not yet been scertained by any of the "Life Insurance" members.[21]

SEVEN

Marching South

The morning of July 5 dawned clear and hot, with every indication that it would become even hotter as the day went on. The weeks of planning and waiting ended when Mower's division broke camp in La Grange and commenced marching south on the Salem Road behind the Jayhawkers of the 7th Kansas Cavalry. Smith's plan was simple: the infantry, artillery, and supply trains would march south to Salem, then southeast into Ripley, and then south to the high ground known as the Pontotoc Ridge. Grierson's cavalry would ride on a parallel road out of Saulsbury and then south to cover the front and left flank of the infantry, and Winslow's brigade would lead the first day's march down the Ripley Road and make camp in a convenient place, "so as to communicate with us tonight." Datus Coon's brigade would follow from Grand Junction and make camp near the junction with the LaGrange–Ripley Road, with the two columns meeting at Ripley and from there marching on together. [1]

On the morning of the 5th, Smith's infantry was ready to move. But Grierson and his cavalry were not. Smith had intended to leave LaGrange shortly after dawn, but the horse soldiers put a serious hitch in his plans. For some reason the cavalry's movement out was held up, and at 8:00 A.M. Smith complained to Washburn, "General Grierson is now delaying me." Whatever the problem, it did not cause a great deal of concern with the men in the mounted ranks. Capt. Lot Abraham of the 4th Iowa Cavalry spent the morning peacefully reading the novel *Luona Prescott* and noting in his diary, "All quiet and nothing doing." Pvt. Jacob Gantz of the same regiment took the time to wash his shirt and drawers and set about writing a letter while his laundry dried. General Hatch stopped in camp long enough to give "a little speech" to the men of the 2nd Iowa, his former regiment. While waiting for Mower's division to clear the camps, Moore's division kept busy loading all of the tents, camp equipage, and other supplies being left behind onto a train headed back to Memphis.[2]

While Grierson worked to get his troopers on the road, Smith met with several of his subordinates and offered up an entirely new plan. At 5:00 P.M. he wired Washburn with his idea: "All have concluded, with your permission, to go to Tuscumbia and do all the mischief we can on the route, and from that point I can reach Columbus much easier than by the route proposed." Smith explained that he could live off the country easier in Alabama, avoid crossing the Tombigbee River to reach Columbus, and still draw Forrest out for a fight. "I can get subsistence and coffee by the Tennessee [River], and that is all I want." The message had to have stunned Washburn, who no doubt wondered what in the world Smith was thinking. Smith's new plan would require his columns to march east for an additional hundred miles and then turn southwest through Alabama and approach Columbus and the Mobile & Ohio Railroad from the east. While the essential elements of the raid would remain in place— Forrest would be drawn out to fight, the Mobile & Ohio would be broken, and Sherman's supply line would be guarded—it left Memphis (and Washburn) dangerously exposed. So if Forrest chose to ignore the proffered fight and take a ride into Memphis, there would be little to stop him. Washburn lost no time instructing Smith to continue with the raid as originally planned.[3]

Why did Smith wait until his men were already marching to spring a new plan on Washburn? Did he envision the raid as becoming something bigger and longer-lasting than his commander viewed it? Could he have supplied himself from the Tennessee River, or did he plan on living off the wealth of the Black Prairie region? These questions remain unanswered. It was no secret that Canby wanted Smith's divisions for an assault on Mobile. And if Smith marched the 225 miles from Tuscumbia to Columbus (and defeated Forrest), he would be in an excellent position to move into the interior of Alabama or to move down to the Gulf of Mexico and Mobile, a move that would certainly please Canby. Also, by placing his force on the far side of the Tombigbee River, Smith would increase the odds of his *not* being recalled to Memphis. This was a good move if Smith was trying to put distance between himself and Memphis with the ultimate goal of being sent back to his corps with Sherman. Or he may have even been interested in acquiring an independent command within Alabama. There is even a chance that the message to Washburn was nothing more than a small ruse to confuse the enemy as to the army's destination. There are many questions, what-ifs, and whys, but no answers.

Finally, at 4:00 P.M., Smith gave the order for Moore's division and the supply train to head south from LaGrange. The afternoon was stifling hot, and the passage of Mower's four brigades had left the road several inches deep in dust. The tramping feet of Moore's Third Division caused the dust to rise in a cloud that choked Bouton's USCT brigade marching in their wake. The combination of the intense heat and dust was especially brutal for the men at the back of the column. Chaplain Edwards of the 7th Minnesota observed that "the members of the Black Brigade suffered more in proportion to their numbers than did the Whites." Behind the infantry came the hundreds of wagons loaded with rations, forage, small arms ammunition, as well as the reserve artillery ammunition. The line of wagons stretched for miles. A late-afternoon shower cooled the air and washed some of the grime from the men's faces, but it also turned the dirt road into a narrow ribbon of mud. At 5:20 in the afternoon, Smith rode out from his headquarters in LaGrange and set out after the rear of the column, leaving the 9th Illinois Cavalry to guard the vacated camps. Seven miles away, just across the Mississippi line, the column halted for the night at Davis Mill on the Wolf River. It was a slow start, but there had been no stragglers, and no men were lost to the heat.[4]

The camp at Davis Mill was crowded with men dropping their packs and searching for shade on either side of the Wolf River. Chaplain Edwards described "a cool, clear stream" that was almost immediately polluted with thousands of sweaty soldiers stripping off their clothes and jumping in for an afternoon swim, "utterly regardless of the fact that this was our and their only supply of drinking water."[5]

Two bridges spanned the stream at the abandoned mill site, a wagon bridge and a mile-long trestle of the Mississippi Central Railroad. Davis Mill had been the scene of a desperate fight on December 21, 1862, when 250 men of the 25th Indiana Infantry and the 5th Ohio Cavalry held at bay 3,500 Confederate cavalrymen under the command of Maj. Gen. Earl Van Dorn, fresh from their destruction of Grant's massive supply depot at Holly Springs twenty miles to the south. The defenders on the Wolf River stymied Van Dorn and his command for three hours and forced them to travel west to find another river crossing. In the intervening year and a half the site had served as a campground for passing troops on both sides of the struggle.[6]

At sunrise the following morning, July 6, the march resumed, with the 7th Kansas Cavalry once again leading the infantry south. Moore's Third Division took its turn in front and was first on the road. This set a pattern for the expedition; each day a different brigade from each of the divisions led the morning march. There were advantages to being the first in line: the heavy dust had not yet been churned by the thousands of feet, hooves, and wheels, and so the breathing was easier; the first brigade was also the first to get into camp at the end of the day's walk; and they got the first pickings of the blackberries that grew in hedges and at fence corners on the side of the road.[7]

Sgt. Lyman Pierce of the 2nd Iowa Cavalry recalled how "the weather was oppressively warm, the thermometer being 100 degrees above zero." Because of the relentless heat, Smith called for an easy pace. Rain the previous evening had done nothing to cool the air, let alone settle the dust that again rose in thick, choking clouds. The heat was unrelenting and, despite what should have been an easy pace, as the morning wore on the column began to lose stragglers. Capt. Theodore Carter of the 7th Minnesota Infantry blamed eight months of soft garrison duty for his regiment's poor showing on the march—"we were not able to stand the heat." Chaplain Edwards saw "many fall out of the ranks and lay exhausted and panting by the roadside." Maj. David Reed of the 12th Iowa, a veteran of Fort Donelson, Shiloh, Corinth, and Vicksburg, observed how "the march [was] under the hottest sun and in the deepest dust that we found in all our marching, was trying to the men, and many suffered from sunstroke." The route was soon littered with men who waited for the cool of the day before pressing on and catching up with their regiments. At noon a halt was called by Smith within four miles of Salem, and the men sought whatever shade they could find. The army had advanced a mere twelve miles.[8]

Historians have criticized the slow pace of Smith's advance from LaGrange, one of them going so far as to claim that "it strains definition to call this movement a march; it was more like a tiptoe." Yet, there was little to be gained by a quick march south. Every hour and every day Smith's presence kept Forrest away from Sherman's supply line was a victory for the northern force. As long as he held Forrest's attention in Mississippi, the slower Smith marched the better. Moreover, Smith knew the level of endurance he could expect from his men. If a fight lay ahead of him, he needed to keep every man in his army ready for battle. A handful of men died on July 6 from heatstroke; had the pace been pushed to what was considered "normal" on an average day, say twenty miles, the number of dead would have been in the hundreds. Smith was determined not to make the same mistakes that proved fatal to Sturgis's campaign the month before, when his column had become widely separated. Smith kept his column together by slowing the pace.[9]

One soldier who refused to fall out of ranks was Pvt. Robert Burdette of the 47th Illinois Infantry: "There were times when I was so dead tired and worn out, and faint with hunger that my legs wabbled as I walked, and my eyes were so dry and hot with lack of sleep, that I would have given a month's pay for floor space in Andersonville prison. But whenever I turned my eyes longingly to the roadside, passing a good place to 'drop out,' . . . I braced up and offered to carry my file-leaders knapsack for a mile or two."[10] In the 117th Illinois, Pvt. Ben Hieronymous noted that the blinding heat was only a part of the problem:

> Not a few of the men were sun-struck & numbers were worn out with excessive fatigue & overcome with heat. Four of our boys of our Co[mpany] started on the trip barefoot, two of them succeeded in getting shoes—but my brother Thomas and Billy Sease went the whole trip of near one hundred and fifty miles without a shoe. And many places on the route was rocky—and frequently we had to march through brush & briers. It was the neglect of some Quarter Master that did not have proper clothing.[11]

Under particular hardship during that march were the men of the 33rd Wisconsin. Back in early March, when the regiment was setting out on the Red River campaign, the excess regimental baggage, including knapsacks, was sent to Cairo, Illinois, and stored in a warehouse. After the campaign, while the men were camped at LaGrange, the knapsacks were returned to them—still crammed full with the clothes the men had been wearing the previous winter. Not wishing to risk losing the knapsacks again, the men of the 33rd disregarded the order to proceed with only haversacks and blankets and marched under the broiling Mississippi sun bearing a load of flannel shirts, flannel drawers, greatcoats, and wool blankets on their backs.[12]

For some, though, the extra burden of even a light knapsack was simply too much, given the tremendous heat. Pvt. Johann Schmidt of the 117th Illinois discarded his equipment on the second day of the march, a move that made an impression on Pvt. Louis Hucke, who made note of the lightening of Schmidt's burden in his diary and then the following day chose to follow his friend's lead: "Camped in a dense forest and here I threw away my knapsack and canister and everything that was in it." In the days to come Huch never expressed a single word of remorse for throwing away his gear.[13]

Over on the Saulsbury Road, Grierson's division set a slower pace than the infantry. The cavalry was to rendezvous with the infantry at the junction with the LaGrange-Ripley Road, and since it was only a few miles down the road, Grierson allowed his men to sleep in. At 2:00 P.M. Winslow's brigade left the campsite first and crossed the state line into Mississippi. Within two miles the road forked; the road to the left led directly to Ripley, eighteen miles away; the road to the right led seven miles to where they were to meet the infantry.

There had been some contact with the enemy, but after a bit of light skirmishing the Confederates videttes fell back without either side inflicting casualties. At the road junction, Winslow's men set up their meager camp and waited for Coon's brigade. Back at the LaGrange campsite, the 9th Illinois Cavalry was released from guard duty by troops sent from Memphis and rode out at 6:00 P.M. to catch up with the column.[14]

That night Pvt. Ben Thomas of the 14th Iowa had guard duty at the Third Division headquarters, and though he grumbled about the loss of sleep, he was entertained by the activity. "Made my couch beside Colonel Moore's tent and a number of officers had gathered there after night. I must say I heard some of the most wonderful stories I ever heard told. The story telling and drinking was kept up till after midnight." There is no way of knowing if Col. Ed Winslow of the Second Cavalry Brigade was at the party, but the following morning General Grierson caught the bleary-eyed colonel napping along the roadside.[15]

The first two days of the expedition were relatively quiet, save for a little inconsequential skirmishing by the cavalry. Interestingly, however, one Confederate soldier recalled it quite differently. Sgt. Henry Hord of the 3rd Kentucky Mounted Infantry remembered decades after the war a "kind of guerrilla warfare—capturing pickets, ambushing, night attacks, rushing in while they were on the march, killing the wagon guards, burning wagons, and out again before they could get a whack at us." As a response to these alleged Confederate activities, he remembered, Smith's column was forced to slow to a mere six or seven miles a day, and their back trail was scattered with dead mules, burnt wagons and freshly dug graves. "All the way from La Grange to Harrisburg we acted as an invisible escort to Gen. Smith. He could not water his horses without taking his army to the creek with him, and he camped every night in line of battle, with heavy skirmish lines thrown around him." Capt. Theodore Carter of the 7th Minnesota responded to Hord's 1905 letter printed in *Confederate Veteran Magazine*, noting, "We were never disturbed, never camped in line of battle, and made as long marches as the men could endure in that hot climate." Indeed, Carter's comments are backed by scores of diaries and letters, while Hord's recollected account is more fiction than fact.[16]

Reveille came early in the Union camps. Smith roused the men at 2:00 A.M. on July 7 to take advantage of the cool morning air. At dawn the cavalry division, which had spent the night at the crossroads rendezvous, mounted up and set out, and for the first time it led the infantry and shared the Ripley Road. Captain Abraham of the 2nd Iowa Cavalry observed, "We came into the road we *retreated* over June 11th." There was plenty of evidence of the Brice's Crossroads rout—bits of equipment and burned wagons as well as several shallow

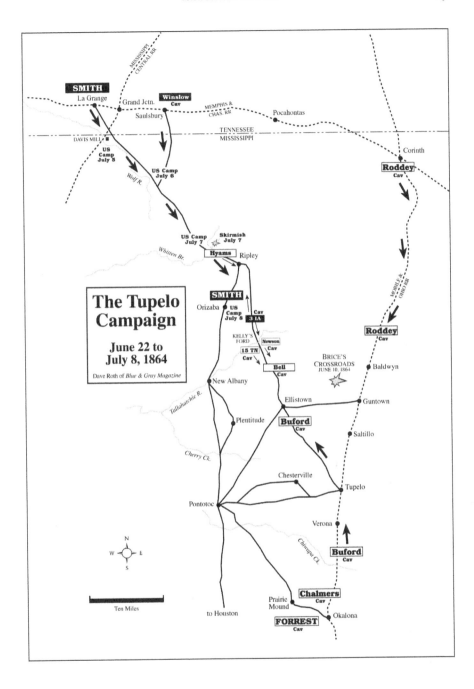

The Tupelo Campaign

June 22 to
July 8, 1864

Dave Roth of *Blue & Gray Magazine*

graves that had been dug up by rooting hogs. The line of march passed the well-tended graves of four privates and a captain of a Kentucky regiment and then the unburied remains of three Union soldiers. Murmuring and cursing rippled through the Federal ranks as they passed.[17]

Coon's Third Brigade's 2nd Iowa Cavalry, under Maj. Charles Horton, led that morning, closely followed by the ranks of infantry, artillery, and wagon trains. The 9th Illinois, which had camped at Davis Mill on its ride to rejoin its brigade, rode at the rear of the formation. By early afternoon, however, it reached the head of the column and took a position in line with Coon's brigade.[18]

When the 9th Illinois made the move forward from the rear of the column, the seventeen men of Company H, 7th Kansas Cavalry, dropped back to the rear. The 7th was driving a herd of some 100 cattle (an important food source for the the army) when, without warning, a Confederate patrol swooped onto the road, pushed the Jayhawkers down the road, and absconded with the cows. The remaining men of Company H, along with the balance of Company A, were summoned from the front of the infantry column and sent off in pursuit of the rustlers.[19]

At the head of Smith's column, the 2nd Iowa Cavalry also made contact with the enemy, when two videttes discovered four mounted Confederates and rashly charged them with the hope of trying out their new Spencer carbines. The southerners were the lead element of an eight-man detail under the command of Lt. V. A. Grace of the 1st Mississippi Partisan Rangers. The Confederates outnumbered the audacious Iowans two to one and held their ground, expecting to take a few foolhardy prisoners. But then the Federals lifted their carbines and "pumped lead therefrom." Two of the southerners were unhorsed, and the other pair put the spurs to their mounts and took flight. The four-man Confederate reserve heard the firing and joined their two comrades, who were galloping away from the scene. Alerted by the firing, a second pair of Iowa troopers arrived and charged after the retreating Confederates, who could not be caught. When they rounded up the two prisoners, one of them asked to see one of the guns the Federals had fought with. Impressed with the weapon, the Confederate observed, "It is no use for us to fight you'ens with that kind of gun."

Lieutenant Grace and his remaining men rode south and found the bulk of the Partisan Rangers with the 3rd Tennessee about three miles north of Ripley. At the far end of an open field, Lt. Colonel Samuel Hyams, commanding the small detachment from McCulloch's brigade, decided to make a demonstration in front of the advancing enemy, posting his men on a commanding hill.[20] Major Horton was notified of the Confederate defensive position and led six companies of his 2nd Iowa to investigate. Horton ordered his men to dismount and form a line of battle in the trees on the near side of the field. Every fourth man in line held the horses of the other three, and in this manner three-quarters of Horton's men prepared to advance into the field on foot. When the Union troopers reached the midpoint of the field, the Confederates fired "volley after volley." Firing downhill with a muzzle-loading weapon at a moving target can be difficult at best, and, luckily for the Iowans, the first volley went well over their heads. Before the Confederates could fire again, the Federals had taken cover in "a friendly ditch." From the protection of the makeshift rifle pit, they returned a hot fire and masked Horton, who took one of his battalions on a flanking movement to the left. As Horton ordered the battalion to charge, the rest of the regiment burst out of the ditch and charged headlong up the hill.

Hyams was outnumbered, but he would not have stayed to fight even if the odds had been in his favor. Forrest's orders were clear: observe the enemy but don't make a determined stand. The evolving plan was to draw the enemy closer to Okolona, where Forrest would attack and defeat them, just as he had Sturgis. Hymans, however, misjudged Horton's response and ended up with casualties disproportionate to the importance of the engagement. Had he obeyed his orders, he would have pulled his men off the hill earlier and avoided the fight altogether. The small dustup, dubbed "the Battle of Whitten Branch" by the *Southern Sentinel,* claimed the lives of ten Confederates and left four Federals slightly wounded.[21]

By the time the field and the hill had been swept for casualties, Mower's infantry division arrived, and the army set up camp for the night. But a serious problem now presented itself, as Fletcher Pomeroy of the 7th Kansas Cavalry recorded in his diary: "There is no forage to be found for our horses here." Just a few days earlier General Hatch had disregarded the warnings of Sturgis and Sooy Smith and assured Smith of the plentiful forage to be found on the Ripley Road. The hay and grain in the supply wagons was never meant to be the sole source of forage for the animals but, instead, to augment what could be taken from local farmers along the way. If a steady supply of forage could not be found in the countryside, the expedition could be in jeopardy.[22]

The heat on July 7 was intense, and despite the slow pace, men had again succumbed to heatstroke during the march. Sgt. Harrison Chandler, in charge of the 114th Illinois wagons, gave up his horse so a few tired soldiers could ride and take a short rest. Other stopped in the shade of the roadside trees, too exhausted or overcome by dust to continue. The straggling became so widespread that Col. William Marshall of the 7th Minnesota issued an order requiring any man who had fallen out of the regiment to have a pass. Captain Carter of the 7th anticipated another tough day of marching and spent the evening writing out passes in advance, leaving the name to be filled in the next day when men began to straggle once again.[23]

Other soldiers fell out of ranks for different reasons. The sight of the debris left from the Brice's Crossroads retreat fueled the men's anger, and some burned and pillaged the homes and farms along the route of march. Chaplain Edwards of the 7th Minnesota attempted to explain the actions:

> This burning of buildings, and other destruction of property is apologized for as an act of retribution for atrocities committed by residents upon the road from Guntown to Memphis who fired from their houses upon the Union troops as they were retreating from Guntown after their defeat at that place. It was for this reason that the torch was applied to every house from whose windows a gun had been fired at a Union soldier.

Chaplain Edwards, so new to the army he did not yet have a uniform, was witness to a great deal of plundering of which, "I had neither the ability or authority to prevent." The soldiers plundered houses of whatever food could be found, and what they could not carry away they usually destroyed—"Family pictures, old daguerreotypes, etc. they crushed under their heels." At the whim of the sackers, they would then put the building to the torch or leave it for others to comb through. The chaplain witnessed a great deal of such plundering, writing, "I am loth to report these despicable outrages, but am glad to report that strict orders have been issued from headquarters strictly prohibiting these practices."[24]

However, General Order No. 5, issued by Smith prior to the Red River campaign and though technically still in effect, was not stringently enforced.

Some of Smith's regimental commanders gave strict commands that the General order prohibiting pillaging be followed while others simply ignored it. The 35th Iowa's Pvt. George Brockway recorded, "The orders from head quarters is on this march that if any one is found behind without a pass from the Cap he is to be severely punished and if found straggling away from the road burning any property or destroying anything what ever he is to be hanged or shot on the spot."[25]

With some men slipping away to pillage and burn, the column continued south. At noon Smith called a halt for the day four miles north of Ripley, and for the next several hours the army marched into the camp on the north bank of Tippah Creek.[26]

The march of July 8, which began early, at 4:00 o'clock, proved to be the hottest. By 10:00 A.M., Captain Carter began to have difficulties keeping his men in ranks. One overheated private told him, "It's of no use to try anymore, I simply can't keep up any longer." The captain handed the man a pass and continued down the road, doing his best to hide the fact that he, too, was suffering from the heat. By the time a halt was called at midday, half of the company, including Carter, was missing from the ranks.[27]

Hours earlier, and just before daylight, two companies of the 7th Kansas Cavalry rode out under Maj. Charles Gregory to look for the stolen cattle, though few held out any hope that the rear guard would be successful. Chaplain Edwards spoke for many when he wrote, "This sounds fishy since our rear guard is not likely to distinguish itself by capturing cattle or anything else." At dawn, Smith's column set out for Ripley with Winslow's brigade and the 10th Missouri Cavalry leading the way. Three miles down the road the troopers found a fork in the road. The road to the left led directly to Tupelo by way of Ellistown, and the main road continued south to Pontotoc. Since the army was headed for Pontotoc, the troops continued the march without a halt.[28]

General Grierson paused at the crossroads long enough to brief his brigade commanders on some new instructions. He ordered Winslow and Coon to use parallel roads as much as possible, staying on the left flank of the advancing column, something they'd done at the start of the campaign. This maneuver would not only protect the left flank as the army marched farther south, but it would also cut back considerably on the dust generated by 12,000 hooves. In addition, Grierson had a special assignment for one of Winslow's regiments.[29]

He pulled Col. John Noble and his 3rd Iowa Cavalry out of the line and sent them down the left road, known as the Ellistown or Tupelo Road, on a reconnoitering mission to Kelly's Ford on the Tallahatchie River.[30] The reconnaissance was to scout out enemy activity on the road south to Ellistown and Tupelo and, more importantly, confuse the enemy about Smith's intentions. Smith was an old campaigner and did not have to be told that Forrest was drawing in his detachments to make a stand somewhere up ahead. He hoped that the presence of Noble's men on the Tupelo Road would cause Forrest to converge on Ellistown while the Federals continued unimpeded on the road to Pontotoc. Colonel Noble set out with a heavy advance guard and within a half-mile came across a "very considerable earthwork" on the brow of a hill.[31]

The approach to the breastwork was exposed and presented difficulties for the advancing cavalrymen, who did not relish riding across an open field under fire. They had nothing to fear, however, since the Confederate defenders of the road block had fled when they saw the two Federal companies sent out to flank the position. Noble assumed that they were "also intimidated no doubt by the appearance of our other troops on the main road." The Iowans continued south on their scout and noted how the road was heavily marked with horse tracks. Obviously, the road had been used recently by enemy cavalry, and they made the same observations at every junction along the route. After advancing a total of four miles, Noble could confirm that the southerners held a good position at Kelly's Ford and numbered at least 1,000 strong. The experienced soldier must have felt some trepidation as he observed the area and been sure that there was an even larger force hovering at his flanks.[32] With the information in hand, Noble reversed his route and began a "leisurely" return to the cavalry column. No sooner had the regiment turned than Noble's instincts were confirmed, and it was attacked by a detachment of Confederates bursting out of the woods. Noble's men opened fire with their Spencers, and as fast as it started, the fight was over. One southerner was killed, one wounded, and one captured, while the 3rd Iowa rode on unscathed.[33]

While the 3rd Iowa was on the Ellistown Road, Smith's infantry and artillery continued to pass through Ripley, which one soldier saw as a little town "with several fine residences" and another described as "a small dilapidated village." Chaplain Edwards remarked, "This village impressed me as more than usually attractive embowered as it was with semi-tropical shrubbery." While trudging through town several soldiers noticed a cavalryman standing at the front gate of a house, as if on guard. The trooper held his carbine in a menacing fashion and refused to allow any Union troops to enter the home or even approach the well in the front yard. Captain Carter of the 7th Minnesota struck up a conversation with the young horse soldier and learned he was a self-appointed guardian of the home of a local physician. Apparently the trooper had been wounded at Brice's Crossroads and the good doctor had not only dressed his wounds but cared for the soldier in his home and then, when sufficiently recovered, taken him most of the way to Memphis in his buggy. The trooper stood guard until the entire column had passed then remounted and returned to his regiment.[34]

Chaplain Edwards noted that "from appearances I feared some of our stragglers had been committing depredations although it was done before we came." The *Southern Sentinel* reported the burning of the Tippah County Courthouse, the Methodist and Cumberland Presbyterian churches, the Mason's and Odd-Fellow's halls, a drugstore, and at least four private residences. Judge Orlando Davis of Ripley noted how it took from 7:00 A.M. to 3:00 P.M. for the Federal army to pass through town. "The scenes of this visitation were the most terrible we have ever experienced in Ripley. The Yankees were infuriated because of their former defeat here and came swearing vengeance on the town."

Just outside of Ripley a modest white house stood on the west side of the road. Captain Carter told about a hog that had wandered out of the yard and into the road, where a Union soldier shot and killed it. The lady of the house heard the commotion in her front yard and came out on the porch to see her hog being butchered. She told the offending soldier to take all the pork he wanted, that it had not cost a thing to raise it, since "it was fattened on dead Yankees and niggers." For the "insulting remark," the soldiers burned the house to the ground. Another house nearby was torched when soldiers marching past found a human skull set on a stake in a fence corner.[35]

Excessive foraging and depredations had been rampant since leaving La-Grange, but the burning of Ripley went above and beyond any such behavior during the campaign. When ordered to burn a public or private building, the soldiers involved either relished the task or were sickened by it. In either case, the perpetrators recorded the events in letters, diaries, or official reports. But few men took credit for the burning of Ripley, and neither Smith nor any of his officers mention the details of the event in their reports. Soldiers did freely burn public buildings, and Smith was under orders to burn the homes of citizens known to be assisting Forrest. But churches, even in enemy territory, were still considered to be sacred and were rarely set aflame.

There was a single soldier who had no reluctance about admitting to the burning of Ripley. Pvt. Hans Danielson of the 7th Minnesota Infantry "passed Ripley at noon where the command burned several fine houses for the out-rages committed on the men returning from the ill-fated Sturgis raid in June." Whether he meant it was Smith's army or specifically the 7th Minnesota that did the burning is unclear; but in defense of the Minnesotans, neither the regi-ment's chaplain, Edwards, nor the captain, Carter, mentioned their participa-tion, and Edwards dutifully recorded the depredations he observed. Carter later recalled having seen only one burning building during the whole expedi-tion, and it "was so close to the road as to endanger the ammunition train." Carter obviously downplayed the destruction and was quick to blame any and all such burnings on the cavalry, which was always in the advance.[36]

Another soldier who mentioned the burned buildings was Fletcher Pome-roy of the 7th Kansas Cavalry, who placed the blame on Grierson's brigade. The Jayhawkers of the 7th were in an unattached status and had a well-de-served reputation for arson and theft. Pvt. Ben Thomas, marching at the head of the column with Moore's division, blamed Bouton's brigade, writing, "We heard that as the negro troops passed through Ripley they were fired upon by parties concealed in some of the houses and that they in return set fire to the town and burned it to the ground. Hoped this was one of the false rumors we had so many of. There was too much property destroyed from necessity without being obliged to fire as nice and seemingly as quiet a place as Ripley." This claim was seconded by David King, commissary sergeant of the 89th Indiana, whose wrote in his diary on July 8 that "the 89 guarding the train, passed through Ripley at noon. The rear guards burnt the town."[37]

Chaplain Edwards, new to the army and not yet hardened to war's horrors, was convinced that the acts were not initiated by Smith: "One thing is reasonably certain, that the firing was not done by special order." Edwards heard a great deal of grumbling by the men in ranks prior to the entry into town, and therein lay the key to the destruction of Ripley—the near-universal belief that local civilians had fired on the soldiers withdrawing through town in June. Reverend John Aughey, a local clergyman, confirmed these reports when he wrote of the retreat from Brice's Crossroads: "As a squad of these panting fugitives passed through Ripley, the women from their windows and doors shot them as they passed along. A young soldier begged a young lady who was seated on a veranda to give him a glass of water, as he was perishing from thirst. She walked into the house, brought a glass of water, and while this young patriot was drinking she drew a pistol and immediately shot him." As the story of the shootings by the local citizens was passed from soldier to soldier, the men became "phrenzied," and the fate of Ripley was sealed.[38]

Evidence of the violence that accompanied the retreat was all along the road. Surgeon Bartlett of the 33rd Missouri noted a scattering of broken muskets along the road and "a grave which had been made so shallow that a portion of a human skeleton protruded." The column passed a mass grave along the roadside that purportedly held the remains of five soldiers, further fueling the anger smoldering in the ranks. "We found where several of our men had been buried that was killed on the stugis retreat," recorded Jacob Gantz of the 4th Iowa Cavalry, "and there had been a little hole dug & them thrown in & the hogs had dug them up & eat them & their bones was laying around the hole." When the 89th Indiana marched past the scene, Cpl. Cornelius Corwin looked on and later described it in his diary, writing, "Passed several graves of our men that had been killed on the Sturgis Expedition they had not been only a little dirt thrown over them and the hogs had rooted them out and there was nothing left of them but the clothes & bones." Pvt. Thomas Hawley of the 11th Missouri later tried to explain the effects of these discoveries on the local inhabitants:

Rebel property suffers and we passed over part of the same ground crossed as part of General Sturgess' forces. Could often see the wreck of a wagon, the skeleton of a mule or horse, a few muddy army blue rags. Looking closer in the bushes and gullies, we often saw bones of the human skeleton. A skull or other bones were distinguished. Some never buried at all, others in shallow pit that the pigs routed out and devoured the flesh. Then to hear the tales of many of the men who had run the gauntlet of death was truly distressing and exasperating. We could see houses burn without any compunction of conscience.

But there were few men in the Union ranks who had any pity for the fate of Ripley. "Retribution will certainly be metted out to both armies for such conduct," mused Sgt. Harrison Chandler, "on our part for vandalism, on theirs for *murder*."[39]

As the morning of July 8 wore on, the head of the column reached Orizaba and a halt was called for the day, the army having advanced another ten miles. Shade was abundant at the site, and there were several springs of clear, cool water as well. A surprise mail call reached the 4th Iowa Cavalry, though how it appeared is a mystery (probably an overlooked sack was found in one of the wagons). For spiritual comfort as well as entertainment, there was preaching in the camp of the 122nd Illinois Infantry. There was extra rejoicing among the 7th Kansas Cavalry, since a large field of oats and corn was found for the horses, and Major Gregory and his patrol returned in triumph with all of the recovered cattle. In the 178th New York camp the mood was more subdued; Pvt. Martin Koch had died of sunstroke during the day's march.[40] Aurelius Bartlett, the surgeon of the 33rd Missouri treated three cases of heatstroke that day, one of them so severe the soldier was unable to speak for several hours after reaching camp.[41] Some from the 114th Illinois made an attempt to have fresh beef for supper. Sgt. Harrison Chandler, the acting quartermaster for the regiment, spied a cow in a nearby pasture. The poor creature had only one eye, so he bravely snuck up on the "blind side" and grabbed her by the horns. The cow hadn't seen him creeping up and panicked, bucking wildly. Chandler hung on for dear life. After being dragged around the field a few times, he and a few comrades succeeded in overcoming the animal, and the men of the 114th dined on fresh meat.[42]

There was little to see in Orizaba in 1864. The town was dying; few of its 150 inhabitants remained by the time Smith's column came to spend the night. The Cumberland Presbyterian Church and the Masonic Lodge were surrounded by a cluster of homes and small businesses, and the town, which had survived off the trade of the local planters, was nearly deserted.[43] A soldier of the 122nd Illinois went exploring in the community and in a smokehouse discovered what he believed to be a barrel of molasses. His friend, Cpl. William Ibbetson, hoisted the load onto the soldier's back and then watched as he staggered back toward camp with his prize. Wishing to share in the treat, Ibbetson found a jug and convinced his friend to set the load down long enough to draw off enough for his own use. "We turned the tap & lo out came, well, varnish. We were sold. We left that & got some apples & a sheep & had a good supper & went & washed & went to sleep."[44]

The march continued the next morning, Saturday, July 9. Reveille sounded at 2:30, and by 4:00 the southward trek continued with David Moore's Third Division leading the infantry column. Smith planned to march no farther than New Albany on the south bank of the Tallahatchie River, an easy twelve-mile trek. Moore set a quick pace, intending to take advantage of the cool morning air before the heat of the day made marching intolerable. He should have started earlier.

"It's terrible hot & we march like the deuce," wrote Ibbettson, "if we had not good roads to march on we could never have stood up to it." Harrison Chandler, who was lucky enough to ride a horse, saw men dropping out of line by the dozen. "It is hard to see poor soldiers falling senseless by the wayside as I have seen them today—completely exhausted, overcome with heat." There were several rumors of fighting off to the left or to the right, but it was always some other brigade or division doing the fighting, and the day passed with no enemy contact worth reporting. Before noon Moore was crossing the Tallahatchie at Williamson's Mill and setting up camp on the high ground of the opposite bank. The bridge over the river had been burned, but the army managed to cross on the remaining timbers.[45]

The day's march had been easy for Moore's men, but not so for Mower's division, which brought up the rear. As the morning went on and the thermometer continued to climb, men were overcome by heat and began to straggle. "I was probably the last man to reach camp," recalled Capt. Ted Carter of the 7th Minnesota, "and it was past midnight when I arrived. Had the Confederates had a force in our rear they would have captured many who were unable to keep up, myself among the number." The heat had yellowed the grass and wilted the leaves, but the farmland bordering this section of the Ripley-Pontotoc Road had fared better than any the men had seen thus far on the expedition. Pvt. James Krafft of the 117th Illinois recorded in his diary, "Country more improved than any we have seen in Northern Miss, nearly every farm having an orchard." And Corporal Ibbetson noted, "We are passing through some very nice country."[46]

Once the column had passed through Ripley and marched south on the Pontotoc Road, it departed from what had been the main line of advance and retreat taken by Sturgis during the Brice's Crossroads affair. There was no longer the detritus of battle scattered along the route, and this section of Tippah County appeared relatively untouched. Though the hungry foragers still hit the farms like a swarm of locusts, they torched no barns or buildings. "Crops have been splendid all the way through, corn, wheat & potatoes," noted Ibbetson. "We are in on the potatoes." Moore's men quickly cleaned out all the food to be found around New Albany, and those who followed were forced to hunt farther from the main road or eat their army rations. This presented a potentially disastrous problem; Smith's army was running out of rations.[47]

The men had been given a three days' supply of food and told to make it stretch for six. "Rations short," wrote a Missouri soldier, and "drew ½ rations for 3 days" from a man in the 33rd Wisconsin. Some regiments were unaffected for the first several days, since the rations were liberally augmented by foraging. But as early as July 6, the day after the column left LaGrange, John Keltner of the 24th Missouri noted "rations short"—and six of the men from the 7th Minnesota had been captured while foraging too far from the column—and then "rations out."[48]

Smith had left LaGrange with what he believed was twenty days' rations of hardtack. Each soldier received a daily ration of one pound of hard bread, which worked out to about ten crackers per man. Dispersed among the supply wagons were 140 tons of hardtack as well the other daily rations of beef, salt pork, coffee, sugar, and salt. The hardtack had come to LaGrange by way of Memphis and should have been inspected by any number of commissary officers before it was accepted for use by the army. But three days before the column left LaGrange, Smith contacted Washburn and reported, "I have just discovered that a large portion of my ammunition is worthless. I have ordered an examination of all the boxes and will retain and send in special train this evening with that condemned. I am happy that I have made the discovery this early." With the inspectors busy looking at boxes of ammunition, they neglected to inspect the boxes full of hardtack. Had anyone bothered to inspect the bread, he would have discovered the majority of it to be moldy and unfit to eat. But the worthless food had been loaded on the supply wagons, and Smith was forced to pay the price for his staff's shoddy work.[49]

Smith could have turned the column back to LaGrange on July 6 or 7 and arranged for more bread to be sent out from Memphis and been back on track within a week. But having started out, the old soldier was intent on holding the initiative and not letting it go. The men could forage for their rations, he maintained, and even if the bread gave out completely he was adamant about continuing on until he got his fight out of Forrest. The move was risky, but still a calculated gamble. Luckily the foraging was good, and that evening Pvt.

Charles Tiedman of the 178th New York could brag, "lots of potatoes here." Those regiments that strictly forbade foraging, however, began to suffer for the want of food.

The bivouac site near New Albany was a "fine camping ground," and by nightfall Chaplain Edwards noted its "rather picturesque appearance." Men flocked to the Tallahatchie for a swim and a chance to wash out their salt-stiffened uniforms. While the shirts and pants dried on bushes and trees, the men went after the itchy chiggers they had been invested with in Tennessee. Ben Thomas of the 14th Iowa commented,

> Its choice location was between the shoulder blades. I do not know how it learned that one spot of the human body that was out of reach of the hands, but there it located and there it stayed in spite of the victims' efforts to remove it. Some one told us to scour with fine sand and it would cut them off so while in the river we scoured each other to remove them. It was amusing to see a long row of men each rubbing his file leaders back with sand.[50]

A cool rain fell on the camp during the evening of the 9th. The shower settled the dust but did not disturb the sleeping army.

EIGHT

Pontotoc

For six days the opposing forces had been gradually converging—the Federals from LaGrange and Saulsbury and the Confederates from Tupelo, Okolona, and Corinth. Smith's army slowly made its way along the Pontotoc Road, conserving its strength in the summer heat, and Forrest shifted troops across the countryside while trying to determine Smith's intentions. Forrest had become so proficient at predicting what his enemy was doing, where they were going, that it seemed almost instinctual.

This was no longer the case, however. When Smith sent John Noble's 3rd Iowa Cavalry as a diversion down the Ripley–Tupelo Road, Forrest responded appropriately by directing Buford to send a brigade up the road to investigate. Early in the morning of July 8, Col. Tyree Bell's Tennessee brigade went to Ellistown. It was grueling twenty-five mile march that wore down men and horses in the unrelenting heat. When they arrived, Bell dispatched the 15th and 19th Tennessee to continue on to the ford of the Tallahatchie River and report on enemy activity. There was nothing to report.[1]

Despite the fact that no Federals had been sighted near Kelly's Ford for more than twenty-four hours, Forrest concluded that this was the route Smith was taking. In the morning hours of June 9, he ordered Buford to take Lyon's brigade of Kentuckians and meet up with Bell in Ellistown. He ordered Mabry's Brigade out of their Saltillo camps as well. By nightfall an entire division lay ready to intercept an enemy that was not there.

When Forrest finally realized that Smith was not on the Ellistown Road, he made another bad assumption in concluding that Federals had been on the road but were now headed southwest on a road that connected Kelly's Ford with New Albany and Pontotoc. In order to confirm Smith's position, Forrest gave an order to Buford to "hang upon his flanks and to develop his strength, but to avoid a general engagement by gradually falling back toward Okolona if the enemy pressed him." But since Smith was not on the Ellistown Road—and never had been—or on the path leading out from Kelly's Ford, it was impossible for Buford to "hang on the flanks" of Smith's army. Buford figured the only road Smith could be on was the Ripley–Pontotoc Road, and his instincts were proven correct when he received the scout's report.[2]

Colonel Bell ordered Pvt. D. B. Willard, a farrier in Company C, 2nd Tennessee, to "go till you find them." Along with two other privates, Willard rode for hours and finally discovered the enemy column in camp at New Albany, more than twelve miles from where they were thought to be. Willard left his companions and rode at a horse-killing pace to relay the vital information.[3]

General Buford dispatched his findings to Forrest before setting out to get ahead of Smith's column. Two roads went south out of New Albany: the Pontotoc Road led directly south to Pontotoc before continuing on to Okolona, and the Plentitude Road ran twelve miles southeast to the hamlet of Plentitude and then arced back to the southwest where the two roads came together again before the crossing at Cherry Creek. To determine Smith's strength and exact position, Buford had to place a force on each road and wait for the enemy to come to him—if he could get there first.

While the northerners slept on the heights above the Tallahatchie, Buford sent messengers through his own camps preparing his division for a night march southwest on the road to Pontotoc. The men fed and watered their mounts and, almost as an afterthought, ate a few bites of food themselves before climbing back into the saddle. Bell's 2nd Tennessee and Mabry's 6th Mississippi led the column out of camp and then set a faster past, soon outdistancing the rest of the division. Buford ordered these two regiments to ride fast to Pontotoc and then turn north until they made contact with the enemy.[4]

The 2nd Tennessee, under Col. Clark Barteau, were to ride through the night and take a position on the New Albany Road, while Col. Isham Harrison's 6th Mississippi would take the parallel Plentitude Road to the east. Shortly after dawn the two regiments splashed across Cherry Creek and rode on diverging paths toward New Albany. "We reached there just in time to meet the [Federal] advance crossing the Tallahatchie," recalled Pvt. George Hager of the 2nd Tennessee.[5]

That morning in the Union camps, soldiers attended to their morning duties and waited for the day's march to begin. Harrison Chandler, quartermaster sergeant of the 114th Illinois, wrote in his diary, "Indications of a clear bright

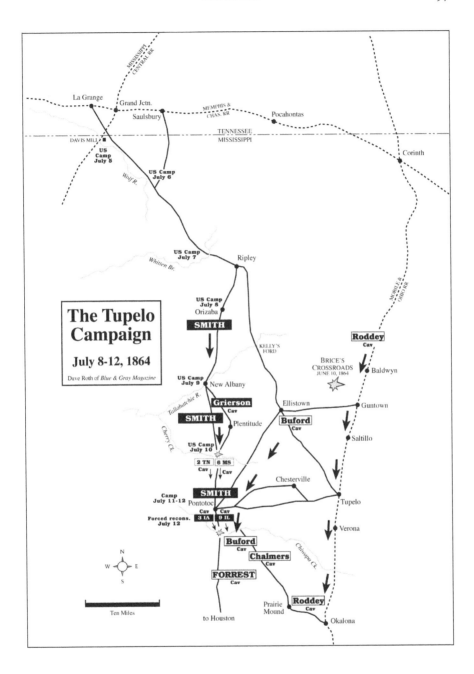

The Tupelo Campaign

July 8-12, 1864

Dave Roth of *Blue & Gray Magazine*

sunny day—too warm for comfort, even now while the sun is at rest. The eastern sky begins to redden and a beautiful sight will be the first appearance of
this morn's sun."[6]

The cavalry was in the saddle and moving by 3:00 A.M. Just beyond their
bivouac, at the fork in the road, they turned southeast in the direction of Plentitude. The cavalry was ordered to cover the left flank of the army, and since
the roads were within a few miles of each other across flat fields, they were
within easy supporting distance. Over on the Pontotoc Road the infantry set
out with Col. Herrick's 7th Kansas Cavalry in the lead. Behind the Jayhawkers
came J. J. Woods's brigade from Mower's division, grateful to be at the head of
the column and free of the choking clouds of dust.[7]

"Had an early start this morning," wrote Chaplain Edwards, "The day was accompanied with the usual scenes of pillaging and burning." Edwards was deeply
affected by the daily scenes of destruction. He had yet to see an enemy combatant (though a bullet had "whizzed very close to my ear" a few days before), but
he had seen plenty of the senseless and brutal destruction levied on the old men
and the women who had the misfortune of living along the army's route.

> The horrors of war have for the beholder a horrible fascination like that which
> an envenomed serpent exercises upon an unwilling spectator who has fallen
> under its spell. I can no more turn my eyes from these things than I can pre-
> vent them. Underneath all this horrible sameness of pillaging and burning
> there are new revelations of human character, or that character in new lights
> as affected by the passions of greed, of lust, of revenge; and shall I say it? A
> grim sense of humor. The humor of war rises in the concept that it is in itself a
> huge joke, and the roughest campaign is thereby turned into the wildest frolic.
> Some in spirit of malicious deviltry had carried away the toys and playthings of
> poor little children. One made a turban of a snowy tidy which he wore proudly
> as though it was a badge of chieftanhood. There seemed to be among this class
> of soldiers a spirit of unwonted hilarity. I wonder if this portends that battle
> that we are daily expecting.[8]

The disillusioned Edwards, who was also something of an artist, made a
sketch of Smith's column marching on the Pontotoc Road. The soldiers in
the sketch are marching four abreast past a two-story house fully engulfed in
flames. In the center of the dark and brooding landscape are four figures, obviously the residents, with arms outstretched in hopeless supplication while the
army passes by without turning a head. Explaining his wartime artwork, He
said he "preferred throwing light upon its more noble aspects upon the hero-

Chaplain Elijah E. Edwards, 7th Minnesota Infantry (DePauw University Archives and Special Collections)

ism, self sacrifice and patriotism of its heroes." But he also noted that he did not write for entertainment but to accurately describe what he saw: "There is a dark side of army life, and I could not avoid sometimes peering into its depths and revealing some of its horrors."[9]

The first action of the day came on the road to Plentitude. The 6th Mississippi Cavalry under Harrison passed through the hamlet of Plentitude and set up a road block. Then they waited. As the morning wore on, Company D of the 4th Iowa Cavalry found the Mississippians four miles south of New Albany and "began skirmishing with quite a force of Reb Cav." Harrison made his stand from a hill, forcing the Hawkeyes to dismount and charge the enemy on foot. They gamely rushed up the hill—"to ascend which, dismounted, was most exhausting on that very warm day"—but by the time they reached the top the enemy was gone. Harrison was under orders not to bring on a general engagement, and so he and his men gradually fell back through Plentitude.

As it pushed through the deserted town, the exhausted Union advance guard was relieved by a squadron of the 3rd Iowa Cavalry, Companies I and M under the command of Capt. George Johnson. The skirmishing continued for about three hours as both forces slowly moved south down the Plentitude Road. When the Confederates waded across the waters of Cherry Creek, Colonel Harrison pulled his troopers back into the saddle and rode south beyond Pontotoc.[10]

The results of the fighting on the Plentitude Road were negligible. Lt. Col. John Peters of the 4th Iowa claimed to have killed one Confederate and wounded four others, as well as captured a horse. The animal possibly replaced the mount of Pvt. Thomas Brown of the 3rd Iowa, whose horse was shot dead—the only Union casualty of the morning.[11]

A few miles to the west, Colonel Barteau's 2nd Tennessee set off shortly

"On the Road to Pontotoc" (DePauw University Archives and Special Collections)

after dawn to perform a similar mission on the Pontotoc Road. Barteau's plan for slowing the enemy force was decidedly different from that of Isham Harrison. He divided his regiment into detachments of one to two companies and positioned them 200–300 yards apart. His plan was to engage the enemy with his first detachment, and when the fighting became too warm, threatening to overwhelm the small force, that group would ride south and take a new position at the end of the regiment. This would slow the Federals and, hopefully, would compel them to quit marching in column on the road and deploy in line of battle so the size of their force could be confirmed.[12]

Clark Barteau was a bit of an anomaly in the southern army. By most standards, he was a Yankee. He was born in Cuyahoga County, Ohio, not far from Cleveland, and attended Ohio Wesleyan University. A year after he graduated, Clark took the job of principal at the Male Academy at Hartsville, Tennessee, and from that moment he was a southerner through and through. In 1858 he became the publisher of the *Huntsville Plaindealer*, a decidedly pro-Democrat, pro–states' rights paper. When the war broke out he enlisted as a private in the 7th Tennessee Cavalry Battalion; when the unit was consolidated with another to form the 2nd Tennessee Cavalry Regiment, he was promoted to lieutenant colonel. Known for his modesty and bravery, Barteau was wounded at Shiloh and again at Murfreesboro. As so often was the case during the Civil War, his only brother, Harrison, was a sergeant in the 103rd Ohio Infantry, which was fighting deep in Georgia along the Chattahoochee River.[13]

At dawn, the 7th Kansas Cavalry watched Grierson's division head down the Plentitude Road as they readied their mounts to lead the infantry down the Pontotoc Road. The first contact with the enemy came at 10:00 when Company "E" discovered a thirty-man company of the 2nd Tennessee and chased it down the road. The Jayhawkers came to a sudden halt when they reached Barteau's second line of "several hundred rebels in a defensive position." Barteau later wrote of the Federal charge, "which we very successfully checked by having a good position behind a bridge, which we destroyed, and thus impeded his progress for two hours and a half."[14] He commended Lt. Thomas Atkinson for "coming in hand-to-hand contact with the advance of the enemy's charge and emptying their saddles with his own pistol. His conduct seemed to be much admired and applauded even by the Yankee troops, and served as an incentive to my own men." A northern account by Pvt. Fletcher Pomeroy is far less dramatic, noting that after "considerable maneuvering and some pretty sharp skirmishing," the Confederates were pushed back beyond Cherry Creek. The regimental historian of the 7th Kansas, Simon Fox, recorded that the enemy was "badly whipped" and left five dead on the field of battle. Both Fox and

Barteau wrote their accounts long after the war, so Pomeroy's account, written the night of July 10, is probably closest to the truth.[15]

By noon the two Federal columns were converging at Cherry Creek. Grierson's cavalry continued down the road and went into camp a mile east of the road under the shade of a line of trees. The 7th Kansas maintained a watch near the stream as the infantry column slowly made its way across it. Once the entire column crossed the stream, the line continued on for another mile or so before setting up camp. The army had marched twelve miles, and the men who found shade south of the creek were within six miles of Pontotoc.[16]

Colonel Barteau led his men south to within a mile of Pontotoc and allowed them to dismount and rest in the shade. It had been a long night and morning for the Confederates, and they slept off the afternoon heat. Despite the close proximity of the forces, neither side seemed inclined to engage in any further fighting.

Aside from the action on the roads to Pontotoc, the Confederates had been very active since before dawn. Buford's division arrived in Pontotoc not long after daylight; with a shortage of forage for the animals, Tyree Bell's brigade was ordered southeast to Okolona to find some.

A new set of orders from General Forrest awaited Buford, directing him to send a squadron of "100 good men" into the rear of the enemy to cut their communications back into Tennessee. With four brigades of veteran cavalry at hand, Buford wasted no time pondering who should carry out this dangerous assignment. The order went down the chain of command through General Lyon of the Kentucky brigade to Col. William Faulkner, commander of the 12th Kentucky Cavalry, and on to Maj. Thomas Tate Jr., who detached Capt. Henry A. Tyler of Company A with "100 picked men."[17]

Captain Tyler of Company A chose the 100 most likely troopers and ordered them to mount up. While the 2nd Tennessee and 6th Mississippi were preparing their roadblocks on the roads to New Albany, Tyler led his hand-picked detachment northwest out of Pontotoc on the King's Ferry Road. The road the Kentuckians took was two and a half miles west of and parallel to the main Pontotoc–Ripley Road, and so they were well away from the roads being used by the Federals. Along the way they met up with "two marauding parties of the enemy." Tyler easily brushed aside the foragers and continued on his trek to the rear of the Union column.[18]

Two days earlier, Smith had fooled Forrest by sending the 3rd Iowa Cavalry down the Ellistown Road, and Buford's three brigades had been rushed to Ellistown in response. Once Forrest discovered the diversion he was convinced that Smith was headed south on the Pontotoc Road with an aim of striking the railroad at Okolona. He was absolutely correct, and the prolonged skirmishing by the 6th Mississippi and the 2nd Tennessee confirmed this. His decision to move Buford's brigades from Ellistown had been timely, and the division arrived in Pontotoc on the morning of July 10 well ahead of the enemy.

The Confederate commander continued to consolidate his forces as Smith's intentions became clearer. Not long after Forrest sent Buford on his all-night ride, he ordered James Chalmers to roust his two brigades in Verona and put them in motion. He sent Black Bob McCulloch's brigade up the road to Pontotoc with orders to "precede the enemy there." Behind McCulloch's troops came Chalmers's ordnance and supply trains, which Forrest wanted moved up to Garvin's (Gorman's) Mills. With the arrival of Buford's command, this shifting of troops placed four Confederate brigades in Pontotoc. Forrest ordered Chalmers to take his other brigade, Col. Edmund Rucker's, and ride the six miles northwest to the dismounted cavalry camp about six miles west of Tupelo at the intersection of the Pontotoc–Tupelo Road and the Chesterville–Okolona Road. Not altogether comfortable with his orders—"I had not been connected with the front in any way up to this time and knew nothing of the strength, position, or movements of the enemy"—Chalmers sent Maj. Brodie Crump, a member of his staff, up the tracks to Tupelo to speak directly to Forrest and ask for more detailed instructions. In the meantime, Chalmers rode off into the night in the direction of the dismounted camp.[19]

James Chalmers did not look like a military man. He was thin and stoop-shouldered, had a pointy chin and baggy, hound dog eyes. His men called him "Little 'un." Looks can be deceiving, however. When Chalmers enlisted he had a healthy round face and body; three years of war had taken a toll.[20]

If the war had not come along, Chalmers would have remained happy living as a lawyer in Holly Springs, Mississippi. He started the war at the head of the 9th Mississippi Infantry, and by Shiloh he was wearing the stars of a brigadier general. His division commander, Jones M. Withers, described him as "gallant and impetuous." He was a good fighter but not a consistent one, and though he made a good showing at Shiloh, he was bested by an inferior force at Booneville two months later. Again, at Munfordville, he turned in a lackluster performance followed by a courageous showing at the hard-hitting conflict at Stone's River. It was during this battle that an exploding artillery round struck Chalmers down, a wound that spared his life but ended his days with the infantry.[21] By February 1863 he had recovered enough to take command of the cavalry in the northern counties in Mississippi. For nearly a year he performed this duty competently, and so there was an understandable touch of resentment when he was handed a subordinate roll under the newly assigned

Brig. Gen. James R.
Chalmers (Library
of Congress)

Forrest. The two got off on the wrong foot. Forrest took Chalmers's only tent away and gave it to his brother, Lt. Col. Jesse Forrest of the 16th Tennessee, which prompted the general to write a sharply worded letter of protest to Forrest. General Polk mediated this test of wills by two senior officers, neither of whom liked serving under the other. In the end, Forrest came out on top, and Chalmers proved a faithful and able lieutenant.[22]

Forrest devised a plan for how to deal effectively with Smith's column: if Chalmers and Buford could slow Smith's advance, all the while drawing him south to Okolona, Forrest and Lee could prepare a strong defensive position and lure an unsuspecting Smith into an ambush. There was plenty of merit to the plan. Fighting defensively could reduce the advantage of Smith's greater numbers, and the proximity to the railroad at Okolona could provide quick reinforcements from Mobile if necessary. It was a good plan *if* Smith would cooperate by acting as expected.

In preparation for a battle near Okolona, Stephen Lee moved his headquarters down from Tupelo and supervised work on entrenchments. He impressed slaves from local plantations to dig the fortifications, sending the men in the dismounted camp to help. Another source of labor came from James Neely's

First Brigade of Chalmers's Division, which had just returned from Lafayette, Georgia. The hot ride across Alabama had proved too much for the mounts, and they were sent away for forage and rest. Samuel Ray of the 15th Tennessee recalled, "We were dismounted at Columbus, Miss and placed on flat cars as the emergency was very great, to Okolona." At the same time the dismounted men of Samuel Gholson's brigade were arriving from Canton, and both groups were hustled up the Pontotoc Road to Prairie Mound where construction of another line of earthworks was commenced. Lee was pleased with the preparations being made at Okolona and wrote to Braxton Bragg in Richmond, "Will fight here; convenient to railroad in case Mobile is assaulted."[23]

The increased activity and the threat of imminent battle prompted Forrest to send his wife south to Columbus, out of harm's way. Belle Edmondson, the young Memphis socialite, was a member of a party hurrying to catch the morning train as well. "Met Mrs. Forrest, the Gen. and two companions Miss Montgomery and Miss Grant. We did not get off for some time, Gen. Forrest had a fight with the conductor before he would get off." Forrest's legendary temper was beginning to show.[24]

Meanwhile, Chalmers was waiting restlessly at the deserted dismounted camp. At daylight a tired Major Crump returned from his mission to meet with Forrest and brought with him a clearer picture of Chalmers's responsibilities. Forrest gave Chalmers new orders to ride ahead to Pontotoc, where he would take command of Buford's division as well as his own. Forrest wanted him to "skirmish with the enemy, and make him develop his strength, but not to bring on a general engagement." Buford was a hard man to track down, however, and it was early evening before Chalmers met up with him and began to carry out Forrest's instructions.[25]

Per Forrest's order, Chalmers assumed command of all the southern troops around Pontotoc. He sent a regiment from McCulloch's brigade in the direction of Cherry Creek to determine where the enemy was and in what numbers.[26] As McCulloch's men moved north toward the enemy lines, they passed Barteau's 2nd Tennessee still resting in the shade after their prolonged skirmish on the Ripley Road. Learning that McCulloch's brigade had assumed responsibility at the front, Barteau put his men back into the saddle and rode east on the road to Tupelo. Chalmers sent orders for Barteau to watch for any movement along the road, and the regiment settled into camp six miles east of Pontotoc.[27]

Late into the evening Union regiments were still arriving at the bivouac site. The day's long, hot march had the column stretched out like an accordion, with the line alternately surging forward and stopping when the mules and horses crossing Cherry Creek halted for a long drink of water. Many of the leading regiments had been in camp since noon and had time for a good rest and a bite to eat. At 5:00 P.M. two companies of the 7th Kansas rode south on the Pontotoc Road to reconnoiter and establish a picket line. Maj. Francis Malone and his detachment were three miles from the main encampment when they ran into McCulloch's men—"Met about 300 rebels and a sharp fight ensued." Men fell on both sides. Colonel Herrick soon learned of the fight and ordered the two companies back, and Malone established a new picket line within a mile of camp.[28]

Joseph Woods's Third Brigade of Mower's division had arrived at the bivouac site relatively early in the day and had chosen a nice spot. Many of the men were enjoying a cool bath in a creek when "suddenly the bugle sounded the assembly." And in the 7th Minnesota camp Chaplain Edwards was making his nightly journal entry when he was startled by "the long roll of drums,—the call to arms."[29]

Whether due to the activity of the 2nd Tennessee earlier in the day or in response to the scrape with McCulloch's men near dusk, Smith was not taking any chances and at sunset ordered Woods's brigade to march two miles in the direction of Pontotoc and deploy in a line of battle, spread out in a long line perpendicular to the road. Pickets went out in advance of the main line, and the whole brigade lay down for the night on its arms. After six days of marching in enemy territory, this was the first time Smith thought it expedient to deploy one of his brigades.[30] The movement was a severe irritant to Pvt. George Brockway, who had just milked one of the cows brought along for fresh beef: "You better believe we got up a good supper. We killed nine beaves for supper and breakfast. Just before sundown orders come to march which went against the grain as we had to leave our fresh beef."[31]

As usual, reveille came early for the Federals camped below Cherry Creek. The bulk of Mower's division was up and moving by 1:00 A.M. Nine miles to the south James Chalmers was waking his troopers as well. While McCulloch's men seemed to have things well in hand north of town, Chalmers ordered Buford to move three miles south on the Okolona Stage Road to the commanding heights of Pinson's Hill. The previous morning Buford had sent Tyree Bell's brigade ahead to Okolona for forage, and so he made this trip with just Mabry's and Lyon's brigades.[32]

Pinson's Hill was a naturally strong position on the south side of Chiwapa Creek. The approach to the hill was "on the opposite side of a low swampy bottom through which run two creeks. This bottom was about a mile and a half in width, densely timbered, and which the enemy had rendered almost impassable by felling trees across the road." General Lyon put his men to work building two lines of defense, the second, which was on the crest of the hill, being the more formidable. The Pinson's Hill breastworks were not designed to be Forrest's main line of defense in the upcoming battle; their purpose was merely to slow Smith in his descent toward Okolona.[33]

While Lyon's men sweated at their job of building fortifications, McCulloch's troops prepared to meet Smith's advance north of Pontotoc. Forrest's orders to Chalmers were unchanged: develop the enemy's strength and do nothing to bring on a general engagement. Early in the morning Chalmers had sent a message to his commander, "that the enemy was moving very slowly, and usually with a line of battle and skirmishers about one mile in length, and that I could not without artillery make him develop his strength." The division commander erred in noting that the Federals were "usually" moving in a line of battle, but he was new to the front, and it was a logical assumption.[34]

McCulloch's brigade was a mixed bag of regiments in a corps where the brigades were usually composed of units from the same state. His own 2nd Missouri Cavalry, led by his cousin Red Bob was the only group of Missourians in Forrest's legions, and Willis's Battalion Texas Cavalry was the only representative of the Lone Star State. Mississippi was represented by Hyams's 1st Partisan Rangers (also known as the 7th Mississippi Cavalry) and the 5th Mississippi under Lt. Col. Nathaniel Wickliffe. McDonald's Battalion of Tennessee Cavalry (also known as the 3rd Tennessee, or Forrest's Old Regiment) rounded out the brigade.

Black Bob McCulloch was quite possibly the toughest, rumble-tumble fighter to serve under Forrest, though he was "modest almost to a fault." It was later said of him, "Although a man of strong personality and a strict disciplinarian [he] was as gentle and tender as a woman." On at least three occasions the "gentle" McCulloch had personally led mounted saber attacks, a rare activity at any time during the war. He and his cousin Red Bob were Virginians by birth, though both were raised in Missouri. The two were very close and had traveled to the California gold fields together and then on to Kansas, where they stood on the slavery side of the question. Black Bob was in a score of battles, and after Van Dorn's Holly Springs raid in December of 1862, his regiment was permanently transferred to Forrest's command.

While McCulloch's men were deployed north of town, Chalmers scribbled a message to Forrest describing the situation as he understood it. Chalmers had been ordered to "develop his strength," but Smith had deployed only a single brigade, making it difficult, if not impossible, to gauge his true numbers. Chalmers was an experienced soldier and knew how to develop, or compel, an enemy force into revealing its size and strength; present a strong, wide front that forces the enemy to reciprocate or run the risk of a flank attack. Such a maneuver wasn't possible with just McCulloch's understrength brigade. In order to force Smith to deploy, he needed artillery, and Chalmers wasted no time in making his request in writing to General Forrest. While waiting for the cannon to arrive, McCulloch would just have to do his best.

Chalmers talked at length with Buford about the tactical situation and readily accepted the reports of action at face value, and in so doing he misinterpreted the situation. Both Chalmers and Forrest believed the skirmishing was causing Smith to act in a cautious, if not timid, manner. "The enemy was easily held in check," recalled Forrest, a belief echoed by Chalmers in his own report. It was true enough that Smith was advancing very slowly, but the lack of speed had nothing to do with anything the Confederates were doing. When the southern commanders compared the poor performance of both Sooy Smith and Sturgis with A. J. Smith's slow descent from LaGrange, they logically assumed that they faced yet another timid Union general, and Smith's behavior on July 11 did nothing to convince the Confederate commanders otherwise.[35]

Col. William McMillen's First Brigade of Mower's division had the Federal advance that morning, led by the 7th Kansas Cavalry. McMillen, who had been given any number of second chances, was working on yet another. A native of Ohio and a graduate of the Starling Medical College in Columbus, he volunteered as a surgeon with the Russian Army during the Crimean War. At the outbreak of the Civil War, he accepted the surgeon post with the 1st Ohio Infantry but soon wrangled the colonelcy of the 95th Ohio. McMillen was present at the two most decisive Confederate victories of the war: Richmond, Kentucky in late August 1862 and Brice's Crossroads in June 1864. After Richmond, he was court-martialed for cowardice but later acquitted. At Brice's Crossroads he commanded the infantry division and saw his brigades cut to ribbons. He was a hard drinker (some said he was drunk at Brice's) and had a volatile temper. He had been reduced to brigade command and knew he was on probation.[36]

McMillen deployed his brigade on the morning of July 11, his left resting on the Pontotoc Road. His five regiments—72nd and 95th Ohio, 114th Illinois, 93rd Indiana, 10th Minnesota—were accompanied by Lt. Orrin Cram's two guns of Company E, 1st Illinois Light Artillery. Smith gave the order to advance, and the line moved slowly forward. The skirmishers of the 7th Kansas immediately drew the fire of their counterparts in McCulloch's brigade, and the action continued for five long miles. When the Federals were within a mile of Pontotoc, the Kansans came on McCulloch's main line, "800 strong, drawn up in line of battle in a strong position," along Lappatubby Creek. Colonel Herrick halted his regiment and waited for McMillen's infantry.[37]

A mile to the east, on a parallel road, Grierson's cavalry column stood poised on McCulloch's exposed right flank. At the head of the cavalry was Colonel

Coon's Third Brigade, consisting of the 2nd Iowa and 9th Illinois with detachments of the 3rd and 7th Illinois. Coon's Civil War career was tied to the 2nd Iowa, and the former newspaperman had been commissioned as one of the original captains in the regiment.

The purpose of advancing the cavalry and infantry on parallel roads was so that they could provide mutual support if one of the columns ran into trouble and take advantage of any opportunity that presented itself. Such was the case when Coon observed McCulloch's brigade deployed across the Pontotoc Road. Coon turned to Capt. Jacob Bandy of Company K and told him, "Captain take your company and put the rebels through that town." Unsure of just what the colonel wanted, a charge or a general advance, Bandy asked, "Shall I charge them?" Coon impatiently replied, "I don't give a damn what you do," as long as he made a move against the enemy.[38]

Bandy led his company forward in a platoon column, the textbook response to an advance on a restricted front across difficult terrain. Lt. James Crawford of Company L quickly followed with his command in the same formation. McCulloch, a pretty savvy cavalryman himself, had posted dismounted troopers along nearby fences and houses to keep an eye on his flanks. They met Bandy's lead squad with a ragged volley, prompting the captain to change tactics and order the charge—again, the proper response. But armed with their "invincible seven shooters," the Hawkeyes closed with the Confederates, who slowly gave ground.[39]

McCulloch's orders were straightforward, and, to the best of his ability, he had developed the enemy force and resisted the offer to be drawn into pitched battle. His withdrawal through town and then down the Okolona Road was orderly, though the excited men of the 2nd Iowa claimed that the enemy "hurried with all haste to the rear." Sgt. Lyman Pierce, caught up in the moment wrote, "The chase through town was truly exciting; the rebels freely using the spur, while our boys followed closely pumping a continuous stream of lead after them." Several Federals recalled hearing cannon fire during the engagement, though no one took the time to identify the battery doing the firing. It certainly was not the Confederates, as Chalmers was still waiting for a reply to his request for artillery support. The guns were most likely Battery K, 1st Illinois Light Artillery, assigned to Grierson's cavalry. Those few rounds made a big impression on Chaplain Edwards: "The roar of these guns was the most thrilling sound I had ever heard, and seemed most inspiring to the men who heard it many times before."[40]

By noon the Federals were moving through town. As Smith's brigades moved through town and set up camp on the south side, the 2nd Iowa Cavalry followed McCulloch's retreating troopers. Coon kept the men spread out in a line of battle for two hours before turning and rejoining the rest of the army in camp.[41]

While all of the excitement was occurring on the north side of Pontotoc, Capt. Henry Tyler and his 100 "picked" men were seeing some action of their own. Sgt. Z. N. Wright described how "the enemy had one hundred Confederates in their rear, cutting them off from communication from that point; and we had about sixteen thousand Federals between us and the main Confederate army, thus cutting us off from communication with our army."[42] Tyler began a thirty-minute skirmish with the Union rear guard, but "failing to make an impression," he led his detail over to the Tuscumbia–Pontotoc Road. Grierson's cavalry took this route into Pontotoc earlier in the day, and Tyler followed at a discreet distance. Eventually the Kentuckians got a little too close, and Grierson's rear guard lashed out, killing one of the Confederates before driving them off to the east. If Tyler had learned anything during his ride around Smith, it was that the Federals were not keeping a line of communication open with La-Grange, and there was no point in maintaining a watch in the Federal rear.[43]

By noon McCulloch completed the withdrawal beyond Pontotoc and passed through General Lyon's defenses on Pinson's Hill. General Chalmers stood nearby and directed McCulloch to take his men over to the west and block the Houston Road leading south out of Pontotoc. Rucker's brigade maintained a watch on the Cotton Gin Road, another path leading down to Okolona, and stood ready to assist Barteau and his 2nd Tennessee, who were maintaining a vigil on the Tupelo Road. Chalmers was effectively watching all of the roads leading south and east from Pontotoc, ensuring that Smith could not make a move without being seen. Meanwhile, the Kentuckians had nearly completed their breastworks and stood ready. But the Federal response was almost anticlimactic. A single battalion of the 2nd Iowa cavalry rode forward in the direction of Lyon's fortifications, but it was merely a feint to confirm the Confederate position, and the northerners quickly returned to Pontotoc. The sun was still in the sky, but the activity was done for the day. The Federals began to settle into camp, and the Kentuckians went back to work strengthening their breastworks.[44]

General Forrest was pleased with the day's action and the resulting troop dispositions, which he deemed "most satisfactory." He was feeling confident that the enemy was doing just what he wanted and that the Confederates were nearly ready to meet them on the road to Okolona. He was sure he had a lock on the Federals' intentions and saw no reason to shift his troops, noting, "As all the approaches south were strongly guarded I made no change." Smith was pleased as well, and aside from ordering Grierson to send out patrols in all directions, he gave no specific orders or directions before the army bedded down.[45]

NINE

Pinson's Hill

The men of Smith's army enjoyed a day of rest on July 12. Accustomed to 2:00 A.M. reveilles, they relished the opportunity to sleep in and then eat a leisurely breakfast. The soldiers of the 122nd Illinois found some apples and blackberries and stewed them together into a compote. But only those who went out and foraged for food were able to feast. "We draw three days rations. Scant," recorded one hungry soldier. The daily ration of hardtack was growing ever smaller, and most of the regiments were down to a half or even a third of the normal amount of the army staple.[1]

In the bivouac of the 7th Minnesota, the regimental chaplain made special note of the most unusual sight he awoke to: "The camp this morning is white with cotton scattered about it. The cotton sticks tenaciously to everything it touches, especially to the uniforms of the soldiers. They have reveled in cotton; rolled in it, covered them selves over with it till the pale dusty or dirty blue of their uniforms is scarcely discernible." The 10th Minnesota had also taken advantage of the cotton beds they'd foraged, and Sgt. Amos Glanville laughed at the appearance of his comrades: "Each particular one was a study for an artist—pinfeathered and festooned in white all over, including eyewinkers, beard and hair. You couldn't recognize your dearest friend."[2]

Though the men certainly needed a day of rest, Smith had not halted his column out of the kindness of his heart. Through his field glasses, he had carefully studied the approaches to the Pinson's Hill fortifications the previous afternoon. He then spoke to Grierson and listened to the reports of the evening patrols. The results were not unexpected: Lee and Forrest had finally appeared in strength, and a battle appeared imminent. But he was unwilling to push headlong down the Okolona Road and into a likely trap. The lessons provided by Sturgis were still fresh in his mind, and Smith paused to weigh his options. At the end of the meeting he instructed Grierson to prepare for an early-morning reconnaissance.[3]

Not long after dawn, Grierson summoned Col. John Noble of the 3rd Iowa Cavalry and Lt. Col. Henry Burgh of the 9th Illinois for a briefing at his headquarters. He ordered Noble to lead the 3rd Iowa directly south down the road toward Houston to investigate an enemy roadblock and Burgh to take his men across Chiwapa Creek and turn southeast on the road to Okolona, where they were to cautiously probe the defenses on Pinson's Hill. The 52nd Indiana Infantry would stand by to help either regiment if things got out of hand.[4]

Grierson rode out with Burgh on the Okolona Road, the direct and preferred route if Smith continued south. No sooner had the 9th Illinois passed the Union picket line then they began to take fire from Lyon's skirmishers, some of whom were hunkered down inside a nearby log house. The Federals quickly rousted the Kentuckians from the building and continued their advance. Grierson believed Burgh had matters well in hand and trotted off with his staff to check on Colonel Noble over on the Houston Road.[5]

Capt. Tom Harwood's Texas Cavalry positioned itself in the earthworks atop the hill at Lochinvar Plantation, and the battalion's fire was sufficient to prompt Noble to dismount his lead battalion on the right side of the road and order them up the heights on foot. "I pushed forward the main column and succeeded in getting possession of the hill without loss, but with great physical labor to the dismounted men on account of the heat of the weather and the roughness of the ground." Grierson arrived in time to see Noble's men crest the hill; he then posted pickets under the command of Capt. John Brown. The Texans withdrew down the road, where they were reinforced by the balance of McCulloch's brigade, but they declined to renew the fight.[6]

The men were winded from their charge up the hill, and Noble allowed them to sit in the shade, where they uncorked their canteens for a cool drink and to wash the choking dust out of their mouths. The assault had been free of casualties, save for the 3rd Iowa's Sgt. Reuben Delay, who was accidently shot in the leg while removing fence rails so his squadron could pass though. After an hour, the sound of firing over on the Okolona Road increased in volume, prompting Grierson to order the men back into the saddle. The column advanced a short distance and found a small crossroad connecting the two main roads.[7]

Not long after Grierson had ridden away from the Okolona Road, Burgh and his 9th Illinois ran into trouble. The Confederate pickets had retreated from the log house with Burgh's advance battalion in pursuit. The battalion, which consisted of Companies B, G, H, and I under the command of Captains Henry Buel and Anthony Mock, had orders to develop the strength of the enemy on the hill. Near the top of the hill, the Federals fired a few shots, and the southerners disappeared into a dense thicket of young trees. The small group of Federal horsemen, no more than eighty in all, did not hesitate and rashly followed the enemy into the brush. Their overconfidence bordered on arrogance, as one of them stated: "As we were armed with repeating rifles we gave but slight consideration to a moderate disproportion of our numbers." Buel and Mock must have realized the danger and called a halt in the heart of the thicket. They ordered the men to load the empty chambers in their revolvers and to ensure that their carbines' magazines were full.

But just beyond the thicket, no more than 250 feet away, was a long, open field along which ran a rail fence that had been strengthened with logs and more rails "to render it a bulletproof breastwork." Whatever risk Mock and Buel had sensed was now ignored. They abandoned all caution and ordered their dismounted troopers to charge the Confederates behind the works.[8]

The opposing forces were so close that when Buel ordered "Forward!" the command was clearly heard by the Confederates crouching behind the fence. As the first of the Federals ran toward the clearing, someone yelled "Fire!" and a volley tore into the 9th Illinois. Men fell in every direction. Two troopers were killed instantly, and more than two dozen lay wounded. One soldier, Pvt. Jesse Haws, passed through the thicket and was within an arm's distance of the breastwork, with the enemy just feet away shouting, "Shoot him! Shoot him!" Haws's salvation came in the form of a burly Kentuckian who reached across the barricade and pulled the soldier into captivity. Mock and several of his men found themselves pressed against the outer wall of the fortification, the enemy mere inches away. The firing was so heavy they couldn't do a thing but keep their heads down and hope for the best. Eventually the captain made an attempt to break free of the trap. "Mock arose and waving his sword attempted to rally his men for the charge, but the hail of lead was too hot; only one man Sergeant [John] Showalter arose from cover, and the brave leader was obliged to give up the attempt."

Regimental lore had it that the captured Haws informed the Confederates there were several regiments of Union cavalry poised to attack the position. Supposedly this information caused the confused southerners to stop firing, thus allowing the battered battalion to escape to safety. As improbable as it sounds, the Confederates did stop their fire, but not as a result of Haws's story. Burgh and the balance of the 9th Illinois, attracted by the sound of heavy firing, had arrived on the scene.[9]

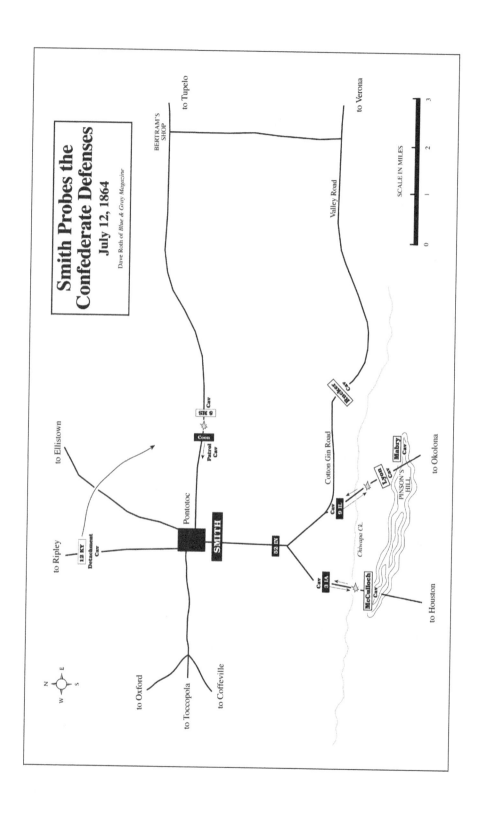

Smith Probes the Confederate Defenses

July 12, 1864

Dave Roth of *Blue & Gray Magazine*

SCALE IN MILES

0   1   2   3

The Confederate position was not the main line of defense on Pinson's Hill but, rather, a fortified picket line. Lyon's pickets followed Forrest's orders to make a show of resistance before falling back to the stronger secondary line. After a brief defense the works on Pinson's Hill were supposed to be abandoned, like the picket line had been, and the Federals were to be led southeast toward Okolona. The southerners never intended to hold the forward position; it was merely a ruse to deceive the enemy.

Colonel Burgh wrongly believed that he had driven the enemy from their works and was preparing for a follow-up charge when General Grierson arrived with the 3rd Iowa. Noble's regiment dismounted and came up on the right of the 9th Illinois, the advance companies immediately drawing heavy fire from the main Confederate line. Grierson wisely called both regiments to a halt. Though the arrival of the Hawkeyes "caused some confusion among the rebels," Grierson could clearly see he was outgunned and faced a strong defensive line. "Having developed the enemy's force and observed their strong position, thus accomplishing the object of the reconnaissance and not wishing to jeopardize the lives of the soldiers unnecessarily, I ordered Colonel Burgh to withdraw slowly from his engagement and directed Colonel Noble to return to his camp, the pickets on all roads being at once strengthened."[10]

Yet, a third Union patrol, much smaller than Noble's and Burgh's forces, was sent from Coon's brigade and ordered to head east on the Tupelo Road with instructions to look for enemy forces. No more than five miles from town they came across Col. William Duff and his veteran 8th Mississippi Cavalry. Duff's regiment easily brushed aside the Federal patrol, sending them scurrying back to Pontotoc.[11]

The opposing cavalry forces came away with distinctly different impressions of the morning's events. Henry Burgh's narrative of the action was reduced to a single sentence in his official report, and in it he managed to stretch the truth twice, if not outright lie: "Morning of the 12th made a demonstration on the Okolona road, met Lyon's rebel brigade and drove them about three miles, with a loss to us of 1 killed and 1 taken prisoner and several wounded; the enemy's loss not known." Although he had certainly driven in Lyon's pickets, he had not budged the Kentucky brigade an inch from its hilltop defenses, and he carefully avoided the fact that he lost nearly half of his advance battalion. For their part, Forrest and Chalmers were correct in reporting how Lyon's brigade had easily driven back the enemy, as had Duff on the Tupelo Road. But both erred in stating that the Federals on the Houston Road were "forced to make a hasty retreat." The 3rd Iowa had bested the Texans on the road to Houston, and, instead of being "driven" from the field, the Iowans had galloped off to the east to reinforce Burgh on the Okolona Road.[12]

A. J. Smith's record of the day's events was short and to the point: "As they had a very strong position on a hill on the other side of the bottom, I did not deem it prudent to attack the position from the front if it could be flanked. I, therefore, caused demonstrations to be made on the Okolona Road during the day, and held the skirmish line during the night." In studying the Pinson's Hill defenses, he took careful note of the approaches he would have to cross if he were to make a frontal assault. A swampy stretch of bottomland, two creeks, and an obstacle of fallen trees awaited anyone headed south on the road. An advance across these bottoms, under a plunging artillery fire with an enemy dug in on the heights, was not much of a plan for success; it was more like the makings of another Federal disaster. But Chalmers and Lyon had performed their duty too well. Forrest had directed Chalmers to hold the enemy back for forty-eight hours while he prepared to meet Smith farther down the Okolona Road. The Confederates were successful in this regard, but the Union commander paused, unwilling to snap at the bait. As indicated by his mention of a flanking movement and the cavalry excursions being only "demonstrations," Smith had already decided not to assault the Pinson's Hill defenses. The reconnaissance by Grierson's troopers had been nothing more than a diversion.[13]

According to Grierson, Smith summoned him, Noble, and Burgh to his headquarters to discuss the day's actions. In his memoirs, written long after the war, Grierson recalled convincing Smith of the futility of advancing on the Okolona Road. "I talked freely with General Smith on the subject," who apparently favored attacking the enemy "at all hazards, where he was then." Grierson went to great lengths to take credit for Smith's subsequent actions. Noble, who based his reports on his detailed diary entries, made no mention of any such meeting, let alone Grierson's claim of being the author of the subsequent Union activities.[14]

Grierson's memory, or at least his personal account, is flawed; the actions during the morning were obviously mere diversions. Although he does not say as much in his official report, it is clear that Smith decided on a flanking movement after viewing the Confederate position through his binoculars, not after sending out his patrols. If he had been adamant about forcing any one of the three roadblocks, he would not have had his army sitting idle in camp all morning. He would have made a serious attempt using an entire brigade, with the remainder of the army standing by to exploit any gains. The only one of the three patrols that was actually a reconnaissance was the smallest out on the road to Tupelo. Smith needed to discover the strength of the enemy between his army and Tupelo and whether there were any breastworks blocking his route. Had he sent only the one patrol on the Tupelo Road, he would have been revealing his intentions; Lee and Forrest would have been able to deduce his plans and act accordingly. Smith had kept his adversaries guessing ever since he left Memphis, and he had no intention of letting up.

The general dismissed Noble and Burgh after the meeting and requested that the two other division officers, Mower and Moore, join him and Grierson. By the end of this second meeting, the officers were fully aware of Smith's plans and had their orders. The army would remain in Pontotoc for another night, and at 5:00 A.M. the column would march east on the Tupelo Road. Cavalry pickets would maintain a presence to the south of town, effectively screening the movements of the main column. Smith hoped to steal a march, to slip out of Pontotoc and be well on his way to Tupelo before the enemy knew he was gone.[15]

The change of direction indicated no real deviation from his original plans, since Okolona had never been Smith's target. The goals remained unchanged: to engage Forrest and break the Mobile & Ohio Railroad. By marching to Tupelo, he could still destroy a section of the railroad, and now, more importantly, rather than attack Forrest under unfavorable conditions, Smith hoped to compel his opponent to attack him on ground of his own choosing. Waiting till dawn to move out had its advantages. First, the air was cooler in the morning, and the men had eighteen miles to march, the longest single-day march since leaving Memphis. Second, Smith hoped that by sitting quietly in camp after the morning action he would confuse the Confederate leadership. A lack of activity in the Union camp would certainly cause Lee and Forrest to debate whether it was Smith's intention to attack Pinson's Hill with a larger force or that he had lost his nerve and was preparing for a return to Memphis. Smith's plan to generate confusion, or at least consternation, succeeded handsomely.

In Okolona, Lee and Forrest had completed their preparations to meet Smith. The earthworks at Prairie Mound were complete, and it was time to allow their quarry to advance. Forrest sent new orders to Chalmers:

> If the enemy moves on you this morning, let him come, keeping his flank and rear well watched and guarded, so that you may know promptly of any changes of direction. Skirmish slightly with him. A section of artillery has been sent up which you will use occasionally, as though feebly resisting his advance. . . . Should the enemy turn back, you will attack and hold him until the General can move up with the balance of his troops.

The message arrived too late, however, because Smith had already decided to detour onto the Tupelo Road.[16]

In anticipation of abandoning the Pinson's Hill line and drawing Smith down the Okolona Road, Forrest ordered Chalmers to send Rucker's brigade to the rear. Forrest wanted Rucker's men to be in place at Prairie Mound when he sprung the trap, but this move unwittingly opened the door for the enemy when Duff's 8th Mississippi was removed from their position on the Tupelo Road. Barteau's 2nd Tennessee was camped along the road as well but rode off in search of Bell's brigade the previous night. This meant that the one road Smith planned on using for his flank march did not have so much as a single Confederate guard on it after noon on July 12.[17]

When Rucker's men rode away from their posts on the Tupelo and Cotton Gin roads, Chalmers's ordnance and supply wagons also turned around and headed back toward Okolona. Forrest was removing all of his resources beyond the Prairie Mound line, counting on Lyon and McCulloch's brigades to slowly fall back and draw Smith into the trap. Men and animals had been marching and countermarching for days, and the hot sun was beginning to take a toll on the Confederates, just as it had on the Federals. There was a difference, however; Lee's dismounted troops, unused to marching on foot, were quickly exhausting themselves, whereas the Federals had become acclimatized in the twenty days since leaving Memphis and were no longer troubled as much by the heat.

By late morning Lee and Forrest knew about the enemy's weak demonstrations against the Confederates guarding the three roads leading south and east from Pontotoc. Lee was puzzled by the withdrawal of the Federal cavalry back to the Pontotoc camps; he could not fathom what Smith was up to. He was hoping for a quick battle that would enable him send troops off to the other threatened areas of his department. Each day he was bombarded with messages warning him of imminent disasters. From the west 10,000 Union infantry were poised to cross the Big Black River and raid the state capital at Jackson. To the south, General Maury continued his cries of warning from Mobile: spies in New Orleans and Baton Rouge had observed light transports being fitted out to carry horses, and several heavy steamers had arrived in the Crescent City loaded with enemy troops. The intelligence indicated a movement against Mobile by General Canby with 20,000 men. Maury sent several messages every day to Lee, and in one telegram, sent on July 11, he raised the specter that perhaps Smith's raid was only a diversion and that Canby's looming attack was the actual threat. Whether or not Lee believed this to be the case is uncertain, but he was still feeling the burden of commanding an undermanned department with Federals threatening from too many directions.[18]

Despite the threats, real or perceived, Lee had to act on the situation before him. A decision had to be made, and Smith's activities over the last few hours did not make the decision any easier. The relative quiet following the reconnaissance of the roadblocks was disconcerting and led Lee and Forrest to discuss the evolving circumstances. The weak demonstration against the Pinson's Hill defenses was not followed by a stronger effort to dislodge Lyon's Kentuckians. The skirmishes on the Houston and Tupelo roads had likewise failed to stir Smith into real action.

As they saw it, Smith had two options: first, to push through the Pinson's Hill defenses and continue his advance; or, second, to turn his column around and head back to Memphis. Confederate strategy for the last forty-eight hours had been based on the assumption that Smith would continue southeast in the direction of Okolona. Southern troops were in motion to ensure that the Federals received a warm welcome at Prairie Mound. If, however, Smith was making a turn back to Memphis, the Confederate troops were headed in the wrong direction. Therefore, any and all troops used in a pursuit would have to be turned around immediately and marched back up the Pontotoc Road.

"The delay of the enemy at Pontotoc," explained Forrest, "produced the impression that he designed to fall back toward Memphis, and after a short consultation it was determined to accept battle wherever he offered it, and to attack him if he attempted a retreat." Lee was unwilling to allow Smith to escape unscathed and so directed Forrest to move all available men to Pinson's Hill. Col. Matthew Galloway of Forrest's staff went racing up the Pontotoc Road with orders for Chalmers to "resume his former position if he had retired, and to hold it at all hazards until I arrived with the artillery and infantry re-enforcemnts."[19]

Lee's headquarters was a hive of activity, with a stream of orders issued to officers and commands. Within a matter of hours, all available units were headed to Pinson's Hill. Tyree Bell's brigade of Tennesseans, only recently arrived from Pontotoc, was put back in the saddle and ordered to report to Chalmers posthaste. Likewise, Edmund Rucker's brigade was sent back to its previous post on the Cotton Gin Road, but no provision was made to return Duff's 8th Mississippi to its post on the Tupelo Road.[20] Only recently arrived from Alabama via Corinth, Roddey's Division, along with John Morton's artillery battalion, rolled out of camp as well. Bringing up the rear were the dismounted brigades of Samuel Gholson and James Neely, the heavy artillerists from Mobile and the 1st Mississippi Infantry under Lt. Col. Marshall Polk, the only infantry unit in Lee's small army. The regiment had been captured over a year before when Port Hudson, Louisiana, fell in a protracted Union siege. The enlisted men had been exchanged, but the officers of the regiment were still in northern prison camps.[21]

Polk, an 1852 graduate of West Point, saw duty in California as a young lieutenant; was shipwrecked off the coast of Acapulco, Mexico; and fought the Sioux at the Battle of Blue Water. When the Civil War commenced he became the captain of Polk's battery, Tennessee Light Artillery, and lost a leg in the fighting at Shiloh. After a lengthy recovery, he took a promotion and an assignment as chief of artillery on Lt. Gen. Leonidas Polk's staff. (He and his commander were kin, Leonidas being the second cousin of President James Polk and Marshall his nephew.) The active life of campaigning was likely too much for the amputee, and in February 1864 Polk was sent to command minor postings at Port Marion, Alabama, and later at Aberdeen, Mississippi. As Smith's column approached from LaGrange, Lee ordered the 1st Mississippi and Reynolds's Battalion brought up from Meridian, and Polk was directed to take command. Shortly before leading his new command up the road, Polk took a few minutes to write his wife Evalina: "We will probably fight tomorrow. Pray for us that we will be successful. I have been thinking of you ever since leaving Aberdeen. If it is fated that I never see you again you must be sure that my heart has always been yours & has never gone out from you. Take care of yourself my darling and think of me kindly."[22]

Lee and Forrest accompanied the mounted troops riding out of Okolona, deeming it the right time for them to finally move up to the front. While on the ride to Chalmers's roadblock, Lee penciled an order directing an administrative change to his small army. He relieved Gen. Hylan Lyon of duty with the Kentucky brigade and placed him in temporary command of the dismounted division, with command of the Kentuckians passed to the senior regimental commander, Col. Edward Crossland. Lyon had his work cut out for him. His new command—nine regiments of dismounted cavalry, two of heavy artillery, one infantry, and assorted dismounted troopers who had lost their horses to death or exhaustion—was scattered for miles along the Pontotoc–Okolona Road and had never fought as a unit, let alone marched together on foot.[23]

In direct contrast to the flurry of Confederate activity, it was a relatively calm and relaxing day in the Federal camps a mile south of Pontotoc. A few of the diarists commented on the cavalry getting into a bit of a scrape, but most made entries about Tuesday being a day of rest and napping. Chaplain Edwards took the chance to stroll through Pontotoc and record his thoughts and worries about the near future in his diary.

> It was formerly a beautiful place of about 500 inhabitants, but is now war-worn and half in ruins. It has [not] suffered so much as Ripley, but is still in a pitiable condition. I called at several residences, but found only women, children and

negroes, and one aged man, Rev. Mr. Blackburn, a Methodist Minister resident here. I found him in a sad plight, his house having been remorselessly plundered & his furniture including an old fashioned piano reduced to splinters. He was in pitiable straights. His horse and carriage had been stolen and there was no food left in his house. I reported the matter to Colonel [William] Marshall who was furiously indignant at this outrage and sent out a posse to find and restore the aged man his horse and carriage; which was done. More than this it was not in his power to do. Strict orders had been issued against pillaging in which we were encamped, and guards stationed at many of the dwellings, and there was not time to spare as we were on the eve of battle the horrors of which might prove greater than the pillaging of a poor little country town.[24]

Edwards was not alone in his belief that the army was "on the eve of battle." That afternoon he was repeatedly approached by soldiers bearing messages to be sent to their homes should something happen to them in the looming fight. "Some of the presentiments are gloomy forecasts of disaster, while others are more hopeful," he noted. Two men in particular, Cpl. Archibald Savidge of Company K and the regimental surgeon Lucius Smith, were convinced they would soon be killed or wounded.

Others, though, had just the opposite feeling and were brimming with optimism. One, recalled Edwards, "bore himself very bravely and impressed me as a man without fear. He remarked with the most confidant air that the bullet had not yet been molded that would kill him in the coming battle."[25] Indeed, the overall mood in the camp was one of confidence and even cocky anticipation. As a group, the men were unsure of where they were going or why they had stopped. Dr. Henry Murdoch of the 8th Wisconsin spread the rumor "that we are booked for Mobile and that this is a temporary stopping, and we are to fight our way thither." Ben Thomas of the 14th Iowa was sure the column would continue to the southeast: "We had lots of faith in General Smith and believed he would not undertake what he could not accomplish, yet it looked to us like a pretty big contract to try and capture Okolona. But if General Smith said we could capture the place we believed we could and would do it." And the possibility of returning to Memphis was discussed by others. "It is rumored we return tomorrow but I guess it is all a hoax," wrote William Ibbettson. "But where we are going is entirely in the dark. Old Smith knows how to keep his own secrets." Pvt. Ezra Fish of the 114th Illinois agreed, "We move again tomorrow, but the direction taken will be a question unsettled by the boys around the campfires."[26]

The peace of the Federal camps was broken at 2:00 P.M. when "ten or fifteen bushwhackers" disturbed a group from the 59th U.S. Colored Infantry that was out berry picking. A private was wounded in the scuffle, and the party returned to camp, passing Company C of the regiment, which had been sent out to deal with the enemy. Capt. Henry Fox and his men engaged the Confederates, who withdrew with no further bloodshed on either side.

The "bushwhackers" were probably Henry Tyler's Kentuckians, who had left their bivouac in the afternoon and reported engaging enemy pickets on the Chesterfield Road. After the dustup, Tyler moved over to the Pontotoc–Tupelo Road and took a position to observe the path for enemy movement. The road had been unguarded since Duff's 8th Mississippi had pulled out earlier in the day, which meant Tyler's 100 picked men were all there was between Smith and the town of Tupelo.[27]

Several miles to the south, the traffic on the Pontotoc–Okolona Road increased considerably. Through the afternoon and into the evening, thousands of men, horses, and mules were traveling northwest to Pinson's Hill, and the numerous and inevitable bottlenecks resulted in frustrating delays and frayed tempers. Roddey's Division, as well as Rucker's and Bell's brigades, was mounted and had a relatively easy time of it. It was a different story for Lyon's dismounted division, including the infantry and heavy artillerists. It had been another hot day, and though the 1st Mississippi Infantry was used to hard marching, the men had been languishing for a year in northern prisons and were unable to maintain the pace. Soldiers began to straggle and fall by the roadside. Most of the dismounted cavalrymen wore clumsy cavalry boots, a poor substitute for the brogans worn by the infantry. Luckily, the frequent stops allowed the stragglers to catch up with their units as the column continued to inch forward as the sun went down.[28]

As Morton's artillery battalion, with its twenty guns and attending limbers, caissons, and ammunition wagons, passed Chalmers's supply train at Garvin's, the supply wagons fell into the long line as well. The combination of cavalry, artillery, foot soldiers, wagons, dust, darkness, and a narrow road resulted in a logistical nightmare of traffic jams and delays. With just a touch of understatement Chalmers noted that the march "produced some confusion." Among the confused were the troopers of the 2nd Tennessee who had been looking for their brigade, Tyree Bell's, since their skirmish on the Pontotoc Road two days before. Colonel Barteau had first taken his men to Verona for a well-earned rest and then moved to Okolona, where he learned Bell had already departed. The Tennesseans joined the column with orders to move to the front, where, within four miles of Okolona, they met Lee and Forrest at the head of the column. "Turning again," wrote Pvt. Richard Hancock, "we halted and fed at Prairie Mound, seven miles from Okolona. By this time it was dark. We remained there until our brigade, and in fact most of the command, had passed. Swinging ourselves into the saddle again, a little after midnight, we moved out to overtake our brigade." It would be dawn before the exhausted 2nd Tennessee rejoined Bell's brigade.[29]

Lee and Forrest arrived at Pinson's Hill at 9:00 P.M. and found that all the troops had retaken their positions held earlier in the day. Rucker's brigade assumed its posts on the Cotton Gin Road, but without orders Rucker was unwilling to send the 8th Mississippi back to the Tupelo Road. Aside from Tyler's small force, the road continued to go unguarded.

The Confederates' morale was high. Certainly they were tired from all the marching and countermarching, but they had driven the enemy back into Pontotoc and had every reason to think the Federals had lost their nerve. And just as at Brice's Crossroads, they were about to chase the enemy all the way back to Memphis. But as if to spoil the mood, General Buford reined in next to his commanders and offered his observation. "I reported to them all the information in my knowledge, and the fact that up to that time I had discovered no evidence of the demoralized condition of the enemy, but had found him ever ready for action."[30]

TEN

The Road to Tupelo

"The bugle call sounded early this morning and the drums beat a rousing tattoo," wrote Chaplain Elijah Edwards. It was back to business as usual in the Federal camps, the previous day of rest already no more than a pleasant memory. With the morning routine of roll call, breakfast, and hitching mules and horses complete, the men waited away the predawn darkness of July 13 unsure of what the day held in store. Smith had briefed his division and brigade commanders the previous afternoon, but, as always, the men in the ranks were kept in the dark lest the plans fall into the hands of the enemy.[1]

General A. J. Smith's plan was bold, and to be carried off it would require speed and organization. His army would be strung out for miles along the narrow route, and he could expect Forrest's much-faster mounted brigades to attack his right flank from the south as well as his rear guard. As a precaution he ordered the column to stay tight "and to move steadily forward without halting, unless absolutely necessary." The danger lay in stopping to fend off flank attacks, which would cause large gaps to form in the column and thereby create an opportunity for the Confederates to divide and conquer their numerically superior foe, a proven formula of Lt. Gen. Thomas "Stonewall" Jackson, who wrote, "Once you get them running, you can stay on top of them, and that way a small force can beat a large one every time."[2]

Smith ordered the cavalry to lead the advance, with Winslow's Second Brigade in the van, followed by Coon's Third Brigade. Col. David Moore's Third Division would fall in behind the cavalry, with his three infantry brigades (Murray, Gilbert, Wolfe) marching in numerical order. The division trains would follow closely behind and precede Mower's division. He divided up the

First Division trains and had them march directly behind their respective brigades, also in numerical order (McMillen, Wilkin, Woods, Ward). Bouton's Colored Brigade would march in the rear of the infantry column to fend off attacks from the enemy coming up from behind. Smith positioned the 7th Kansas Cavalry at the very end of the line.[3]

"Moved out just at daylight. Our brigade is in front," wrote Captain Abraham of the 4th Iowa Cavalry. At the head of Winslow's brigade were two battalions of the 3rd Iowa followed by the 4th Iowa and the 10th Missouri. The missing battalion of John Noble's 3rd Iowa was still manning the picket line on the Houston Road, where it had driven back Willis's Texans the day before. Noble instructed Capt. John Brown to maintain a presence on the Houston Road until the rear of the army had passed through town and turned east toward Tupelo. Over on the Okolona Road the pickets of the 9th Illinois Cavalry provided a similar screen. As Moore's division made the turn east, Colonel Bouton ordered the 61st USCT to the high ground vacated by the Third Division. The low ridge covered the Okolona Road, which was the most direct route for Forrest's troops to follow when they found the enemy had pulled out. This redeployment freed up the men of the 9th Illinois who had been picketing the Okolona Road, and they quickly mounted up and rode off to join Coon's brigade near the front of the column. For a second precious hour the Union army continued to march unobserved.[4]

In fact, however, there had already been contact between the two forces. Smith's column had been spotted moving out of Pontotoc at dawn, but the vital information had gone unreported. Capt. Henry Tyler's 100 men of the 12th Kentucky had spent the night on the Tupelo Road, the only Confederate troops on Smith's route of march. On the morning of July 13, five miles east of Pontotoc, Tyler met the advance of Grierson's mounted division. "I promptly ordered the men in line and engaged the enemy, not knowing whether it was a movement in force or just another foraging party."[5]

A few scattering shots soon became heavy skirmish fire, and the Kentuckians, convinced this was no mere foraging detail, began a fighting withdrawal in the direction of Tupelo. In his official report filed a week later Tyler exaggerated the action: "After a brisk engagement of twenty-five minutes the enemy threw a heavy column of cavalry around both my flanks and advanced their infantry immediately on my front." The "heavy column" was really just the two battalions of the 3rd Iowa Cavalry, and it was such a minor scuffle that they didn't ask for help from the rest of the brigade let alone the infantry. The 4th Iowa Cavalry, the next regiment in line, never broke its marching order and continued steadily on to the east. Tyler did all he could to hold back Grierson's

cavalry, but with only 100 men in the ranks, it was a doomed effort. Unfortunately for Generals Lee and Forrest, the brave captain was too distracted by his
skirmish to send a messenger with the news that the enemy was on the move. It
was another two and a half hours before the Federals' movement was detected.[6]

At 2:00 that morning, Buford had placed Hinchie Mabry with three of his
regiments (14th Confederate, 4th and 38th Mississippi) in front of the Pinson's Hill line. Mabry's other regiment, the 6th Mississippi, had been resting in
Okolona ever since its fight on the Plentitude Road. At 6:00 A.M. Mabry's pickets
became curious about the lack of activity from the Federal pickets. They edged
closer and discovered that their counterparts were no longer on the high ground
across Chiwapa Creek. They immediately sent for the colonel, who "at once
notified General Buford of the fact and began to follow up the foe."[7]

At about the same time, Lt. William Pirtle of the 7th Kentucky was with
his Company A near the Pinson's Hill breastworks, where he "could hear a
commotion about the yankee camps, could not tell what it meant, but after a
time General Chalmers rode up to left of the line the highest ground about
there, put his field glasses to his eyes, and decided the yanks were moving east
in place of coming out to meet us." The general rode away at a gallop.[8]

James Chalmers was very confused by what he observed and what he understood to be the Confederate strategy. His subsequent report revealed how
little he knew of Lee's and Forrest's plans. "I supposed that we would fall back
to the place selected for battle near Egypt Station," he wrote, "and that the
enemy was attempting to get there before us." (Egypt Station was a depot on
the Mobile & Ohio Railroad eight miles south of Okolona and had never been
a part of the recent Confederate strategy.) Apparently, Chalmers knew nothing about the previous night's forced march to Pinson's Hill, about the revised
plan to give battle to Smith "wherever he offered it and to attack him if he attempted a retreat," or about the scrapped plan to lure Smith to Prairie Mound.

Granted, as the day broke on the 13th, the generals were not altogether
sure if Smith was retreating or preparing to attack. What Chalmers saw convinced him that Smith was attempting to flank the Confederate army, but he
believed Smith to be heading southeast instead of due east. His orders to his
subordinate officers confirm this misunderstanding: "I therefore took Roddy's
and Rucker's brigades and moved at once to the fords on the Chuappa [Chi-
wapa] Creek, with a view of preceding the enemy and holding him in check
until our forces could get into position to receive him." Had Chalmers's movement gone unchecked, it would have resulted in a sizable portion of the Confederate army guarding fords the enemy had no intention of using.[9]

Lee and Forrest received word of Chalmers's discovery at about the same time they learned the news of Mabry's scout. They met hurriedly on realizing they were wrong about Smith's intentions. Lee told Forrest to set out in pursuit with a force consisting of Forrest's Escort, Mabry's Brigade, McDonald's Battalion (which he still referred to as Forrest's Old Regiment), and Capt. Edwin Walton's four guns of the Pettus Flying Artillery. He ordered Forrest to find and engage the rear guard of Smith's column with the intent of forcing the Federals to turn and fight.[10]

Lee took Buford's and Chalmers's men "with the view of attacking the enemy's flanks at every vulnerable point." Chalmers recalled Rucker's brigade before it could reach the Chiwapa Creek fords and directed it to set out southeast on the Verona Road. McCulloch's brigade still held a position on the Houston Road, and Chalmers instructed the men to mount up and follow as best they could. Without waiting for Black Bob, Chalmers set out with Rucker's troopers.[11]

Buford received his marching orders as well, which were basically the same as Chalmers's. "I was immediately ordered to move on his [Smith's] flank on the Pontotoc and Camargo Ferry road, known as the Chauappa Valley road, leading via Doctor Calhoun's house to Verona." This road, two miles to the south, roughly paralleled Smith's route, with several smaller roads leading north that crossed the Tupelo Road. Though the distance both armies had to march was fairly equal, the Union had a sizable head start. Even though the Confederates had the advantage of being mounted, they would still have to ride hard in order to catch their prey. Buford set out with Bell's and Crossland's (Lyon's) brigades. The still-exhausted dismounted cavalry and infantry fell in behind Forrest, as did the balance of the artillery.[12]

Forrest's blood was up. As he rode down from Pinson's Hill he could not help but think that once again he had guessed wrong about Smith's plans. He had marched and countermarched his men and only succeeded in tiring them out, while Smith's men had been resting. Now his men would have to ride, march, and fight in order to stop the enemy. It was imperative to stop Smith before he could reach good ground and compel the Confederates to attack him.

To begin the pursuit, Mabry deployed and advanced his three regiments in line of battle. South of town they met the Federal rear guard, which let them know there was still a Union presence in Pontotoc. Capt. Lorenzo Jean and Company A of the 61st USCT stood their ground as Mabry's mounted advance hove into sight. Shots were fired, and two Confederates fell from the saddle. This was the baptism by fire for the 61st, which had only seen garrison duty in west Tennessee prior to the expedition. Col. Frank Kendrick of the 61st withdrew Jean's company before Mabry could bring up the balance of his brigade, but not before delivering the message that there was a vigilant rear guard on duty. Once the Union infantry and supply trains had cleared Pontotoc, Kendrick gave the order for the Colored Brigade to fall back through town. The rear guard duties were passed to the 7th Kansas Cavalry, which watched the roads from the south as the black soldiers fell in line at the end of the column.[13]

When the last of the black soldiers made the turn onto the Tupelo Road, Col. Hendrick of the 7th Kansas called his horse holders forward, and the regiment rode through Pontotoc, the last of the Federals to pull out of town. But whether Hendrick simply forgot or had never been informed of their presence, the word to pull out never reached the battalion of the 3rd Iowa Cavalry picketing the Houston Road. "The picket on the Okolona Road," explained Colonel Noble, "did not act in harmony with my companies, but retired sooner, the enemy were enabled to get between the main army (retiring) and Captain Brown." Brown's four companies (A, I, K, L) were intently watching the Houston Road expecting McCulloch's men to make an appearance from the south. The young captain grew concerned, aware that the army was marching away. And then he heard the musket fire on his left. He waited patiently, but no orders to pull out ever came. At some point Brown (or one of his troopers) looked back toward town and was astonished to see a "line of the enemy, some 300 strong," behind them. Brown had been in tight spots before and called his men in from their picket posts and formed them in a column. There were not a lot of options, so, "with his usual coolness," Brown "determined to charge through them and break through to the army." He gave his men a quick pep talk, explained the situation, and warned each man to keep his saddle. With pistols and carbines at the ready, Brown's bugler blew the charge, and the column raced full speed into Pontotoc. "Our men, cheering, firing, and thundering down the hill with so much audacity, surprised the rebels, who at once broke and fled in apparent amazement." Despite all the high drama, there were no casualties on either side. Free of danger, Brown slowed his battalion to a brisk walk, not resting until they had ridden the length of Smith's column and rejoined Noble and the rest of the 3rd Iowa Cavalry. Noble was delighted with Brown's charge through Forrest's line: "The battalion met with no loss, but the situation was one of a more difficult nature than it should have been thrown into, as I submit it was, unnecessarily."[14]

Surprised by the charge of the Iowans, Mabry halted in town to wait for his 6th Mississippi, which was hurrying forward to join the brigade. In Pontotoc the women and children came out to praise their liberators as the last of Brown's men were chased out of town. Years later Pvt. F. Holloway of the 38th Mississippi mused, "Do you remember how the ladies shouted and waved their handker-chiefs as seeing the boys in gray after them?" It was then well past 7:00 A.M., and Grierson's cavalry had already covered more than half the distance to Tupelo.[15]

Most of the men in the Union ranks were experienced enough to know that General Smith had just commenced a flank march and that they were continu-ing their advance into Mississippi rather than falling back. Ben Thomas of the 14th Iowa could have been speaking for the entire army when he wrote,

> Well, we were surprised this morning when we started on the march to retrace
> our steps through Pontotoc and as soon as we were through the town to strike
> out due east toward Tupelo. We had no doubt the rebels were surprised by the
> move. The air was fresh and fairly cool and our boys spirits were high. They
> felt that victory was more than half won by this strategy. Frequently the boys
> would cheer as we marched along. The cheering would begin in front and
> gradually pass along the line to the rear.

"We rejoiced to know we would fight an open battle instead of butting our heads against fortifications as we expected to," wrote a private of the 14th Iowa. Johnson Paisley of the 117th Illinois observed, "General Smith out generalled the rebs as they were expecting us to attack," a thought echoed by seventeen-year-old Otto Wolfe of the same regiment, who wrote his folks about how "Gen'l Smith outgeneraled Forrest at Pontitic, he was badly fooled for we turned around and took the other road." Otto's brother, Adolphus, made a simi-lar comment in his letter home, when he wondered aloud, "But what must have been their mortification in the morning when they found we had given them the slip. Now we had the rebels in our rear, & if they wanted to whip us, they had to do the attacking." Charles Tiedman of the 178th New York quipped delightedly, "The rebels are 'fooled.'" Surprisingly, the Federals were not the only ones impressed with Smith's gambit. John Hubbard of the 7th Tennessee grudgingly praised Smith, saying, "A tactician thoroughly aquatinted with the topography of the country could not have made a more judicious move, or taken more proper steps to select his own position for battle."[16]

Compared to Lee, Forrest had the shorter distance to cover in reaching the enemy, and on the arrival of Harrison's 6th Mississippi he set out in pursuit of the Federal rear guard. The 7th Kansas was not far ahead, so he quickly made con-tact. "The enemy soon became aware of our movement and followed us closely from the town out. We had pretty sharp skirmishing," recounted Colonel Her-rick, "which increased as we went on." The 7th Kansas was well known for its liberal foraging and wanton destruction, but the Jayhawkers could also fight.[17]

Lt. Simeon Fox, the adjutant of the 7th Kansas, later tried to explain how the regiment as rear guard fended off six regiments and two pieces of artillery personally commanded by Forrest: "It was done, how it was done is difficult to understand; it was the accomplishment of a seeming impossibility." Herrick detached companies, squads, and platoons at every defensive position he could find. As the Confederates approached, the dismounted Kansans fired, jumped back in the saddle, and rode past their comrades to another likely position. This leapfrogging went on for over a mile, a tactic that forced Mabry to deploy his men in line of battle and slow their pursuit, taking advantage of "every hill and grove that offered a good position." When the Confederate line threatened to envelop his own, Herrick sent squadrons out on either of his flanks to give the impression of a much greater force. At about 10:00 A.M. Herrick dismounted three companies (A, F, H) and set them in an ambush on the north side of the road. As the southerners advanced, the Jayhawkers unloaded a volley that, while not stopping the enemy, caused them to be a bit more cautious.[18]

Eventually Forrest wearied of the slow pursuit and ordered Mabry to make a charge and scatter the Federal rear guard. It was all Herrick could do to keep the enemy at bay, and two miles from Pontotoc he called on Col. Ed Bouton for help from the 61st USCT, which was bringing up the rear. Lt. Col. John Foley took two companies back down the road to prepare an ambush. He found a likely spot and hid his men on either side of the road. The tail end of the 7th Kansas passed. When the pursuing enemy had advanced to within twelve paces, the black soldiers let loose "a well-directed volley, which emptied 15 or 20 saddles and threw [Mabry's] column back in confusion." The ambush bought Kendrick some time, and he used it to fall back a mile and prepare another ambush. The southerners had grown wary, however, and the second encounter met "with partial, but not so complete success."[19]

The fighting between the Confederates and the rear guard caused a gap to form between Bouton's black soldiers and Mower's First Division. Smith had ordered the column to stay closed up and to keep moving forward without halting, unless absolutely necessary. So in order to close the gap, Bouton's brigade had to quicken its pace and cross Ben Miller Creek, five miles east of Pontotoc. The road led down a hill into the small creek valley and then up the opposing ridge. The 59th and 68th USCT had gained the opposite heights, and the 61st was crossing the stream when Mabry's brigade struck hard, tumbling back the 7th Kansas Cavalry. Company C was on the south side of the Tupelo road in an isolated position and was nearly cut off and surrounded. Herrick waited until the last moment before ordering the men to cut their way

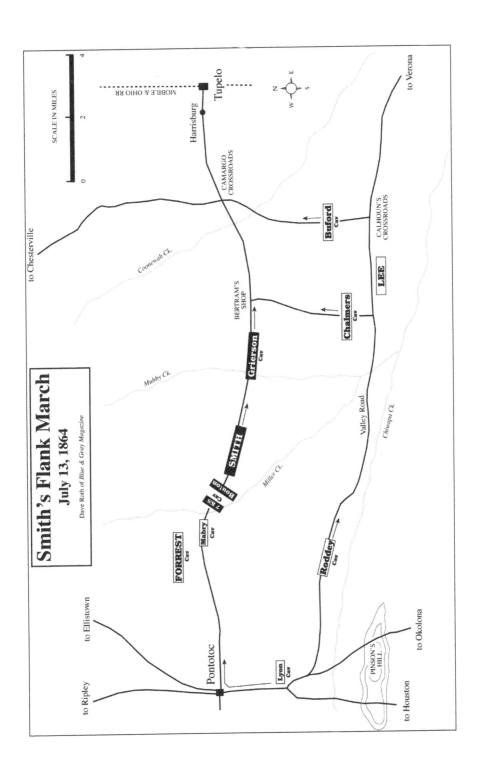

Smith's Flank March
July 13, 1864

Dave Roth of Blue & Gray Magazine

SCALE IN MILES

0   2   4

to Chesterville

to Ellistown

to Ripley

Pontotoc

FORREST
Cav

Mabry
Cav

Bouton
7 Ks

SMITH

Grierson
Cav

Lyon
Cav

Roddey
Cav

PINSON'S HILL

to Houston

to Okolona

Valley Road

Chiwapa Ck.

Miller Ck.

Mubby Ck.

Coonewah Ck.

BERTRAM'S SHOP

CAMARGO CROSSROADS

Chalmers
Cav

LEE

Buford
Cav

CALHOUN'S CROSSROADS

to Verona

Tupelo

Harrisburg

MOBILE & OHIO RR

N E S W

out and escape. It was a close call, but the Kansans were able to splash across the creek and up the hill behind the USCT regiments.[20]

The Confederates sensed an opportunity and pressed even harder. Forrest arrived on the heights to the west of Miller Creek and began shelling the Federals furiously with two cannon of the Pettus Flying Artillery. But for all the noise, they did little actual damage. It was there Bouton made his most stalwart defense of the morning. The men of Battery I, 2nd U.S. Colored Artillery, unlimbered four guns in the road and began to return fire at a range of 800 yards. The 59th USCT formed a line of battle on the left of the battery, while the companies of the 61st deployed to the right. Behind them the relatively inexperienced 68th stood ready as a reserve. Herrick divided his 7th Kansas and posted them on either flank of the black infantry line.[21]

This Union line high on the ridge presented an intimidating sight. The Confederates had grown cautious after the two ambushes and were in no hurry to charge recklessly into a third. "The enemy approached this time very slowly," reported Bouton, "and only engaged [us] at long range." In fact, the southerners took so much time crossing Miller Creek that Bouton became nervous about the gap that was again forming between his brigade and Mower's division. So after a short wait he ordered Jones's 58th to turn about and resume the march, followed by the 61st and two of the artillery pieces. Capt. Louis Smith, the battery commander, stayed behind with his remaining section of guns, and Bouton placed the rear guard in the capable hands of Maj. James Foster, commander of the 59th USCT.[22]

James Foster had started the war as a nineteen-year-old private in the 53rd Ohio Infantry. He saw his first action at the Battle of Shiloh as a first sergeant, a fight in which his regiment was disgraced through the conduct of their commander, Col. Jesse Appler. With his regiment, and a new commanding officer, Foster fought at the Siege of Corinth and in Grant's overland campaign against Vicksburg and garrison duty in LaGrange. His traits as a leader were noted, and he was commissioned as a second lieutenant. In May 1863 he was detailed to recruit for the 1st West Tennessee Infantry of African Descent, a black infantry regiment later designated the 59th USCT. The unit fought at Brice's Crossroads, and he was one of the few officers to come out of the disaster with a glowing account of his actions. The commanding officer of the 59th, Lt. Col. Robert Cowden, was wounded in the hip at the close of the fight, and command passed to Foster. The 59th remained with the rear guard throughout the retreat, fending off Abraham Buford's cavalry until the beaten army limped back into Tennessee. Within days Foster was wearing the gold oak leaves of a major.[23]

Major Foster acted quickly to position his regiment on the heights above Miller Creek while the balance of the brigade marched away to the east. Capt. Henry Fox and two companies remained on the south side of the road while Capt. Noah Smock and three companies moved across the path and took the place of the 61st regiment. Foster held the remaining five companies in reserve. The men of the 7th Kansas Cavalry, dismounted and with their carbines at the ready, maintained their vigil on the flanks of the 59th. Foster and Bouton noted a cloud of dust rising rapidly across Miller Creek: "It was evident the enemy was advancing in force." Captain Smith began to discharge his 12-pounders, but it was impossible to tell if they were having any effect on the enemy. Under the cover of his own two guns, Forrest was changing his tactics. "The Confederate advance was made in three columns," explained Lieutenant Fox of the 7th Kansas; "if you checked one the others came on and threatened your flank." In a move to counter this threat, Foster took two companies from the reserve under Capt. Maurice Covan and extended his line into the underbrush on the right, and Lt. Jacob Swartz took his company into the bushes on the left.[24]

It was close to 1:00 when Mabry's Mississippians, along with McDonald's Battalion and Forrest's Escort, finally pushed forward in force, crossing Miller Creek and into a cornfield. Bouton described how the enemy felt "their way with scattering shots until within fifteen yards, when they were met by a deadly volley, quickly followed by others, which seemed to tell on them with terrible effect, throwing them into confusion." No sooner had the Federals beaten back Mabry's column on the road than they discovered another force advancing on their right flank. Bouton was feeling the continuous pressure and sent a request for Mower to send help. But one wonders why he did not recall his own two regiments, the 61st and 68th. Fortunately for Bouton, the Confederate flank attack failed to develop, and the need for help passed.

The rear guard was able to withdraw and close in with the rest of the column, and Bouton took advantage of the lull to limber up Louis Smith's two cannon. As the battery horses trotted up the road, Foster pulled back his regiment, leaving Captain Fox to form a skirmish line with his companies (B, H). "But before the movement began the enemy fired on us," wrote Capt. Robert Cowden, "which we returned with considerable effect, checking the advancing columns after a few minutes of hard fighting." Once again the Confederate advance halted, and Bouton's brigade finally pulled back and scurried across Mubby Creek to set up yet another defensive position on the far bank.[25]

Forrest had been stymied in his attempts to break through the Union rear guard and to force Smith to halt and engage him. In his report, he grudgingly complimented Smith, noting, "He took advantage of every favorable position, and my artillery was kept in almost constant action." He had to have been frustrated by his inability to crack the Federal line, but he was also growing concerned that there had been no sound of an attack on the enemy's flank. Where was Lee with Chalmers and Buford? Forrest began to think the lack of activity of the Federal flanks was due to his own activity on the Tupelo Road: "I had driven the enemy ten miles, and as his flanks had not yet been attacked I was fearful that he was driven too rapidly." But Smith was not being driven at all. The column was moving at a quick pace that forced Bouton's rear guard to hustle to keep up. If anything, Forrest's men had slowed the column slightly. Rather than being driven, the Federals were making remarkable time and had yet to meet any real resistance at the front or on the flanks.[26]

Ahead of the Union column, Captain Tyler's Kentuckians did the best they could to hold back the Federal onslaught, but their best was not nearly enough. They kept up the skirmishing until just before 9:00 A.M., when they reached a fork in the road twelve miles east of Pontotoc. The route to the southeast led to Verona, and Captain Tyler, unsure which direction the Federals would turn, took this road. Colonel Noble kept his 3rd Iowa on the main road, prompting Tyler to ride hard for Verona to spread the word of the enemy's advance.[27]

It did not take long for Grierson to discover that the enemy had disappeared from his front and taken with them any remaining opposition on the road to Tupelo. The division was called to a halt for a well-deserved rest and to feed and water the mounts. The men were stretching their legs and backs when Grierson called for a group of them to remount and ride the remaining five miles into Tupelo to secure the town in advance of the main column. The detail of Maj. Martin Williams, commander of the 10th Missouri Cavalry, and Capt. Benjamin Crail and two squadrons of the 3rd Iowa rode into an undefended Tupelo and found it deserted of enemy forces. Without delay Williams picketed the roads leading into town while another working party dismounted and piled obstructions on the tracks of the Mobile & Ohio Railroad. By noon the remainder of Winslow's cavalry brigade arrived in town, followed soon after by Coon's regiments. Grierson set them all to destroying the railroad.[28]

In the cavalry supply wagons there were pry bars and picks, and the men knew how to use them. They pried up individual rails and threw the wooden ties into piles, which they then set on fire. A detachment of the 9th Illinois Cavalry was sent four miles south of Tupelo to Stanislaus Station, where they systematically destroyed the depot and a series of trestles.

This detail had just completed its work and gotten back in the saddle when Henry Tyler's men arrived on the scene. Tyler and his men had arrived in Verona at noon. While the young captain was busy sending reports, the men took an hour off in the cool shade. Barely refreshed, the men and animals headed north up the tracks in the direction of Tupelo. Hardly a mile up the tracks they came upon the men of the 9th Illinois leaving the scene of the destruction at Stanislaus Station. Too late to stop the Federals, they drove the enemy north from the depot, which was fully engulfed in flames, and then rode back to Verona.[29]

Grierson kept his troopers busy tearing up thirteen miles of track between Stanislaus to the south and Saltillo to the north. At 3:30 P.M., while the destruction was still in full swing, Grierson received a dispatch from Smith ordering him to send a detachment of cavalry to the rear of the column to assist the exhausted 7th Kansas. Lt. Col. John Peters took a battalion of the 4th Iowa Cavalry and joined two battalions of the 9th Illinois, all under the direction of Col. Henry Burgh, and within minutes the relief column set off for the rear at a gallop. In the distance they could hear the sound of heavy musket and cannon fire.[30]

ELEVEN

Bertram's Shop and the Camargo Crossroads

In the predawn light of July 13, hours before Forrest began his pursuit, a lean, dusty company of Kentuckians rode up to his headquarters. They were refugees from Brig. Gen. John Hunt Morgan's command and were at the end of one of the longest and most daring rides of the war.

On June 11 Morgan had led 1,200 men into Cynthiana, Kentucky, sixty miles south of Cincinnati. The day went well for Morgan, and with little effort he brushed aside the understrength 168th Ohio Infantry and set about burning the town. Union brigadier general Edward Hobson arrived with reinforcements, the 750 men of the 171st Ohio National Guard, who had enlisted for only 100 days of service and who were no match for the veteran raiders. Morgan managed to trap Hobson in a turn of the Licking River and by sunset had taken nearly 1,300 prisoners.

The following day the tables turned when Brig. Gen. Stephen Burbridge and 2,400 men from Ohio, Kentucky, and Michigan attacked an ill-prepared Morgan and sent his dismounted cavalry reeling. The Confederates retreated through the smoldering town but could not escape Burbridge's cavalry, which surrounded and captured the bulk of the southerners. Morgan managed to slip away with a handful of his staff, and several hundred others ran off in all directions. Union troops from across the state were called in to hunt down the fugitives.[1]

Beyond the Confederate lines, and unnoticed during the sharp fighting, 106 southern soldiers serving as horse holders waited, each man holding his own mount as well as four others. Capt. William Campbell had observed the destruction of Morgan's troops and ordered the men into the saddle and away from the scene of the disaster. To speed their escape and distract any pursuers, they turned the extra horses loose. Campbell made a decision that day to lead the small force to Mississippi and there join up with Forrest. "Now we need not have gone to Forrest all," explained Pvt. John Johnson. "We could have turned to the east and gone back to Va., but none of us saw it in that light, so we made haste to reach Tupelo and offer our services to Gen. Forrest."[2]

The odds were against them. Only fifteen of the men were armed, and those few had little or no ammunition. The route they followed was hardly "as the crow flies" and meandered over 550 miles through three states. They headed due west and reached the broad waters of the Ohio near Louisville, where they turned south. At the small town of Bardstown, Campbell bluffed the Union garrison into thinking he was at the head of a large and well-armed force. Lt. Fenney Driskill and Company I of the 48th Kentucky were completely taken in by the ruse and surrendered to the lightly armed Confederates. Campbell supplied his men with arms and ammunition and released his prisoners. They left Bardstown with the 9th Michigan Cavalry in pursuit but by nightfall had eluded their foes.

The long route led the men west to Owensboro, where they again paused along the Ohio and then turned south to cross the Green River at Calhoun. Just west of Cadiz the men forded the Cumberland River, the normally deep waters made shallow by the summer drought. The greatest challenge lay just ahead at the crossing of the Tennessee River, eight miles north of the state line, where Union gunboats were patrolling the river and keeping a close watch on river traffic. Campbell and his men slipped into the water and swam the wide distance. Actually, the horses did the swimming while the men clung to manes, tails, and saddles. Several horses and at least one soldier drowned in the crossing. On the other side, the small column made its way into Tennessee, the men foraging and begging food to keep up their strength. They traded the exhausted horses with local farmers, a practice known as "exchanging," which gave the soldiers nice fresh horses and left the farmers with broken-down animals.

Eventually the riders crossed into Mississippi, and at the outskirts of Corinth they made contact with a small unit of Forrest's scouts. "They were hard looking and very dirty," recalled Johnson, "but I can never forget the joy, the delight and happiness it gave me to see them. I could have put my arms around them and hugged the last one of them. Safe at last! Within the lines of good old Dixie!" Forrest's men must have indeed been a sight for this ragged group to notice how hard and dirty they looked. The refugees continued on to Tupelo, where Campbell presented his little band to General Forrest for duty. Private Johnson recalled the meeting:

I remember quite well what Capt. Campbell told us when he returned from his interview with Gen. Forrest, in which he tendered Forrest our services. "Gen. Forrest accepts our services and pays us the compliment to make us a part of his body guard but gives us to understand that his bodyguard has to fight." These were near his words as I can recall, It may have been a figure of speech as to the honor and bodyguard of it, but it was a literal fact as to the fighting.

Forrest assigned Captain Campbell and the rest of Morgan's refugees to the 8th Kentucky of Lt. Colonel Absalom Shacklett. Of the 106 men who had left Cynthiana, ninety were still in ranks when they joined the chase after A. J. Smith on July 13.[3]

James Chalmers was first down the Chiwapa Valley Road with Rucker's brigade of men from Mississippi and Tennessee. Behind them came Buford's division accompanied by General Lee. The first opportunity to strike the enemy column came eight miles west of Tupelo where a small farm lane turned north off the Valley Road. The lane meandered for two miles and eventually intersected with the main Tupelo–Pontotoc Road, on which Smith's army was rapidly marching east. Chalmers directed his troops onto the connecting path.[4]

The main road ahead was clogged with the men and wagons of the First Division. The march had been fairly uneventful for Mower's four brigades. The rear guard was doing some fighting, and the sounds of rifles and artillery could be heard as the column pushed forward. The brigades were marching in numerical order, with Col. Lyman Ward's Fourth Brigade bringing up the rear. Mower's regiments were guarding the individual wagon trains assigned to the brigades as well as the "general supply train" near the end of the infantry column. Ward's deployment was typical of the division: "I divided my command into companies of about twenty five men each, and distributed it along the right flank of the supply train and the train of my brigade, one company to each six wagons." Ward's was the smallest infantry brigade in Smith's army, numbering no more than 700 men. At the head of the brigade was a detachment of the 41st Illinois Infantry. (These fifty "nonveterans" of the regiment had declined to reenlist and were awaiting their discharges while the bulk of the regiment was home in Illinois on furlough.) Behind it came the 14th and 33rd Wisconsin. All three regiments (even the 41st, despite the nonveteran tag) were filled with seasoned fighters, veterans of Shiloh, Corinth, Vicksburg, and the Red River campaign.[5]

At 1:00 p.m. Mower got the urgent call for help from Colonel Bouton and the embattled rear guard. The general responded by ordering Ward to drop back with the 33rd Wisconsin and provide whatever assistance was needed. The brigade and its trains were just crossing Mubby Creek and climbing the slope on the opposite bank. Before he rode away, Ward ordered the 14th Wisconsin and the detachment of the 41st Illinois to spread out and cover the right flank of the train as best they could. They had too few men to guard the wagons, 250 at the most, which left more than a quarter of the wagons with no guard at all.[6]

While Ward and the 33rd Wisconsin dropped out of the line, Mower sent an order to Col. Joseph Woods, his Third Brigade commander, whose regiments were marching just in front of Ward's brigade. As an added precaution, he ordered Woods to let two of his largest regiments fall back in the line to help fill the gap. The 12th Iowa and 7th Minnesota were already marching in the woods on the right of the road, and rather than march back down the road they simply stopped where they were until the tail of the column reached them. From his position near the head of the division Mower listened intently to the firing in the rear and headed in the direction of the fighting. This was no surprise to his staff, who followed in his wake; Joe Mower always rode toward the sound of fighting.[7]

Joseph Anthony Mower, the thirty-seven-year-old commander of the First Division, was a native of Woodstock, Vermont, and a born soldier. He was raised in Massachusetts and spent two years at the Norwich Academy in Vermont, but he dropped out of college and took on work as a carpenter. His true calling came with the outbreak of the Mexican War and his enlistment as a private in the Corps of Engineers. He returned to civilian life for a brief time before wrangling a lieutenant's commission in the First U.S. Infantry, and by the outbreak of the Civil War he had advanced to captain. In May 1862 he was commissioned colonel of volunteers and given the helm of the 11th Missouri Infantry; command of a brigade soon followed. He amassed an impressive combat record at Iuka, Corinth, Vicksburg, and the Red River. The *New York Times* claimed he was brave to a fault, "absolutely without any sense of danger, he seemed to relish above everything else the tumult of battle." Cloyd Byner, the historian of the 47th Illinois Infantry agreed, saying that there was "no lover more impatient for his mistress than Mower for war's troubles." He had a dangerous tendency of riding far forward to observe the fighting, "an almost uncontrollable impulse to mingle with the skirmish line." Not only was he a hard fighter, he was an equally hard drinker, often combining the two activities. On the morning of October 4, 1862, at the Battle of Corinth, he was drunk when he led a patrol that skirmished with the enemy and ended up with a nasty neck wound and a few hours as a prisoner. A month later he was a brigadier general. Capt. Theodore Carter of the 7th Minnesota made a canny observation of his division commander when he said, "Gen. Mower was a good military man, when he was sober. But he could not stand success. If he accomplished his designs one day, the next he was quite sure to get 'full.'"[8]

Brig. Gen. Joseph A. Mower
(Library of Congress)

While the men of the 7th Minnesota enjoyed their rest, waiting for the rest of the column to catch up, Chaplain Edwards took the time to write in his journal, noting, "The Union and Confed forces are today racing on near, and convergent roads to see who shall reach Tupelo first, and get into a favorable position for the real struggle that must come tomorrow." Satisfied with his grasp of the tactical situation, he decided to take a walk up the road while the men ate. On the right, or south, side of the road was a large field with a dry brook running through it east to west with a small fringe of undergrowth. The field was enclosed by a rail fence to keep the livestock away from the crops. But what had once been planted in corn had given way to tall yellow grass. The men resting alongside the road relaxed with confidence; unlike the overextended 14th Wisconsin behind them, they had flankers several hundred yards off to the south to warn of the approach of the enemy. Besides, thought the chaplain, "what could mar the sweet serenity of that hour of rest?"[9]

Edwards strolled past Lucius Smith, the regimental surgeon, who was resting in the shade with Surgeon Aurelius Bartlett of the 33rd Missouri. A quarter mile down the road Edwards came on a blacksmith shop on the left side of the road and a small cabin to the right. A short distance ahead was another cabin at a fork in the road, the path to the right a small farm road winding away to the southeast. The tiny community was known as Bertram's Shop.[10]

The Union column was crossing the plantation of James D. Brame, a wealthy landowner whose property stretched across both sides of the Tupelo–Pontotoc

(18)

At about two o'clock, P.M, a halt was called which lasted about an hour. This was much appreciated by the weary ones in line and mounted, for our pace had been rapid and we had no other interval for rest or lunch. Our mess-chest having been overturned in a ditch we had no sumptuous meal this day. I was tired of riding horseback, and besides began to have some scruples about the propriety of riding a white horse into battle. I felt that the color of the horse might attract undue attention from the Rebel sharp shooters who were blazing away at us on our line of march. I did not want to attract too much attention even from our enemies; and for that reason went on foot the rest of the way to Tupelo. It would have been heroic to ride that white horse into the thickest of the fight; but I did not want to ride in the thickest of the fight. I didnot want to be a "hero in the strife, and I preferred safety to making a display. Really I was not thinking of the battle at all. We had found by the wayside in a field such a quiet resting place. And rest was sweet. What could mar the sweet serenity of that hour of rest.? The 7th Regiment was serving as Train - Guard to day and for that reason was somewhat scattered, being broken up in detachments, and there being no necessity for my keeping my position in the line, I strolled forward nearly a quarter of a mile thinking to fill my canteen at a farm house that I saw a few rods beyond the bend of the road. There was a cabin on the right hand side of the road inhabited by two or three women. Some bummers were plundering this house, apparently for mere mischief as there was nothing worth carrying away. On the left side of the road stood an empty blacksmith shop. A few rods beyond was the farm house I have mentioned. The bummers had not troubled the inmates and I was hospitably received by the inmates and allowed to fill my canteen with the purest sweetest I thought I had ever tasted After a short talk, I left thinking to return to

Chaplain Edwards's map of Bertram's Shop (DePauw University Archives and Special Collections)

Road. The plantation house stood to the west, overlooking Mubby Creek, and had escaped the plunder and burning that had become so common. The small blacksmith shop that stood near the intersection was owned by a man named Bertram, a former slave. Bertram maintained the tools and farm implements of the Brame plantation and, after he was freed, his former master allowed him to set up his own business. Bertram's Shop (also known as Bartram's, Burrow's or Barrow's) was open for the local trade between Pontotoc and Harrisburg. The road which led off to the south of Bertram's Shop was a farm lane that connected the Tupelo Road with the Valley Road, and coming up the lane were the troopers of Edmund Rucker's Confederate brigade.[11]

Several hundred yards south of the Tupelo Road, Rucker directed his men off the road and into a line of battle. Duff's 8th Mississippi was on the left, Duckworth's 7th Tennessee on the right, and Chalmers's 18th Mississippi coming up in support. The men dismounted and came quietly through the brush and tall grass. In front of Duff the 14th Wisconsin had taken in their flankers to extend their line of wagon guards, which left no one to warn of the Confederate approach. On the right, while the 7th Minnesota and 12th Iowa were resting in the shade, vigilant flankers were out in the brush. The southerners could just make out the white covers of the wagons rolling by on the road.[12]

At 2:00 P.M. Sgt. William Tucker of the 14th Wisconsin was marching on the right side of the Fourth Brigade's wagon train. The gap between the Third and Fourth brigades was about closed, and just ahead he could see the men of the 7th Minnesota relaxing in the shade and finishing their lunch. He recalled how then "all at once, bang, bang, whiz, whiz came the minnie balls thick and fast." Duff's men had taken advantage of the high grass and attacked with virtually no warning. The few men guarding the wagons fell back to the far side of the road and disappeared into the trees. Within moments the Confederates were among the wagons shooting the braying, panic-stricken mules. Several of the teamsters panicked as well and tried to escape the attack by passing around the disabled wagons in their front, in the process whipping the mules mercilessly and crashing several wagons into each other as well as the trees along the road.[13]

Further up the road Duckworth's Tennesseans were not so lucky. The flankers of the 7th Minnesota had discovered the Confederates and given a warning before they ran to the safety of their regiment on the Tupelo Road. The 7th Tennessee halted and unleashed a crashing volley, wounding several northerners. Surgeon Lucius Smith, a conspicuous target in a wide straw hat, was hit in the neck, the bullet cutting the carotid artery and killing him almost instantly. The Minnesotans formed a single-file line along the right side of the road and began to return the heavy fire pouring into their ranks. To the left of the 7th

Minnesota the 12th Iowa waited silently in the thick undergrowth as its own flankers ran back to the road. Col. John Stibbs allowed the Confederates to approach to within twenty paces before "suddenly pour[ing] a sweeping volley full in their ranks. This threw them into confusion."[14]

The continuous enemy fire reminded Chaplain Edwards of "the long roll beaten on a tenor drum." Aside from the light skirmishing on the Ripley road this was the first real small-arms fire he had ever experienced. "The bullets whistled through the trees like a storm of hail, some coming unpleasantly near." Having wandered away from his regiment while his 7th Minnesotans relaxed and waited for the rest of the column to catch up and feeling particularly exposed on a white horse, he was at a complete loss as to what he should do. He spurred his horse back down the road and soon came on a familiar face. Capt. John Kennedy of Company F and Albert Stevens and Company B were hurriedly escorting the threatened wagons up the road. Edwards chased after them, catching up at the bend in the road. Kennedy and his men were breathing hard, and it took a few minutes before he could tell the chaplain that he had been ordered to lead the wagons to safety while the other eight companies of the 7th Minnesota had been sent into the woods to drive away the enemy. Still unsure of what to do, Edwards turned and once more led his horse through the gauntlet of fire, searching for his regiment. What he found was Sgt. Maj. Orin Richardson lying in the middle of the road "moaning piteously." A bullet was buried in his heel, and since Edwards's duties included caring for the wounded, he stopped to aid the stricken soldier.[15]

The 14th Wisconsin had run into the woods at the start of the action but had not run away. Lt. Col. James Polleys rallied his regiment, and the men who had been spread out in detachments of twenty-five came together and formed a ragged line of 200 rifles, still well outnumbered by Duff's 8th Mississipppi. "They had us at a great disadvantage," acknowledged Sgt. Bill Tucker. But Mower and Ward had heard the firing, and help was on the way.[16]

Col. Fred Lovell's 33rd Wisconsin was still marching to the relief of Bouton's brigade when the fighting commenced. Bouton's crisis had passed, and the new clash of arms took Ward's full attention. He ordered Lovell's command to make an about-face and "at the double-quick" ran them back to their former place in the line. As they approached the fight, Lovell ordered his forward companies off the road and into position behind the rail fence on the west end of the field. This movement placed the 33rd Wisconsin at a right angle to the road and directly on Duff's exposed left flank. Duff's men scattered a few shots at them, but the men of the 33rd reached the cover of the rail fence and from there unleashed "a murderous fire" on the Mississippians.

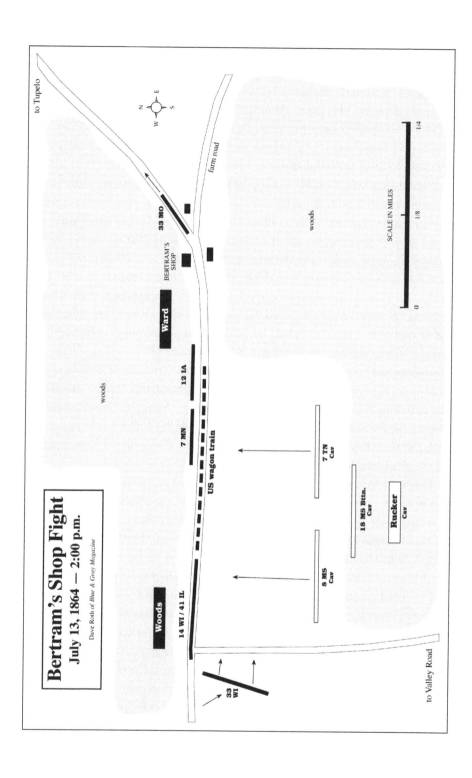

Bertram's Shop Fight
July 13, 1864 — 2:00 p.m.

Dave Roth of Blue & Gray Magazine

to Tupelo

N E S W

farm road

woods

SCALE IN MILES

0   1/8   1/4

33 MO

BERTRAM'S SHOP

Ward

woods

12 IA

7 MN

US wagon train

7 TN
Cav

18 MS Bttn.
Cav

Rucker
Cav

8 MS
Cav

Woods

14 WI / 41 IL

33
WI

to Valley Road

Ward rode back and forth behind the line directing volleys from first the right wing and then the left.[17]

A score of Duff's men fell, including Duff, who left the field with a severe wound in the arm. When Lt. William Barr, who carried the regimental battle flag into the fray, fell, the flagstaff became wedged between the rails on the north side of the fence, holding the banner upright throughout the engagement. The 7th Tennessee's attack had ground to a halt, and they were unable to help Duff's men. Maj. Charles C. Clay, still recovering from a head wound received at Okolona, went down with a second dangerous gunshot wound. The tide had shifted, and Rucker's men were in trouble.[18]

Colonel Ward saw that the time was right to put an end to the fight and ordered Polleys's 14th Wisconsin to charge from the road and push the Confederates back through the field, "which he did in fine style." Capt. Menomen O'Donnell of Ward's staff rushed over to Colonel Marshall of the 7th Minnesota with an order for them to charge the enemy as well. "This was promptly done, the line charging at the double quick across an old field." The men of the 33rd continued to pour a hot fire into the Confederates, who were beginning to fall back. Lt. John Reed, a member of Ward's staff, had his eyes on the 8th Mississippi's battle flag and rode back and forth shouting "Hurrah! Hurrah! A stand of colors for the Thirty-third!" Others saw the flag and wanted the trophy as well. Lt. Col. Stibbs of the 12th wanted to take the colors, but he was ordered farther up the line and was unable to send anyone into the field. Capt. Carlos Mansfield of the 14th Wisconsin cut a mule loose from one of the damaged wagons, swung up on its back, and urged his company forward. To the anguish and anger of the 33rd Wisconsin, Mansfield rode up the rail fence and plucked the flag up and waved it over his head. For years the veterans of the 33rd Wisconsin claimed that the 14th had stolen the trophy that was rightfully theirs. Later in the day the flag was inspected and found to have been pierced by thirteen bullets.[19]

The fight was over, and General Chalmers ordered his men back. "Superior numbers forced us to retire." It was a hasty withdrawal, and Chalmers had to leave his dead and severely wounded on the field temporarily: 47 men of the 8th Mississippi and an unknown number of casualties from the 7th Tennessee, though Sgt. Richard Hancock admitted that "the loss to the command in this brush was severe." On the Union side, J. J. Woods's brigade suffered 2 killed and 27 wounded, and Ward reported another 14 wounded.[20]

Mower arrived at the scene and directed Ward to get the damaged wagons sorted out and the column moving again. The soldiers moved supplies out of the broken wagons and unhitched the mules. Eight wagons were badly damaged, and once their wheels and other useable parts were removed they were burned.

Captain Carter of the 7th Minnesota blamed the loss on "the cowardice of the drivers ('levee rats' from St. Louis), who cut the traces and tried to get away."

Once the last of the Federals had left the field and passed beyond Bertram's Shop, Chalmers returned to the scene to tend to his wounded and bury his dead. The seriously injured were taken to the Brame plantation house, which was pressed into service as a hospital. Before long Forrest arrived with his force, and Chalmer's men fell into line with his comrades still harassing the Union rear.[21]

Just as Chalmers's attempt to strike the flank had failed, Forrest's rear-guard attacks had been blunted without too much effort. Confederate hopes to break the Union column shifted to Buford's division, which had followed Chalmers east on the Valley Road. When Chalmers had veered off to the north toward Bertram's Shop, Buford, with Bell's and Crossland's brigades, marched on to Calhoun's Crossroads, two miles west of Verona. Buford was running out of time. The sun was getting lower in the western sky, and Smith's infantry was beginning to enter Harrisburg, a mere two miles from Tupelo. He knew that if he was going to strike at Smith's flank, it had to be done immediately.

At the heart of Calhoun's Crossroads stood the elegant mansion of Dr. William H. Calhoun, nephew of noted South Carolina politician and U.S. vice president John C. Calhoun. From there, a road led north two miles to a crossing over Coonewah Creek and another half-mile to a junction with the Tupelo–Pontotoc Road and then continued as the Chesterville Road. Because travelers headed for the town of Camargo took this route, it was often referred to as Camargo Crossroads. If there were to be any hope of striking the Federal column short of Tupelo it would have to there.[22]

The Confederates in Buford's column caught a break as a result of Rucker's attack at Bertram's Shop. Mower's division had come to a halt, spread out over three miles of the road. The Federals lost time loading the wounded into ambulances and clearing away the damaged wagons. When the column again got under way, Mower ordered the wagons to move to the front of the division while the infantry maintained its positions, standing by watching the wagons roll by. The delay had bought Buford a full hour in which to get his two brigades into position, but they were still making their way north from Calhoun's when the Federal column lurched back into motion.[23]

Buford rode near the front of the Confederate column. Lt. Mercer Otey, a member of Forrest's staff, described the impressive figure:

> Buford presented a queer appearance, either mounted or afoot. He weighed
> something over three hundred pounds, of powerful frame, a round, ruddy
> face, covered with a short, stubby, red beard, dressed in brown butternut Ken-

tucky jeans, his pants invariably stuck in his boots, he was the most perfect picture of the Jack of Clubs. With all his weight he was the most graceful dancer I ever saw swing a lady on the light fantastic.

Chaplain James McNeilly of the 49th Tennessee Infantry described him more succinctly: "He was a big man on a big horse. He looked as big as the proverbial 'skinned elephant.'" Though he was easily twice the size of the average trooper, what really set Buford apart was his relationship with his commander: he was among that small number of West Point–trained officers Forrest respected, let alone trusted.[24]

Abraham Buford was born in Woodford County, Kentucky, in 1820 to a family well known for breeding racehorses. When he was seventeen he entered the U.S. Military Academy and graduated next to the last in the class of 1841. Such a low standing should have consigned him to the ranks of the infantry, but Second Lieutenant Buford somehow wrangled a spot in the 1st Dragoons, the same regiment as A. J. Smith. Buford earned a brevet as captain at Buena Vista during the Mexican War but resigned his commission in 1854 to return home to raise horses and cattle. When the war broke out he tried to remain as neutral as his home state, which didn't last too long for either of them. In the fall of 1862, when Braxton Bragg's Army of Tennessee entered the state, Buford cast his lot with the Confederacy, unlike his two cousins, John and Napoleon, who became Union generals. He raised and led a brigade of Kentucky cavalry but in early 1863 was transferred to Mississippi and the command of an infantry brigade. He served nearly a year as a foot soldier until he was transferred in March 1864 to Forrest's corps and the command of a division. His superior performance at Brice's Crossroads cemented his bond with his commander.[25]

It was nearly five in the afternoon when Buford's lead brigade under Tyree Bell splashed across Coonewah Creek and dismounted. Buford was optimistic about breaking the Union column and capturing some of the wagons. He rode among the men, telling them, "Boys, do not kill the mules, but turn them down this way." The dismounted troopers began the half-mile march to the road junction with Col. Clark Barteau's 2nd Tennessee in the lead.[26]

On the Tupelo Road Mower's division had finally resumed the march, with the last few wagons just passing the 93rd Indiana Infantry, the lead regiment. Mower assigned the protection of the trains to Col. David Moore's Third Division, which had halted at Harrisburg three miles up the road. William McMillen's First Brigade marched through the muddied waters of Coonewah Creek and on through the Camargo Crossroads. For some reason the 2nd Iowa Artillery was bumped up from the head of Wilkin's brigade and placed ahead of the 114th Illinois, the rear regiment in McMillen's command. For whatever reason the move was made it would prove fortuitous.

The mood was light, and despite the hot weather the men seemed to be enjoying the march. "The boys were talking pretty loud. An occasional snatch of a song could be heard, and again a loud peal of laughter would begin at one end of the company at a bright jest of one of our wits, to be taken up as often as repeated to the other." On the left of the road was a large open field recently used by the Confederates as their camp for the dismounted cavalry. On the right side was a large field planted with corn but long ago stripped of any ears.[27]

At just past 5:00 P.M., Barteau's dismounted Tennesseans began to deploy on the right side of the lane and parallel with the Tupelo Road. The unsuspecting men of McMillen's brigade were only a few hundred yards north. Content with the regiment's position, Buford turned to direct the 15th Tennessee to fall in on Barteau's left. Only two of Col. Robert Russell's companies had taken their place when, without warning, Barteau's line surged forward. The 15th Tennessee was not yet deployed, and the 16th and 19th were still strung out down the road. Whether through a misunderstanding of orders or the impulsiveness of the men, the 2nd Tennessee made an unsupported charge against two brigades of Federal infantry. Providentially, they hit a weak spot in the Federal line.[28]

Lt. Joseph Reed's 2nd Iowa Battery had crossed the creek and was approaching the crossroads when he was met by his first sergeant, John Coons. Coons was concerned. While riding up ahead checking on the battery wagons, he had noticed Confederates lurking in the woods no more than 300 yards south of the road. Reed shared this information with the brigade commander, McMillen, who assured his lieutenant that "he had a regiment deployed on that flank which would protect his column from surprise." But the flankers McMillen was depending on were the men of the 72nd Ohio, who were only five yards from the road and in no position to give warning if the enemy attacked. The nearest infantry to the west was the 114th Illinois, which had just crossed the creek and was still some distance behind. The small regiment numbered no more than 150 men, the ranks thinned down from 411 at Brice's Crossroads.[29]

Barteau's regiment was within fifty yards of the road before it stopped and delivered a crashing volley. Unfortunately for the Confederates, they directed their volley between the two-gun section of the 1st Illinois Light Artillery and the flankers of the 72nd Ohio Infantry and so did relatively little damage. Captain Reed called his battery to halt and saw squads of the 72nd break for the woods "as fast as their legs would carry them." McMillen's brigade, Reed explained, "had been with Sturges, and it is probable the men had not yet recovered their nerve. The situation was extremely critical." But if the men of the

72nd Ohio lost their nerve they found it again just moments later when they and the 95th Ohio formed a line on the road and stood their ground, returning Barteau's fire. At the head of McMillen's line the 93rd Indiana continued forward with the last of the wagons, while the troopers in the 10th Minnesota stopped to assist their comrades. McMillen's left was secure.[30]

The right of the line, however, was in trouble. When the first volley from the 2nd Tennessee came crashing through the woods, Orin Cram's section of Battery E, 1st Illinois, was caught in the open. The lack of cover scared Cram, though, with the old dismounted camp on his left and the cornfield to his right, he was actually in an excellent position, with plenty of room to maneuver and a clear field of fire. With no infantry support closer than the 72nd Ohio, and the enemy only fifty yards away, Cram ordered his pair of 12-pounders to continue down the road at the double quick. Reed watched Cram's flight in amazement— "He attempted to carry his section across the whole front of the enemy." Having run the gauntlet, Cram brought his guns in on the right of the 72nd and tried to bring the weapons into position. But the road had narrowed, and the trees lining it obstructed his movements. Lewis Philips of the 2nd Iowa could see that "the section of artillery was badly demoralized and could do nothing." The horses attached to one of Cram's caissons bolted in terror and turned toward the enemy. But before they could run more than a few feet, all six horses were shot down by the Confederates. The panicked gunners placed one of the artillery pieces into position and began a rapid fire with canister on the enemy. However, when bringing up the second gun, one of the wheel horses (the pair closest to the limber) was shot and killed; and as it fell and twisted in the traces, the whole assembly of limber, gun, and horses went awry, and the gun carriage overturned.[31]

"If Bell had followed his volley with a rush," admitted Reed, "he could have captured the section and seized the road, for there was a wide gap in the column behind McMillen." As for Reed, he was in an excellent position to confront the attacking Confederates. Barteau's exposed left flank (the two companies of Russell's 15th Tennessee) was no more than fifty yards from the road, though somewhat shielded by the rail fence around the cornfield. The enemy apparently paid no attention to anything except the road in their immediate front, which allowed Reed to place his four Napoleons in the road facing south. Private Phillips, who stood by with his lanyard and friction primers, recalled how "Captain Reed now turned around and gave his order in a low, distinct voice: 'In battery left oblique, fire with canister, load.' This order pointed the guns sharply to the left, a position we had never taken before in battle."[32]

The first volley of canister sent 108 iron balls tearing into the Confederate flank from a range of only seventy-five yards. As fast as they could, the gunners sponged the smoking tubes and rammed home another load of the deadly shot. The artillerymen were too busy to notice that the 114th Illinois Infantry had closed the distance and formed a solid line behind the guns. And from the end of Wilkin's line the detachments of the 8th Wisconsin and 5th Minnesota double-timed up the road and fell in on the right of the 114th, which extended the lines and ended any hope of a Confederate success.[33]

What had seemed like a golden opportunity only minutes before had turned disastrous for Bell's brigade. While Barteau's regiment was being cut to pieces, the balance of the 15th Tennessee finally came up on the left, but it was too little too late. Col. Robert M. Russell, West Point class of 1848, ordered his regiment forward and charged headlong into a solid wall of blue. The men did not gain a foot of ground. The 9th Minnesota had come up between the 114th Illinois and the 8th Wisconsin and began an immediate advance through the cornfield toward Russell's Tennesseans. The 47th Illinois came up on the right of the Minnesota infantry, and the 11th Missouri filed into line behind both regiments to act as a reserve. The small gap Tyree Bell's brigade had found in the Union line was gone and had been replaced by two full brigades of infantry.[34]

There was some confusion as the 9th Minnesota entered the cornfield. Lt. Colonel Josiah Marsh explained how "a small force of the enemy, thirty or forty in number, soon appeared in my front, not more than eight or ten rods distant. We at first took them to be our skirmishers falling back, and they evidently took us to be a portion of their own force." Col. John McClure, commanding the 47th Illinois, saw the enemy as well, but since they were "so much dressed like our own men," he held his fire. Col. Alexander Wilkin reined in his horse behind the 9th Minnesota to get a better look just as the 15th Tennessee was drawing a bead on the 2nd Iowa battery. Yelling out above the noise of the fighting, Wilkin called out for the 9th to fire, and a volley tore through Russell's men. "It is believed that few, if any of this party escaped."[35]

Barteau and Russell could take no more. On their right the 1st Illinois Light Artillery had flipped its second gun right side up, and the Confederates were being bracketed by artillery fire. One Federal regiment had already advanced against them, and several more stood poised to charge. "The result was we were encompassed and cut to pieces," bemoaned Barteau. The 16th and 19th Tennessee, still trying to come up, were met by the 2nd and 15th falling back.[36]

Across the way the Federal artillery fell silent, and the long line of infantry pushed south into the woods and cornfield. The 114th Illinois passed among Reed's four cannon. A portion of Russell's 15th Tennessee made a last-ditch effort to change their front and face the charging 9th Minnesota, but it was to no avail. "Under the storm of iron to which it was exposed," noted Reed, "the

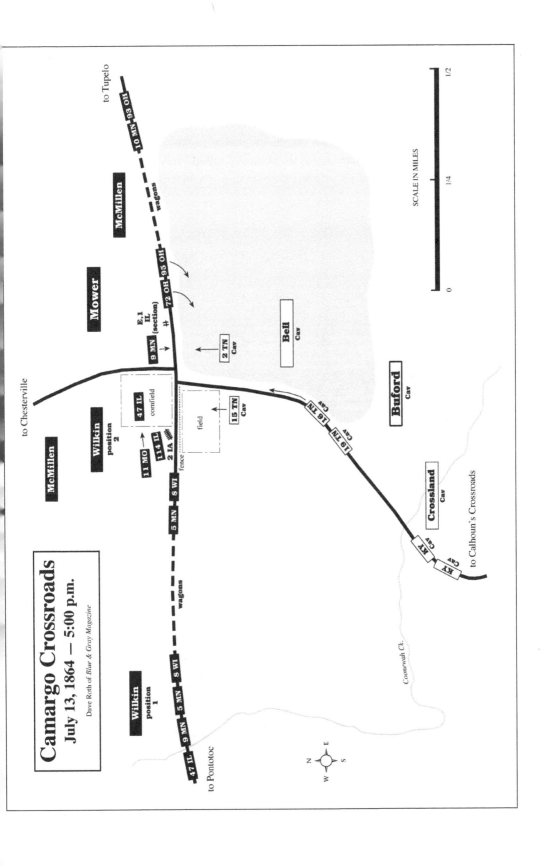

Camargo Crossroads
July 13, 1864 — 5:00 p.m.

Dave Roth of Blue & Gray Magazine

to Chesterville

to Tupelo

10 MN · 93 OH

McMillen

wagons

Mower

72 OH · 95 OH

E, 1
IL
(section)

9 MN

2 TN
Cav

Bell
Cav

McMillen

Wilkin
position
2

47 IL

cornfield

11 MO

114 IL

2 IA

fence

field

15 TN
Cav

8 WI

5 MN

16 TN
Cav

19 TN
Cav

Buford
Cav

Crossland
Cav

KY
Cav

KY
Cav

to Calhoun's Crossroads

Crooewah Ck.

Wilkin
position
1

8 WI

5 MN

9 MN

47 IL

wagons

to Pontotoc

N
E
S
W

SCALE IN MILES

0   1/4   1/2

effort was futile, and in the effort to withdraw the line, the whole force broke in confusion." Too late to assist in the assault, a section of Morton's Tennessee battery unlimbered in support of Bell's withdrawal and began throwing shells into Mower's ranks; its timely arrival undoubtedly saved dozens of men. "These cannon shot came square across the column," noted Phillips. "This made us feel a little lonesome and we wondered where they would strike us next."[37]

ON THE WAY TO TUPELO.

"The men behaved most gallantly, and ran like htroes across the Zone of Death, Page 20.

Battle Field of Tupelo. House of the Tnree Chimneys.

"On the Way to Tupelo" (DePauw University Archives and Special Collections)

The first few rounds from Morton's guns scattered the men on the road, who ran into the woods for protection. The aim was high, but the soldiers were taking no chances. General Mower and his staff were sitting on their horses just off the road cajoling the men, "Boys, what do you duck your heads for? These things never do any harm." The next shot was lower and tore the leg off Pvt. George Blackwell of the 7th Minnesota. Morton's battery was masked by the high corn, and while their fire could not be accurately aimed, the Union soldiers could not see the cannoneers. Chaplain Edwards watched as "a perfect storm of grape and canister shot tore its way through our ranks; shells burst to right, to left, over us and in our lines. Heavier shot ploughed furrows in the road beneath our feet. It did not however stop for an instant the movement of the column forward. The men as a rule behaved most gallantly, and ran like heroes across the storm-swept zone of danger, stepping high as they went."[38]

The men from Bell's brigade made their way back to Coonewah Creek, where they met up with the horse holders and Crossland's Kentucky brigade coming up the road from Calhoun's. The 2nd Tennessee was a wreck. Three captains were down with wounds, one of them mortally, and three lieutenants had fallen as well. Anderson French took a wound thought to be mortal but he eventually pulled through. James Lawrence had to be carried from the field unconscious with heat stroke. Lt. Francis McRee, who was knocked down by a canister round, was so stunned he had to be helped away by his men. Pvt. Monroe Paschal was captured when he surged past his comrades and into the Union lines, where he was forced to surrender. Lt. George Hager of Company G later told how private James Drury, "a noble and brave soldier," had become convinced he would be killed in the next engagement and asked Captain, J. M. Eastes to send his possessions and his horse "to that faithful and loving wife in her lonely home in Tennessee." Hager asked Drury if he wanted to be excused from the next fight. Drury shook his head. He died that afternoon next to the Tupelo Road. A few feet away Captain Eastes was shot down and killed still holding Drury's belongings. Capt. Moses McKnight of Company C miraculously survived his third major wound of the war. Shot in the chest at Okolona, he had refused to leave the field. At Paducah, Kentucky, his skull was fractured when a chimney was hit by a shell, and he was covered in a shower of falling bricks. And on the afternoon of July 13 he was struck by a bullet in the lower right leg, shattering the fibula bone between the ankle and the knee.[39]

There was no count of the Confederate killed and wounded in the official reports other than Buford noting "considerable loss" and Bell stating that his loss was "quite heavy." In a postwar manuscript Clark Barteau related the loss of "some of my best officers and thirty men." Barteau's account gives the impression that his regiment was ordered in without support and that "had the attack been made by all of Buford's division at once at this place, as Forrest was then on the rear, I have reason to believe the enemy would have been thrown into great confusion, and would probably have retreated during the night." One person who did not agree with Barteau's assessment was General Buford. His flank attack had been carried out poorly, he maintained, and only a fraction of his division was in place when the fighting began. In his report he gives credit for his defeat to his former comrade in arms Gen. A. J. Smith. "At no time had I found the enemy unprepared. He marched with his column well closed up, his wagon train well protected, and his flanks covered in an admirable manner, evincing at all times readiness to meet any attack, and showing careful generalship." Thomas Jordan, Forrest's biographer concurs: "Bell's Tennesseans went into action with their accustomed alacrity and courage. But the odds were too heavy, and after considerable loss Buford was compelled to withdraw from the combat."[40]

Buford's wounded were taken south down the road to Calhoun's Crossroads. Officers knew the resident of the home was a doctor, but they were unaware he was nearly bedridden and on the verge of a nervous breakdown. He reacted to their arrival by staggering to a back bedroom and throwing himself across the bed. He told his wife, "I'm done Jane, I can't do it." She quietly responded, "Get up doctor. This is our day." From somewhere deep within he found his courage and soon came out the front door and joined a group of Confederate surgeons and local doctors who were preparing an impromptu surgery in the yard. Men laid planks across wooden benches and the operating commenced. More than 300 wounded were brought in during the afternoon and evening.[41]

The supply train was up on the Pontotoc–Tupelo Road in the vicinity of the old dismounted camp, and no one had thought to bring rations down for the wounded. Not bothering to wait on the army, Mrs. Calhoun put together a stew, throwing every vegetable in the kitchen and springhouse and the children's pet goat into the large wash pot. Neighborhood women brought bowls, pans, anything that would hold stew, and they made sure that every man got a bit of the goat stew. As the sun began to set, several of the women held lanterns over the operating tables so the surgeons could work through the night, while others tore sheets and cloth into bandages.[42]

On the Union side, McMillen reported thirty-five casualties. Col. John McClure of the 47th Illinois ended up writing the report for Wilkin's brigade and made no mention of casualties, though there was at least one killed and a handful wounded. One of the wounded from Wilkin's brigade was young Louis

Phillips of the 2nd Iowa Artillery. In his memoir Phillips invariably wrote in the third person, frequently referring to himself as "our boy."

Our boy was that day acting No. 4. His duty was to fire the gun when it was ready, and one time, while he had his hands close together in front of him in the act of inserting the lanyard hook into the primer ring, a rifle ball struck a tree ten feet to the right of him, glanced off and struck him on the right wrist and cut a ragged gash to the bone. Then he knew how rebel lead felt, but he paid no attention to this until the little squabble was over with, when he noticed he was bleeding quite freely. Then he wrapped his wrist with his handkerchief and let it go at that.[43]

McMillen was delighted with his brigade's performance, commending them "for the gallantry with which they met the enemy and the handsome manner in which he was repulsed." He and Mower both took a few moments to praise the 114th Illinois, which had been so prompt in coming up to support the 2nd Iowa Artillery. Harrison Chandler's diary entry bragged, "Commander of Brig. [and] Div. complemented our regiment. Commander of Brig. Says we 'saved the day.'" The historian of the 47th Illinois Infantry laid the success of the engagement solely on the shoulders of Lieutenant Reed and his cannoneers: "The 2nd Iowa battery was doing terrible execution. Lieutenant Joseph Reed, ever cool and intrepid inspired his men with the same qualities and they manned their guns earnestly and well." Reed recalled that the battery was "engaged on many fields, but it never rendered a more important service than on that occasion." Perhaps the praise went to his head, as he also claimed that "the fight was ours. Not another organization or man fired a shot in repulsing the attack." There were plenty of men in the two brigades who could dispute such an unfounded claim.[44]

The Federals loaded their dead and wounded into ambulances, and the column of the First Division lurched into motion once again. It was 6:00 P.M., but the men didn't have much farther to march. A. J. Smith had found the ground he was looking for two miles west of Tupelo at the little town of Harrisburg.

TWELVE

Harrisburg

Harrisburg, Mississippi, was a dying town even before the Federals arrived, though it was still relatively young. The little crossroads village was named for Judge W. R. Harris, a local planter who provided the land for the blossoming community. The first resident was a shopkeeper named George C. Thomason, who opened his doors for business in 1847. Three years later another merchant opened a small store, and three years after that a third shop made wares available to local residents. These were the boom years for Harrisburg. The hamlet grew to include a Methodist Church, a Masonic hall, a saddler, a blacksmith, a justice of the peace, a hotel, a school, and a scattering of homes. At its greatest the population never exceeded 100 residents.

Harrisburg's death knell was neither the roar of the cannon nor the crash of a rifle but, instead, the whistle of the steam locomotive. In 1860 the tracks of the Mobile & Ohio Railroad were laid two miles to the east, where the town of Tupelo sprang into existence. Harrisburg became a suburb of Tupelo and then dwindled into insignificance when most of the residents made the two-mile move to the burgeoning railroad town. Named for the Tupelo Gum trees found in the area, the town was founded near land long claimed by the Chickasaw Indians. Not far away was the battlefield of Achia, the site of a 1736 victory of the Chickasaw Nation over the French under Bienville. Old lead musket balls, bayonets, and arrowheads could still be found in the fields. For generations the native Chickasaw had used a nearby trail later known as the Natchez Trace, a path frequently used by boatmen and farmers traversing the overland route between Natchez, Mississippi, and Nashville, Tennessee.[1]

Tupelo had not been given much of a chance to get off the ground. The town had not yet incorporated when the war came, bringing with it tens of thousands of soldiers and scaring away many of the residents. The people who stayed watched in fascination as train after train brought soldiers up from the Deep South in March 1862, but that fascination turned to horror in April when those same trains returned filled with wounded men from the Battle of Shiloh. In the wake of the Siege of Corinth in May 1862, Gen. Pierre G. T. Beauregard had retreated south to Tupelo with his Army of Mississippi and pressed the homes and buildings into service as hospitals, headquarters, and warehouses. Aside from a few Federal raids passing through, Tupelo had been in Confederate hands throughout the war.[2]

On July 13, as the fighting sputtered to a close near Camargo Crossroads, Tyree Bell ordered his battered brigade to fall back beyond Coonewah Creek and form a defensive line. The enemy, intent on resuming the march, did not pursue. As the men from Tennessee slowly fell into ranks, Crossland's Kentucky brigade finally arrived from Calhoun's Crossroads. Crossland had been expecting to assist in the flank attack only to find the assault had been made without his regiments. "When I arrived Bell's brigade was falling back in confusion. I dismounted, formed line, and covered his retreat, and awaited an attack from the enemy." Bell reformed his brigade on Crossland's line, and Buford's division was ready for whatever might come down the road. But nothing did.

Mower's Federals were again moving east. Col. W. W. Faulkner's 12th Kentucky was sent forward by Crossland as skirmishers and came into contact with the 7th Kansas Cavalry bringing up Smith's rear. Before Faulkner could organize an attack, Mabry's Brigade came up the road from Pontotoc driving the Kansans away from the crossroads. General Lee arrived at the crossroads at sundown and called a halt to all Confederate activities as Chalmers's and Buford's divisions reunited at the old dismounted cavalry camp.[3]

Forrest and Lee met to discuss the day's disappointments and determine the next step. And there were the wounded to tend to. Those who could ride were helped onto their mounts and led two miles down the Verona Road to the Calhoun place; others were treated on the scene until ambulances could be brought up. The men in the ranks took the opportunity to unsaddle and feed their horses, and only when that was done did they tend to their own needs. The day that had seemed cool to the Federals was remembered as being brutally hot by the Confederates. Many men had fallen out of ranks and straggled into camp over the next several hours. The footsore dismounted cavalrymen were still miles away but had reached the end of their strength. General Lyon called a halt, with plans to resume the march at midnight.[4]

In Harrisburg the Union infantry was in far better condition at the end of their day's march. But they were no less tired and looked forward to a night's rest. It had been the longest march of the campaign, but they had become accustomed to the heat and the marching and had finished the day without any straggling. Smith would have probably continued the march on to Tupelo, where the cavalry was busy destroying the tracks, had he not noticed the defensive qualities of the land around Harrisburg. It was just what he was looking for. The Tupelo Road rose to the crest of a modest ridge, made a short jog to the northeast, and then continued east on a low extension of the ridge. The approach to Harrisburg from the west was an assortment of fields, several sown in corn and the others thick with weeds. The ground was rolling and broken but offered little to no cover. There were a few patches of woods on the north and south side of the road, but enemy approaching from the west would be exposed for a minimum of 200 yards and in most places for up to a mile. It only took a moment for Smith to make a crucial decision: "I immediately passed the train to the front through the First Division and parked it about two miles west of Tupelo, at the same time forming line of battle with the Third Division on the left of the road."[5]

The men of Col. Charles Murray's brigade had seen no action during the march and, other than a few dead Confederates left by Grierson's cavalry, had seen little sign of men fighting and dying throughout the day. The first infantry to enter Harrisburg, they situated themselves south of the road along the low concave ridge. Murray's line extended farther south to the edge of a creek bottom lined with willows. To its front were open fields and behind it was a cool, shaded wood. The wagon trains made their way past the infantry and came to a halt two miles from Tupelo in a huge field on the south side of the road. The ground to the east sloped off to King's Creek, and the teamsters unhitched the animals and took them down to the water for a long drink.[6]

Next came Col. James Gilbert's Second Brigade, which had also had an easy day. A man in the 14th Iowa had heard the fighting in the rear and supposed it was General Mower "teaching the rebels not to encroach on land he was occupying. He was always a little particular about his rights." The brigade marched into the field where the trains were parked and bivouacked between the wagons and a small peach orchard on the west side of the field. (The orchard was a welcome sight to the men of the 3rd Indiana Battery; they had managed to forage some corn and watermelon and were pleased to add peaches to the evening's menu.) Then "the ambulances began to pour in with wounded & the chief surgeon ordered the hospital to be established right by us & the groans of the poor fellows was sorrowful indeed. We soon concluded there was no sleep for us if we remained there & we moved head quarters."[7]

Edward Wolfe's Third Brigade brought up the rear of Moore's division and filed off the road to the right. It took a position in the woods beyond the creek on Murray's left. The bulk of the regiment set up its meager camp in the woods while the 117th Illinois advanced to "a splendid position on some hills," where its men served as pickets for the brigade. The remainder of the brigade and the division set up their camps not near water and shade but in a long continuous line. Louis Hucke of the 117th told his diary, "Throughout the night we laid low in the line of battle, 1 mile from Tupelo."[8]

For the next several hours, the men of Mower's First Division made their way into Harrisburg and filed into their camps on the north side of the road. McMillen's brigade was first into town and positioned itself on the heights facing north, where a cornfield separated them from the upper reaches of King's Creek. The site suited Lt. Henry McConnel of the 10th Minnesota, who described it as "a fine position on an elevation covered with woods with an open field in our front and on both flanks."[9]

Col. Alexander Wilkin's Second Brigade followed, and his five regiments found a nice campsite in a small hollow between the road and McMillen's brigade. The pugnacious colonel, just over five feet tall and barely a hundred pounds with his uniform on, saw to his men's needs and then set a guard about the camp. A Yale lawyer and president of the St. Paul Fire and Marine Insurance Company, Wilkin was an outstanding soldier. He was a captain in the Mexican War and one of the first sons of Minnesota to volunteer after Fort Sumter fell. He had seen combat at Bull Run, Mill Springs, and Corinth. He was also one of the few officers to come out of the Brice's Crossroads fight with both his brigade and his reputation intact. His men had seen no fighting during the march from Pontotoc, and they were ready to make up for it in the morning.[10]

Close on the heels of the Second Brigade came Joseph Woods's Third Brigade. Fresh from their fight with Tyree Bell's Tennesseans, they were dirty, tired, and hungry—but proud of their day's work. Mower selected an important piece of real estate for the four regiments and placed Woods's left on the Tupelo Road, where it made its turn to the northeast. It was an admirable location, sitting on high ground overlooking the remnants of Harrisburg with wide fields open to their front. If the Confederates followed the Tupelo Road, they would have to face the Third Brigade

The last of Mower's brigades, Ward's Fourth, arrived at Harrisburg well after dark and found its campsite (which had been reserved for them) on the ridge between McMillen's and Woods's brigades. Sgt. William Tucker of the 14th Wisconsin described the site as "a long ridge sparsely covered with scattering trees and faced a large opening of cotton and corn fields, on the other side was heavy timber. This opening was from half a mile to a mile wide." The brigade strutted into camp displaying the colors of Duff's 8th Mississippi Cavalry. The flag drew so much attention it prompted young James Newton to write, "I really believe we are getting to be notorious."[11]

Bouton's Colored Brigade arrived at 9:00 P.M., the last of the infantry, and went into bivouac on the far left of the army beyond Moore's division. Not quite as desirable as the campsites claimed by the brigades arriving earlier, the brigade's camp was on high ground south of the small creek and the willow bottoms, with open fields to the left and the rear and the front and right covered with thick oak brush. Vigilance would be necessary lest the enemy approach unobserved from the south.[12]

Bringing up the rear was the 7th Kansas Cavalry. Along with the Jayhawkers came a battalion of the 4th Iowa Cavalry that had been ordered out to assist in pushing back the Confederates when the pressure from Forrest was its greatest. By the time Lt. Col. Peters and his men had backtracked to the rear guard, the line had stabilized, and they were not called on to help. At 11:00 P.M. the last of Smith's men passed through the lines and into their camps. An exhausted Sergeant Pomeroy of the 7th Kansas managed to stay awake long enough to make a detailed diary entry of the day's activities: "Our horses got no feed and the men were too tired to get supper."[13]

With the army gathered, most of the men tucked in for the night. But not all. Forrest was still out there somewhere, and no one—least of all A. J. Smith—had forgotten it. Each regiment lay in the line of battle, with the wagon trains situated securely behind the center of the line and reserves camped nearby to assist if any part of the line called for assistance. Cavalry guarded the army's flanks and the rear. To ensure that there were no surprises, a strong force of infantry pickets advanced beyond the main line, with cavalry videttes posted even farther out. Three companies each from the 3rd and 4th Iowa Cavalry were selected for the job. One of the unhappy troopers chosen for this duty was Jacob Gantz of the 4th Iowa Cavalry, who had been looking forward to a good night's sleep: "We went out on the Pontotoc Road 2 miles, placed the companies around in the best position could be done to prevent the enemy coming in, then sent out videttes to alarm us of any approaching enemy & the rest of us dismounted & held our horses until morning."[14] And there was considerable activity in the makeshift hospitals. "Camp was reached at a late hour," recalled Aurelius Bartlett of the 11th Missouri Infantry, "and it was about 11 o'clock at

night when our labors with the wounded began; and daylight on the next morning when the last wound was dressed." A surgeon, Bartlett worked throughout
the night, treating more than seventy men. "When I sat down on the morning
of the 14th, the thought occurred to me that I had not taken a moments rest, or
been off my feet during the entire night. I have often wondered what became of
those severely wounded men and the question has presented itself—are any of
them still living?"[15]

Confederate scouts watched the Federals bed down for the night on the
heights beyond Harrisburg. They could see the hundreds of campfires flicker-
ing in the distance and observed the pickets and videttes taking their positions.
As the darkness of night fell over the landscape, the scouts pulled back to inform General Forrest of their observations.[16]

The report from the scouts was too vague to suit Forrest. How were the
enemy posted—in lines of battle or in camps? What was the location of the
artillery and cavalry? Were they sleeping or building breastworks? Were they
vigilant? These were questions needing answers before he could make decisions
or make suggestions to General Lee. So he ordered Mabry to rouse his men
from their slumber and direct them to saddle up. The Mississippians walked
their horses down the Tupelo Road in the direction of Harrisburg, stopping
in the woods well short of the wide fields. Skirmishers went out cautiously to
determine if the enemy was watchful. They were. Light firing broke out up
and down the line. But if Mabry and Forrest had hoped to develop the enemy
forces with the threat of a night attack, they were sorely disappointed. The
Federal pickets did not fall back to their main line, which remained quiet and
untroubled. The four guns of Morton's Tennessee battery that accompanied
Mabry were unlimbered to have a go at the enemy, firing several rounds at the
high ground hoping to draw a response from the Union artillery. The only
response from the Federals was a few diary entries noting how the sound of the
artillery disturbed their sleep. The Union batteries stood silent, their positions
remaining a mystery.[17]

The lack of information troubled Forrest. His success as a commander had
always been based on observing the enemy and exploiting any and all weak-
nesses. In this he had few peers. But he had thrown his men at Smith's rear and
flank and could find no soft spot, no flaw. To make matters worse, the enemy
had failed to panic, as they always had in the past. "Putting the skeer" on
the enemy and "keeping the bulge on 'em," maintaining continuous pressure,
were the hallmarks of Forrest's style of warfare. For this method to be effective, it required a bit of a bluff, some showmanship, and the ability to bring
overwhelming and continuous firepower on key enemy positions. It was also

necessary for the enemy to lose heart and break ranks. Despite the best efforts of Forrest and his men, this had not happened so far.[18]

If there was to be any chance of success the following day, Forrest knew that he had to find a weakness. The greater numbers of the Federals could be overcome, just as they had at Okolona and Brice's Crossroads, if he could determine Smith's Achilles' heel. Mabry's dismounted cavalry and Morton's guns had not found the weakness; in fact, they had not even been able to determine the enemy's position.

Forrest went to Lee's headquarters to confer and plan. He found the general seated on the ground with his back against the trunk of a tree. Nearby was John Morton, the youthful artillery chief who observed the scene with interest. It had been a long day. The heat had yet to ease and the night was hot and sultry; the humidity was stifling. Forrest eased down from the saddle quite slowly; his boils had been bothering him again. He pulled off his uniform coat and spread it on the ground next to Lee, rolled up his shirtsleeves, and stretched out under the branches. He lay still, but his mind was racing. He needed more information. With no warning he suddenly rose up, put his coat back on and swung back up on his horse. He called for Lt. Samuel Donelson, and the two men rode off into the night. Forrest decided he would do his own reconnaissance.[19]

Morton wrote much later about the evening scouting trip, based on Lt. Donelson's account.

They made a wide detour through the woods. General Forrest remarked to Lieutenant Donelson that his scouts brought in word that the Union forces were encamped about a mile ahead. He also stated that he had neglected to put on his holster, and was therefore without his pistols. Lieutenant Donelson offered him one, but it was declined, General Forrest saying he did not think they would be needed. In about an hour they came up well within the rear of the Federal lines, and soon found themselves among the wagons and teams. The friendly darkness concealed the Confederate uniforms, and, keeping well away from the camp fires, the two daring officers rode leisurely through nearly every portion of the enemy's camp. Having satisfied himself of the position and resources of the enemy, General Forrest turned in the direction of his own camp. They had proceeded about two hundred yards when they were suddenly halted by two Federal soldiers who were on picket duty. Riding directly up to these men, General Forrest, affecting intense anger, said, "How dare you halt your commanding officer?" and without further remark put spurs to his horse, an example quickly followed by Lieutenant Donelson. The sentries did not discover the ruse until the two horsemen were some distance away, and on account of the darkness could not now be seen. Anticipating that they would be challenged, General Forrest and Lieutenant Donelson crouched down upon their horses, put spurs to them, and broke into a full gallop along the narrow roadway through the woods. The pickets fired, but the bullets fell wide of the mark, and the two officers returned in safety to their own camp.

General Forrest related this occurrence with great gusto, declaring jocosely that a bullet might have done him some good, as it might have opened one of his boils, which would have been a relief.[20]

It was an incredible exploit, a singular act of daring and bravery. And yet the vast majority of the details could have only occurred in the mind of Lieutenant Donelson. Forrest never spoke of such a dangerous ride, though he and Donelson did in fact carry out a reconnaissance. In his official report he merely noted, "At a late hour in the night, accompanied by one of my staff officers, I approached Harrisburg and discovered the enemy strongly posted and prepared to give battle the next day." And in their biography of Forrest, which the general read, Thomas Jordan and J. P. Pryor describe how

> Major General A. J. Smith immediately set his troops to improving, as far as practicable, during the night, by breastworks made of rails and logs, and the materials of cabins and outhouses, torn down for that purpose, and covered with earth. This was discovered by General Forrest in a reconnaissance, which, accompanied by Lieutenant Sam Donelson, of his staff, he made about midnight, to within fifty yards of the Federal position, riding along and reconnoitering the lines for nearly a mile.

There was no talk of a leisurely ride through the enemy camps or of "the position and resources of the enemy." In fact, the details of the scout, which Donelson claimed Forrest laughed and bragged about, were never recorded by any of his men until Robert Selph Henry published the embellished account in 1907. Since then it has become a widely accepted anecdote furthering the Forrest mystique.

Even if the story were true, which it most certainly is not, Forrest failed to share the intelligence with his commanding officer. Had Lee and Forrest known the position of Smith's infantry and artillery, they would have repositioned their troops in preparation for the morning's activities. Indeed, had they known in advance of any earthworks or breastworks, they would have likely called off the attack. As it really was, Forrest's only orders after his scouting trip were for General Buford to relieve Mabry's tired troopers with the Kentuckians of Crossland's brigade.[21]

Jordan and Pryor's subdued narrative of the late-night reconnaissance also took a few liberties with the facts, though not on the scale of Donelson's. The account of the Federal breastworks, "made of rails and logs, and the materials of cabins and outhouses, torn down for that purpose and covered with earth," was a good description of the defenses the Confederates found *after* the battle. On the night of the 13th and in the early hours of the 14th the enemy was engaged in a far less threatening activity than building earthworks; they were sleeping.[22]

Interestingly, there are two other accounts of midnight scouts of the Union lines. Pvt. Henry Hord of the 3rd Kentucky Mounted Infantry told a fanciful tale. According to Henry, he and two of his comrades were sent out individually to reconnoiter the enemy position. He was given a Union uniform to wear over the top of his own clothes and told to "bring one pistol if you want to; we are going afoot." The three men were instructed to penetrate the enemy lines and learn as much as they could. "It was a dangerous mission and meant death sure and swift if we were caught."

> As soon as we separated I went to where I was certain the enemy's skirmish line would be, and managed to locate it without being heard or seen. I then crawled up close to the sentinel and waited till the relief came around. The weeds were about as high as oats. When the guard was changed, I heard the countersign given, then I slipped back and went to another sentry, was challenged, gave the countersign, "Grant," bold as brass, told the fellow I had been outside scouting for Gen. Smith, and then, just for devilment, told him the Rebs were out there in the weeds, and he had better keep his eyes "peeled."
>
> I made my way to where I thought Gen. Smith's main line was, and by good luck struck one end of it. They had thrown up breastworks about four feet high, stacked arms, and were all soundly sleeping around the guns. I did not see any guards at all except one sentry in front of a new tent, with a light burning in it; and as that was the only tent I saw, I supposed that it was Gen. Smith's headquarters. I went from one end of the line to the other, got the exact position of each battery, the number of guns, where the negro brigade was, etc. I got out about daylight by doing some of the fastest running a boy ever did.[23]

Hord maintained that he made it back to his own lines in time to brief Forrest, Buford, and their combined staffs. Yet somehow Bedford Forrest neglected to mention this extraordinary intelligence coup in his official report. Nor did he or Crossland or Col. Gustaves A. C. Holt, the 3rd Kentucky's commander— mention the valiant Private Hord.[24]

A third account of a scouting trip that night, the most plausible of the trio, was made by Lt. William Pirtle of the 7th Kentucky Mounted Infantry, who much later wrote out his version of the events he witnessed in the "war of the sixtys."[25] He recalled the evening of July 13 after Lee's army had been reunited at the dismounted cavalry camp, when General Forrest sent a verbal order to Colonel Crossland to send a company "around south of the yanks and establish pickets as near to them as safe and watch their movements just as close as possible." Pirtle was on his horse next to Crossland when the messenger arrived, and he and his Company A were sent out to fulfill the order. The captain led his men south on the road to Calhoun's but cut off the path into the woods to the east before reaching the crossroads. They had gone only a short distance when his and Sgt. Wilson Edwards's horses began to act nervous. The enemy was close. Pirtle and Edwards rode out alone away from the group for a bit and then determined that the best course of action was to return to the road and go south a little further. They returned to find all the men in the company sound asleep. "Wilson and I had a hard job to wake up the boys and get them to understand the situation without making any noise, as we feared any disturbance would bring the yanks upon us and we did not want any fight at that time."

Eventually they got the company moving again and soon reached Calhoun's Crossroads and turned east on the road to Verona. Wherever a road or lane intersected their path, Pirtle left a few men behind as pickets. After two miles he was down to just six men. At the intersection of the next road leading north, he left Lt. B. P. Willingham with three men and proceeded up the road with Sergeant Edwards and a private. Soon the horses became nervous again. Pirtle dismounted, handed his reins to Edwards, and set out on foot through the woods by himself.

[I] ran perhaps two hundred yards came to the field and there sat a yankee on his horse some two hundred yards up the rise in the field. I watched him closely for a time, he seemed to be riding his beat of about two hundred yards a little quartering from where I was at the edge of the bushes.

Saw a tree about a third of the way to the yank, decided I could reach the tree by starting when he would turn his back to me and away I went to the tree, stood against the tree next to him. As I knew it was darker where I was than on top of that hill where he was and as a man cannot see out of light into the dark, knew he could not see me. Here I stood for quite awhile listening to the nois in camp and watching my yank.

I had just about decided in my mind that the yanks were crossing old town creek as the nois sounded just like wagons on a bridge. But became very tired set down to rest a little and about the next I knew it was getting light so I could see the buttons on my yanks coat.

I was now in a dilemma as to what to do, but when he turned his back slipped around the tree and kept it between me and him until I reached the woods, then ran to where I left the boys with my horse.

To his dismay, his horse and his men were gone. Lieutenant Willingham, fearing Pirtle was captured, had returned to Calhoun's, gathering up the pickets along the way. Pirtle walked the two and a half miles back to the crossroads. He was relieved to find his men clustered around the Calhoun place, which was being used a hospital, but by the time he made it back to his regiment the battle was in progress and his information was of little use.[26]

THIRTEEN

Opening Moves

Capt. Benjamin Crail of the 3rd Iowa Cavalry got little, if any, sleep that night. He was in command of a section of the Union pickets composed of companies E, F, and H of his own regiment as well as C, L, and M of the 4th Iowa. The pickets were placed well out from the sleeping army, nearly a mile to the west of old Harrisburg, and he posted them in a long line to cover each side of the Pontotoc Road. On the right side of his line, two companies of infantry from Mower's division extended the line farther north.[1]

The picket line Crail commanded was typical of the guards employed by either army during the war. In essence, it was a layered alarm system to provide warning to the army should the enemy advance. Farthest out were the videttes, mounted soldiers who remained in the saddle throughout their designated watch, and they constituted the first line of warning. Behind the videttes at an interval of 150–300 yards were the pickets or advance guards. These soldiers were placed in positions chosen by the officer in command, a position he determined to be best suited for the job, whether it be a road, path, bit of high ground—whatever offered a wide field of vision. A few hundred yards behind each picket was the reserve, a group of three or four soldiers who took turns relieving the picket. At any given time during the night, one or two men of each reserve would be allowed to catch a little sleep, though they were expected to wake at a moment's notice if the alarm was given. At no time was the picket or the videttes allowed to sleep; and no one, including the reserve, was allowed the comfort of a campfire. In theory, a vidette would note the enemy's advance and give the warning by firing his weapon or falling back to the picket line. The pickets would engage the foe and, if necessary, fall back on the reserve. The reserve could make a stand against any but the strongest advances and would only return to the main line if forced or ordered back.

In the middle of the night of July 14, this theory was put to the test by the advance of the Confederate pickets of Crossland's brigade. "At two o'clock I was suddenly aroused from a nap into which I had fallen, by the firing of our videttes," remembered Cpl. Simon Duck of the 4th Iowa Cavalry, who was resting with the reserve when the alarm was given. Rather than wait to see if the pickets would be driven in, Captain Crail sent Company L forward, "across to the brow of a hill," to bolster the picket line and engage the Confederates. Company C came up on the left, and the combined force was ample to check the advance of the Kentucky pickets. Company C soon withdrew to its previous position in the cover at the edge of the woods. The light skirmishing between the two lines was kept up until dawn.[2]

Two miles away at the dismounted cavalry camp, General Lee could most likely hear the firing in his front. It's doubtful whether he slept at all that night. The events of the last thirty-six hours dominated his thoughts and taxed his strength. The fighting, the marching, and the near-constant flow of reports on enemy movements forced him to focus on the battle with A. J. Smith, but as departmental commander he had much more to contend with. Near Vicksburg, Union general Henry Slocum had led his infantry on a second diversionary expedition, and Wirt Adams's Confederate cavalry had no idea where the column was headed or how to stop it. To the northeast, in Decatur, Gen. Lovell Rousseau was preparing for a thrust against Opelika, Alabama. From his headquarters in New Orleans, General Canby had dispatched a cavalry expedition to cut the Mobile & Ohio Railroad near Meridian, and he continued his buildup of cavalry and infantry at Pensacola in a threat to Mobile. And perhaps the biggest threat Lee faced, apart from Smith, was the Federal fleet sitting outside of Mobile Bay poised to seize the port from the skeleton force left behind to defend it.[3] Lee had taken a sizable gamble bringing together so many troops to confront Smith, and the longer he kept them in north Mississippi, the greater the likelihood of a disaster occurring in another sector of his command. But he could not dare transfer a single man until he knew Smith was no longer a threat. "On this occasion," he explained, "not to fight would have been to have given up the great corn region of Miss., the main support of other armies facing the enemy on more important fields." Sometime before dawn Lee decided that if Smith could not be induced to attack him, he would take the offensive and go after Smith at Harrisburg.[4]

Eventually the eastern sky began to lighten, and Lyon's Division arrived from the west. They limped into camp at dawn and promptly lay down to rest or sleep. It was obvious they would be of little use for hours to come. The dawn also brought General Forrest to Lee's headquarters. The two men discussed their options: should they dig in and wait for Smith to attack them, or should they march across the open fields and take the fight to the Federals? Taking a defensive stance was the more desirable of the two plans, but neither man believed Smith would be foolish enough to give up the high ground. They had tried a similar tactic two days before at Pinson's Hill, and Smith had reacted by stealing a march on them.

Of course, waiting Smith out was a third choice, and probably the best option. Eventually the Federals would run out of rations and be forced to either forage from the countryside or return to Tennessee. Forrest was all for waiting and striking Smith when he was once again stretched out on the road and in a vulnerable position. Maj. Charles Anderson, Forrest's assistant adjutant general, heard his commander attempt to persuade General Lee:

> The enemy have a strong position—have thrown up defensive works and are vastly superior in numbers and it will not do for us to attack them under such conditions. One thing is sure, the enemy cannot remain long where he is. He must come out, and when he does, all I ask or wish is to be turned loose with my command. I will throw Chalmers' Division on the Ellistown Road, and if Smith undertakes to cross the country to Sherman, turn south to devastate the prairies, or return to Memphis, I will be on all sides of him, attacking day and night. He shall not cook a meal or have a night's sleep and I will wear his army to a frazzle before he gets out of the country.[5]

If either man had been aware of the serious shortage of the Federals' rations, Lee would have probably followed Forrest's recommendation. But he did not know, and the pressures being placed on Mobile, Vicksburg, and other areas of his department outweighed any desire to wait and see. He had to act. Moreover, the conditions Forrest had asked or wished for had been present for the last week, and still he had been unable to capitalize on them.[6]

There was still a small chance that Smith could be influenced to take the offensive, so Lee ordered his troops into a line of battle to try to provoke the Federals into action. If nothing developed, they would attack. It is not known whether or not Forrest agreed with this course of action. In his official report he merely stated, "On the morning of the 14th Lee ordered the attack to be made, and the troops were disposed for that purpose."[7]

Forrest's duty was to support General Lee and to do everything in his power to make the attack successful. If he had any reservations about Lee's orders, he kept them to himself. Forrest never had a problem expressing his opinions concerning orders he did not agree with, and on several occasions he told his superiors just what he thought of them. So if he had sharply disagreed with Lee, he would have let the general know in no uncertain terms. Lee wrote, "Whatever others may say, Gen. Lee and Gen. Forrest were in perfect accord as to delivering battle, and gen. Forrest personally never shrunk from this responsibility before or after the bloody battle."[8]

Yet, when Lee directed Forrest to carry out the plan, Forrest balked and declined to take command on the field, citing Lee's superior rank as the reason. It must have come as a shock to Lee.

> I said to General Forrest that a large proportion of the troops now on the ground belonged to his immediate command, had served under him in his recent successful campaigns, and had just won the splendid victory at Brice's Crossroads, having beaten some of the troops that they would have to encounter to-day, and that, knowing Forrest better than myself, they would have more implicit confidence in his leadership. General Forrest, however, positively declined to take the command, saying I was his senior, and that I should take the responsibility.[9]

Lee's request was not only a gracious admission of Forrest's skills; it was logical and not the least bit untoward. With the exception of the 1st Mississippi Infantry and the artillerists from Mobile, every man on the field was under Forrest's command. While it was not strange for Lee to expect Forrest to command his own troops, it is perplexing that Lee even bothered to ask him. True, he was the senior man on the field, and the responsibility for success or failure was ultimately his, but his presence did not relieve Forrest of his own responsibilities. In a very technical sense, the chain of command that morning had only two individuals in place to receive orders directly from General Lee: Forrest in command of his cavalry corps and Lyon's dismounted division. Therefore, Forrest's refusal to take command of his own corps is puzzling and might suggest that he did not agree with Lee's decision to attack. Or perhaps it was his poor health that prompted him to pass tactical control of the fight to his commander, though his painful boils didn't stop him from taking the saddle for the remainder of the day.

In command or not, Forrest worked quickly to prepare for the battle. Lee explained the line of battle he envisioned, and Forrest took issue with the alignment. James Hancock of Roddey's Division recalled the exchange between the two generals:

G[eneral] L[ee]—"Let Roddey's Division form on the left and Buford's on the right."

G[eneral] F[orrest]—"No, I want Buford's Division on the left and Roddey's on the right."

G.L.—"As Roddey is here, why not let him form on the left, and Buford can fall in on the right as he comes up?"

G.F.—"No, I want Buford on the left."

G.L.—"Very well, have your own way then."

Buford took the left, Roddey the right, and Chalmers and Lyon the reserve.[10]

Buford had been given orders during the night by Forrest to have his men ready at Camargo Crossroads at dawn. Mabry's and Bell's brigades were on time and set out on foot at first light, leaving their mounts back at the camp with the horse holders. Within the hour they were approaching Crossland's Kentuckians, who had stood picket throughout the night.[11] Buford's division deployed first. The division commander placed the Kentucky brigade, already on the field from the evening picket, on the south side of the Tupelo Road about a mile and a half west of the abandoned town. A thick belt of black jack oak screened them from the watchful eyes of the Union pickets. "We dismounted and moved forward," wrote Private Johnson of Morgan's refugees, "We all felt or seemed to know that the supreme hour had come. The generals may write the history and tell you one thing or another, but they can never take away from the men that intuition that one feels, that something is going to happen and it is going to happen immediately."[12]

Buford positioned the four Mississippi regiments of Mabry's brigade north of the road, on Crossland's left flank. Just down the line Albert Gardner stood quietly and listened to the occasional artillery round passing over head: "By and by the report came along the line that Gen. Stephen D. Lee had taken General Forrest's place. We were told that he was a nephew of 'Marse Robert' and a West Pointer." The commander of the 4th Mississippi was Col. Thomas Stockdale, a native Pennsylvanian who had come to Mississippi at the age of twenty-eight to become a teacher but instead attended the University of Mississippi and became a lawyer. At the outset of the war he turned away from his three brothers and three sisters back home in Pennsylvania and accepted a commission in his adopted state. An imposing figure, his friends called him "the Tall Pine of Mississippi."[13] Farther down the ranks was Maj. Robert Mc-Cay's 38th Mississippi, 279 rifles strong. And behind the Mississippians, Tyree Bell's Tennesseans began to fall into line as a reserve.[14]

As Buford's division marched into position, Buford rode with Forrest and

Lee to the front and voiced his concern about the plan of action: "I modestly expressed the opinion that the attack should not be a direct one, but the majority of the forces should be thrown forward on the Verona and Tupelo roads, and a vigorous assault made on his left flank; that a direct charge was what the enemy most desired, and for which he was strongly posted both by nature and art." General Chalmers was also riding with the group, and he recalled the scene years later.

> Lee, Forrest, Buford and I were riding to the front when the battle was about to begin. Buford said to Lee and Forrest who had spent the night and morning together in consultation: "Gentlemen, you have not asked my opinion about this fight; but I tell you, we are going to be badly whipped." Forrest replied, sharply: "You don't know what you are talking about; we'll whip 'em in five minutes." Buford replied, "I hope you may be right, but I don't believe it."[15]

As the last of Buford's troopers took their places, the Alabama regiments of Roddey's Division began to file into place on the right. Roddey's was the smallest division in Forrest's Corps, and since it had seen no service the day before, it was the freshest. Colonel Josiah Patterson's brigade, the 5th and 10th Alabama, and Stuart's Battalion, numbered 700 men, while Col. William Johnson's brigade, the 4th Alabama, and Moreland's and William's battalions combined numbered 800. Philip Roddey had grown up dirt poor in northern Alabama. His saddle-maker father was murdered when Philip was five years old, leaving his wife and son penniless. Before the war Roddey found work as a tailor, a sheriff, and, in the western waters, as a riverboat captain. He was the first colonel of the 4th Alabama Cavalry, and though most of his activities in north Alabama were independent, he was occasionally called to assist in larger operations in Tennessee, Mississippi, and Georgia.[16]

Lee placed Chalmers's two brigades, Rucker's and McCulloch's, in reserve behind Buford's columns. They also left their horses behind at the dismounted camp and walked to the staging area, "and as there was some change in the orders about our position after we came upon the field, there was consequently marching and countermarching, which proved very exhausting to men unaccustomed to marching on foot." Lyon's dismounted cavalry, infantry, and artillerists fell in behind Chalmers's Division, where they also took a reserve position well back from the front.[17]

Forrest's artillery was under the command of twenty-one-year-old Capt. John W. Morton Jr. Only seventeen when his home state of Tennessee seceded, Morton was captured in February 1862 at Fort Donelson along with the rest of his unit, Porter's Tennessee Battery. After his brief stay in prison and exchange, he was thereafter associated with the artillery of Forrest's command. In his own words, Morton was "full of enthusiasm and eagerness to go into battle commanding a full battalion of artillery, it being the first opportunity he had of the kind. It was a chance he coveted." The arrival of Ferrell's Battery (Company C, 14th Battalion, Georgia Light Artillery) with Roddey's Division brought the artillery up to five batteries.[18]

Morton had his twenty guns on the Tupelo Road before the sun came up. He reported to General Forrest for orders; but, having declined to command any of his own troops, Forrest sent the young captain to General Lee, who directed Morton to Maj. Jefferson L. Wofford, his chief of artillery. Wofford told Morton, "The artillery is all yours. You report to General Lee for orders." Morton sought permission from the commanding general to mass his twenty guns behind Bell's brigade on the left center "and make a breach in the Federal lines, creating confusion in their ranks, which would give the Confederate cavalry easy work."[19]

Wisely, and much to Morton's disappointment, Lee disregarded the suggestion. Massed artillery may or may not have softened the Federal lines, but it would also attract counterbattery fire from the high ground. With the Confederate guns concentrating on the infantry, the Union gunners could fire on Morton's artillery without fear of reprisal. The southern guns would be silenced one by one, and the infantry would charge without support. Instead, Lee chose to distribute the batteries to support the individual brigades on the field. Morton complained bitterly, but Lee's decision was not to be taken lightly; he had commanded an artillery battalion himself in Longstreet's Corps during the 2nd Manassas campaign, and his performance played a pivotal role in the victory.[20]

Morton directed his Tennessee battery of four 3-inch rifles to fall in on Mabry's right flank. Lt. T. Sanders Sale, commanding, placed the pieces just north of the Tupelo Road and awaited the advance. Capt. Alfred Hudson's Mississippi battery took its place on Roddey's left and waited to assist the Alabamians with two 10-pound and two 12-pound howitzers. Finally, Capt. Thomas Rice's Tennessee battery of 6-pound smoothbores stood ready to support the center of the Confederate line from the Tupelo Road. The cannoneers in Rice's battery had begun the war in early 1861 as infantry, rather than artillery. The "Sumter Grays," or Company A, 38th Tennessee Volunteers, fought at Shiloh and did well. Their stint as foot soldiers ended shortly thereafter, however, and during the Siege of Corinth they were given three large-caliber cannon and redesignated as a company of heavy artillery. After the siege they went into garrison duty in Columbus until early 1864, when they were given field pieces and redesignated as light artillery.[21] Morton placed the remaining two batteries, Thrall's from Arkansas and Ferrell's from Georgia, in reserve with Chalmers's division. While they were awaiting orders, the gunners built "slight intrench-ments of rails and logs," the first breastworks to go up on the field.[22]

Writing about the battle many years later, Stephen Lee stated, "Every pre-caution was taken to accomplish this general movement. Both Gen. Lee and Gen. Forrest understood the desperate venture." Lee's plan was simple, but it still required careful coordination and execution. He would begin by ad-vancing a portion of his troops close enough to the enemy to engage them with long-range musketry and artillery. If this movement went off as planned, Smith's army would be coaxed off the high ground and the Confederates could fight on the defensive from the edge of the woods. If Smith would not be drawn out, Lee would take the offensive and attack on the left with Buford's division. Once the battle was under way, Roddey's Division would strike on the right, and the Federal line would be broken.[23]

Lee assigned the only serious attempt to draw out Smith and his Federals to Col. William Johnson's small brigade in Roddey's Division. Johnson sent More-land's Battalion of Alabama Cavalry, Maj. J. N. George commanding, to occupy a small hill in full view of Smith's left flank. Joining the Alabama troopers were Captain Henry Tyler and his picked men from the 12th Kentucky, who had spent the night in Verona and picketed the road leading north to Tupelo. Just how this small detachment came to be teamed with Johnson's brigade is unclear, though they were probably on their way back to their own brigade (Crossland's) when Tyler learned of the movement and threw in with the Alabamians.

It was Captain Tyler's boldness that had led General Lyon to select him four days earlier to lead the scout around Smith's column. And, not surprisingly, it was Tyler who led the forced reconnaissance to draw out the enemy the morn-ing of the 14th. Two and a half miles southwest of Tupelo, near "Mr. Thomas's place," Tyler found the enemy pickets and firing commenced.[24]

* * *

A. J. Smith was not a prolific writer. He wrote detailed after-action reports and carried on typical military correspondence, but he left no memoir, diary, or let-ters home. After the war he never engaged in refighting the old campaigns in the pages of the newspapers, and he never gave addresses at the veterans' reunions. During the war he played his cards close to the chest and never held councils of war. What was going through his mind on the morning of July 14 is a mystery.

Reveille came at 3:00 A.M. in the Union camps. The men were allowed a hasty breakfast but kept their place in line facing the enemy. General Smith had had time to observe his alignment, and though the army had spent the night in line of battle, he was not content with their position by the morning light. The lines did not conform to the topography as much as he would like, and changes needed to be made to ensure the best use of the high ground. So when it was light enough to see, he ordered his line forward. "The next morning," explained Mower, "the general commanding the expedition indicated the position he wished my division to occupy."[25]

Mower's First Division maintained its presence north of the Tupelo Road, but Smith moved most of the regiments, particularly those in Woods's brigade, as much as 400 yards closer to the enemy. This positioned the Federals on the crest of the low ridge overlooking the fields the Confederates would have to cross. Had the Federals constructed any breastworks or entrenchments during the night, they would have proved worthless as the line moved forward into the new position.[26] Woods's brigade, posted at the bend of the Tupelo Road, held the key position to Mower's division, if not the entire army. The 12th Iowa formed in the woods and faced an open field, with its left firmly planted on the Tupelo Road. The 7th Minnesota formed behind the 12th, acting as a ready reserve. "In front of and running parallel with our line was a heavy rail fence," noted Capt. Jonathan Stubbs, "which we threw down in such a manner to form a good protection against small arms." The fence did not impress Captain Carter, however, who was nearby with the 7th Minnesota: "In front of the Twelfth were the remains of a rail fence, much of which had furnished fuel for the campfires of at least two regiments. Being entirely used up in some places and not so much in others. This was torn down and used to protect the men but was of little consequence." At the far right of the regiment, Company B of the 12th Iowa was "refused," or bent back at a right angle to the rest of the regiment, and connected with the 33rd Missouri and, beyond, the 35th Iowa. The brigade's was a strong position with good interior lines and a strong reserve but, save for the rail fence that protected only 300 men, had no breastworks.[27]

On the right of the Third Brigade, the 2nd Iowa Battery was brought up to plug the gap between the 3rd and 4th brigades. Private Philips of the 2nd Iowa recalled,

We looked off to the west, and about a third of a mile away saw a line of skirmishers standing there like statues. They were also looking to the west. We remarked to the boys that that looked like there would be something doing around here before long. "Yes," they said, "the Johnnies are just over there in the timber to the west and are getting ready to come out and take us in." Well, we said, when they came they would find us here, and as for the taking of us, that might not be so easy.

Because the Tupelo Road made a four hundred yard diagonal turn to the northeast before resuming its easterly path, Woods' brigade was able to anchor both its right and left flank on the road and Capt. Reed was able to place his guns almost directly in the road facing northwest.[28]

The 33rd Wisconsin took up a position in the yard of a log house on the crest of the hill. The 14th Wisconsin formed on its right, and the small detachment of the 41st Illinois fell in behind as the reserve. On the far right the four guns of the 6th Indiana Battery unlimbered on the edge of the woods overlooking a wide cornfield, a good position if the enemy attacked from the northwest. Commanded by Capt. Michael Mueller, the 6th was in a rather unique situation during the expedition. It had been forced to abandon its guns during the retreat from Brice's Crossroads and had yet to procure replacement pieces. On this outing, the gunners were borrowing the four cannon of Battery M, 1st Missouri Light Artillery (and many of the subsequent reports refer to them as Battery M).[29]

Beyond Ward's position, McMillen's First Brigade stayed in its position overlooking King's Creek. The only change Smith made in McMillen's line was shifting the 93rd Indiana over to the far left of the brigade to support the 6th Iowa Battery. Likewise, Wilkin's 2nd Brigade, the last of Mower's force, maintained its reserve position in the hollow behind McMillen's regiments. With these late changes, Smith had his largest division formed in an unusually compact line with plenty of reserve and artillery support, and the odd zigzag shape of the line created numerous deadly fields of interlocking fire.[30]

To the south of the Tupelo Road, Smith repositioned David Moore's Third Division as well. He first moved Charles Murray's First Brigade, advancing it "some 300 yards toward Pontotoc to a more advantageous position." The new position pleased Moore, "our lines being concealed from their view by the brow of the hill." Murray's right-hand regiment, the 122nd Illinois Infantry, set its flank on the Tupelo Road, where it was supported on either side by the 3rd Indiana Battery. Battery commander Lt. Richard Burns placed the first gun directly in the road on the right of the 122nd and the other three cannon on its left. He positioned the three guns so that one faced directly west while the other two covered the left and right oblique. The remaining regiments of Murray's brigade—89th Indiana, 58th Illinois, 21st Missouri, and 119th Illinois—extended his line to the south, hugging the top of the ridge, which bent inward slightly and ended alongside a tributary of King's Creek.[31]

Smith left Gilbert's brigade in reserve at the wagon park and was about to reposition Wolfe's Third Brigade when the enemy was seen advancing on his left flank. "The battle opened by the enemy attempting to secure a commanding position on our left."[32]

Captain Tyler's Kentuckians moved quickly once contact was made. "Hastily dismounting my detachment, I advanced at double-quick, driving pickets of the enemy posted in the houses and behind the fences on Mr. Thomas' place. Here posting my men behind crest of hill 300 yards in front of enemy's position they opened a heavy and rapid fire, warmly responding to the foe."[33]

Smith sent the Third Brigade to meet the threat by advancing it several hundred yards to the crest of the ridge. Capt. George F. Young led the 178th New York forward "into the open field." The 178th stopped midway across the field and connected with the 119th Illinois of Murray's First Brigade on its right. The remaining three regiments of Wolfe's brigade—the 52nd Indiana, 117th Illinois, and 49th Illinois—stretched the line off to the southeast toward the far end of the field. The Third's position was so long that the addition of this single brigade nearly doubled the length of Smith's line. Lt. Col. Zalmon Main of the 52nd Indiana described the position as being "across a large uncultivated field, facing westward, with a dense strip of woods some 600 yards in front." Pvt. Otto Wolfe of the 117th Illinois was very pleased: "Our brigade had a splendid position on some hills where we could overlook the battlefield."[34]

Between the 117th and the 52nd Indiana, Wolfe posted Battery G, 2nd Illinois Light Artillery. Lt. John Lowell brought his four guns up to the line, where he was ordered to post his cannon in front of the Third Brigade.[35]

But before Lowell could bring his guns into action, the threat to Smith's left flank had passed. Henry Tyler was chagrined as he watched a brief window of opportunity open and then quickly close. He had taken the high ground, as ordered, and called for Maj. J. N. George to bring up Moreland's Battalion in support. George absolutely refused to come forward, and any chance of engaging the enemy while the Union troops were in motion was soon gone. The Alabamians sat on their horses 600 yards behind Tyler, who groused, "I deemed it imprudent to advance farther, or charge [the] enemy's position with so small a force as my command."[36] The high ground to the south of Harrisburg had been left exposed for a short time, but without support, or a general advance with the Confederate right, Tyler's command was easily pushed aside. As a consequence, Smith held all of the high ground when fighting commenced.

While Wolfe's brigade was moving forward, Smith called up his final infantry brigade. Bouton's Colored Brigade had spent the night alongside the wagon park near the junction of the Tupelo and Verona roads. Soon after daylight they moved 1,200 yards south to the far end of the field where Wolfe was deploying. One of Bouton's regiments extended the main line to the extreme southwest corner of the field and lined up with the field behind them and the dense woods in front. It was an unenviable position, but it had the benefit of being on the far edge of the higher ground.[37]

The field ended, and the high ground leveled off into the surrounding countryside. If Smith continued to extend his line southward, he would do so by placing the remainder of Bouton's brigade directly in the scrub oak with no natural
protection. Instead, the old veteran chose to refuse his left flank by bending the
left of his line back 90 degrees. In this way, he would anchor his left flank on the
swamp beyond the Verona Road while still maintaining use of the higher elevation and the open field. It was a good piece of soldiering. He placed the remaining two regiments facing south, and Capt. Louis Smith's four guns of Battery I,
2nd U.S. Colored Light Artillery, unlimbered facing southeast.[38]

Smith's cavalry had finished its destruction of the railroad and maintained a
guard of the army's flanks, Winslow on the right and Coon on the left. A single
cavalry regiment, Henry Burgh's 9th Illinois, dismounted and positioned itself
on the extreme left of the Union line alongside Smith's battery. A battalion of
the 9th Illinois advanced as skirmishers and videttes, while the remainder of
the regiment threw up "temporary works." Captain Carter described the works
as "a slight barricade on our extreme left, which was not used or needed."[39]

Stephen D. Lee was still attempting to draw Smith off the high ground as
the last of the Federals filed into line, and with the southerners distracted, the
northerners had time to redeploy. Smith's men had only to sit and wait as the
scorching sun rose in the sky.[40]

FOURTEEN

"A Medley of Blunders"

The Confederate attempt to draw the Federals off of the heights did not end with the failure of Tyler's company and Moreland's Battalion. Buford's and Roddey's skirmishers had reached the edge of the timber facing the open field, and the soldiers began a long-range fire with their rifles. The Union response was less than Lee was hoping for and was conducted by the cavalry skirmishers and not the main line. Because the Confederates did not immediately advance, Captain Crail and his companies of the 3rd and 4th Iowa Cavalry believed they were holding their own. Within a few minutes, however, the small-arms fire became an exchange of artillery as cannon from both sides joined the action.[1]

The artillery duel went on for the better part of an hour with neither side making any headway. For the spectators, however, the artillery fire was impressive. Chaplain Frederick Humphrey of the 12th Iowa observed how the "artillery opened with terrific earnestness at quarter after seven, throwing canister, grape and shell. Gun succeeded gun with rapidity of musketry." Once again, though, the Federals refused to take the bait and held to their position on the heights.[2]

The Confederate plan to draw the enemy from the heights beyond Harrisburg had failed, and, as a consequence, Lee resolved to attack Smith where he was. He directed that once all his troops were in position, a "signal gun was to be fired on the Pontotoc Road between Bell and Crossland as the order for a general and simultaneous advance to attack the enemy." Lee recalled these events thirty-seven years after the battle, and his recollection had undoubtedly dimmed, since the statement cannot possibly be true. The battery in question, Rice's Battery, was posted on the Pontotoc Road with Crossland's brigade on

the right, but it was Mabry's Brigade on the left, not Bell's, as Lee stated. Fur-
thermore, the front-line Confederate batteries had been firing for an hour, and
it would have been impossible for anyone to discern the individual discharge
from a 6- or 12-pounder in the middle of all that noise. When Lee's belated
version of the battle was published in 1901, Capt. John Morton, the Confederate artillery commander, took issue with Lee's explanation. Morton, writing in
the third person, countered with his own account: "He was never directed by
General Lee, to whom he reported and from whom he was receiving orders,
to fire a signal gun for opening the fight. He received no intimation of such an
order from General Lee or any one else."[3]

Lee was still making final preparations for the assault when two "reliable
scouts" reported that Smith was withdrawing from the field and preparing to
march north to Memphis via the Ellistown Road. Lee described how Forrest
"felt and believed" that

> all that could be done was to fight Smith and risk the results. He advised im-
> mediate attack; his blood was up; the fire of battle was in his eye. He said that if
> he was in command, he would not hesitate a moment, that his scouts reported
> the enemy preparing to retreat on the Ripley Road. Gen. Lee ordered the at-
> tack and said:—"If it is to be a fight, let us fight to the bitter end, the troops are
> yours, select which wing you will command in person, and I will take the other."

Though Lee had failed to convince Forrest to take tactical control of the coming fight, his statement left no room for Forrest to decline leadership of at least
a portion of the troops on the field. Forrest chose Roddey's small division on
the right to "swing around the enemy's left flank."[4]

Lee's description of Forrest—"with the fire of battle in his eye" and his
desire to hit the enemy in a frontal assault before they could commence a retreat—is in direct contradiction to that of Maj. Charles Anderson, Forrest's assistant adjutant, who remembered his commander wanting to strike the enemy
only after they had left Harrisburg. The previous night Forrest had badgered
Lee to wait until Smith was returning to Memphis and then attack his column.
Why Forrest would change his mind in the space of a few hours and want to
strike Smith in a frontal assault is hard to grasp. Whether he was eager to begin
the attack or was being carried along reluctantly, we will never know.[5]

In his official report Forrest stated that "Lieutenant-General Lee gave the
order to advance, and directed me to swing the right around upon the enemy's
left." If Forrest expected to unleash a crushing flank attack on Smith's left, Roddey's Division was completely out of position to make it happen. In a footnote

to General Forrest's biography, Thomas Jordan claimed. "General Lee's orders really were that his centre should stand still while the right (Roddey) should have time to swing around into a position as near to the enemy as that held by Buford." Roddey's Division was on the right of Crossland's Kentucky brigade, and because the Union line bent back away from it, Roddey's Division was not as close to the foe as was the rest of the southern army. Jordan's statement questions whether Forrest was to lead an attack on Smith's left flank or to merely attack the left of the enemy line—two actions that sound similar in theory but were far different in execution. If Forrest was to advance against Smith's left, he had only to move the division forward a few hundred yards and wait for the general advance to begin. If, however, a flank attack was called for, Roddey's two brigades would have to move over a mile and a half to a position south of the enemy line. The first could be accomplished in minutes; the latter would take at least an hour. [6]

Forrest's subsequent actions would imply that he was preparing a flank attack. He "immediately repaired to General Roddey's right with all possible speed, which was nearly a mile distant, and after giving him the necessary orders in person I dashed across the field in a gallop for the purpose of selecting a position in which to place his troops." If Forrest was merely leading an advance on the Union left, he would have stopped at the center of the division and directed Roddey to move his men forward. A ride to the far right would have been proper if he was intent on moving the division to the south. [7] If Lee's plan had any hope for success, it would require careful timing and coordination. The attack had to be made simultaneously with four brigades of dismounted cavalry.

The general was making a few final troop adjustments when things began to go terribly wrong. Roddey's Division, still under cover of the timber, began to make its way to the right in anticipation of the attack on the enemy's left. This movement opened a gap between Roddey's Division and Crossland's Kentucky brigade. The Kentuckians were moving forward in the woods when they noticed the gap and began marching to the right oblique to maintain their alignment with Roddey's Alabamians. Apparently no one had informed Crossland of the flank attack, and if he continued to oblique, he would end up pulling his brigade right out of position. Meanwhile, Hinchie Mabry's Mississippians, for some unknown reason, began to oblique to the left. Buford saw the problem developing and knew it would lead to trouble if not checked: "Observing these intervals, I reported the fact to General Lee, who immediately ordered Colonel Bell to move forward and form between Mabry's and Crossland's brigades." The battle had yet to begin, and the southern line had fallen into a dangerous state of disarray. But before Bell could carry out his orders and restore the line, the Kentuckians emerged from the woods and began to advance against the enemy. [8]

This was not part of the plan. The attack had to be a hammer blow by both divisions and from two directions, not a piecemeal assault by a single brigade. One of the keys to Forrest's success, he knew, was getting the "skeer" on the enemy: hit them hard enough to make them *believe* they were going to be beaten, which would cause them to panic and run away, as they had so many times before.

No one recalled hearing a signal gun or even an order to charge. Whether he really did give the order or not, General Lee took responsibility for the premature advance, saying, "At the signal agreed on Gen. Lee ordered the left wing to attack." But this was not what had been planned; none of the other brigades was yet in position.[9] Henry George, historian of the Kentucky brigade, attempted to explain:

> It must be borne in mind that there was no time indicated when the battle should begin, nor were there any arrangements for a signal to commence marching. The lines were simply moved forward, and everybody understood that it was for the purpose of engaging the enemy in battle; therefore when the Kentuckians were marched under fire of the enemy, it was natural for these veterans to suppose the general in charge had everything ready for an immediate engagement. They could not afford to halt or retire, and it had been the custom of the brigade to always advance, under fire, double-quick; and at this point Major Tate says that Colonel Faulkner, the gallant commander of the Twelfth, ordered his bugles to sound the charge. Whether it was the bugle or the general impulse, the whole brigade started forward in their charge to death to so many . . . I am forced to conclude the movement of the Confederates was a medley of blunders.[10]

Lt. William Pirtle of the 7th Kentucky laid the blame on confusion and overconfidence.

> I have heard much censure and criticism about that days work, as to who was to blame I do not pretend to say. But have my doubts as to the intension of making a charge on their works that they had all night to build. But think most likely that the Ky brigade being flushed with victory over Sturges only a month previous, had such great confidence in themselves thought they could whip the whole federal army. And some one heard someone hollow and thought charge, and hollowed charge then repeated along the line, and charge it was with the Ky brigade alone. I have never heard of the man that gave the order or authorized the order to be given.[11]

At any rate, someone gave the order to advance, and Crossland's men marched through the trees toward the field. Pvt. John Johnson of Morgan's cavalry described how they "moved forward thorough the narrow strip of woods in quick time under heavy shell fire that tore the trees till the limbs looked like flying ax handles. When we reached the open field it was a frantic double quick charge under a heavy fire from the enemy." As the line emerged from the woods the Kentuckians let loose a "loud and hearty cheer" and opened fire on the Federal skirmishers in the field.[12]

"Of course we had to fall back," admitted Simon Duck, a skirmisher with the 4th Iowa Cavalry, "but we did it in order, giving them a volley at every good position until we came to our infantry lines." Unable to hold back the Confederates advancing across the field, the Union cavalry skirmishers mounted up and rode through gaps in the main line opened for them by the infantry. Artilleryman Phillip Lewis joined in the taunting of the often maligned Union cavalry: "They passed within ten feet of our gun. We told them they couldn't fight with their little short pop guns and that they were afraid and always ran away when they saw a rebel. They replied that they had already whipped [the Confederates] and were just drawing them on for us to finish up."[13]

Shortly after entering the field, Crossland's line began to come apart. The colonel said, "Though ordered to move surely and steadily, it was impossible to restrain the ardor of my men. Believing that they were strongly supported both on the right and left, raising a shout they charged forward on the enemy's line, keeping a constant and destructive fire." But they were not being supported, and they entered the field alone. Their confidence surged as they looked across the open space and saw no enemy, other than the skirmishers hustling over the ridge. Yet, a single battery was plying their ranks with deadly effect, and it was these four cannon that became the focus of the Kentuckians' charge.[14]

Moments before the Confederates commenced their charge, Lt. Richard Burns, in charge of the four guns of Battery G, 3rd Indiana Light Artillery, was ordered by Colonel Murray to send a single gun to the right of the First Brigade, and Lt. Phillip McPherson was dispatched with a 6-pounder James rifle, which was unlimbered square in the middle of the Pontotoc Road. The remaining guns, another 6-pounder rifle and a pair of 12-pounder smoothbores, were "brought to bear on the columns of the enemy, as they advanced, with as much accuracy as the nature of the ground and other circumstances would permit."[15] The Confederates were charging directly at Charles Murray's First Brigade, though they could not see any of the Federals on the ridge. Murray had ordered all five of his regiments to lie down, where they were concealed by the corn and bushes on the crest of the slope. Pvt. Luther Frost of the 119th Illinois explained, "We were formed on a ridge just over the brow of the hill so when the rebels fired at us the balls passed over us. We lay down and let them come up."[16]

As Crossland's men approached midfield, they began to receive artillery fire on both flanks. Lt. McPherson's gun in the Pontotoc Road fired shell and canister as fast as the piece could be served, and further to the south the four guns of Battery G, 2nd Illinois Light Artillery, joined in, having unlimbered in front of Wolfe's Third Brigade with an unobstructed view of the Kentuckians' right flank. Since there was no enemy in their own front, Wolfe's two right-hand regiments, the 52nd Indiana and 178th New York, advanced their lines into the field, turned slightly to the right, and began firing thunderous volleys of musketry into Crossland's ranks.[17]

Pvt. John Johnson observed the carnage unfolding around him: "We had not fired a shot while the enemy had been inflicting serious damage upon our ranks." As the Kentuckians drew closer to the Union lines, still ominously quiet directly ahead, they faced an unavoidable obstacle: a deep ravine running north and south that emptied into a wide ditch to the south. Johnson described the scene: "As we came up out of the ravine, which was not over 12 to 15 feet wide and 7 to 8 feet deep, it seemed as if the doors of Hell had been suddenly thrown open. The cannon and musketry bullets swept us like hail." Pvt. Henry Hord of the 3rd Kentucky recalled how he was nearly killed by the intense cannon fire:

> Five hundred yards or so from the Yankee lines a shell burst just as it passed between [Private] John Duke's head and my own. We were both in the front rank, and the concussion knocked us both down, the fragments killing the two men in the rear rank. I was the first to come to, with my face turned toward the woods from which we had come. My first impression was that the fight was over and I could see nothing of the command and could hear no firing. I happened to turn around and look the other way, and saw them about two hundred yards off, going as regular as clockwork on to the Yankee line. The concussion of the exploding shell had destroyed my hearing.[18]

The only support for the Kentucky brigade came from artillery captain John Morton. Morton ordered Rice's Battery to advance with the attack, "pushing his guns forward by hand, keeping pace with the rapidly advancing line of battle." It was unspeakably hard work, with temperatures already in the nineties. One of the guns was quickly silenced and disabled by counterbattery fire, with seven of its crewmen wounded. Horses fell so fast that only a single section could advance with the dismounted cavalry.[19] When Morton saw the concentrated fire being directed on Rice, he ordered James Thrall's Battery up from its reserve position. The combined artillery fire from front and rear forced Pvt. Gabriel Puryear of the 12th Kentucky to throw himself to the ground: "There was such a storm of shot and shell that all who were not killed lay down. I never heard any command to lie down, but I lay down and everybody else did." Though they were still a hundred yards short of the enemy line, the Kentuckians were running out of steam.[20]

A conspicuous mounted target in the center of the Confederate line was Colonel William W. Faulkner, the commander of the 12th Kentucky, who was valiantly trying to get the men moving again. At the top of his lungs Faulkner shouted, "Forward men; forward!" Private Johnson saw Faulkner, though being from Morgan's cavalry he did not know who he was. "On my left, 20 or 30 steps away a Colonel on his horse went down and our ranks were being fearfully thinned." Faulkner went down with two wounds, and his horse was killed by an artillery shell. But his desperate plea to the men had worked, and as a body they began to rise. "Now began our fatal charge into the very jaws of death," recalled Johnson. The 12th Kentucky swept by a barn and a cotton gin and up the slope covered in high weeds.[21]

Charles Murray had shown admirable patience as he waited for the Confederates to approach his brigade line. He kept his men out of sight and had walked up and down the line admonishing them not to fire. Finally, when the enemy was no more than fifty paces off, he ordered his regiments to rise and fire, "which they did with the greatest gallantry and courage, meeting on the crest of the hill the advancing and confident enemy." The resulting volley was thunderous, and when the cloud of white smoke cleared, hardly a Confederate was still on his feet. One of the few still standing was Private Johnson: "I saw all, I thought it was all, of my comrades fall. I thought they had fallen just to dodge the first fire of the enemy. It was our custom under similar circumstances to drop down on the ground and let the first fire pass over us, then rise and charge, but alas! Those who fell today never rose again."[22]

Though the first volley sealed the fate of the Kentuckians, they continued to move ahead. Shacklett's 8th Kentucky "pressed forward until within thirty yards . . . when a terrific fire of musketry compelled us to retire." Maj. Thomas Tate became the commander of the 12th Kentucky when Faulkner went down, and he continued to lead his men forward. He recalled, "The fire was the most destructive I ever saw, yet not a man wavered, but all went forward, charging to the front." Tate was on the left of the regiment, where the main body pressed to within thirty yards of the enemy. Pvt. A. P. Hill made it to within twenty

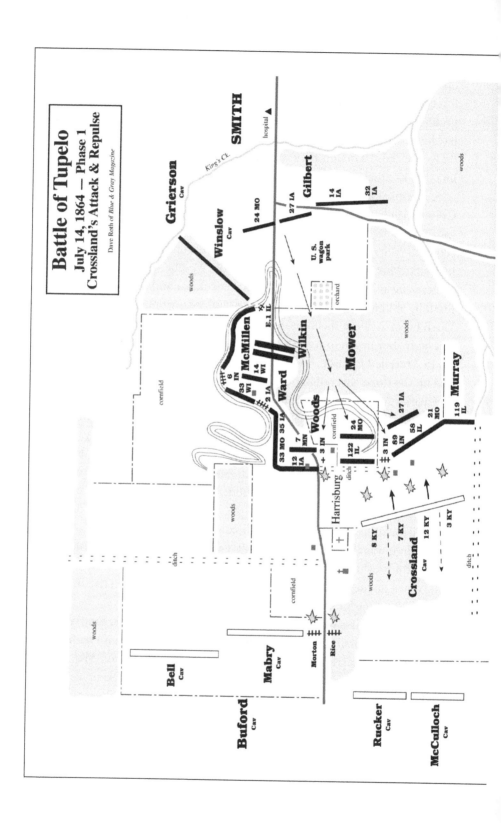

Battle of Tupelo
July 14, 1864 — Phase 1
Crossland's Attack & Repulse

Dave Roth of Blue & Gray Magazine

SMITH

Grierson
Cav

Winslow
Cav

King's Ck.

hospital ▲

24 MO

27 IA

Gilbert

14 IA

32 IA

woods

woods

U.S.
wagon
park

orchard

McMillen

6 IN

33 WI

14 WI

2 IA

E. 1 IL

Wilkin

Ward

Mower

cornfield

33 MO 35 IL

7 MN

3 IN

Woods

cornfield

24 MO

27 IA

21 MO

Murray

58 IL

119 IL

12 IA

122 IL

3 IN

89 IN

ditch

Harrisburg

8 KY

7 KY

Crossland
Cav

12 KY

3 KY

woods

ditch

woods

cornfield

ditch

woods

Morton

Rice

Mabry
Cav

Bell
Cav

Buford
Cav

Rucker
Cav

McCulloch
Cav

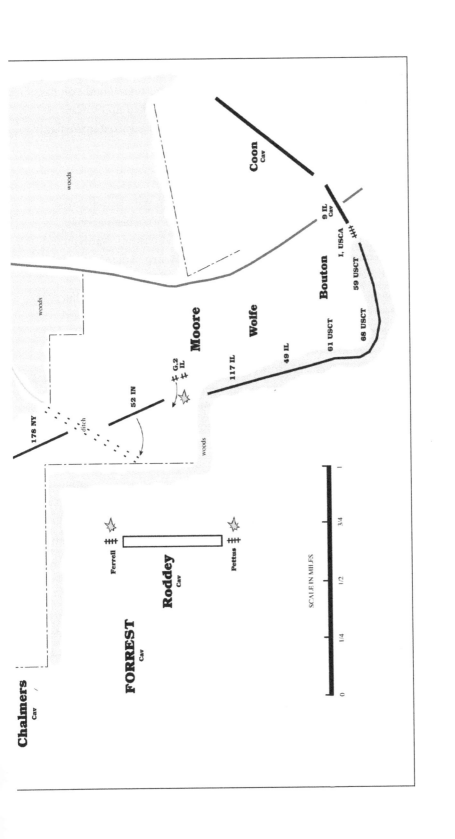

Chalmers
Cav

woods

woods

178 NY

ditch

52 IN

G,2
IL

Moore

Ferrell

Roddey
Cav

Wolfe

117 IL

49 IL

61 USCT

68 USCT

59 USCT

I, USCA

Bouton

9 IL
Cav

Coon
Cav

FORREST
Cav

Pettus

woods

SCALE IN MILES

0   1/4   1/2   3/4   1

yards when he was cut down; no one in the 12th made it closer. Ensign G.W. Dunn was nearly as far along when he fell carrying the regimental colors. The flag fell into the dust but was almost immediately picked up by Capt. J. F. Melton, who pulled the banner out from under Dunn's body. Later the flag was found to have been pierced eighteen times. [23]

Private Johnson was in the thick of the fighting:

> There is an indescribable swish in close quarter fighting. It was a dreadful reality, a pandemonium of lead and steel and screams and a sort of hissing sound. It was a place for Veterans only. I had run in a double quick charge towards the enemy for a half mile or more and had been shot at every step of the way and I was now confronted by a wall of fighting men, and good fighting men at that. I had seen Yankees break and run long before we got that close to them, but these stood their ground. God knows they had but little now to stand against. We were more than decimated and forced back.[24]

Inevitably, the Kentuckians began to give way. Major Tate heard his men shouting "that they were falling back on our right, and on looking found the regiment on my right had fallen back in great confusion. I ordered the left to fall back, as we were without support, and moved to the right to rally the men who were falling back." Within moments the entire brigade was in full retreat.[25]

On the heights, David Moore watched from horseback as the advancing Confederates were hit by the first volley, "causing them to flee in the utmost disorder, exclaiming, 'My God! My God!'" Moore sensed an opportunity and ordered Murray to send his brigade forward and sweep the enemy from the field. The order was passed up and down the line, and the wall of dusty blue soldiers set off down the sun-baked slope at the quick step. "Our lines continued to follow them up," reported Murray, "pouring deadly volleys into their rapidly thinning ranks."[26]

The casualties on the Federal side were light. One of the wounded was Sgt. Bailey Bowden of the 122nd Illinois, who had stopped to assist a wounded comrade and was accidently stabbed in the face by the man's bayonet. As he reeled back in pain and surprise, a shell from a Confederate gun exploded above him and a piece of shrapnel struck a glancing blow in the back of his head. Others fell as well, but they were a mere fraction of the number of Confederates that lay dead and wounded across the slope. Indeed, for most of the northern soldiers, it had been no more than a hot run down the slope: "The field was cleared of the rebels in front of us in less than ten minutes after we fired the first shot."[27]

There was little resistance left in the southern soldiers as the Kentuckians ran through the dry weeds for the shelter of the trees. Men who had survived the charge collapsed, overcome by the relentless heat. Pvt. Johnson ran an obstacle course of bodies and noticed how he could have walked back on them without ever touching the ground. He was halfway to safety when he once again had to navigate the ditch in the center of the field: "I got back to the ravine, and as I attempted to climb the other side of it a solid shell, just missing my head, struck the bank, penetrated the earth and exploded. One piece struck my left foot, another my left shoulder, throwing me backwards some distance into the ditch, unconscious and covered with dirt and dust."[28]

The only credible resistance to the counterattack came on the extreme right of Murray's line, against Col. John Rinaker's 122nd Illinois. Confederate sharp-shooters in the church and other town buildings began an annoying harassing fire which lasted for several hours. Murray said, "The right of my line was directly fronting the church and other buildings in the deserted village of Harrisburg, where the enemy attempted repeatedly to force and hold a position, but the fire from the One Hundred and twenty-second Illinois and the battery compelled them to abandon any serious effort in that direction."[29] Murray's brigade finally came to a halt at midfield, but the heat was so intense the men soon retired back up the slope to their first position at the edge of the woods. With them came thirty-five prisoners, lucky to be alive. The small-arms fire petered away to almost nothing, though the Confederate artillery continued to fire away in support of the last of the retreating Kentuckians.[30]

Crossland's brigade was in rough shape. Fewer than 800 men had begun the charge, and at least 200 never made it back to the trees. "The ranks were decimated," Crossland lamented, "they were literally mowed down." He laid blame for the disaster squarely on the shoulders of the division to his right: "The failure of Roddey's division to advance, and thus draw the fire of the enemy on my right flank, was fatal to my men."[31]

Crossland's anger was somewhat justified. Roddey was in position to attack the Union left and had already begun to move forward. Union skirmishers were falling back as he advanced. The Pettus Flying Artillery threw shells into the Union line as fast as they could load them, though the casualties they inflicted on the 117th Illinois were very light. Pvt. Sidney Robinson wrote how "J. G. Sandbach was lying down on his side taking a chaw of tobaccer & a small piece of shell took out his front teeth & cut his arm. A shell struck a rail & a piece of the rail struck Jr. Shukel on the shoulder & Frank Davis on the arm, bruised them up some."[32]

Forrest selected the position from which he wanted Roddey to begin his attack and then, inexplicably, had him stop. Roddey said that he was advancing "when General Forrest ordered an immediate retreat to the horses, saying that Buford was badly cut up." In his report Forrest explained that he had only just arrived at Roddey's position and was personally scouting a place from which to begin his attack, "but on reaching the front I found the Kentucky brigade had been rashly precipitated forward, and was retiring under the murderous fire concentrated upon them." After ordering Roddey to retire from the field, he rode over to Crossland's brigade, where he found the men exhausted and demoralized. To rally them, the general snatched a battle flag and rode up and down the line calling the men back to their ranks. His presence was electrifying. When they realized who was calling out to them, men who had fallen to the ground stood to their feet, dressed their lines, and turned to face the enemy. Lt. William Pirtle of the 7th Kentucky was just returning to his regiment after his overnight scout when he came on the scene: "General Forrest seemed to be directing in person, I think he had lost his hat, could see his white locks flowing in the air."[33]

Forrest, who earlier in the morning had refused to exercise command of his own troops, then made a command decision.

> The terrific fire poured upon the gallant Kentucky brigade showed that the enemy was supported in overwhelming numbers in an impregnable position, and wishing to save my troops from the unprofitable slaughter I knew would follow any attempt to charge his works, I did not push forward General Roddey's command when it arrived, knowing it would receive the same concentrated fire which had repulsed the Kentucky brigade.

On the surface, it was a sound military maneuver, but there were serious consequences to the decision. Forrest's failure to support Crossland's right flank actually *added* to the Kentuckians' casualties; without Roddey's brigades on the field, Wolfe's Third Brigade entered the field and flanked the attacking line. As for the reasons Forrest gave in his report for not attacking, Smith did not have overwhelming numbers of troops in that part of the field—a circumstance that had never bothered Forrest before anyway—and the Federals were not in an impregnable position or behind any works. Most importantly, the decision was not the move General Lee was waiting for or, for that matter, what Forrest had been ordered to perform. And finally, he ignored the fact that he had waived his authority as field commander, and, to make matters worse, he failed to inform either Lee or Buford of the change in plans. Two brigades on the Confederate left were about to advance not knowing that, for all practical purposes, the fight on the right was already over.[34]

Across the open field, Smith was no doubt pleased. The battle had been going on for less than an hour and the threat to his left had already ended, at least for the time being. The enemy brigade that advanced against Moore had been easily repulsed, and the division that made a brief appearance farther to the south had withdrawn after an inconsequential exchange with his skirmishers. There was never any real danger of the line being broken; the few regiments of the reserve brought up to support Murray's brigade never actually engaged.

Col. John Gilbert's brigade, the Third Division's reserve, spent the morning guarding the wagon train. The wagons remained in the protected field south of the Tupelo Road, and though he was away from the action, Gilbert took his responsibilities seriously. He placed his four regiments in a line of battle ranging north to south on the west side of the wagons. He ordered the 32nd Iowa, on his far right, to about-face and send skirmishers east in the direction of Tupelo.[35]

The wagon park was screened from the enemy by the ridge to the west as well as a thick belt of timber. However, as Ben Thomas of the 14th Iowa explained, "During the battle the enemy threw their shot and shell at our lines and as they came over or through them they struck the trees above our heads, for we were on lower ground than our army was, and cut off large branches which sometimes fell upon our men. In this manner we had in our regiment two men killed and a number wounded by falling timber striking them." When Murray's brigade counterattacked the Kentuckians, the 24th Missouri and 27th Iowa moved up in support.[36]

Maj. Robert Fyan of the 24th was in command of his Missourians as well as Capt. Amos Hasley's 27th Iowa. He placed the two small regiments on either side of Burn's 3rd Indiana Battery. From the heights they watched Murray's men sweep the Kentuckians toward the far end of the field, but they were not called on to assist. For the time being they remained in reserve.[37]

A few hundred yards to the north, Mower's men had waited and listened to the roar of battle as Crossland's Kentuckians attacked Moore's division to the south. Some of Crossland's artillery landed among the First Division, but there was nothing to do but wait it out. As Captain Carter tried to explain, "The worst place for a soldier in battle is where he is liable to receive wounds or be killed, but can do nothing but *think*. Men that will stand that will generally perform their full duty when called upon to face the fire of small arms, shells, grape or canister." The men of the 12th Iowa could hunker down behind the questionable cover of the split-rail fence, but the other regiments were exposed to the fire and simply had to bear it. Luckily for the front ranks, the Confederate artillery was firing too high; but this proved unlucky for Wilkin's Second Brigade in reserve behind the front ranks. "We were, while there, under a heavy fire from the guns of the enemy," said Lt. Colonel John McClure of the 47th Illinois, "their shell, canister, & c., passing over the advanced forces and exploding around us."[38]

The Confederate artillery fire had also created trouble for surgeon Aurelius Bartlett of the 33rd Missouri. At the operating table throughout the night, the exhausted doctor had just lain down to get some sleep when he was awakened by the exploding shells: "At first there was considerable confusion in the rear and some delay about the choice of a site for the field hospital, and the first place selected was exposed to the shot and shell of the enemy, necessitating the removal of the wounded to a point further in the rear." The hospital would have to be moved twice more before a safe location could be secured.[39]

* * *

Buford had watched helplessly as his brigade under Crossland advanced prematurely and was cut to pieces. The only thing he could do was urge his other two brigades forward to take some of the heat off of the Kentuckians.[40] Earlier, when the general advance through the timber had begun, Mabry's Mississippians made an oblique to the left and broke contact with the Kentuckians. Buford had responded by ordering Bell's Tennesseans up from their reserve position to fill the gap created by the movement. As a consequence, Mabry arrived at the edge of the field in advance of Bell, who was still maneuvering through the trees and into position. Without waiting for Bell to come up on his right, Mabry repeated Crossland's mistake and led his brigade into the open field without support on either flank.[41]

As he walked his horse into the field, Mabry could see the Federals waiting up ahead. In the enemy's front "were large, open fields with occasional small skirts of woods. The ground was gently undulating, affording no protection to our troops on any part of the line." Mabry was on the extreme left of his army and was headed for the compact line held by Fighting Joe Mower's First Division.[42] Directly in front of Mabry was Lyman Ward's Fourth Brigade, still flush from its victory the previous day at Bertram's Shop. Ward's brigade was sandwiched between McMillen on his right and Woods on the left, and it held such a small portion of the line that only a single regiment was at the front line. Col. Frederick Lovell's 33rd Wisconsin had the front position with Lt. Colonel James Polley's 14th Wisconsin, and the nonvolunteer detachment of the 41st Illinois was a few paces to the rear. A small log house was on the left of Ward's position, and in the yard were the four guns of the 2nd Iowa Light Artillery. To his right were four more guns of Capt. Michael Mueller's 6th

Indiana Light Artillery with its four borrowed "Rodman" rifles.[43] To the left of Ward's command, Woods's Third Brigade was in a similarly compact line, with the 33rd Missouri and the 35th Iowa facing north and the 12th Iowa looking due west. With no place for them in the front rank, the men of the 7th Minnesota formed a second line directly behind the 12th Iowa. Captain Carter of the 7th recalled, "As the Twelfth Iowa was about half the size of ours, two of our companies formed on their left." Capt. Ralla Banks and Lt. Loel Hoag aligned their men on the left of the 12th Iowa between a small house and Lt. Philip McPherson's rifled 6-pounder of the 3rd Indiana Battery.[44]

It was a deadly position for the enemy to approach. There were three distinct ninety-degree angles within a 400-yard line, creating a murderous converging crossfire. Mower's last brigade, Wilkin's, waited in reserve only yards behind Ward's. Mabry, alone and unsupported, was unwittingly leading his men into the strongest sector of Smith's line.[45]

Mabry's Brigade, fully 100 yards in advance of Bell, set out from the cover of the trees for the Union lines. From the outset, it was in range of the Federal artillery, which began to tear holes through the ranks. Men began to fall at a terrible rate, but still they moved forward, pushing the enemy skirmishers back into their main line. Pvt. Albert Gardner of the 4th Mississippi was stunned as men began to fall on either side of him: "I took an ardent notion to help some poor fellow off the field; but the loud voices of those in the rear saying, 'Close up! Close up!' reminded me that I had no crape on my arm and that my principal business was to fight. I was in a pickle, for I wasn't a bit mad. I was always a poor fighter when in good humor."

But it wasn't only the enemy fire that was dropping the southerners. It was only ten o'clock in the morning, but the heat had once again mounted from oppressive to deadly. Men were collapsing from sunstroke and heat exhaustion. Private Gardner was overcome with cramps and nausea—"I reckon the heat and the sight and smell of blood did it"—and for five minutes he retched and vomited on the field. When at last the spell passed, he had lost his good humor—"I was mad and cool as a cucumber."[46]

From the heights, A. J. Smith watched the second attack of the day unfold. The open field offered an exceptional view, and it was easy to follow the course of the action and the deadly effect his guns were having on the enemy. "At first their lines could be distinguished separately," he noted, "but as they advanced they lost all semblance of lines and the attack resembled a mob of huge magnitude."[47]

Mabry's desperate attempt to keep his brigade in formation was hindered when his horse was killed, throwing him to the ground. The dazed commander lurched stiffly back to his feet and continued to urge the men forward. Two young staff officers rode up and down the line conveying the colonel's orders.

Mabry ordered the brigade to charge the last seventy yards, but there was only so much his men could do. He blamed the heat of the day and the distance the men had to cross: "These two causes of depletion left my line almost like a line of skirmishers."[48]

The casualties began to pile up at an incredible rate, particularly among the officers. Col. Thomas Stockdale, the Pennsylvanian commanding the 4th Mississippi, went down with a severe wound. He was the luckiest of the four regimental commanders. A bullet went through the head of Maj. Robert McCay of the 38th Mississippi Mounted Infantry, and he fell backward into the arms of Colonel Mabry. Not far away Col. Isham Harrison of the 6th Mississippi fell mortally wounded. Lt. Col. Thomas Nelson took command of the 6th, but soon he, too, was fatally wounded. And not far away lay Col. John B. Gage of the 14th Confederate Cavalry, his life's blood seeping into the parched earth. In a matter of minutes, three of four regimental commanders were dead and the remaining one was being carried from the field.[49]

When Mabry's men reached the middle of the field, the Union skirmishers fell back with the main line and the artillery switched over from shell to canister. Nothing stood between the Mississippians and total annihilation but a chance quirk of geography. "There was between their line and ours a little ridge, and just beyond that a hollow," explained Lewis Philips of the 2nd Iowa Artillery,

> as they came down through this hollow out of our sight all was quiet for a few moments, but they came to the brow of the hill, where they could see us and themselves partially hidden they stopped and delivered their fire and received ours. Here for half an hour or more we were under the heaviest musketry fire of any place during the war, not excepting Corinth and the assault on Vicksburg.[50]

The gunners of the 2nd Iowa were fighting with their brand-new 12-pounder Napoleons, with Private Philips on gun number 4, of which he noted, "We found them much heavier to work than our former guns and with greater recoil, but the way they would sling canister would delight any artillery man's heart." The battery was just over the reverse side of the ridge, and the ground they were on sloped gently away behind them to the east. With every shot the guns recoiled sixteen to twenty feet and had to be rolled back up to the firing line. With a hint of pride Phillips recalled, "In that blazing sun this was work for giants to do, but the 18 and 20-year-old boys from Iowa were giants in those days."[51]

Philips was amazed that any "person or thing" could live in such a place. Bullets were flying and knocking splinters from the wooden cannon carriages. One ball creased his cheek and left an angry red welt across his face. Another bullet slammed into the torso of the man in the number-one position, making him drop his sponge/rammer and grab his side screaming in pain. "On examination he found the ball had only skinned his fifth rib, when he turned to us with a broad grin, picked up the staff and resumed his occupation of ramming shells into old No. 4."[52]

As the Confederates continued to fight from the nominal shelter of the hollow, the aspect of the attack changed; though the charge had ground to a halt, the Union line was taking heavy casualties for the first time.

On the right of the 2nd Iowa battery the 33rd Wisconsin was fighting gamely, as fast as their guns could be loaded. Pvt. Alexander Gray was slightly wounded in the right hand when a ball struck his "middle finger on the nuckle and went throo it and cut three others." Two men in his company were killed, and nearly a third; "The ball that killed one of our boys struck Charley Matthews in the pit of the stomack and nocked the breath out of him for a little while." In a letter to his mother he later confessed, "That was rather the tightest place that we were ever in."[53]

Off to their left the firing was so heavy that within a half hour the 12th Iowa had shot away all of its ammunition. Lt. Col. John Stibbs ordered his men to the rear, and the second rank, Marshall's 7th Minnesota, stepped up to the slight rail barricade. Stibbs led his Hawkeyes back several hundred yards to replenish cartridge boxes and to clear their badly fouled rifles.[54]

While the 12th Iowa moved back for a resupply of ammunition, General Smith ordered two regiments from the reserve to move to the east and, as an added precaution, moved the trains out of range of the Confederate cannon. Smith shifted the 47th Illinois and the 11th Missouri of Wilkin's Second Brigade to the right of the new wagon park, away from the fighting, in anticipation of a possible enemy thrust from the direction of Tupelo. But it was a phantom threat, and they saw no action. [55]

Col. Alexander Wilkin had gone with his two regiments to place them in their new position. When all was well he turned his horse and while he rode back to the brigade, he was struck by a bullet that passed through his body from the left side to the right. The diminutive colonel slid out of the saddle and fell lightly to the ground. He died a few minutes later in the arms of one of his soldiers.[56]

The 7th Minnesota's advance to the front line took place during the slackening of enemy fire, as Mabry's brigade sought cover in the hollow and Bell's regiments were just emerging from the woods. General Smith watched as Bell's brigade moved across the field, too late to support Mabry.

There was no skirmish line or main line or reserve, but seemed to be a foot race to see who should reach us first. They were allowed to approach, yelling

and howling like Comanches, to within canister range, when the batteries of
the First Division opened upon them. Their charge was evidently made with
the intention to capture our batteries, and was gallantly made, but without
order, organization, or skill.[57]

The 7th Minnesota settled in behind the rail fence alongside Companies E
and H of the 12th Iowa, which had been resupplied with cartridges and did
not need to fall back with their regiment. The 7th was a larger regiment than
the 12th Iowa, and there were nearly twice the number of guns being fired; the
sound of the crashing musketry swelled dramatically.[58]

From the cover of the hollow, Mabry yelled over to Capt. Jasper Green, the
only officer of the 38th Mississippi not killed or wounded, and asked if his men
could stand another charge. Green, a Baptist minister, yelled back, "Colonel, we
have exhausted every round of ammunition, but if you say so, we will try again
with empty guns." With nothing to be gained, Mabry replied, "We can't stay
here and live. Order your men back."[59]

The order was given, but it could not be obeyed. Any man who tried to
move, whether forward or back, was shot down. Even so, some still pressed on.
Pvt. F. Holloway of the 38th Mississippi took a bullet to the left arm trying to
reach the shelter of the hollow. Pvt. John Snell of the 6th Mississippi charged
forward toward the enemy line, but before he could cross the open ground he
was hit by a round of artillery, a solid shot, which tore his leg off and threw his
body into the dust.[60]

The remnants of Mabry's Brigade, unable to retreat or advance, fought on
with renewed tenacity and were proving difficult to drive away. Marshall, riding back and forth behind the 7th Minnesota, advised the company commanders to have their men aim low to the ground. (The colonel, sitting high on his
horse, made a tempting target, but he was never touched, though there were a
couple of close calls: his horse was wounded, and a spent ball lodged in his felt
hat.) Most of the men in Marshall's regiment escaped injury by lying on the
ground to shoot over the rails and then rolling onto their backs to reload. Two
men in Company K refused to lie down and fought on one knee, where they
said they could see better. Another man in the same company rose to his feet
and began hurling curses across the field at the enemy. A musket rammer had
streaked across the field and pierced his bicep, and he stopped to pull the long
bloody piece of steel from his arm. Captain Carter remembered laughing at
the sight: "It was ludicrous to hear him use strong invectives against the 'rebel'
who was so careless as to leave his ramrod in his gun after loading."[61] Carter

also commented on one of his men who lay flat on his face without moving a muscle, though he did not appear to have been shot.

> I asked the man next to him if he were dead, and he said he had not noticed anything wrong with him, and shaking him, he put his mouth near his ear and spoke to him. Looking up at me he said, "Fruits (the recumbent was a German named Fruechte, which our boys called 'Fruits') claims that he cannot get his gun to go off," and picking up the gun and looking at it, he found that the cap had never been snapped. He told Fruits that his gun was so dirty that he could not use it, and he would use his (Fruits) during the battle, which he did. This was the only case of physical cowardice that I ever saw.[62]

Colonel Marshall had anticipated that the rapid fire would quickly shoot away the 7th Minnesota's forty rounds per man and had sent to the rear for more ammunition, so boxes were piled up behind the firing line. Marshal split open the crates with his saber, gathered up the paper-wrapped bundles (each containing ten cartridges), and passed them out to the company captains and file closers, who then distributed them to the men. The firing continued without pause.[63]

However, a new problem presented itself: bad powder. An unscrupulous contractor had added an unknown substance to the powder in an effort to fill more cartridges at less cost and pass it off as acceptable powder. Undoubtedly, he had paid off an inspector, and the inferior powder made its way to the army. Whatever the additive was, it prevented the powder from fully igniting, and once fired, the guns immediately began to foul and clog the barrel, "so that many became unserviceable, the balls sticking halfway down." The same thing had happened to the men of the 12th Iowa, who had just spent the previous forty-five minutes cleaning their guns before they were once again ready to return to the firing line. It was providential that the guns of the 7th Minnesota became unserviceable just as Mabry's attack ground to a halt.[64]

FIFTEEN

"Endurance Had Reached a Limit"

Unable to advance or retreat, the surviving soldiers in Mabry's Brigade prayed for a miracle. The answer to their prayers was Tyree Bell's brigade, which came up on the right and drew the fire away from the beleaguered Mississippians.

When Bell's brigade finally entered the field, it was moving obliquely to the right to follow Buford's original order to plug the gap between Crossland's and Mabry's brigades. Though such a move was no longer necessary, the Tennesseans continued on in the same southeasterly direction and, as a consequence, spent a much longer time than Mabry's Brigade in the field and were under enemy artillery fire from the start. On the left was Clark Barteau's 2nd Tennessee; extending the line to the right was Col. John Newsom's 19th Tennessee, Andrew Wilson's 16th, and Robert Russell's 15th Tennessee. As Russell's regiment passed through a skirt of trees, the line was dressed and the diagonal movement ceased. They faced forward and, in quick time, headed out into the field.[1]

As the brigade emerged from the trees, Lt. Tully Brown, commanding the right section of Morton's Battery of Tennesseans, limbered up his two cannon and kept pace with the left of Bell's line. Rice's Battery had earlier accompanied Crossland's attack, but the guns had been laboriously rolled forward by hand, a deadly feat in the heat. Brown's two guns were drawn onto the field by horses (eight per gun, rather than the usual six). This increased mobility brought his guns up quickly, but it also made them a tempting target for the enemy. The other two guns of Morton's Battery stayed well back from the fighting and took up a post on the far left where Bell had emerged from the trees.[2]

As with the two previous charges, when Bell's brigade reached midfield, the enemy's artillery switched from shell to canister. Two batteries fired into their ranks without pause, and they were soon joined by the small arms of the infantrymen. "Never had such an appalling fire of musketry and artillery blazed and gushed in the face of the Second Tennessee," claimed Sgt. R. R. Hancock, "and notwithstanding in spite of the fact that their ranks had never been so fearfully thinned on any previous field, yet they had never more coolly and deliberately faced the missiles of death than on this memorable occasion."[3]

The arrival of Bell's brigade provided the support needed for Mabry's men to escape the meager shelter of the hollow and make their way back to the tree line. Unfortunately, the additional firepower concentrated on Bell made his attack falter, just as the others had. Col. Clark Barteau made it to within twenty yards of the enemy and was still waving his men forward when a bullet crashed into his wrist and opened an ugly gash. The loss of blood, along with the heat and fatigue, forced him to relinquish command to Lt. Col. George Morton. But the lieutenant colonel was not fully recovered from a wound he'd taken at Paducah, Kentucky, and he was unable to stand up to the exertion of the charge. Soon he, too, headed to the rear. Within minutes the senior officer in the 2nd Tennessee was Lt. George E. Seay, all of the others having been killed, wounded, or disabled. In less than twenty minutes more than 400 of Bell's men had fallen, including all four of his regimental commanders.[4]

Nor was Lt. Tully Brown's section of artillery spared the carnage. At just one of his guns, six of the seven cannoneers were wounded, and all eight of the horses killed. The other piece was disabled when a Union artillery round scored a hit and shattered one of the wheels. Sgt. J. W. Brown, with blood flowing from three wounds, calmly ordered a spare wheel to be brought up from the caisson and personally directed its replacement in the middle of the firestorm. With one of his limbers completely disabled by dead horses, Lieutenant Sale, commander of Morton's Battery, called for the other limber to come up and draw off the stranded cannon. While waiting for the limber to arrive, Sale rode his horse onto the little knoll where his two guns were drawing such a heavy fire. Sgt. Frank Reid described the scene:

> The air was dark with a storm of bullets and shells. It seemed certain death to sit there on horseback, and [Lt.] Brown remonstrated with him against the rash act; but his eye had caught sight of a very small pony that had been harnessed to the limber in the place of a big wheel horse disabled. An amused expression came over his face, and, pointing to the pony, his answer to the remonstrance was: "Brown, _____ if he don't believe he's a wheel-horse!"[5]

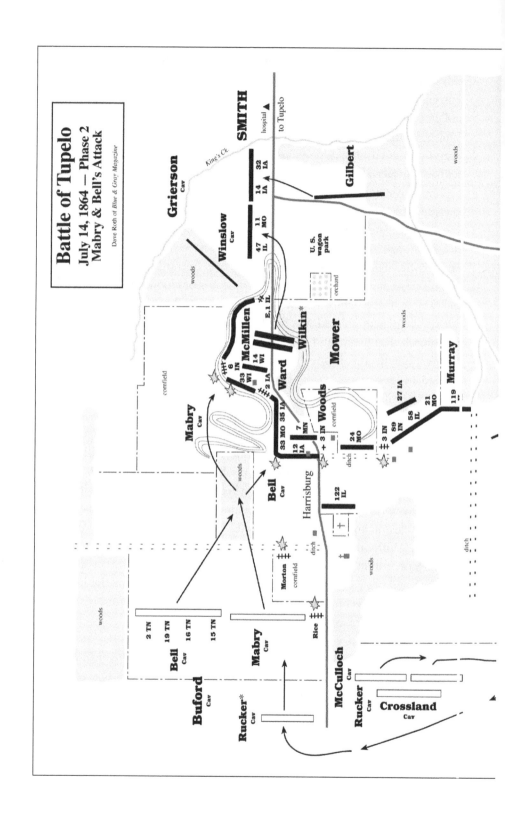

Battle of Tupelo
July 14, 1864 — Phase 2
Mabry & Bell's Attack

Dave Roth of *Blue & Gray Magazine*

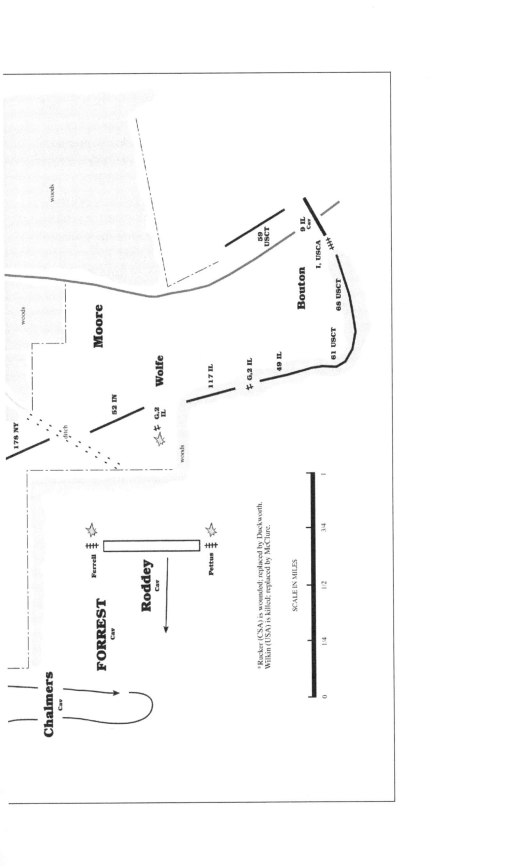

Chalmers
Cav

FORREST
Cav

Roddey
Cav

Ferrell
‡‡‡

Pettus
‡‡‡

178 NY

52 IN

Wolfe

Moore

woods

woods

G.2
IL

117 IL

G.2 IL

49 IL

61 USCT

68 USCT

Bouton

59
USCT

I, USCA

9 IL
Cav

woods

ditch

*Rucker (CSA) is wounded; replaced by Duckworth.
Wilkin (USA) is killed; replaced by McClure.

SCALE IN MILES

0   1/4   1/2   3/4   1

Help came from the most unlikely of sources. Two days before the battle, Jim Titus of the 3rd Tennessee was promoted from corporal to captain and given command of a "temporary experimental organization" composed of soldiers being held for trial for various crimes "and other grave military offenses." Thomas Jordan explained, "In organizing the company, General Forrest told these men that he would not return them to fight with their companies as yet, but would place them on probation during the impending battle." Oblivious to the fire and the heat, the men of Titus's company surged forward, several of them clapping onto the cannon, and began pulling and pushing the damaged piece toward the woods. Fifty-odd men had set out with Captain Titus, and by the time the cannon had been hauled to safety, a third of them had fallen.[6]

There was nothing more Bell's men could do. Like Mabry's Brigade before them, they began to fall back across the field or seek shelter behind whatever scant cover they could find. Those who stayed kept up an ineffectual fire while they hoped and prayed for help.

In the woods behind them Rucker's brigade of Chalmers's Division was preparing to make their charge across the open field. It would need plenty of luck if it was to have any hope of succeeding where three other brigades had failed. The Union line had been tested by veteran troops and, though it had been bloodied, it had not been broken; it had not even bent. Each of the previous charges had been launched squarely at the Third and Fourth brigades (Ward and Woods) of Mower's First Division. These were the same two brigades that had thwarted the Confederate attempts to break the column on the Tupelo Road less than twenty-four hours earlier. Mabry and Bell had wrecked their brigades attempting to break the enemy line and had not even come close. For a second time the Confederate fire slackened as Bell's brigade stopped its charge well short of Mower's line. Those not injured fell back or sought shelter among Mabry's remaining men in the hollow.

Chaplain Humphreys of the 12th Iowa watched them flee: "Again they break and fly for safety beyond the reach of the 'boys' guns." The timing of their repulse worked well for the men of the 7th Minnesota, who had shot away the last of their tainted ammunition. In his memoir, Carter bragged about how each man "fired from sixty to eighty rounds in all." When the ammunition was used up, the 7th Minnesota marched back to its reserve position and the 12th Iowa returned to its place behind the low barricade. "After our guns were cleaned," explained Captain Reed, "we returned to the front just in time to repel a charge from one of Chalmers brigades." The Minnesotans moved back less than a hundred yards and quickly set about cleaning their own fouled rifles.[7]

Lee called on Chalmers to help, with his two brigades in reserve. Though the division had seen no fighting that morning, the men were growing weary. He explained, "As there was some change in the orders about our position after we came upon the field, there was consequently marching and counter-marching, which proved very exhausting to men unaccustomed to marching on foot." As Chalmers moved up to support Buford, the confusion and lack of communication reached its zenith: "From General Forrest I received an order to move to the right and support General Roddey; from General Lee to move to the left and support Colonel Mabry, and from General Buford an order stating that I should move by direction of General Lee, to relieve him on the center. Major-General Forrest being my immediate superior, I obeyed his order and moved to the right." The bitterness felt by the Kentuckians is evident in the tone of Henry George of the 7th Kentucky, when he wrote, "I presume it will never be known why General Chalmers was ordered from the rear of the Kentucky Brigade, at a time when it was being slaughtered, to support a division that never fired a gun in the battle."[8]

Once again Forrest overstepped his self-imposed, limited authority by issuing orders directly to Chalmers. It is curious that Chalmers even paused to decide which order to follow. Under normal circumstances, Forrest was his direct superior and his decision would have been correct. But on the morning of July 14, Forrest commanded only Roddey's Division, and Chalmers answered to General Lee. Either he chose to disregard Lee's order out of loyalty to Forrest or someone had neglected to tell him of the modified chain of command. Either scenario was testimony to the breakdown of communications in Lee's army that morning. Why Forrest gave the order to Chalmers when he had already withdrawn Roddey is even more puzzling. Chalmers was marching his tired troopers away from the fighting when their presence was greatly needed in the other direction.

As the minutes ticked away with no sign of Chalmers or his division, Lee turned his horse to the south and rode off to find them. He found Chalmers at the head of his marching column. A direct verbal order from the commanding general split the division; McCulloch's brigade was to return to the reserve position, and Rucker was "to charge at a double-quick and with a shout."[9]

In his written account of the battle, Lee described meeting with Forrest and bluntly asking him what had gone wrong.

Lee: "Why did you not carry out the plan of attack?"

Forrest: "Buford's right had been rashly thrown forward and repulsed. In the exercise of my discretion I did not move Roddey forward but I have moved him to the left and formed a new line."

Lee: "In doing as you did, you failed to carry out the plan of battle agreed upon, and have caused the loss of many men in the left wing."

Forrest: "If so Gen. Lee, it has been an error of the head and not of the heart."[10]

It's unknown how General Forrest reacted to this rebuke but for the next several hours he did little more than place Roddey's Division along the Tupelo–Verona Road and reposition Pettus's battery. For the rest of the morning Forrest was out of the fight.[11] Before they parted, Lee conceded to Forrest that the attack had failed: "It was too late to remedy the matter, and he ordered the three brigades of Bell, Mabry and Rucker to withdraw." Unfortunately, the order came too late, as Bell's Tennesseans were pinned down and Rucker's men were about to enter the field.[12]

If the men of Rucker's brigade believed that Mabry and Bell had softened the Union line in front of them, they were terribly mistaken; the only differences they would encounter was an air temperature that had become even hotter and a field now strewn with bodies. This "proud little brigade" was composed of Duckworth's 7th Tennessee, the 8th Mississippi under Capt. Charles W. Johnston (standing in for the wounded Colonel Duff), and the 18th Mississippi Battalion under Lt. Col. Alexander Chalmers. Many of the men wore bloody bandages on their arms and heads, a reminder of their fight at Bertram's Shop. And now, across the field, were the Third and Fourth brigades of Mower's division, the very men who had handled them so roughly the day before. But somewhere up ahead were the captured colors of the 8th Mississippi, and the men of that regiment were determined to take them back.[13]

In order to come up behind Bell's brigade, Rucker's men had to cross through the woods to the south and west of the old church. Pvt. John Somerville of the 7th Tennessee wrote how the "ground over which we passed was covered in many places with such a thick growth of blackjack bushes a man could not be seen two steps in our advance distinctly." As they struggled through the scrub oak, Chalmers ordered his Second Brigade, led by Black Bob McCulloch, forward on their right to attack the line where Crossland had been driven back. Before the Second Brigade emerged from the woods, however, both Lee and Forrest called on McCulloch to halt "this hopeless enterprise" and to remain in place "to support the centre, and cover the retreat in event of disaster." For the fourth time that morning, a lone brigade was hurled against the Union line without support on either of its flanks.[14]

Gen. James Chalmers, a gifted and able soldier, was not at the top his game that day or the preceding days. He had misunderstood enemy movements and exhausted his men and horses in near constant marching (often in the wrong direction), and his effectiveness had been minimal in the flank march and the resulting fight at Bertram's Shop. As his men in Rucker's brigade marched toward their probable doom, he exchanged ineffectiveness for recklessness. While Rucker took his place on the right of the line, Chalmers rode up to take charge on the left. Such a move was inspiring to the men and was something Forrest often did, but on this day it was particularly foolhardy given the horrendous casualties the division had already taken.[15]

The advancing Confederates passed out of the woods and crossed over to the north side of the Tupelo Road and into the plowed field. The atmosphere in the woods was stifling; hardly a breeze stirred the leaves. But as the men entered the clearing, the heat reflected off of the baked ground hit them like a fiery wall. Every breath was tortured, and they too soon emptied their canteens of their tepid water.[16]

During the first two attacks the Federals had allowed the Confederates to approach to within yards of the Union line before firing, but this time they began to open fire the moment Rucker's men came into view. Chalmers kept the men at a walking pace as they passed through the plowed ground and into the cornfield "in full view of the enemy for 2,000 yards." He could not take the risk of calling the charge with a mile of open ground still ahead of them. Had he done so, none of them would have survived such a distance under those conditions. They had to remain at a walk until at least within 100 yards of the enemy, all the while being shot at.[17]

Despite the measured pace—or perhaps because of it—men began to fall at an alarming rate. Heat and Federal bullets were opening huge gaps in the line, and there were no reinforcements or reserves to fill them. They pressed on with "resplendent courage" to within sixty yards of Mower's line and finally charged forward. On the hill, Mower noted how the Confederates' line extended farther north than in the two previous attacks and ordered McMillen to detach one of his regiments and extend the blue line to the right.[18]

Lt. Colonel Samuel Jennison and his 10th Minnesota Infantry, 666 officers and men, were posted on the left of McMillen's line and spent the morning overlooking an empty cornfield to the north. Jennison's left flank was tight against the 6th Indiana Battery, and though the fighting had been raging only yards away, his men had been mere spectators. This easy duty ended, however, when the enemy emerged from the trees and Colonel McMillen ordered a left wheel, with the left flank of the regiment becoming a pivot point while the right flank moved in a circular movement to the west (much like a door swinging on a hinge). When the order came to halt, the 10th Minnesota had changed its front ninety degrees and, as a consequence, extended the Union line an additional hundred yards to the north. Although Companies A and E were performing picket duty in the King Creek bottoms, the remaining eight companies presented a formidable front of more than 400 rifles, one of the largest regiments in Smith's army. "Their new position," Jennison explained, "was concealed from the enemy by the crest of a ridge, upon which Mueller's battery of Rodman guns had been doing excellent service. I awaited the enemy until I was satisfied I could reach them with the fire of my riflemen, when the regiment rose as one man, developing a line of greater extent to their left than the enemy had yet seen, and gave them a volley."[19]

Rucker's men, who were then moving up the slope, turned as many of their guns as they could muster toward the new threat and delivered a ragged fire. On the other side of the battery, Colonel Lovell ordered the men of the 33rd Wisconsin to their feet in response. Capt. George Carter wrote, "Up rise our death dealing lines of blue and such volleys and such cheers as would deafen a mute. Their lines halt, waver, try to fire, go down like grass before a scythe."[20]

The valiant survivors of Rucker's brigade were too exhausted and too few to pierce the Union line. "The brigade charged up the steaming slope by the right flank," recalled Private Young of the 7th Tennessee, "the men falling everywhere from the murderous fire of the enemy's infantry and fainting by dozens from the intense heat and thirst." One of the stricken was Pvt. John Somerville, who was "struck in three places and so completely exhausted by fatigue and the oppressive heat of the day, that it was with the greatest difficulty that I got off the field."[21]

Within sixty yards of his goal, Colonel Rucker went down with two wounds and had to be helped to safety. Col. William Duckworth moved over to the right and assumed command of the brigade. Fully a third of the brigade's men were down, with more falling every minute. Lt. Colonel Bill Taylor took over the 7th Tennessee from Duckworth, and next to him Color Sgt. Egbert Shepherd was hit while carrying the regimental banner. Unable to continue on, he called out for someone else to take the flag, and a dozen men sprang forward to protect the regimental pride. Sgt. Maj. Charlie Clairborne was also mortally wounded. Yet, somehow the men found the strength to fight on. John Hubbard of the 7th Tennessee thought the men "fought as if they expected some supreme moment was near when they would repeat the work of Brice's Cross Roads." But that moment never came, and the men of the 7th Tennessee continued to fall without making a single gain.[22]

Chalmers refused to admit he had been defeated by the enemy; even long after the war he placed the blame on the relentless heat: "So great indeed was the distress from thirst that, for some moments, all organization was at an end." Miraculously untouched, Chalmers had seen enough and called for his men to

fall back. As Pvt. John Hubbard of the 7th Tennessee observed, "Human endurance had reached a limit." What was left of Mabry's and Bell's brigades staggered back with Rucker's. McCulloch's men provided an ineffective long-range
fire from the far edge of the field to cover the withdrawal. Men moved out of
the clearing as best they could, running, walking, or crawling. Private Hubbard
explained, "[We] retreated with no attention to order. To save individual life
was now all that could be expected of the living." Some used the last of their
strength to run for the woods; others simply turned their backs and began the
long walk back. Those who could do neither crawled away or simply lay where
they fell. Very few had enough fight left in them to fire back at the enemy.[23]

Mower and Smith, with their combined staffs, peered through the smoke at
the far end of the field to see if another charge was in the offing. To their disappointment, they saw nothing, and it was too much to hope the enemy would
continue the futile assaults. After a few minutes, and "losing all hope of their
attempting any closer quarters," Mower called for a general advance of his line.
Men who had been lying down to fight rose to their feet and dressed their lines.
At the command, the long, dusty, blue line moved forward at the double quick
and counterattacked down the slope.[24]

Woods's Third Brigade almost immediately began to lose its alignment.
When the brigade started out, it was still formed at a right angle with the 12th
Iowa facing due west and the 33rd Missouri and 35th Iowa to the north. Because of the alignment problems, a gap formed immediately between the 12th
Iowa and the rest of the brigade. Luckily, the men of the 7th Minnesota, having
finished cleaning their fouled rifles, returned to their supporting position when
the charge commenced. Colonel Marshall ordered them to move in to fill the
gap, along with a company of the 33rd Missouri, thus preserving the line.[25]

Col. John McClure, elevated to command of the Second Brigade after
Wilkin's death, was determined to not be left behind. His brigade had remained
in a reserve status throughout the morning and had seen no action. He had
sent half the men away to guard the wagons, and McClure had been waiting impatiently to bring up his remaining regiments. When the counterattack
commenced, he led what troops he had on hand—the 9th Minnesota with detachments of the 5th Minnesota and 8th Wisconsin—and set out to help drive
the enemy back.[26]

The crooked Union line advanced at different rates; some units double-
timed while others held to a steady walk. In front of Woods's brigade was the
hollow that had sheltered the Confederates, and the first troops to reach it were
from the 33rd Missouri Infantry. Lt. Col. William Heath had sent Capt. William McKee and Company D to the front to act as skirmishers. There, McKee

and his men came on "a party of the enemy's sharpshooters," who they charged and chased away from the cover. The Confederates were men of the 6th Mississippi, Mabry's Brigade, who, in an extreme act of bravery, were simply attempting to find their colors and remove them from the field. Unable to complete their mission, the Mississippians were either shot down or captured as the Federal advance passed through the hollow and continued down the slope.[27]

There were bodies everywhere—in the hollow, the fields, the skirt of woods, everywhere. Dead soldiers lay in every conceivable position, and wounded men were scattered where they had fallen or were gamely trying to crawl away. The Federals stepped over and around them but otherwise ignored the fallen men. Their attention was focused on the wood line at the far end of the field. Thousands of eyes peered through the smoky haze to see if the Confederates were rallying for a defense or if reserves were coming out to meet them. Southern resistance in the field itself was practically nonexistent, and only a few Confederates turned to fire at the blue line. At first there was strong artillery fire from Morton's, Rice's, and Thrall's batteries, but it soon dwindled to a few shells and then stopped altogether. These guns had advanced into the field, and the retreat of the dismounted cavalry left them exposed and vulnerable. They limbered up and disappeared into the trees.[28]

Mower had ordered the charge with the hope of not only driving the enemy from the open field but also of coaxing the Confederates out of the woods for another fight. The southerners, however, had had enough. With little to no organization left in their ranks, those still on the field were doing their best to reach their own lines. As Chaplain Humphreys of the 12th Iowa said, "The rebels, swift of foot, escape the steel of our bayonets and seek safety in the timber."[29]

The Union line came to a halt midway across the field and just north of old Harrisburg. Mower explained, "I had two field officers and several men sunstruck during the charge, and the enemy having fallen back to their led horses, disappeared from our front, I did not attempt to pursue them any farther, as my command was well nigh exhausted with the march of nineteen miles and the fighting of the day before; in fact, it would have been useless to pursue mounted infantry with troops on foot under any circumstances."[30]

What Mower had seen to make him believe the Confederates were mounted up and withdrawing is a mystery. The enemy directly in his front, Buford's and Chalmers's men, were still on foot, as their horses were better than a mile away at the old dismounted camp. And the two division commanders, along with members of Forrest's staff, were rapidly pulling the men into a defensive line should the northerners attack.[31]

In his biography of Forrest, Thomas Jordan was blunt in his assessment of the day's fighting: "The Confederate attack had now failed at all points, and it was manifest the Federal position and force was impregnable to any offensive operations of the Confederates arrayed against them. General Lee, therefore, ordered his whole force to retire from the field, and occupy the position held at daylight." Lee directed Forrest to fall back to the farm of the Widow Sample and to form a new line fronting a large open field. It was a strong position. There was no timber in the front to obscure vision or fire, and it commanded every approach for several hundred yards. Forrest ordered the construction of temporary fortifications there, "and in a short time the men along my entire line were protected behind strong works erected out of the rails, logs and cotton bales which the premises of Mrs. Sample so abundantly furnished."[32]

These fortifications were an extension of the earthworks thrown up by Gen. Hylan Lyon's command. The exhausted division had reached the front at 9:00 A.M., and despite the fatigue of the men in ranks, they were given only a brief rest before being put to work. When Lyon had been given command of the dismounted troops, Lt. Col. Thomas Barnett of the 3rd Kentucky Cavalry had gone along to command the contingent of men from his own regiment, who were also active in constructing the new breastworks. "Here I formed line of battle and threw up some defenses formed of rails," reported Barnett. "After remaining here a short time I moved in line across an open field and threw up a second line of defenses." In a short time, the western edge of Mrs. Sample's property, and the adjoining property of Dr. Ledbetter to the north, were adequately fortified to withstand an attack. In fact, the Confederate works were much stronger than the small rail barricade erected by the Federals on the heights.[33]

It was possible the mounted troops Mower saw were Roddey's Division or even Crossland's Kentucky brigade, which had been resting in the woods south of the Tupelo Road since their failed attack. Because Crossland's men had served as pickets the previous night, their horses were close at hand. Near the end of the fighting on the left, the Kentuckians were ordered to mount up and move over to the Verona Road. By noon they had arrived at Calhoun's Crossroads.[34]

The soldiers of Mower's division, clad in blue wool, stood sweltering in the sun for the better part of an hour. Details walked over the battlefield and helped the Confederate wounded back to the Union field hospitals. Others went out to collect the weapons that had been dropped or abandoned and were now littering the field. Smith did not have the transportation available to carry away all of the small arms, so he ordered the details to destroy the captured weapons. For a solid hour the men smashed wooden stocks and beat the hammers and lock plates into junk. Among the weapons left on the field was a Confederate artillery piece. The only battery in the immediate path of the advancing Federals had been Morton's Battery of Tennesseans, which had struggled to withdraw its shattered crews and guns from the field. Capt. Joseph Reed of the 2nd Iowa Light Artillery described a Confederate battery in the position Morton had taken and the devastating fire the two units exchanged. "One of its guns was dismounted and abandoned, and later in the day Lieutenant Chas. F. Reed, of the Second Iowa, with a squad of his men, brought it into our own line and carried it back to Memphis." A. J. Smith confirmed that his men had taken a cannon from the field, though in his report he gave credit to the cavalry for pulling it from the scene of the action.[35]

The men who went out to help with the wounded were stunned by the carnage. "They left all of their dead and most of their wounded in our hands," recalled Sgt. William Tucker. "The rest of the afternoon was occupied in bringing in and caring for the wounded." Robert Burdette of the 47th Illinois was also surprised at the number of dead he came across, writing, "It seemed to me that nobody was wounded that day. It was as though every man that was hit was killed. The taste of blood was in men's mouths."[36]

James Harrison of the 14th Wisconsin described it as "a fearful sight, after the battle, to see the Dead & Dying & Wounded, all stretched out in the broiling sun. Some of the wounded men would beg us not to kill them, said they were conscripted. We told them we did not intend killing them, but treat them as Prisoners of War. Almost every prisoner we took would beg us not to kill them nor let them be put in the niggers charge." Harrison speculated that the affair at Fort Pillow had prompted such requests. Another common claim made by the prisoners was their belief that, until the attack began, they thought the Union army was composed of only "100-days men and negros," neither of which had been expected to put up much of a fight.[37]

Captain Carter of the 7th Minnesota, who noted how "a person could walk a long distance without touching the ground if he stepped on the dead and wounded," stopped to talk to a desperately wounded Confederate from Mabry's Brigade who had fallen not far from the rail barricade.

He lay with his head propped up by some article, I have forgotten what, and as I stopped and asked him if I could do anything for him, he said he had a great curiosity to know what took place to cause such an increase in our fire after the battle had been on about an hour. He said he had been in many hard battles, but never saw or experienced such a fire as that before. I told him of our taking the place of the Twelfth Iowa and of our watching the men to make them fire low. He said that must have been the cause, for he was in the low ground. He was white as snow from loss of blood, having received four wounds. He first received a wound through one lung and tried to leave the field, but was hit by a bullet in one thigh. Still trying to get off the field, he received another bullet through the other lung, but was still able to crawl. A bullet through the other thigh caused him to cease his efforts to leave the field. He realized his condition and bravely and cheerfully awaited the end. I did what I could for him, but was obliged to leave before he was picked up and taken to the hospital. I think he was a lieutenant, and his residence was Ripley.[38]

By 11:00 A.M. General Mower finally acknowledged that the Confederates were not coming out on the field again, and he withdrew his division to the ridge. There, the overheated soldiers were given a brief rest. Once they were rested and had refilled their canteens, cartridge boxes, and percussion cap pouches, they picked up picks and shovels and went about building breastworks along the ridge of the high ground. If the Confederates attacked again, they would find conditions even worse than before—if that was possible.[39]

Col. Thomas Kenney of the 119th Illinois Infantry looked across the field with pity and compassion. After sending out skirmishers, he directed squads of men to bring in more of the enemy wounded for care. He even went so far as to ride out into the field and direct the activities in person. "While engaged in this humane act of administering to the wounded rebels on the field," he later wrote, "we were fired upon by the enemy from the woods, some 300 yards distant. This caused us to cease our acts of kindness for a time, but after a time we resumed the efforts, and succeeded in carrying from the field all the wounded, who were duly cared for by our surgeons."[40]

As the afternoon shadows lengthened and the work on the breastworks continued, many of the Union soldiers took a break from the digging for a walk across the battlefield. Some fell in to help with removal of the Confederate wounded, while a few took the opportunity to search for souvenirs. Most wandered about in a daze, unable to fully comprehend the devastation around them. Pvt. Sidney Robinson of the 117th Illinois tried to draw a comparison his mother could understand; "Here the Rebs lay scattered around like Pumpkins in a field."[41]

Many noticed the body of Col. William Faulkner of the 12th Kentucky. At least five diary entries make note of Faulkner being dead on the field (and two of them, including A. J. Smith's, gave him a posthumous promotion to brigadier general). Pvt. Charles Tiedman of the 178th New York remembered him as "the Butcher of Fort Pillow." But apparently none of them looked too closely; if anyone had, they would have noted that there was still life to be found in Faulkner. He had been shot in the right arm and the left thigh and had passed out from shock or loss of blood, but he was still breathing. He would pass a night and a day on the battlefield before he was finally found and taken to a Confederate hospital for care. The twice-wounded officer recovered quickly and returned to the head of his regiment.[42]

Chaplain Edwards of the 7th Minnesota commented on the scene.

> I came back to the field, shortly after its close and during the lull which had followed the battle. Except for the removal of the wounded the field was as it was left after the charge. The dead seemed very numerous, but I only looked closely at a few of them. Those that I saw were mostly boys, far too young for such a fate. One I noticed with a smooth girlish face, fixed as marble with a smile frozen upon it. The body was only half reclining. It appeared as though when mortally wounded the boy had crept to a tree, and died while leaning against it and gazing at his hand. The hand had a finger extended and a circlet of deadlier white than that of the hand showed where a ring had been. The thieves that plunder the dead on battle fields were already at work. They had taken the ring but it had left its impress. It had told its story. Before leaving the field I saw another pathetic spectacle. Three women had somehow made their way through the lines, and as they passed from place to place, bent over the dead and peered anxiously into their faces. When at last they recognized the object of their search bowing over their dead they gave utterance to the most frantic screams.[43]

The wounded, Federal and Confederate alike, were taken to the field hospital set up in a house alongside the Tupelo Road. There they were cared for without regard to the color of their uniform—the worst cases given priority no matter who they were. They arrived on foot under their own power, helped by friends or strangers, carried on stretchers, or riding in ambulances. Otto Wolf, the seventeen-year-old drummer boy of the 117th Illinois, was one of many who helped the injured from the field.

> I went out with them and helped load one ambulance and went back with it to the Division Hospital where all the wounded were taken and staid there all day helping the doctors to Amputate arms and legs. I helped take off fifteen or twenty legs and arms the yard looked more like a butcher shop than anything I can compare it with; it is an awful sight to see the Doctors sawing and cutting away at a man's arm or leg it is sickening.[44]

(29)

Notes Continued.

.Company C.

Sergeant Andrew C. Colby, wounded 'uly 14th. Left in Hospital and removed with other wounded and prisoners to Mobile Ala. where he died and was later buried in the National cemetery there.

Corporal Perer Anderson . Died at St Louis Oct.8th 1864. Company A.H.Fuller Wounded at Tupelo July 15h died on July 16th.8 cannot find other mention of Corporal Fuller.

Melzer Button Wounded July 14th or 85th.)eft in the Hospital.Fate unknown but supposed to have died in Madon Ga.

Assistant Surgeon Percival O.Barton was detailed to re-main with the wounded prisoners and assist in caring for them.Sergeant David A. Caneday of Co.C. was detailed for the same purpose by Col. Mar-shall;but through some defect in his papers,was afterwards subjected to much difficulty in clearing his record,though after being exchanged he promptly returned and served with his regiment until the close of the war.

I must apologize for deficiencies in my record of the battle of Tupelo on the ground that the service was entirely new to me,I having been but eight day in the service when the Battle begun and owing to the strenuousness of our rapid march had made but few acquaintances amongst men or officers.

A MEMORY OF TUPELO.

"A Memory of Tupelo" (DePauw University Archives and Special Collections)

Indeed, soldiers with minor wounds frequently wrapped them up on their own and stayed with the regiment rather than face the hell of the hospital.

Yet, Surgeon Bartlett of the 33rd Missouri was not an ordinary battlefield sawbones. Though often amputation was the only option, whenever he could he operated to save the limb. That afternoon he performed a resection on one man's shoulder and set a compound fracture of another soldier's thigh, two cases that would have normally been, and under others' care, quick saw work and on to the next patient. He had grown so used to the sight of blood and dying it was hardly worth the mention, but even he could be touched by the sights around him.

> William Garbee's wound was of such a nature as to render recovery impossible under any circumstances hence nothing was done for him except to make him as comfortable as circumstances would admit of. He was probably unconscious from the moment he was hurt. My recollection of this short, red-faced, good natured German drummer-boy is distinct, and—as in many other instances—a very trifling incident led to a somewhat intimate acquaintance and made a permanent impression upon my memory. Garbee once requested me to pull a tooth for him and his molars were so interlocked, or so tightly wedged together, that two were taken out instead of one. The sound tooth was replaced in the jaw; and upon the testimony of Billy, as we familiarly called him, its usefulness in grinding 'hard tack' was not in the least impaired.[45]

It was late in the afternoon when Chaplain Edwards took a final look over the quiet field of battle. "At a distance a thin bluish cloud hung over the crest of the hills, nor was the air yet clear of the battle smoke anywhere," he wrote. "I saw the field as through a haze that only partially veiled the horrors of the scene; for I was able to recognize the gray blotches that spotted the grass as the dead bodies of the enemy, enemies no more."[46]

SIXTEEN

"Who Will Care for Mother Now?"

Critics of A. J. Smith point to the feeble Union counterattack as one of the biggest flaws in his campaign. They argue that if Smith had only pushed forward with the offensive movement, Lee and Forrest would have been crushed. Thomas Jordan, a firm believer in this theory, wrote, "General Smith appears to have been satisfied with being able to foil the attack of his daring assailants, and adventured no offensive movement at all." Or, as Robert Selph Henry stated, "There is no doubt it was a defeat for the Confederates which, with more dash and boldness on the part of A. J. Smith, might have been turned into disaster." Armchair generals point out that there was nothing to stop the Federals from achieving their own Brice's Crossroads victory—nothing, that is, but the lack of "dash and boldness."[1]

It is a valid question whether Smith could have completed the victory if he had only continued the charge to the end of the field and into the trees. It is possible that he could have; but it's also possible that he would not have. Buford's division was a wreck, but Lee and Forrest had other troops to throw into the fray, and though they were in no position to turn the tide of battle, they could easily inflict heavy casualties on a reckless enemy. Oddly, it was the seemingly impotent dismounted division that brought strength back to the defeated Confederates.

While the fighting raged a little over a mile to their east, the men of General Lyon's dismounted division had been busily digging earthworks and building fortifications. These men were mainly cavalry troopers who had either lost their horses in battle or to sickness or had them sent away to regain their health. The soldiers of Colonel Gholson's Mississippi brigade had come up from the Jackson area, while Colonel Neely's brigade of four Tennessee regiments had trekked west from Alabama. There were nearly enough dismounted men from Crossland's Kentucky brigade to form a large regiment, and Lt. Col. Thomas Barnett was detailed to lead them. Col. Charles Fuller had arrived from Mobile with the heavy artillerists of Beltzhover's Battalion, and the 1st Mississippi Infantry provided the only contingent of bona fide foot soldiers in the entire army. In all, there were 2,100 men under Lyon, and they were ready and waiting behind strong defensive works.[2]

Hylan Benton Lyon was another one of those rare West Pointers who was able to stay in the good graces of Nathan Forrest. He had graduated from the academy in 1856 and spent the prewar years at a variety of western outposts. In 1861 he resigned his commission to join his fellow Kentuckians in the Confederacy. He was appointed lieutenant colonel just in time to be captured at Fort Donelson and spent the next seven months in Federal prison camps. He avoided a similar fate at Vicksburg when he led his men out of the trap and eventually wound up with Gen. Joseph E. Johnston in Georgia. He was sent back to Mississippi in early May 1864 and put at the head of the brigade of Kentucky Mounted Infantry. He did so well at Brice's Crossroads he was recognized for his abilities and promoted to brigadier general a mere four days after the fight. When it came to selecting a senior officer to lead the dismounted division, his was the only name on the list of candidates—he being the only brigadier general not already in command of a division.[3]

Alongside Lyon's men, Roddey's Division was digging across Mrs. Sample's property. Roddey's men had done some marching earlier in the morning, and though they had come close to making an assault, they had engaged in no real fighting. Roddey added an additional 1,500 rifles to the Confederate defenses. Not counting Buford's and Chalmers's divisions, Lee and Forrest had 3,600 men entrenched or waiting behind barricades on the widow's farm just west of old Harrisburg.

Though they were still outnumbered by the Federals, the advantage might well have shifted to the Confederates if the Union had continued its charge that day. Frontal assaults against a well-manned entrenched position were nothing short of suicide. Smith's men had been successful in assaulting Fort Derussy, Louisiana, and would be again at Nashville, but in both instances the Confederate earthworks were woefully undermanned. Lee and Forrest had just learned this lesson in the worst possible way, and Smith's position could hardly have been considered fortified. Smith could not see the earthworks the Confederates had constructed, so his decision not to advance could not have been affected by their presence. But what some have characterized as fear, or at least timidity on Smith's part, was no more than common sense and prudence.[4]

A charge into the woods without a reconnaissance or scout report would have been foolhardy. Forrest had built a reputation on seemingly reckless, hell-bent attacks, but they were invariably preceded by highly accurate scouts and surveys of the battlefield; his success depended on knowing where his enemy was and how many there were. In this way he was able to overcome larger numbers in a multitude of engagements. To expect Smith to do differently belittles his abilities as a soldier.

At 11:00 A.M., when Mower's two brigades moved back to their positions on the high ground, Lee and Forrest moved to consolidate their own position, care for the wounded, and try to figure out what to do next. In a foul mood, Forrest stalked back and forth near the new earthworks. Not only had the best of his corps been decimated, but his own son, Lt. Willie Forrest, lay dazed in a field hospital. One of his soldiers passing by noted that Forrest was "so mad he stunk like a pole-cat."[5]

Buford's division, by far the most shot-up of the army, limped back beyond the breastworks and took a position in the Confederate rear. In advance of the earthworks was Chalmers's Division. And so for the better part of an hour the southerners, arrayed in three lines, waited for an enemy that did not come. Once it was clear that there would be no more fighting, at least for the present, men began to venture out to the west side of the field to bring in the dead and wounded. They could see the enemy on the far side of the field engaged in the same activities.[6]

During Bell's attack, Sgt. Richard Hancock of the 2nd Tennessee had led his wounded brother, W. C., off the field to the field hospital set up "under some beautiful shade trees" in a yard on the Tupelo–Pontotoc Road. Rather than return to the fight, Richard decided to stay with his brother.

> After cording his leg better and giving him some stimulants, one of the doctors remarked that he was too much fatigued to stand an amputation just then. So we removed him from the table to a blanket spread upon the ground in the shade of a tree. Perhaps he had not been lying on that blanket over forty-five minutes when he fainted, as I thought. I called the attention of a doctor, who on feeling his pulse, remarked, "HE IS DEAD." These words were like a "clap of thunder in a clear sky" to me. I had no thought of his dying this suddenly; in fact, I thought that he would get well. . . . I know of no language by which to express what I felt while *kneeling by the side of a dying brother*.[7]

Another visitor to the hospital that afternoon was John Somerville of the 7th Tennessee, who was seeking treatment for his three wounds, none of them life threatening, when he came on the body of his friend, Sgt. Maj. Charlie Claiborne. Later he took on the painful duty of writing Jane Claiborne, the dead soldier's grandmother, telling her, "My heart bled when I looked on the noble form of my friend and comrade your beloved grandson and I thought of you, I stooped and clipped from his head the hair that I enclose you. It is wrapped in a useless portion of the bandage that covered his wounds."[8] Ordnance Sgt. Daniel Farrar of the 4th Mississippi, Mabry's Brigade, also wrote a painful letter to the wife of Sgt. John Cato:

> It is with sorrow that I announce to you the death of your dear husband. He was killed in battle on the 14th inst. near Tupelo. The fight was a terrific one . . . Our regiment was ordered to storm the hill where the enemy was posted, and finding their numbers too great, we retreated, and in the retreat your husband was shot down . . . his pockets were rifled, and nothing could be found, but a copy of a song he used to sing, "Who Will Care for Mother Now?"[9]

After an hour or so, Bell's Fourth Brigade moved back two or three miles to the wagon train to draw forage and rations. Once man and beast were satisfied, Lee ordered Buford's entire division south to Palmetto Church at Calhoun's Crossing, where the division had paused the day before prior to the fight at Camargo Crossroads.[10]

As the afternoon passed on and the shadows began to lengthen, the men of Chalmers's Division noted a building burning in old Harrisburg. John Hubbard of the 7th Tennessee claimed that the Union soldiers were not just burning but "literally tore up the town by tearing down the houses and using the lumber for breast-works." Chaplain Edwards of the 7th Minnesota also noted that the rail barricade in front of his regiment was strengthened with the "debris of the farm belongings." Which buildings were burned is unknown. General Chalmers reported, "The enemy commenced to burn the houses in Harrisburg." There could not have been too many houses; the town was pretty much abandoned before the war, and most of the farms that were still occupied were within the Confederate lines. One of the buildings that was most likely burned was the old church along the Tupelo–Pontotoc Road. Earlier in the day Confederate sharpshooters had been posted in the church and other surrounding buildings and had maintained a harassing fire for several hours. More than likely, the soldiers of Moore's Third Division burned the buildings to discourage the return of the sharpshooters. There was also a scattering of houses within the Federal lines that may have been burned once the Union soldiers had stripped away the useful lumber for breastworks and campfires.[11]

When Chalmers was made aware of the buildings burning in Harrisburg, he advanced McCulloch's brigade into the field with the 1st Mississippi Infantry acting as skirmishers. In addition, he took along a single piece of artillery, which "obtained a good position and did much execution, throwing shell into the fires which the enemy had kindled, and by the light of which he could be seen moving about."[12] While Chalmers mentions the burning of the buildings as his motivation in advancing McCulloch's brigade, it is hardly a satisfactory reason for the poorly timed move. It was more likely an attempt to ascertain enemy intentions rather than to avenge the burning of a few abandoned buildings. As McCulloch moved forward, the Union cavalry returned to its own lines, and in sporadic firing six of Chalmers's men were wounded before the general pulled them back, confident that the enemy was still on the high ground.[13]

* * *

As darkness fell over the battlefield a hush descended on the two armies. Nightfall was the accepted indicator for both sides to cease hostilities for the day. The occasional pop of a skirmisher's rifle was the only sound other than the normal camp noise and the activity around the hospitals. But the quiet was deceptive. Forrest was on the move. Just as the sun was setting on July 14, Forrest sent an aide over to Rucker's brigade with orders to mount up and meet with him for a nighttime reconnaissance of the enemy's left flank, "with a view of ascertaining his position and strength in that direction."[14]

Twelve hours earlier Forrest had been in the midst of preparing an attack with Roddey's Division against the Federal left flank. The ill-timed and disastrous attack by Crossland's brigade had put an end to those plans. He was considering a similar movement for the next morning and needed to scout the right to see if such an idea was even feasible. His decision to take Rucker's beat-up brigade indicates that he had no thought of any real action that night; if he had contemplated an actual attack, he would have (or should have) taken a more combat-ready force. Roddey's Division had seen no fighting, and the other brigade of Chalmers's Division could have been summoned to assist. At the very least the rest of the army could have been placed on alert to exploit any gains. As it was, the other brigades drifted off to sleep unaware that their commander was off on the kind of mission he excelled in.

Forrest led the mounted brigade on a roundabout route that mirrored the ride taken by Lt. William Pirtle of the 7th Kentucky the previous night. The men kept the horses at a steady walk down the Camargo Ferry Road to Palmetto and past the grisly hospital at Calhoun's Crossroads. There the column

turned to the east and followed the Verona Road and soon turned up the same
narrow farm road Pirtle had taken to scout the enemy left flank. Slowly and
cautiously, Forrest, near the head of the column, led his men into the woods
and toward the unsuspecting Federal left flank.[15]

Grierson's cavalry had seen little of the fighting and excitement around Harrisburg, save for some light skirmishing.[16] Prior to the Confederate assaults,
Grierson had sent Winslow's brigade to guard the right flank and Colonel
Coon's brigade to the left. Subsequently, the 9th Illinois of Coon's command
was pulled from the patrolling duty and sent to help Bouton's Colored Brigade
on the extreme left of the infantry. Col. Henry Burgh kept the regiment busy
digging earthworks that were never used.[17]

The only enemy activity that drew the attention of Grierson's cavalry
was the ever-present and always unpredictable Capt. Henry Tyler and his
100 picked men of the 12th Kentucky. Tyler had last been seen in the morning's first action in his unsuccessful attempt to draw the Federals off the high
ground. When the effort failed, the indefatigable Tyler received orders from
General Lee to "watch [the] enemy's movements closely eastward." Tyler led
his company south to Verona and continued on two miles to Old Town Creek,
where the Kentuckians moved north along the eastern bank of the levee until
they were opposite Tupelo. Once again, Tyler placed his small unit on the far
side of the Union army and far from his friends in gray.[18]

At 4:00 P.M. Tyler made a move toward town and took possession of the
bridges that crossed over into Tupelo, except for one bridge over the slough
on the east side of town. The Federal pickets were in possession of the slough
bridge, but they soon torched it. Tyler's force was so small that he had no hope
of doing anything more than harass the enemy and draw some of the troops
away from the Harrisburg area. Even in this he had limited success.[19]

The 4th Iowa Cavalry had spent the day with Winslow's brigade on the
Union right and had vigorously patrolled the Ellistown Road to ensure that no
flank attack was in the offing. The sudden appearance of Confederate cavalry
on the far side of Tupelo gave Winslow the impression that the enemy was
preparing to attack the wagon park from the rear. Winslow sent a detachment
of the 4th Iowa into town to drive away the enemy or report if it was the beginning of a serious attack.[20] Under the command of Lt. Col. John Peters, the
detachment, comparable in size to Tyler's, arrived to find no real threat to the
Union rear. What Peters did find was a very vigorous show of strength by a
very small force of mounted Confederates. Tyler himself was once again trying
to do a lot with a little: "I here made all the display possible with my little force
so as to deceive [the] enemy as to my numbers, with, I think, complete success,

as they immediately burned the slough bridge and massed a heavy force (fully a brigade) along its banks to prevent my crossing into town." Peters must have been playing Tyler's own game against him; he managed to fool Tyler into believing that his little battalion was an entire brigade.[21] The two opposing battalions skirmished until nightfall, and at least once the fighting became heavy enough for Winslow to report that Peters was "severely engaged." At dusk Tyler disappeared behind the far levee and the excitement was over. Peters posted pickets, the Federals remaining vigilant should the enemy return.[22]

While Peters and Tyler skirmished on the east side of town, Edward Winslow was preparing a Union detachment on the west side with similar goals. Maj. George Duffield of the 3rd Iowa took Companies D, H, K, L, and M and an equal number of troopers from the 4th Iowa and set out across the battlefield to scout the main Confederate position. If Smith had any uncertainty about whether or not the Confederates had actually left the field, the question was quickly answered when Duffield "found the enemy in force, strongly posted behind temporary earthworks."[23]

Skirmishing broke out, and it carried on until near dark. Cpl. Simon Duck of the 4th Iowa concluded he was involved with something other than a mere reconnaissance. "In the evening we were again sent out to feel the strength of the enemy and if possible bring on another engagement; the rebels drove in the pickets, but could not be induced to attack the main line again, their forenoon combats having satisfied them for present, and the day ended without any more fighting."[24] Just after sunset the Union scout was interrupted by the advance of McCulloch's brigade into the field. Duffield began to pull his men back, hastened by the fire of the piece of artillery Chalmers had sent out with his dismounted cavalry. The view of the advancing Confederate brigade was unnerving to the Union skirmishers, and they stepped up the pace as they hurried back to their own lines. Pvt. Jacob Gantz of the 4th Iowa confessed, "We had to use our legs very fast when we were ordered to fall back or we would have been caught but they did not follow us far."[25]

Black Bob McCulloch's men succeeded in driving the Federal skirmishers of Winslow's brigade out of the field in front of Harrisburg, but there was more to this simple action. While neither Forrest nor Chalmers mentioned it in their reports, Chalmers's actions near dark seemed to be a diversion as Forrest rode off with Rucker's brigade to scout the Union left flank. But if it was a diversion, the ploy failed.

At 5:30 P.M., while the Iowa cavalry and McCulloch's brigade were exchanging fire near Harrisburg, General Smith received a report of an enemy column advancing on his left flank. Col. James Gilbert's Second Brigade of Moore's division had been in reserve throughout the day, having done little more than guard the wagon train from threats that never materialized. Gilbert's four regiments, the 14th, 27th, and 32nd Iowa and the 24th Missouri, set out on a march for the extreme left flank of the line beyond Bouton's Colored Brigade. "I immediately executed this order," Gilbert wrote, "occupying an excellent position just behind the crest of a high hill, which commanded the whole field; I threw out a line of skirmishers upon the next hill in advance." Pvt. Ben Thomas of the 14th Iowa, among the skirmishers sent forward, recalled, "We could see the rebel army in the edge of the timber probably a mile and a half away." The "army" he saw was probably just some skirmishers from Roddey's Division.[26]

A. J. Smith, satisfied that the activity had ended for the day, gave an order that had serious consequences for Forrest's late-night reconnaissance: "At sundown, the enemy making no demonstrations whatever, I directed the main bodies of my command to fall back about 600 yards toward the wagons, in order to give the men rest and opportunity to cook their rations, leaving a strong skirmish line to hold their positions."[27] There was no obvious threat from the south, and with Smith's order to fall back, Gilbert pulled back half a mile and set up a temporary camp. Off to the right of Gilbert's men, the soldiers of Bouton's and Wolfe's brigades had fallen back as well. Up and down the line men stacked arms and began to prepare supper.[28]

Unknown to the Federals, Nathan Forrest was less than two miles away and with Rucker's brigade was making a stealthy approach. "By meandering through the woods," said Forrest, "I approached very near his camps before he discovered my presence." As darkness settled over Mississippi, Col. William Duckworth ordered his men to dismount and every fourth man to assume horse holder duty. The men hurriedly checked their equipment and filled cartridge boxes, and just before 10:00 P.M. the order came to advance.[29]

The moon was nearly full and was high in the sky when the sun set. There was plenty of light to guide the Confederates as they made their way through the brush and trees to the Union line. When Duckworth's dismounted cavalry swarmed out of the woods and up the slope, the Federal skirmishers fell back toward the brigade bivouacs. The Confederates confidently thought the main enemy line was on the ridge and that the advance had succeeded in flanking the enemy. The muzzle flashes from hundreds of rifles effectively destroyed whatever night vision the soldiers had, and even the bright moon was of little help in peering through the smoke and darkness. So in the ensuing confusion, the fact that the Federals were no longer in their original position was not immediately apparent to Duckworth and his men. The significance did not escape Private Tiedman of the 178th New York. "Forrest," he explained, "actually made an attack on our camp at night, but we were *not* in camp, but lay in line of battle in a swamp."[30]

The effect in the Union line was electric. Night actions were very rare, and the men sprang into ranks with drummers beating the long roll. The confusion that reigned on the skirmish line was even greater on the creek bed as men groped in the fire light for their weapons and tried to find their place in the ranks. The flash of the rifles up the slope only added to the uncertainty and disorder, and some men began to immediately fire up the slope at what they believed was the enemy. Second Lt. Herman Hemenway of the 27th Iowa was disgusted by the "brilliant operation of shooting a few of our pickets, who were very gallantly holding their own position."[31]

Wolfe's brigade, in the southwest corner of the Union line, was still in its line of battle from earlier in the day and was the first to meet the enemy skirmishers streaming down the slope. Sgt. Richard Saunders of the 117th Illinois wrote, "After dark, our pickets were driven back into our regiment. We came to a left-half wheel facing in the direction of the enemy firing and moved right up. It was said the old 'Sunday School Regiment' did some fierce and determined fighting." Over on the left, the 14th Iowa was only a few moments slower in toeing the line. Bouton's skirmishers came running down the hill and through the forming ranks of the white soldiers: "Here come the negroes closely followed by the rebels yelling like Indians and firing as fast as they could load their guns. Quick as thought our boys had the arms in hand and we went up over the bluff and formed line on the level ground. It was so dark we could not see a man of the rebels but the front was full of the flashes of their guns."[32]

Otto Wolfe off the 117th Illinois could distinctly hear the Confederate officers call for a volley, and the words "Ready, aim low boys, fire!" could be heard up and down the Union line. "As soon as the command was given 'aim low boys' our boys all dropped to the ground and the bullets whistled harmlessly over them." The return fire from David Moore's division was wide of the mark as well. Blind firing at flashes in the night was a chancy thing at best, and Forrest reported, "Not a man was, however, killed as the enemy overshot us." But the response from the Union line surprised Forrest, who was expecting to find a lightly defended flank. The enemy, he said, "opened upon me one of the heaviest fires I have heard during the war. The enemy's whole force seemed to be concentrated at this point. There was an unceasing roar of small arms, and his whole line was lighted up by a continuous stream of fire."[33]

Overleaf: Forrest's flank attack, July 14, 1864 (Map by David E. Roth)

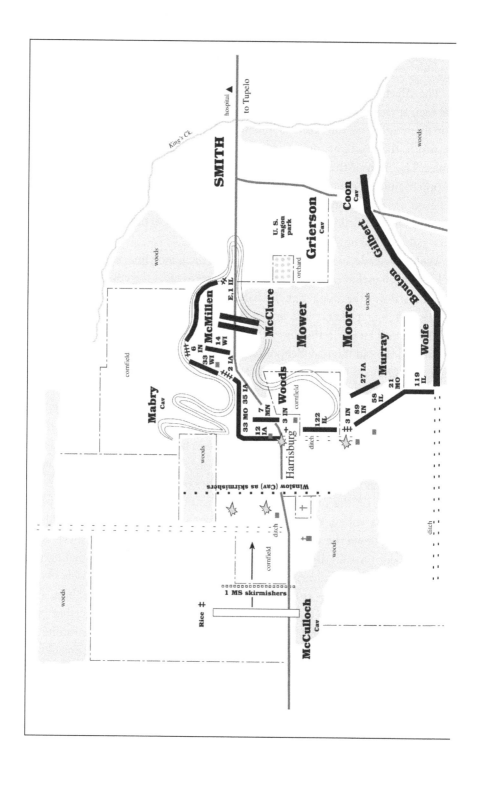

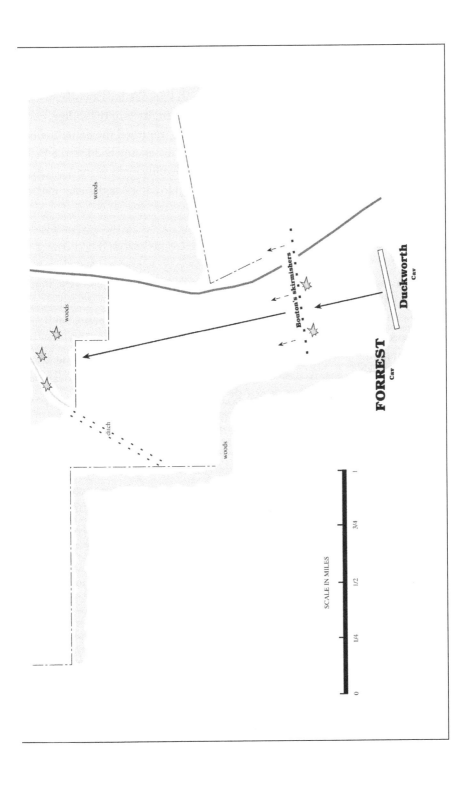

woods

woods

Bouton's skirmishers

ditch

woods

FORREST
Cav

Duckworth
Cav

SCALE IN MILES

0   1/4   1/2   3/4   1

The fire fight went on for the better part of an hour before Forrest yielded the field to the advancing Federals. Moore's men pushed the Confederates far enough to recover their original line and the 9th Illinois's breastworks, which had not been used by either side. Duckworth's men, back in the saddle, rode away to the south. The 117th Illinois, which had "returned the compliment" of the Confederate gunfire, advanced and found the enemy had left the field. This was just fine with Pvt. Thomas: "This was the only night battle I was ever in and I can say I did not like it very well. I would rather see the enemy than only see the flashes of their guns."[34]

It was a minor affair compared to the fighting earlier in the day, and it did nothing to retrieve the waning fortunes of the Confederates. The manner in which Forrest had led the reconnaissance, however, is nothing less than baffling. His stealthy approach from the south had gone unnoticed, and the initial skirmish with the Federal pickets was done in textbook fashion. Granted, the scout had determined that the enemy was heavily posted on their own left flank, but if the Union had been weak in this sector, as Forrest had hoped, the unsupported attack by a shot-up brigade would have accomplished nothing more than alerting the enemy to their own weakness. Even if he had wanted to launch a flank attack in the morning, it was then out of the question. Like a punch-drunk fighter, Forrest had signaled his next blow, and Smith was ready.[35]

Quiet once again fell across the battlefield. Men of both sides wrapped themselves in blankets or curled up against the evening chill. Chaplain Edwards was still awake, but so exhausted that he was of little use in the hospital. A friend, Dr. Murdock, led the young clergyman off to an impromptu campsite. "He took me to a dry bed of a summer stream where the bank undermined by freshets, projected two or three feet over a dry channel of the brook; under which projection we lay down together with our heads as far as possible under the shelving roof of clay and sod and soon as touched the friendly bosom of Mother earth fell into a sleep so deep and trance-like that all the thunders of Forrest's artillery couldn't wake. For all that my inner consciousness could testify, I might have slept there a thousand years."[36]

Sleep would have to wait for Lee, Forrest, and their division commanders, however. Lee called for a meeting to discuss what went wrong and how to prepare for the following morning. Forrest sent a message that he was unwell and could not attend. Lee insisted, and eventually Forrest stomped into the room, saluted General Lee, and sank into a chair, his arms folded across his chest. The conversation progressed without his participation; he didn't say a word. Of course, his input was needed, and eventually Lee turned to Forrest and mentioned that they were in a bad fix. "Yes, we are in a hell of a fix," Forrest barked at his boss. But before the conversation could turn ugly, General Chalmers and Col. David Kelly quickly changed the subject. As it had to, the focus came back to the battle, and Lee asked Forrest if he had any ideas on the subject. Once again Forrest's legendary temper got the best of him and he shouted, "Yes sir, I've got ideas, and I'll tell you one thing, General Lee. If I knew as much about West Point tactics as you, the Yankees would whip hell out of me every day." There was silence in the room. Forrest choked out, "I've got five hundred empty saddles and nothing to show for them."[37]

Nothing could be gained by finger-pointing and blame. Lee ignored the outburst and voiced his concern about Smith's intentions. He believed that his adversary might revert to his advance southward in the direction of Verona, and so he directed Buford to deploy his brigades accordingly. Buford later reported, "During the night I was ordered to mount Bell's brigade and station it at Doctor Calhoun's house, to be in readiness to oppose the enemy if an advance was made toward Verona, and the Kentucky brigade to be thrown between the enemy and Doctor Calhoun's house."[38]

Sometime in those early-morning hours of July 15, Gen. A. J. Smith decided to end the expedition and begin the march back to Tennessee.[39]

SEVENTEEN

The Federal Withdrawal

The decision to turn the Federal army north could not have been an easy one for A. J. Smith. He had just handed Nathan Forrest's vaunted cavalry its first major defeat of the war, and he no doubt sensed that Lee's army was on the ropes. For decades thereafter, armchair warriors debated why Smith settled on such a course of action. Some said he lost his nerve and was frightened about what Forrest would do to him in the morning. Given the fact Smith had out-generalled both Lee and Forrest during those nine days and had ample opportunities to "skedaddle" back to Tennessee, that scenario is highly unlikely. His recent performance at Pleasant Hill during the Red River campaign had demonstrated his fearlessness in combat. "He is a regular trump and has no give up in him," testified Adm. David Porter.[1]

Smith's reasons for quitting the field have been scrutinized and have been laid open to ridicule, if not outright dismissed as cowardly. On close examination, however, his reasoning is straightforward, logical, and the only realistic option he had given the circumstances. "On the morning of the 15th," he explained, "it was found that, owing to the fact that much of our bread was spoiled when drawn from the commissary depot, we had on hand but one day's ration left. Our artillery was also all issued, and we had remaining only about 100 rounds per gun. It, therefore, became a matter of necessity to return."[2]

The first reason Smith gave—the spoiled hardtack—was a falsehood, but a forgivable one. The bread was most definitely inedible, infested with vermin; but rather than having found out about it on the morning of July 15, Smith had been well aware of the shortage as early as July 6. Most of the army had been on half- or even third-rations for a week and had been foraging liberally. Smith had ignored the fact, or at least failed to officially recognize it, until he could engage and defeat Forrest in battle, but he could no longer ignore the situation. He had also been criticized for using the lack of rations as a reason for withdrawing when he was on the edge of the Black Prairie region, one of the most fertile areas of the Confederacy, and what many believed to be Smith's actual goal of the campaign.[3]

Smith's second reason for the withdrawal, the diminished supply of artillery ammunition, has also been called a poor excuse and a subject of mockery. In his history of the battle, John Slonaker, the former historian of the Natchez Trace Parkway, laughed off the claim that only 100 rounds per gun was an insufficient supply: "Only? What would Forrest have done with such a paltry supply? Invade Ohio?" Yet, Smith's assertions were not only practical but completely valid. Nearly half of the available Federal ammunition had been shot away the day before, leaving enough rounds for just one more battle. Smith knew that if he got into another fight and used up the last of his ammunition, he would have been a hundred miles from a fresh supply and would have nothing to fall back on in an emergency.[4]

As early as July 2, Smith wrote to Washburn, "I have just discovered that a large portion of my ammunition is worthless. I have ordered an examination of all the boxes, and will retain and send in a special train this evening with that condemned." It's clear that there was a problem in the Sixteenth Corps' commissary and ordnance departments. Someone, or most likely several someones, had been lax in their duties and allowed bad bread onto the supply wagons and had nearly loaded bad artillery ammunition as well. And exacerbating the situation, a quantity of inferior small-arms ammunition had also slipped by the inspectors and made its way into the cartridge boxes of the 12th Iowa, 7th Minnesota, and 119th Illinois.

As for the artillery ammunition, Smith must have become impatient while waiting for the resupply and chosen to set out on the expedition with far less than the established minimum required on departure. The *Instruction for Field Artillery*, the Federal artillerists' Bible, specified amounts of each type of equipment to be carried with a battery, from thumb stalls to sponge covers. As it informed each battery commander, "The campaign allowance of ammunition is double what has been here prescribed, or about 400 rounds *per piece*, of which about 200 rounds per piece accompany the battery, the remainder being with the reserve parks." If Smith had shot away half his ammunition and only 100 rounds per gun remained, he had left La Grange with only 200 rounds per piece, 50 percent of what he was required to take on campaign. Had the day gone against Smith, he would have been hard-pressed to explain why he had left LaGrange with only a half load of ammunition for his artillery.[5]

* * *

With his mind made up, Smith began preparations for the march north, and his first thoughts were with the wounded and preparing them for the trip north. Working parties began to load the wounded into wagons for the journey, but there were many whose wounds were so severe they would never survive the trip. "I was obliged," explained Smith, "to leave about forty of the worst wounded cases of my command." These severe cases, as well as all of the Confederate wounded, were taken from the field hospitals and transferred to "comfortable quarters" in Tupelo. Two surgeons were chosen to remain behind to care for the injured men until they could be relieved by Confederate doctors. In addition, a number of soldiers from different regiments were selected to stay behind to serve as nurses and to assist the surgeons. Two privates of the 12th Iowa Infantry, Henry Wintersteen and Hiram Andrews, were among those selected. Maj. David Reed, the regimental historian, later wrote about their duty:

> The original order making the detail, written with a pencil by moonlight upon a torn scrap of paper, is now in [Pvt. Hiram] Andrew's possession, and is kept as a relic of a very unpleasant duty, performed for the wounded and dying comrades. When we remember that such a detail meant that these men would remain on the field when their regiment marched away; that they would be taken prisoner by Forrest's men who had, by atrocities committed at Fort Pillow and more recently at Guntown, made a reputation; that prisoners in their hands were liable to be very badly treated, if not murdered, we will understand better the courage and devotion to duty which constrained these men to accept such a detail without a murmur and quietly prepare to accept the fate that awaited them. It is a matter of record that the only protest made by them, when they reported for duty was: "Adjutant, we dislike to be *detailed* for such duty when we would have gladly volunteered, and we only ask you to take back the order and let the record show we volunteered." When it was explained to them that the written order might be useful for their protection they quietly accepted the detail, remained with and cared for the wounded comrades; no doubt saving the life of some of them. They reported afterwards that the written order caused them to be treated as nurses, and not as prisoners of war, and that when their services were no longer needed they were released and came into our lines at Vicksburg.[6]

Not all of the nurses were treated so well, however. Pvt. John Danielson of the 7th Minnesota explained:

Our wounded were left in the field hospital and became prisoners of war as those also, who as nurses were left behind in charge of them. This was no enviable plight to be in but when a call for volunteer nurses was made to the company, John Olson manfully stepped forward for the duty. The abuse heaped upon him by the rebels should deservedly brand them as scoundrels to the end of time. He was robbed of everything, even his clothing and sent to dirty prisons on scant fare.[7]

The decision as to who among the wounded was fit enough to make the journey fell to the regimental surgeons, among them Aurelius Bartlett of the 33rd Missouri Infantry, who wrote, "In this matter I was guided mainly by my own judgment and the wishes of some if not all of the wounded themselves." The transfer of the wounded, whether to the Tupelo hospital or into the wagons for the journey, took hours to accomplish.[8]

Though he had decided to withdraw from the field, Smith delayed the movement—not just for the sake of the wounded but to see if there was any fight left in Lee and Forrest. It was impractical for him to go on the offensive, but it was also foolhardy to begin a departure if his enemy was planning to resume the fight. There was some sporadic firing at dawn by the pickets, but the activity was light as the Confederates also waited to see if their opponents would come down off the ridge. "In the morning we could plainly see the rebels preparing their breakfast a mile away," observed Ben Thomas of the 14th Iowa. The regiment had remained on the Union left flank after the night action and at dawn the men began to stir about. "Sometimes one of them, I suppose to try the range of his gun, would send a shot over our way. While we were trying to start fires to make coffee young [Pvt. Milville] Ingham was on his hands and knees blowing the fire when a ball came with full force and struck among his fire brands, scattering them all about him and filling his eyes with dirt and ashes. A very close call."[9]

Smith was concerned that Lee would attempt another assault against his right flank while he was shifting his troops for the march north. As a consequence, he sent Winslow's cavalry brigade out on the Pontotoc Road to gauge the enemy's intentions. Capt. Theodore Carter had been sent out at dawn to cover the 7th Minnesota's front and watched the cavalry advance, noting, "After awhile a regiment or brigade of cavalry came up in our rear in line of battle, but with ranks opened so that as the front rank fired and halted to load, the rear rank passed through the intervals and fired and halted to load. This was kept up until they had advanced a short distance through our line to the front, when they retired. It was a very pretty drill but of no use otherwise."[10]

As the infantry and cavalry skirmished on the west side of the field, Smith began to pull other troops back to begin the withdrawal. Moore's Third Division would lead the march, followed, in turn, by the wagon trains, the Colored Brigade, Mower's First Division, and the cavalry in the rear. By 10:00 A.M. the regiments of the Third Division were moving out of their places in line and mustering alongside the wagons on the Tupelo Road. First to pull out was Gilbert's brigade and Bouton's soldiers on the far left. Holding the line while the infantry pulled back was Coon's cavalry brigade, primarily the 9th Illinois and the 2nd Iowa—a tall order for the tiny brigade.[11] Moving out next were Murray's and Wolfe's brigades, holding the center of Smith's line on the south side of the Tupelo Road. Mower's men extended their left to fill the resulting gap. McClure's (Wilkin's) brigade marched to the south side of the road and settled in behind the breastworks thrown up by Wolfe's men. To fill the resulting hole, Woods's regiments sidestepped to the left until half the brigade was below the road and the other half remained above it. McMillen's brigade came up behind Woods's left to serve as a reserve, and Ward's brigade simply remained where it was. Once all units were in place, there they waited for their own orders to pull out of line and head north.[12]

Just as Smith had a plan for the morning, so did Lee. His biggest concern was for the safety of the Black Prairie region, and he had doubts about whether his damaged army could fend off a movement south by Smith's army. Still believing that the destruction of the fertile area was the goal of the northern expedition, he had positioned Buford on the Verona Road in a last-ditch attempt to defend it. Bell's brigade had spent the night at Palmetto Church near Calhoun's Crossroads, while Crossland's Kentuckians were posted between that place and the defenses at Mrs. Sample's. Mabry's Brigade had remained on the far left of the Confederate line after the disastrous attack the previous morning. Buford's defensive line was thin at best and could hardly be expected to make much of a showing if attacked. As for the commanders, Lee remained on the left in the vicinity of Lyon's Division, while Forrest stayed with Roddey's soldiers on the extreme right.[13]

Mabry's Mississippians had passed an uneventful evening, getting what rest they could, resupplying themselves with ammunition, and burying the dead they were able to retrieve from the field. Still unsure of Smith's intentions, Lee ordered Mabry to take the bulk of his brigade, three regiments, and ride north of the old dismounted camp to picket the Chesterville Road. His remaining regiment, the 14th Confederate, remained on the field to serve as skirmishers in front of Lyon's Division until dawn, when they were to move through Harrisburg and ascertain the enemy's position. Given the activity in Harrisburg less than twenty-four hours earlier, the orders for the 14th Confederate were more than a single regiment could be expected to handle.[14]

Lyon's dismounted division waited away the early-morning hours in the breastworks constructed the previous afternoon. There were two lines of works, and as dawn approached Lyon withdrew his men to the second line, leaving the skirmishers of the 14th Confederate to hold the first line until orders came for them to move forward. When they did advance, it did not take long for them to learn that the enemy was still in force beyond the abandoned town. In the rear of the second line, the men of McCulloch's brigade, Chalmers's Division, swung into the saddle, ready to assist, but with no specific orders. The morning dragged on as they waited for an assault by the enemy.[15]

By 11:00 A.M., Smith was convinced that the Confederates were not going to make another assault, and he ordered Moore's division to begin the march north on the Ellistown Road, once again led by the 7th Kansas Cavalry. In no time at all, a long blue column snaked out of Tupelo headed north.[16]

As the Third Division began the march, Winslow's cavalry brigade was seeing action on the west side of Harrisburg. Eschewing the dismounted tactics, which were slower but safer, Winslow led the 3rd and 4th Iowa, the 10th Missouri Cavalry, and a two-gun section of Battery E, 1st Illinois Light Artillery, across the battlefield and into the woods beyond. The skirmishers of the 14th Confederate fell back slowly, fighting all the while, and finally took a stand in the first line of works. It was from the cover of these trees the day before that the Confederates had launched the disastrous assaults against the heights. Winslow's advance had taken him into the heart of the enemy's position. But sensing that something was not right, that he was riding into a trap, the colonel called a halt and pulled his men up short of the north-south road fronting Mrs. Sample's property. As a precaution, he directed Lt. Orrin Cram to send a few artillery rounds into the woods, though the crashing shells brought no response from the enemy. The 3rd Iowa pushed hesitatingly on ahead. Colonel Noble took note of the increase in fire on his front and flank. It was apparent to him that the enemy intended to draw him into a general engagement, far enough from the main line of the army to enable them to flank his left with a superior force. Winslow's instincts were correct.[17]

General Lee, watching from the second line of works near Mrs. Sample's, sensed that the Federal cavalry had advanced as far as it was likely to and ordered Lyon's Division forward. The 14th Confederate surged ahead followed by the dismounted cavalry under the direct command of Lt. Col. Thomas Barnett of the 3rd Kentucky, who recalled, "I then received orders to [move] forward, which I did, and kept up a brisk fire upon the enemy."[18]

On the ridge the Union infantry could hear the swell of firing in the woods and soon saw the cavalry emerge from the trees pursued by the enemy on foot. No sooner had the cavalry extricated itself from the trap then Smith ordered them off to the far left of the line to support Coon's small brigade.[19]

Behind the Federal earthworks the soldiers of the First Division watched the Confederate skirmishers continue to advance across the open field, step-ping over and around the bodies of their comrades. Joe Mower rode back and forth behind his men watching the slow progress of the enemy. He dispatched messengers to his four brigade commanders and admonished them "to remain concealed and to reserve their fire until the enemy arrived to within fifty yards of our position."[20]

To the north of the road, the men crouched behind the rail fence barricade and breastworks. The men of Woods's Third Brigade hunkered down behind the works built the previous day by Moore's division. "We had a substantial breast-work of cotton bales formed in our front, which served as an admirable protection against the enemy's sharpshooters." Further down the line John McClure's (Wilkin's) Second Brigade waited in earthworks dug into the hard-baked Mississippi soil. There were substantially fewer Federals on the ridge than there had been the day before, but the strength of the defensive works easily offset any disadvantage posed by their lower numbers.[21]

Out in the field, deployed as skirmishers in the regimental front, Captain Carter and his company of the 7th Minnesota were in an exposed position when the firing began. When his men clambered over the earthworks, he had been assured that there would be skirmishers on each of his flanks, but none had ar-rived. To make matters worse, the Confederate sharpshooters had found their range and were making life uncomfortable for Company K. The only place to take cover was behind tall weeds and southern corpses. He managed to with-draw his men to the shade of the woods and went in search of Colonel William Marshall to complain about his predicament. He found his commander in the earthworks where the regiment waited out of sight with fixed bayonets. Marshall was sympathetic but sent Carter and his men back into the exposed field under a baking sun. In due course, Carter led his skirmishers into the same hollow that had provided the barest protection to Mabry's brigade the previous morning.[22]

The Confederate advance took a long time to develop. Certainly none of Lyon's men were in a hurry to repeat the bloodbath of the day before. For nearly two hours the skirmishers plinked away at each other in the burning sun while the majority of the two forces waited in the shade. And waited. Chaplain Edwards of the 7th Minnesota noted, "Neither seemed in haste to take the initiative." The wait was particularly taxing for General Mower, who Edwards observed, "hated delays. This was probably what put him in such a bad humor,

"General Joseph A. Mower at Tupelo" (DePauw University Archives and Special Collections)

when he was seen prancing about on his steed near the front lines. He was mad. Awfully mad."[23]

Mower was also awfully drunk. At first Edwards was awed by the sight of the brigadier swinging his sword over his head and calling out to his men. He was so impressed he stopped to make a rather dashing sketch of a knightly Mower brandishing his sword over his head while his horse reared up on its hind legs. Under the mistaken belief that Mower was making "brave speeches," Edwards approached and discovered the commander was swaying in the saddle hollering, "Give 'em hell boys! Give 'em hell boys!" The encouragement was so laced with drunken profanities, Edwards was led to record, "Mower was using the King's English in a very free and rather reprehensible manner."[24]

At long last Lt. Colonel Barnett pushed the 3rd Kentucky dismounted and 14th Confederate forward toward the Union line. Only the enemy skirmishers were visible; the main line of the Federals held fire and remained hidden quietly behind works. An order was passed along the Union line, and those who had not already done so drew their bayonets from their scabbards and attached them to the end of their muskets: no one was to fire until the enemy had come within fifty yards of the line. Occasionally a Federal officer would slowly raise his head above the breastworks to observe the enemy's progress across the field, all the while reminding the men to hold fire and remain hidden. Mower's plan was to fool the enemy into believing that the ridge was being defended by a thin line of skirmishers and thus draw them right up to the works. The Confederates continued to cross the open field.[25]

Lyon's skirmishers approached to within 100 yards of the Federal line, and the sharpshooters in the Confederate ranks were making it difficult for anyone reckless enough to expose himself above the breastworks. In response, Mower changed his tactics and ordered up the 2nd Iowa Battery, which was quickly unlimbered and began to fire from an exposed position. In a flash the Confederate skirmishers shifted their attention to the artillerists. Eventually, the exploding shells from the Federal guns silenced the skirmishers, and the 2nd Iowa limbered up and headed back across the Pontotoc Road.[26]

Reed's 2nd Iowa Battery and Cram's Illinois section were not the only artillery active on the field. From beyond the woods an unidentified Confederate battery began to sporadically shell the Union line in hopes of silencing the cannon of the 2nd Iowa. One of these shells fell among the 11th Missouri, dangerously wounding Capt. William Cleland and four privates. It was the third wound for Cleland, who had been injured when his horse was shot out from under him at Iuka in September 1862 and then shot through the thigh the next year outside Vicksburg. A few shells landed among the 93rd Indiana, but they weathered the bombardment without harm.[27]

Any hope Mower had of drawing the Confederates in closer was dashed when Ward's brigade inexplicably unleashed a volley and revealed the presence of Federal infantry on the ridge. The Confederates immediately began to fall back. Col. William Heath of the 33rd Missouri later claimed the volley of the Fourth brigade was the reason for the Confederate withdrawal, though Thomas Barnett, refusing to admit he had been driven away, countered that he had used up all of his ammunition while driving the Federals back into their own lines.[28]

Losing the last of his patience, General Mower—"whose wrath had risen beyond the swearing point," Chaplain Edwards noted—ordered an advance down the slope.[29] Once begun, this counterattack was anticlimactic. The Federals jumped over and across their works and set off down the hill in a line of battle. Lyon's men began to fall back. To the chagrin of Mower's infantry, "the enemy [took] good care to keep out of range of our musketry." The men of the Third Brigade then "charged with a will," and the Confederates took to their heels. "The enemy was driven from the field in confusion, after suffering heavy loss," bragged Colonel Heath, though this was something of an exaggeration. William Marshall, commanding the 7th Minnesota, was closer to the truth when he reported that "the enemy got out of the way, faster than we could pursue." To speed the enemy on their way, a section of the 2nd Iowa Battery was brought up once again to shell the retreating Confederates.[30]

As his division approached the woods on the far side of the field, Mower called a halt and allowed the men to rest. There was no shade, however, and the men sweltered in the sun. Minutes crawled by, and the suffering dragged on for the better part of two hours. The field was still dotted with Confederate dead from the day before, and in the intense heat the bodies were beginning to decompose. A terrible smell blanketed the field. Second Lt. Henry McConnel of the 10th Minnesota, said of the field of battle, "I never want to see another. I counted 40 dead rebels all within as many rods. Some of the killed the dead before are still lying unburied in the hot scorching sun. The scene was fearful heart sickening and I turned back sadly thinking that victory gained by such results was dearly bought." Finally, the division was ordered to move back up the slope and into the shade.[31]

While Lyon had been occupied on the Confederate left, Buford had not been idle on the right. Early in the morning Bell and Crossland had brought their thin brigades onto the Verona Road after passing the night near Dr. Calhoun's place. There they met up with Colonel Rucker's brigade, which had been resting in place on the far right since the night attack. Despite the disappointments of the previous day, the men were in good spirits.[32]

Buford halted his men in the woods, the same spot where the night attack had been launched from. From there, the men dismounted, went to the edge of the large field, the far side of which was planted in corn, and "formed line just on top of a hill on the south side of a dreau [draw]." This had been the Federals' first defensive position the night before, and the field showed signs of the struggle. Crossland formed his regiment in the center, Bell on his left, and Rucker on the right. And then, like Lyon on the far left, Buford waited for the enemy to advance. Roddey's Division remained in reserve in the rear near the horse holders.[33]

While Buford was bringing his men into position on the Verona Road, Col. Ed Bouton had been busy pulling his colored soldiers out of line on the Union left. David Moore's Third Division had begun the march north, and Bouton was to follow and guard the trains. In the place of the black soldiers came Datus Coon's tiny cavalry brigade, the 9th Illinois on the right, and the 2nd Iowa on the left. Coon knew he was too weak to make any kind of a determined stand and appealed to General Grierson for help. In a short time the 93rd Indiana Infantry of McMillen's brigade marched up and fell into line between the two cavalry regiments.[34] Lt. Dorious Neel led the skirmishers of the 93rd Indiana through the corn and crossed over the creek that cut through the center of the field. Almost immediately they came under heavy fire. The Confederate skirmish line had a lot more muscle than the Federals' and began to steadily push them back. Maj. H. S. Hale of the 7th Kentucky led the southern skirmishers across the open space and down the slope to the creek.[35]

Hale's skirmishers were the vanguard of Buford's entire line. Forrest had grown impatient waiting for Smith to come out of his "fortifications" and ordered Buford to attack the enemy left flank.[36] Soon the field was filled with dismounted southern cavalry marching north in a long line of battle. The timing seemed perfect: the Union left flank was held by a thin line of cavalry and infantry, and half of Smith's army was already marching away on the Ellistown Road. This was the very opportunity Forrest had been waiting for, the type of situation he excelled at exploiting. The Federal skirmishers had fallen back into the timber, and the Confederates stood poised on the exposed flank of Mower's First Division. Mower, drunk and preoccupied, was over on the Pontotoc Road advancing on Lyon's Confederates.

But on the battlefield, such windows of opportunity rarely stay open for long, and this was no exception. For while Mower may have been distracted, A. J. Smith was not. The corps commander was riding near the left flank and

"General A. J. Smith" (DePauw University Archives and Special Collections)

saw the predicament Coon faced: the two cavalry regiments had been pushed back into the woods, and were it not for the stalwart 93rd Indiana, the line would have probably collapsed. Smith had few resources to call on. Moore's division was already well up the Ellistown Road, and Bouton's brigade was falling in on either side of the wagon train. Maj. James Foster's 59th USCT had been parceled out, a company to every twenty wagons, and the other two regiments were about to follow. Battery I had already rolled up the road.[37]

Smith calmly called on Bouton to return with the 61st and 68th USCT and shore up the left flank. In a matter of minutes, the black soldiers were taking their place next to the Hoosiers, and the harried cavalrymen of Coon's brigade mounted up and rode over to assist Mower on the right. Soon the 93rd Indiana pulled out as well and went to support the 2nd Iowa Battery, which left the safety of the left flank solely in the hands of the black soldiers. Though he was heavily outnumbered, Bouton worked with quick determination: "The enemy still advancing and driving in the cavalry, I formed the Sixty-first and Sixty-eighth Regiments in line next to timber, and advancing through it in line of battle some 300 to 400 yards, found the enemy occupying ridge where my line had rested previous to its being attacked the night before."[38]

Bayonets drawn and fixed to the muzzles, the Federal rifles waited for a countercharge. Maj. William Burns of Smith's staff was by his commander's side as he rode back and forth admonishing the men to hold their fire until he gave the word, "which he did, and then ordered them to charge,—himself leading them." With Smith recklessly leading the way, the 61st and four companies of the 68th surged forward and drove the Confederate skirmishers back across the creek to the south ridge. Smith was impressed by the performance of the black soldiers: "I am free to confess that their action has removed from my mind a prejudice of twenty years' standing."[39]

Lieutenant Pirtle of the 7th Kentucky was still advancing with his company when the tide of battle began to turn. Many of the skirmishers had broken into a trot as they made for the woods on the north side of the field. But when Pirtle called out, "steady boys, steady," most slowed to a walk. But visibility was poor as they entered the belt of corn, and many of the men were slowed by the tangle of weeds and vines. Pirtle, who was tripped up when a vine caught on his boot and peeled the sole back to the heel, recalled, "We didn't go exceeding ten steps when we met a volley of bullets that seemed to me would cut all the corn in a minute. All broke and fled without any orders from anybody and back to the line." Pirtle flattened himself on the ground as bullets screamed by above him. Eventually he was able to crawl across the field to safety.[40]

Buford waited for a full-scale counterattack to come across the field, but it never came. The black skirmishers made their way nearly across the opening before being called back across the creek. Unsure of what to expect or what the enemy was doing, Buford explained, "I then halted, threw out a line of skirmishers to hold the enemy in check, and rested my division." Eighty of his men had to be carried from the field, "most of whom were insensible." As Forrest recalled, "Few men were killed or wounded in this engagement, but I found the road strewn with men fainting under the oppressive heat, hard labor, and want of water." As the heat-stricken soldiers were pulled into the shade, Col. Gustaves Holt of the 3rd Kentucky noted that the enemy had pulled back as well, "leaving his dead on the field." But according to Pirtle, "If we hurt any yanks, they carried them off, as we marched over the ground and found no dead or cripple yanks."[41]

Bouton waited in the woods to make sure that the Confederates made no further moves on the left. His own men had fared the heat better than the Confederates, but they, too, were sweating and tired and deserved a rest. The enemy troops before him were quiet, but there was continued gunfire over on the right where Mower was still engaged with Lyon's skirmishers. When Bouton had first arrived on the scene, Coon's cavalry had ridden off in response to Mower's call. Mower ordered Coon's two regiments to take a position on the left of his division, plugging a gap between his men and Bouton's soldiers. Col.

Henry Burgh of the 9th Illinois Cavalry was still leading his men across the field to their new place in the line when a messenger caught up with him with an order "to make a charge down the [Pontotoc] road."[42]

Mower's advance down the slope had pushed the Confederates back to the tree line, but when his men abandoned the baked plain and returned to the breastworks, Lyon's skirmishers once again ventured into the field. It was nearly 2:00 P.M. and time Mower's division pulled out of Harrisburg and joined the march north. To mask the movement, Mower ordered a battalion of Burgh's regiment to draw sabers and sweep the enemy from the field a final time.[43]

It had taken years for the armies to learn the lesson that sabers were all but obsolete on the battlefield. Sabers versus rifles was a no-win situation for the horsemen, and such a charge against an entrenched enemy was nothing short of suicide. Many cavalry regiments, North and South, had long since thrown the sabers away and put their faith in carbines and pistols. So when Mower directed Burgh to send four companies headlong down the Pontotoc Road, he found that only two of his companies, A and H, still carried the cumbersome weapons. "It was a very unwise order, but it had to be obeyed." The two companies spaced out in a long line and began the charge across the open field. Burgh was rightly concerned and, as support, wisely sent along a battalion with their carbines.[44]

As anyone could have predicted, the two saber companies were shot to pieces when they came within range of Lyon's men in the breastworks. "It was doomed to defeat," wrote the regimental historian. Capt. John McMahon, leading the charge, was cut down without getting anywhere near close enough for his men to use their swords.[45] The arrival of the battalion under Capt. Llewellyn Cowen saved the squadron. He dismounted his men in the center of the field near a scattering of trees and opened an effective covering fire. Confederate attention turned to Cowen's detachment, allowing McMahon's men to race their horses away. Confederate artillery fire and small-arms rained down on the would-be saviors, and men started to fall.[46] Once McMahon's squadron had withdrawn, Burgh pulled the entire regiment back to the heights and the cover of the breastworks. The returning troopers were met by their comrades in Coon's brigade; the bulk of the infantry division had pulled out. As bloody as it was, the charge had effectively screened the withdrawal of Mower's brigades, and only the 93rd Indiana and 114th Illinois remained behind to cover the army's rear. To assist the rear guard, Mower also left behind two pieces of artillery, Lt. Orin Cram's section of 12-pounders from Battery E, 1st Illinois Light Artillery. Cram requested and received permission to fire on the Confederates to keep up the illusion that the army was still in place on the heights.[47]

There was very little of Smith's army left in Harrisburg or Tupelo, and what did remain was moving out at a sedate pace. Smith had no intention of marching his men hard in the heat when there was nothing to gain for it. The goal of the first day's march was only five miles up the road where the Ellistown Road crossed Old Town Creek. In fact, by the time Mower was putting his men into column, Moore's division was already making camp for the night.

EIGHTEEN

Old Town Creek

Confederate general James Chalmers spent the morning of July 15 on the far left with the men of McCulloch's brigade waiting for the Federals to attack in force. But an attack never materialized. At 11:00 A.M. General Lee directed him to scout out the enemy's extreme right flank "to ascertain where he was and what he was doing." Chalmers's advance coincided with that of Lyon, who was following essentially the same orders. There was some skirmishing with the enemy, and when Mower advanced into the field, McCulloch fell back with the rest of the Confederate line. But rather than take a position in the entrenchments, Chalmers ordered his men into the saddle and to ride directly north. They were clearly seen by the Federals, and Mower later reported that the Confederates had retreated to their horses and fled. Nothing could be further from the truth. Lyon's Division was snugly behind its works hoping the Federals would come into range, and though Chalmers appeared to be riding away, he was doing his best to carry out Lee's orders to scout the enemy's right flank.[1]

McCulloch's brigade stuck to the woods and picked its way carefully through the trees and underbrush. When the men finally emerged from the timber, they were well beyond the Federals' right flank and had an unobstructed view east toward the King's Creek bottoms. What Chalmers and his men saw was the Ellistown Road jammed with blue-clad soldiers marching north. It had to have been a staggering sight: the victorious Federals withdrawing from the field and heading north, not south. Messengers galloped away to inform Lee and Forrest.[2]

Such a discovery was unexpected; no one was prepared for it. Lyon acted first by sending his skirmishers across the field, where they met no opposition. For the first time the Confederates stood on the high ground at Harrisburg and got a look at the enemy's works. And once Forrest learned of the new development, he mounted up and rode with Roddey's Division across the fields to Harrisburg. Before he left he directed Buford to take the brigades of Bell, Crossland, and Rucker to Tupelo and engage any enemy he found there. Within a few minutes all of Lee's army was converging on Harrisburg.[3]

Although Lyon's skirmishers had begun to explore the breastworks, the first regiment to enter Harrisburg was one of Roddey's, the 5th Alabama Cavalry under Lt. Col. James Warren. Over the last forty-eight hours Roddey's cavalrymen had done plenty of maneuvering and a bit of skirmishing, but for the most part they had been a no-show on the battlefield. Warren's regiment hoped to make up for their lack of activity by attacking the Federal rear guard. Unfortunately, the bulk of the Union army was already well up the Ellistown Road, and the only enemy the 5th could find were a few companies of the 9th Illinois Cavalry. A spattering of rifle and carbine fire from both sides resulted in an officer and four enlisted men wounded on the Union side and an unknown number of Confederate casualties. The 9th Illinois, the last Federal unit on the battlefield, broke off the contest, its job finished, and began the trek north. Warren halted his 5th Alabama for orders.[4]

Lee and Forrest, surrounded by their respective staffs and thousands of mounted Confederates, met in Harrisburg. The initial meeting was brief and to the point. Lee ordered General Forrest to take command of all the troops on the field and to "pursue and harass the enemy." There was no protest from Forrest about seniority or any refusal to take command; this was the type of situation he specialized in. It was no secret that he wanted to attack the Union army stretched out in column and drive them headlong out of Mississippi.[5]

Forrest promptly ordered Buford to pursue up the Ellistown Road with Bell and Crossland, to be followed by Chalmers with McCulloch's brigade. He left Lyon's dismounted troopers at the defenses near Mrs. Sample's place. In addition, he ordered Roddey's Division and Rucker's brigade to remain behind in Tupelo until he fully understood the enemy's intentions. Rucker's men had been pretty badly shot up on the 14th, but Roddey had the freshest men in the army; so why they were left behind is a question without an answer. With Mabry's Brigade away on the Chesterville Road, Forrest was setting out in pursuit of the Federal army with only a fraction of his available strength.[6]

Buford directed Tyree Bell's brigade to take the advance and Col. Andrew Wilson to lead off with the 16th Tennessee. He sent the 19th Tennessee under Col. John Newsome into Tupelo "to go to the extreme right and attack the enemy on his left flank." The 2nd and 15th Tennessee made the move to fall in behind Wilson but halted long enough for Rice's Battery of Tennesseans to join the column.[7]

As Buford set out to the north, Forrest accompanied Lee into Tupelo "for the purpose of consulting and receiving orders." After a second short discussion, Forrest and his escort set out on the road in the wake of McCulloch's brigade. Many of Buford's men were still stricken by the heat, and he could barely muster a thousand men to begin the pursuit. McCulloch, however, had not seen as much fighting as his fellow brigade commanders and had just as many men in his one brigade as Buford had in two. Whatever plans Forrest was hatching to harass Smith's column took a turn when he heard the thunder of artillery up ahead; "and as I further advanced I could also hear the firing of small arms."[8]

*　*　*

In the middle of the drought-stricken region, Old Town Creek presented a peaceful, pastoral setting. The land on either side of the Ellistown Road, just south of the creek, was green with the ripening corn of the Rook farm to the west and the Creely farm to the east. Farmer Berry Rook, a South Carolina native, worked his farm with his wife and two sons. At the outbreak of the war the younger son, John, had enlisted in the Coonewah Rifles, Company H, 2nd Mississippi Infantry, and later joined the 1st Mississippi Partisan Rangers. A wound in the arm at Collierville, Tennessee, ended his military career, and he returned to the family farm. On that day, July 15, unknown to him or his family, his old unit was fast on the heels of the Union army and on a path that would lead them to the Rook farm.[9]

The march to Old Town Creek by Moore's Third Division had been without incident, and by two o'clock many of the regiments had passed the cornfields and crossed the rickety bridge over the creek. Just upstream from the bridge, another stream, smaller but with deceptively steep banks, emptied its waters into Old Town Creek. The low valley of Old Town Creek separated modest heights on each bank by roughly 1,000 yards. The stream was bordered by a nearly impenetrable layer of thick trees and brush. About 500 yards from the stream, the land sloped gently down toward the bridge and then leveled off in a jumbled scattering of hummocks and ditches. Within 200 yards the slope again steepened before finally flattening out on the creek bottom. In essence it was a two-step drop from the crest to the creek. Once the Ellistown Road crossed the creek and began to climb the opposing heights, the ridge steepened slightly. Ben Thomas of the 14th Iowa described the setting: "Just north of the creek was a sharp ridge running parallel with the stream through which the road had been cut which produced a passage about eight or ten feet deep." As on the south side, the northern slope flattened out for a brief expanse before reaching the opposing heights 500 yards from the bridge. The road cut described by Thomas was in the steeper upper slope.[10]

Moore's three brigades had set out from Harrisburg in numerical order, with several regiments detailed to guard the wagons following in their wake. One of these regiments was the 14th Iowa, and Private Thomas described the unwelcome duty: "In guarding the wagon train we were obliged to walk beside the wagons and not behind or between them. The orders were if we were attacked for all the troops to come to the side upon which the attack was made. The main object of the rebels now would be to capture or stampede our train and leave us without provisions or ammunition. Our object was to prevent such a 'catastrophe.'" To thwart "catastrophe," detachments of Grierson's cavalry from Coon's brigade rode on both flanks to give ample warning of any attack.[11]

The Ellistown Road was typical of the country lanes in Pontotoc County. "Most of the route lay through timber," explained Thomas, "and the ground was also covered with underbrush so there was scarcely room to walk beside the wagon. When we passed through cultivated land the worm fences on either side left the road so narrow that we could hardly keep our places." The men were keenly aware that it was in similar terrain that the enemy had launched attacks against the First Division on July 13, and they were extra vigilant. Only once did the Confederates appear alongside Moore's column. A small body of horsemen, probably scouts from the 19th Tennessee, rode into a field on the right of the road. A few Union shots scattered them, allowing the column to proceed on without incident.[12]

By 2:00 P.M. the last of Moore's men had passed over the creek, climbed the heights, and moved into a tract of open timber on the left side of the road. After selecting bivouac sites, regiments began to settle into their temporary camps. The wagon train followed and parked in a large field on the right. Skirmishers went out to ensure that there were no Confederates lurking about. While they found no enemy, they did find a gristmill on the Creely property, which had recently ground a quantity of corn into meal. They seized the cornmeal and distributed it among the hungry ranks.[13] Bouton's brigade arrived and settled into a bivouac site to the north of Moore's division, followed closely by Mower's men, whose five-mile walk from Harrisburg had also been uneventful.

The same could not be said for the rear guard, however. William McMillen's First Brigade had been the last of Mower's division to quit the field, and rear-guard duties fell to Capt. Charles Hubbard commanding the 93rd Indiana and Capt. Benjamin Berry leading the 114th Illinois. Berry's regiment set out first, followed by Orin Cram's section of Battery E, 1st Illinois Light Artillery. The guns followed three of Hubbard's companies, while the remaining seven companies of the regiment formed columns and marched on either side of the two cannon. Last came the cavalry, led by General Grierson.[14]

When the Confederates chased the 9th Illinois Cavalry out of Harrisburg, Grierson sent the regiment farther up the line, where they joined the 10th Missouri Cavalry, just recalled from picket duty on the Verona Road. These two regiments reported in to Colonel Coon and began screening the sides of the column. Winslow's brigade assumed the duties of rear guard, with the 4th Iowa Cavalry, along with two companies of the 3rd Iowa, at the extreme end of the line busy "resisting the advance of the enemy, who now began to follow our column closely and in force."[15]

The reinforced 4th Iowa was able to keep the Confederates at bay for the first few miles, fighting relatively lightly with skirmishers and scouts. But at some point between three and four o'clock, Buford, riding in the van with Wilson's 16th Tennessee, ordered brigade commander Bell to engage the Federals. Cpl. Simon Duck of the 4th Iowa recalled, "We were overtaken by a large rebel column which came upon us at a full trot across a large field. The rear guard gave them several shots—I put in three, and closed up with the rest of the company."[16]

The 4th Iowa's commander, Col. John Peters, deployed his dismounted companies individually across the road and began to fall back in a leapfrogging manner: one company fired at the enemy and then retreated up the road to the end of the regiment to deploy once again. When an open field presented itself, the men lay in wait and unleashed an unexpected volley. General Grierson was justifiably proud:

> Never did a small force of our cavalry repel a largely superior force of the enemy more successfully than during the retreat that day. We had repeatedly selected positions where the battalions were well screened from view, and successfully ambushed the enemy, with heavy loss to him. We had some men wounded but none killed. Had a good many horses shot while repulsing the enemy attacks. The rearguard was composed mostly of Winslow's brigade, and never did cavalry perform their duty more satisfactorily. I was present at the rear and clearly observed their movements. Although assaulted by so large a force, no confusion was caused.[17]

Grierson's tactics were especially well-suited for the terrain, and Buford found it difficult to gain any momentum. Thomas Jordan detailed how "a warm volley was suddenly poured into the head of the column from a heavy ambuscade in a corn-field, while his [Buford's] own force was moving along a narrow road through a dense 'black-jack' thicket." He went on to note that "the character of the ground made it extremely difficult to deploy forward any effective body of troops, and Bell's Brigade receiving the first outburst of the ambush, was driven in confusion." The 16th Tennessee quickly rallied and increased its pressure on the Federals.[18]

However, immersed in the details of holding back the advancing Confederates, Grierson made a critical mistake: he failed to maintain communication with the main column. And the timing was crucial. Within a mile of Old Town Creek, he had neglected to inform the army commander of the increased enemy activity, and, even worse, he had no idea that the army had stopped to bivouac on the north side of the stream.[19]

It was five o'clock and the last of Mower's division was crossing over the bridge into the Old Town Creek valley. The First Division had been ordered by Mower to march beyond Bouton's bivouac before setting up camps so it would be in position to lead off the next day's march. Colonel Noble, with the bulk of his 3rd Iowa Cavalry, had begun to dismount at the creek to give the horses a well deserved drink of water when, without warning, the 4th Iowa crested the upper heights and began to fight their way down the slope toward the creek, pursued by the 16th Tennessee. And Grierson was just as shocked to see the army encamped on the opposite bank, "As I received no notice of this halt, the enemy was unfortunately allowed to approach to a good position on a hill south of the creek, within easy range of the train." The cavalry commander left the rear guard and went in search of Smith, whom he found on the north side of the creek with the officers of his staff. Capt. William Burns watched with interest as "Gen. Grierson, very much excited, rode up to Gen. Smith, and reported that we were in great danger from Forrest's army. He had evidently (as we used to say in the army) 'lost his head,' and his actions were demoralizing to say the least. Gen. Smith listened to him a moment and then angrily ordered him to keep quiet, and not expose his fears to the men. That he had just instructed Gen. Mower to look into the trouble at the rear, and if Forrest was there, there was no better man than Gen. Mower to take care of him."[20]

On the top of the south ridge, Bell halted the 16th Tennessee and ordered them to dismount. The 2nd and 15th Tennessee arrived and also climbed down from their horses. A smile had to have crossed Buford's face as he saw an opportunity presenting itself: dismounted cavalry falling back down a slope, more dismounted cavalry watering their horses in the creek, infantry marching in column up the road, and nowhere any enemy troops deployed to meet him. If this was not tempting enough, he could see beyond the opposite ridge to the Federal wagon train clustered in a field. While Bell deployed his troops and sent the horses to the rear, Buford directed Capt. Thomas Rice to unlimber his four guns and shell the enemy wagons.[21]

It was an admirable bit of soldiering by Buford. He had come up on the rear of Smith's army almost unawares and was in a splendid position to launch an attack. Realistically there was no chance for Forrest's depleted ranks to weather another standup fight with Smith's infantry, for, as Pvt. John Hubbard of the 7th Tennessee noted, "Clearly our men were in no condition to make anything more than a spiritless pursuit." But if it was possible to "get the skeer" on the enemy by stampeding the wagon train and causing a panic, the tables could be turned and the victory of Brice's Crossroads repeated. All the elements were in place but one: the Federals had to do their part and panic, a trait they had not displayed thus far in the campaign.[22]

Confederate artillery shells exploding among the wagons was the only warning to most of the Federals that the enemy were nearby. Harrison Chandler, the quartermaster sergeant of the 114th Illinois, had just boiled and sweetened a cup of coffee to go with his supper when shells began to rain down "and came near causing a stampede of our trains. Many teams were out into the road and seemed anxious to get out of the way." Chandler noted that the animals in his care did not panic and were significantly more composed than he was.[23] Other shells aimed farther to the west fell among the men of the Third Division who were busy cooking up their supper.

> Some of us had some meal and some had flour and we was going to make some pancakes. We had it all mixed up when the Rebs began to throw shells right in amongst us. I went to put things on the wagon and picked up the pail full of batter and was going off with it [when] my foot caught in a grape vine and down I went batter and all. The Major was behind me [and hollered] "Dad, let her rip," but I did not like it for we was all out of crackers so we lost our supper.[24]

For his plan to work, Buford counted on the Federals to panic. There was already panic among the civilian teamsters, and if the terror spread to the infantry a rout was almost certain. But that did not happen. As Chaplain Humphrey of the 12th Iowa wrote, "For a few moments all was confusion among the teams. A stampede seemed inevitable. But through the coolness of our men it was prevented." Teamsters and wagon masters regained control of themselves and their teams and began to lead the animals up the road and out of range. Capt. George Carter of the 33rd Wisconsin attributed the sudden order-out-of-chaos to General Smith, who directed the nearby soldiers to shoot any of the civilian teamsters who refused to comply.[25]

In those brief, fleeting minutes, Lee's army came closer to repeating its successes at Brice's Crossroads than at any point in the campaign. But once again the Federals refused to react as they were supposed to; the infantry had remained resolute. On the road south from La Grange, at Pontotoc, Bertram's Shop, Camargo Crossroads, and during the repeated attacks at Harrisburg, the Union cavalry may have been shaky at times, but the infantry had never wavered. And in Old Town Creek, while the shells rained down, a sober Joe Mower wasted no time in throwing forward a defensive line to confront the Confederates coming down the slope.

The 3rd Iowa Cavalry was in the closest position and responded first. Many of Noble's men were already off of their horses and watering them in the creek when they saw the 4th Iowa tumbling over the ridge. Noble dismounted the remainder of his regiment and sent his horses to the rear to form a line of battle on the edge of the cornfield and on either side of the Ellistown Road. It was an exposed position, directly under what Noble deemed a "commanding hill," and the troopers were immediately under shell and canister fire from the artillery as well as musketry from Bell's Tennesseans. The horse holders thundered across the bridge holding the reins of their charges, while the dismounted Iowans sought cover below the first rise, just forward of Noble's position. The creation of the first defensive line was not pretty, what with one group of soldiers retreating down the slope and the horses being galloped up the opposite hill. Noble admitted that the sight "made the assault of the rebels very much like a surprise." Indeed, it was.[26]

In a stroke of luck for the Federals, McMillen's brigade had just crossed the bridge and was passing through the bottom land on the north side. At the tail end of the column the 93rd Indiana halted and deployed to the east side of the road. Cram's detachment of Illinois artillery, being escorted by the 93rd, whipped its horses up the slope and through the road cut, where they were directed to unlimber on the high ground. Possibly spurred on by his own dark memories of Brice's Crossroads, McMillen directed the 114th Illinois and 72nd and 95th Ohio to extend his line to the left of the road. His final regiment, the 10th Minnesota, had been at the head of his column and was too far away to be of immediate use. McMillen was pleased with the rapid deployment: "Notwithstanding the confusion occasioned by a large number of led horses and demoralized cavalrymen passing through my ranks, the heavy artillery fire of the enemy, and a stampeded train, my line did not for a moment falter."[27]

Farther up the road Ward's brigade had been marching in column in front of McMillen's and had just halted when a messenger arrived with orders to move back to the creek and assist in repelling the enemy. Captain Carter of the 33rd Wisconsin recalled, "We had just got our Regt. across the stream and stacked arms when we heard the cavalry skirmishing in our rear. Pretty soon in they came helter skelter running like thunder, the majority of them however being No. 4 with the horses of Nos 1, 2 & 3 who were dismounted. But it was quite evident the rebs were driving them in."[28] Closer at hand was Gilbert's Second Brigade of Moore's division, which was already bivouacked. Gilbert's men had taken shelter as best they could as shells exploded above them, and when the drummers beat the long roll and called them into ranks, they formed up next to the road. Ward's brigade double-quicked past them, not an easy task with the wagons jamming the lane and pushing to the north. [29]

The road south to the bottomland led through a narrow gap that was a potential bottleneck, yet given the gentle slope of the surrounding countryside, it was completely unnecessary for troops moving back to the creek to stick to the road. Gilbert, however, chose to march directly down the road and into the choke point rather than immediately deploy in line of battle. The risky movement was noticed by Private Thomas of the 14th Iowa.

> It was a bad move and might have been fatal to many of us. We were among the first who went through. We met a shell just as we entered the gap but it passed over our heads. A few more steps further and we were startled by a heavy explosion and all dropped to the ground thinking it was a shell burst over us, but next instant we understand the cause. It was one of our batteries that had taken position on the ridge behind the gap and fired their six guns at once. But falling really saved us for the next shell from the rebel guns came an instant after our battery fired and it passed just over our prostrate forms.[30]

The "six gun" battery on the ridge was actually the two-gun section of Battery E, 1st Illinois Light Artillery, under Lieutenant Cram. The two 12-pounder rifles had left the protection of the 93rd Indiana and wheeled into a cornfield on the side of the road, where the crews unlimbered and "commenced replying to their artillery with shell and shrapnel." The Iowans were soon joined by another 12-pounder from Lieutenant Burns's 3rd Indiana Battery. After only a few rounds, Cram "had the gratification of dismounting one of the enemy's guns and killing and wounding several of his men and horses." On the opposite heights Buford was assisting Rice's gunners, yelling out, "Give 'em hell boys!" The Federals' effective counterbattery fire had taken a heavy toll on the Confederate crews and horses, however, temporarily silencing Rice's four guns.[31]

On the east side of the road there was heavy skirmishing between Bell's Tennesseans and the combined guns of McMillen's infantry and Winslow's cavalry. Buford planned to take advantage of the confusion brought on by his artillery and follow it up with a headlong charge into the Federal rear guard. He held Bell's brigade back while Crossland's Kentuckians dismounted and filed into line on the west side of the road. The situation looked promising to the optimistic Confederates, who had driven a panic-stricken enemy from many fields, but somehow, while his own regiments were deploying for the attack, Buford had not observed the three Union infantry brigades that had turned around and were advancing toward Old Town Creek.[32]

It was easy to miss the advancing Federals through the clouds of smoke from the artillery and small arms, as well as the heavy timber and vegetation along the creek. Indeed, Colonel Gilbert and his men had a difficult time reaching the cornfield: "The line scaled the fence, waded a stream nearly waist deep in water and mud, through the thick brush and timber; waded the second stream, as deep as the first, and on through the belt of timber to the edge of a large field of growing corn." Once they came out of the trees, they could see the Confederate line, "with its battle-flags waving in the sunlight."[33]

Buford then ordered his men forward, but the charge was blunted as the line became caught in the thickets and briars on the slope. Blackberry vines and "wait-a-minute" briars with thick, sharp thorns clung to and tore the men's uniforms. Despite the heavy scrub they emerged into the cornfield—the 2nd Tennessee on the far right of the line, the 16th on the left, and the 15th in the center—and easily pushed back the 4th Iowa Cavalry, the most advanced unit of the Union line.[34]

The Tennesseans' success was fleeting. Sergeant Hancock of the 2nd Tennessee sadly recalled, "On nearing Town Creek bottom the enemy, in overwhelming numbers, springing from the cover of the bushes with a yell drove our division back." Alongside the Iowa cavalry was McMillen's brigade, the men who had confronted Bell at Camargo Crossroads on July 13, and they were confident and anxious to once again show their mettle. Reports described the action as an ambush or ambuscade that sent the Confederates reeling back up the slope. Buford and his staff rode into the mess and rallied the men before the confusion could become something worse. The Tennesseans settled in at the top of the first slope and began to send a heavy fire down to the creek. On their left, across the Ellistown Road, Crossland's Kentuckians charged into the fray as well. Like Bell's men, they had some initial success against the cavalry skirmishers but had now come on the Union infantry.[35]

At the far end of the cornfield Crossland found Ward's men, who were being reinforced by Gilbert's Second Brigade. Gilbert's command had passed through the road cut and turned into the field on the west side of the road: "We now deployed [in] line of battle which should have been done in camp and dashed across the creek." Lt. William Donnan of Gilbert's staff recalled a

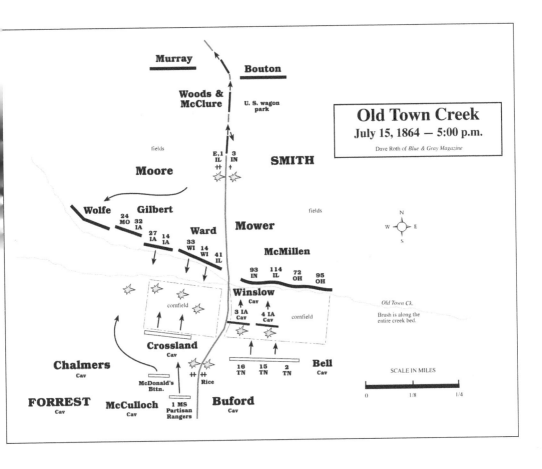

more difficult journey: "The 27th & 14th were ordered out & we charged over two deep creeks, through thick timber, over 3 fences [and] up through a long field of growing corn."[36]

Prior to entering Rook's field, Gilbert called a halt to his brigade and sent his skirmishers into the corn. The skirmishers' job was tougher than usual; the high cornstalks reduced visibility to a matter of yards, and the men gingerly made their way through a sea of rustling green stalks. Unable to learn anything from his skirmish line, Gilbert recalled them and advanced the main line to the split-rail fence at the north end of the field. At his command, "the whole line poured in a volley, raised a shout, scaled the fence, and pressed steadily forward in the open field." It was a hard fight through the corn, admitted Ben Thomas of the 14th Iowa. "They had the shelter of the ridge and poured out a fire upon us that was enough to make veterans quail."[37]

Crossland's men were just as blind and were also startled by the crashing volley that tore through the cornstalks. They retreated a hundred yards to the top of the first rise and began to return the heavy fire coming from the field below them. Gilbert's men pursued, but not very far. "The ground was rough and ascending," explained Gilbert, "the day was very hot. By the time the line had reached the center of the field many had dropped on the ground from heat and exhaustion, unable to rise; not a few had been borne back wounded." Sgt. Bill Tucker of the 14th Wisconsin agreed: "But of all the hard charges we ever made was crossing that small field. The heat was so intense that it seemed that every man would fall before we reached the opposite side." The opponents continued to fire away, almost blindly, for thirty minutes.[38]

The fighting was particularly destructive to the officers of the Kentucky brigade. One of the first to fall was the brigade commander, Col. Edward Crossland. A serious wound compelled him to leave the field, and Lt. Colonel Absalom Shacklett of the 8th Kentucky took command of the four regiments. A few minutes later the 7th Kentucky's Lt. Colonel L. J. Sherrill was mortally wounded, followed by Major Henry Hale. This left the regiment without any field officers; Joel Cochran, the senior surviving captain, took command of the regiment. The unrelenting heat also took a toll, incapacitating dozens, including Col. Gustaves Holt of the 3rd Kentucky, who had to be carried to the field hospital.[39]

When General Forrest arrived on the field, Buford's two brigades were tenuously holding their position on the slope, but it was clear that they would not be able to do so for much longer. The attempts to stampede the Federals had failed, bringing on another pitched fight, another one the Confederates could not win. Buford had been making repeated "emphatic" calls on Chalmers to hurry forward McCulloch's brigade, and these regiments began to arrive at the same time that Forrest was assessing the situation. Seeing that there would be no victory at Old Town Creek, and realizing that the Confederates would be fortunate if they could stave off a rout, Forrest sized up the situation and acted to prevent a disaster.[40]

There was no time for McCulloch's brigade to deploy in line of battle, so Forrest directed Chalmers to feed his regiments into the fight on the left as they arrived. Committing regiments piecemeal into a battle is never a good idea, and the results at Old Town Creek were predictable. Chalmers admitted, "Consequently the advanced regiments were driven back in confusion before the rear could be engaged." While Chalmers was busy dismounting his men and directing them to the left, Forrest set out to reposition Rice's Battery. Before long the Confederate artillery was back in the fight and sending shells down the slope.[41]

The regiments of McCulloch's brigade advanced into a firestorm, a hopeless endeavor if they were attempting to break the enemy's line. But this was not Forrest's intent. He made wise use of his limited resources to prevent Buford from being overrun.[42] Black Bob's men were up to the task. If such a measurement existed, they would have ranked as some of the toughest men in Forrest's corps. Yet, they were a pack of mutts in an army of pure breeds. Every one of Forrest's brigades, except those in Chalmers's division, was composed of regiments from the same state—Bell's Tennesseans, Crossland's Kentuckians, Roddey's Alabamians, and Mabry's Mississippians. The five units of McCulloch's brigade, however, represented men from four states (Missouri, Mississippi, Tennessee, and Texas), and their lineage was as confusing as any in the Confederacy. For example, McDonald's Battalion, led by Lt. Col. James Crews, was known alternately, and quite correctly, as Crew's Battalion, Balch's Battalion, the 18th Battalion, the 26th Battalion, Forrest's Old Regiment, Kelly's Regiment, and the 3rd Tennessee Cavalry. All of these names were perfectly acceptable, and at one time or another were the official designation of the command. Different commanders within the army seemed to call the regiment whichever designation they preferred. To confuse things further, Col. David Kelly, "Forrest's Fighting Parson," had a few weeks before been ordered to recruit the battalion back to a full regiment, and so there was great confusion as to just who the commander was over a unit of uncertain size.[43]

One of the first of McCulloch's regiments to be sent in was Lt. Col. Samuel Hyams's 1st Mississippi Partisan Rangers. Pvt. Jesse Anderson was from Pontotoc County and knew the country well: "We charged them in old man Rook's corn field. My first lieutenant was killed just as we were making the charge. It was a fine field of corn, hardly in good roasting ear. You couldn't see a man twenty steps without you were a squirrel hunter. We charged up within twenty or twenty-five steps of them before we saw them. They were all squatted down with their guns ready to shoot." A quick-thinking officer, most likely Colonel Hyams, shouted out, "Fall boys!" and the men hit the ground. The enemy volley passed harmlessly over their heads, and the rangers returned fire as best they could.[44]

The advance of the Partisan Rangers was a godsend to the 3rd Kentucky, which had held on by sheer pluck and determination. When the Federals had made their charge into the corn, the Kentuckians grudgingly backed up the slope to the first rise. During the retreat the color bearer was shot down and the flag fell among the cornstalks. Lt. John Jarrett reached out to grab the cloth, lost his footing, and fell to the ground. The enemy almost on him, he gathered the colors under his body, where they could not be seen, and played dead.

When Hyams's regiment came through the corn, Jarrett was able to scramble to his feet and run up the slope. The regiment let loose a cheer as he waved the precious banner over his head.[45]

The situation on the Confederate left was deteriorating rapidly, and Mower began to push his men forward to end the engagement. John Gilbert, on the far right of the Union line, was concerned. His two leading regiments, the 14th and 27th Iowa, had been fighting in the cornfield for half an hour, and he was waiting impatiently for his other regiments, the 32nd Iowa and 24th Missouri, to come up on his right. "I sent a staff officer to find out where and why the other two regiments of my command had been detained, and to bring them forward on the right with all possible dispatch." He need not have worried. Col. Ed Wolfe was bringing his Third brigade across the creek and moving into position on the far right. Fully half of Smith's infantry was on the field and prepared to push the Confederates back toward Tupelo.[46]

Forrest either saw or sensed the threat developing on his left flank. He was in the process of drawing his units away from the field but could not allow himself to be flanked. His response was immediate—and improbable. He ordered Chalmers to take one regiment and make a mounted charge through the cornfield. Despite his fearsome reputation as a cavalryman, Forrest was not fond of mounted tactics. His success came in using his horses as transportation and his men as mounted infantry. Chalmers reacted immediately: "Taking Forrest's Regiment (Lt. Colonel Kelly) I went with it myself." The cornfield had already become a slaughterhouse for the soldiers who had advanced through the rows. An advance on horseback was a sign of the desperate action Forrest was forced to take while withdrawing his brigades and saving the rangers.[47]

Forrest's response at Old Town Creek reveals a rarely seen element of his military skills: the ability to fight effectively while on the defensive. It was in his character to take the initiative and bring the fight to the enemy, and he was usually able to dictate the terms of an engagement to ensure his men a victory. Rarely was he in a position where he did not hold an advantage. He also possessed a natural talent for responding quickly to a change in fortune, the very ability that led him to "charge them both ways" when surrounded at the engagement at Parker's Crossroads, Tennessee, in 1862. Though beaten and forced to take desperate measures, Forrest was like a cornered animal: wild and unpredictable.

The Partisan Rangers faced overwhelming numbers in their fight with two Federal brigades. When they began moving back up the slope, they halted with their backs to the rail fence that encircled the field. Hyams ordered them to tear the fence down so that no one would be exposed to the relentless fire while climbing over it.[48]

Not far from the rail fence, Forrest was doing his best to inspire McCulloch's men to hang on a little longer. Despite the heavy fire, the general remained mounted, offering up a tempting target. Moments later a bullet tore through his boot and right foot. It was his fourth wound of the war and, by his own judgment, the most painful. Depending on which of the accounts is to believed, the ball passed through his big toe, cut off his little toe, cut off two toes, or entered the ball of the foot and exited the arch. The ball damaged the myriad of nerves found in the foot, leaving Forrest in excruciating pain. Unable to continue, he sent a messenger to find Chalmers and direct him to return immediately. He sent another to General Lee in Tupelo.[49]

Chalmers was still with David Kelley's men when the messenger arrived with the news of Forrest's wound. At the same time, one of his staff officers rode up and urgently told him that they were in a bad way. "The enemy was 100 yards in my rear and on my right, but I could not see them, nor they me, because of the corn and slight ridge separating us." Rather than threatening the flank of the enemy, he had put himself in a position to be cut off, and he wasted no time in extricating the command from the perilous location.[50]

As Kelly began to pull his men back on the left, Bell's brigade on the far right was also in deep trouble. The three regiments had withdrawn behind the rail fence at the south end of the Creely cornfield. But unlike the Kentuckians in the center, none of McCulloch's brigade had come to their aid. There were no more than 400 men on the front line, and the level of fire that came from down the slope increased by the minute. Bell knew they were going to catch it, and at 5:30 the hammer fell.

On the Union left, McMillen bragged, "With a loud cheer, my men dashed forward." His four regiments surged forward toward the crest under a withering fire. Capt. Benjamin Berry, commanding the 114th Illinois, went down with a wound, as did Maj. Eugene Rawson of the 72nd Ohio. Berry's wound was painful, Rawson's mortal. Capt. Charles Hubbard had let his 93rd Indiana get out in advance of the brigade line and discovered that the enemy—the 2nd Tennessee under Lt. George Seay, standing in for the wounded Barteau—was on his left flank as well as in front. "I ordered an oblique fire to the left when we charged them and forced them from the position," Hubbard reported. He later claimed that the Confederates had retreated in utter confusion, many of them breaking their guns rather than being slowed down carrying them. Alongside McMillen's brigade was Winslow and the 3rd and 4th Iowa Cavalry armed with their rapid-fire carbines. Private Gantz of the 4th claimed that the regiment was "sending balls out of our Spencers 9 inches apart." Col. John Noble could not have been happier: "I feel at liberty, without boasting, to say that few charges during the war could have exceeded this in firmness, spirit, and brilliancy. It was a triumphant vindication of the valor of these regiments from the stigma of defeat on the 10th of June, and must have forever crushed from those rebels' hearts the hope of another victory."[51]

Chalmers returned to the ridge and found the Federals driving up the hill while his own men were falling back. To make matters even more distressing, Black Bob McCulloch, the senior man on the field after Chalmers, went down with a serious wound to the right shoulder. There were men and horses everywhere. Chaos reigned. Chalmers called for Buford to reform his division, but the messenger came back with the news that Buford had nothing to reform, that the division was gone. Chalmers repeated the order, and this time Buford replied that he had managed to rally three companies. The only troops Chalmers could count on were his own men from McCulloch's brigade, command of which had passed to Col. David Kelly. With this painfully small cadre, he withdrew 400 yards from the ridge and formed one last line. The enemy halted and came no farther.[52]

NINETEEN

Return to Memphis

A. J. Smith had sent Mower back to deal with what he considered a minor show of aggression against his rear guard, thinking the Confederates had brought up no more than 1,000 men. His men had not expended much effort driving the southerners away, and his casualties were relatively light. A minor affair, he believed. They had merely turned and struck back at an enemy that was following too closely. But in reality, the Confederates had thrown in more than 2,400 men. Once again Smith had been in a position to deal a death blow to Forrest's cavalry, but, as is evident through the Federals' reports and other writings, none of them realized the opportunity they had missed.

The lack of follow-through shown by the Federals was the only thing that saved the Confederates at Old Town Creek. When James Chalmers took command of the southern force, it was on the verge of collapse. Most of the Kentuckians and Tennesseans had scattered down the Tupelo Road, which left McCulloch's brigade to form the new line on a slight ridge about half a mile south of the creek. After two requests to form his ranks, Buford arrived with all the men he could muster: three companies, something less than 200 men. But since the Federals remained at the top of the second rise, the numbers proved sufficient.[1]

Chalmers kept his men in the saddle for an hour, watching and waiting. The men were jumpy, their confidence low. Making matters worse, a rumor raced up and down the line that General Forrest was dead. But far from lifeless, Forrest was in a field hospital waiting impatiently for the surgeons to staunch the flow of blood and bandage his wounded foot. Eventually the rumor made its way to the commander himself, and painful wound or not, he knew what had to be done. With help from his staff, he hobbled to his horse and climbed up into the saddle. He didn't look at all like a general; only one booted foot was in a stirrup, the other, heavily bandaged, hung loose, and he rode off in shirtsleeves, leaving behind his coat with its brass buttons and wreathed stars. Pvt. C. W. Robertson of the 15th Tennessee saw Forrest ride by: "The effect produced upon the men is indescribable. They seemed wild with joy at seeing their grand leader was still with them." After a few minutes of riding up and down the line, reassuring the men that he was among the living, Forrest turned his horse toward Tupelo and rode away from the field.[2]

With his line stable and the enemy showing no signs of activity, Chalmers was ready to pull out: "I ordered the brigade back to its camp in accordance with instructions I had received to withdraw the troops." General Lee, however, had different plans.[3]

Still in Tupelo when he learned of Forrest's wound, Lee immediately set out for Old Town Creek. He was galloping up the Ellistown Road when he came on squads and companies of Buford's division. With the aid of his staff, he tried to halt the men of Kentucky and Tennessee, ordering them to stop the withdrawal and reform their ranks. He did not have much success. Eventually he made his way up the road and found Chalmers, who briefed him on the situation and told him of Forrest's orders to pull back to Harrisburg. Lee countermanded the order and directed Buford to picket the forward position. Chalmers would rest his men nearby and relieve Buford at 3:00 A.M. But Buford was unable to gather enough of his men, and so the duty passed to McCulloch's brigade under David Kelly.[4]

Abraham Buford's day was over. Just three days before he commanded 3,200 men, the largest division in Forrest's Corps. Over the course of those three days, his men had done the lion's share of the fighting and suffered most of the casualties. One out of every three men was down, and at the end of the third day he didn't have enough troops left on the field to form a decent picket line. When Forrest asked him where his division was, Buford covered his face and replied, "I have no command. They are all killed." At General Lee's order Buford rode down the road with the remnants of his men and returned to his camp beyond Harrisburg.[5]

Joe Mower had called off the Federal counterattack at the top of the second rise. Other than the dead and wounded scattered across the field, there was no sign of the enemy. (Actually, there were a good many Confederates just 400–500 yards to the south, but they went unobserved through the thick screen of undergrowth.) Within a matter of moments, it seemed, the deafening sounds of battle had given way to a quiet calm.

John Gilbert halted the 14th and 27th Iowa and stood to arms, unsure if the enemy had left. It had been exhausting crossing the streams and fences and attacking up the slope. It was nearly six o'clock, and the heat of the day had yet to break. His other two regiments arrived, and he felt confident the enemy had indeed fled the field: "Skirmishers were thrown out, and the exhausted but triumphant line permitted to sit down and rest." Scores of men who had collapsed in the cornfield began to stagger back to their regiments.[6]

By sundown it was apparent that the fighting was over for the day. Smith ordered Mower to cross his two brigades back over the creek and join the rest of the division for the night. In case the Confederates attempted another night attack, like Forrest had the evening before, Smith ordered Moore to leave Gilbert's and Wolfe's brigades on the south side of the creek in line of battle.[7]

As always, in the wake of an engagement or battle, the care for the wounded was the top priority. Among these was Charles Sweney of the 27th Iowa, whose brother Joseph and two other soldiers carried from the cornfield to a farmhouse near the bridge. The makeshift field hospital "consisted of an operating table about the size of a carpenter's bench, put up of rough boards, one end of it being attached to a big tree." Joseph stayed close to his brother and watched the activities on the operating tables, a vision that still haunted him fifty years later.

> On that gallery close to where Charley lay was a wounded man from another regiment; a man whose abdomen was largely torn away by a shell so that his intestines were exposed, and he was suffering about all that man can suffer. This was before dark and very soon after the fighting was over. He asked me when I came there, "How has the fight gone?" I said to him, "We have whipped them, we have driven them off the field, we have won the day!" He said, "Good. I can die contented." Those were his last words, and within five minutes of uttering them he was dead.[8]

Care for the wounded was extended to the enemy as well. When Jesse Anderson of the 1st Mississippi Partisan Rangers was shot in the knee, he collapsed against the split rail-fence at the south end of Rook's cornfield. As a squad of Federals ran past, the last man in line noticed Anderson and called out, "Here is a damned reb in the corner of the fence." The young man's wound was noted and the squad continued up the slope. Anderson waited and spent his time in prayer, convinced the enemy would kill him when they returned. Instead, he found them to be solicitous, their battle fever cooled. An officer stopped over him and said, "Hello my friend, it looks like you are in a bad fix. What can we do for you? Don't you want some water?" By stretcher and ambulance, the

Union soldiers took him to the field hospital, where two surgeons removed his left leg above the knee.

> The next thing I knew I was lying on the ground with my leg off, shaking like a man with hard rigor. Then along came a man and said, "Hello, it looks like you are about to freeze to death, I will wrap you up in my blanket." He did, and after some time he came back by me and said, "You seem to be better" and I said, "Yes, I am about to get warm." I said, "Don't you want your blanket?" And he said, "I believe you need it worse than I do, you keep it." I call him the Good Samaritan you read about in the Bible.[9]

Other men returned to the cornfields looking for the dead and wounded from their regiments. Sgt. Harrison Chandler, quartermaster of the 114th Illinois, was one of these. He took a wagon drawn by six mules and with a number of comrades they scoured the field and found five of their own who had died in the fighting. Chandler was deeply disturbed by the carnage.

> I have heard before the suffering, the groans of the wounded, but never before this trip had I known what it was to witness such a sight and heard what I have heard within the last three days. Have seen humans mangled in every possible way—shell tearing them to pieces and seen them pierced by ball, through every part of the body.

Oddly, the ghastly sights led him to wish for the anonymity of a large army where he believed he would not be subjected to such heartrending scenes: "Give me a position in a large army, where I will have my work in the assaults on Richmond, Vixburg or Atlanta in preference to being connected with a small army like this whose business is to make raids like this." The size of the unit didn't matter; there was no escaping the violent death associated with soldiering.[10]

The lanterns in the field hospital burned late into the night. Surgeons from the various regiments and brigades worked until every last man was treated. Though his regiment was not involved in the fight, Brewer Mattocks, the assistant surgeon for the 7th Minnesota, was busy amputating a man's thumb when, to his surprise, he was joined by none other than Col. William Marshall, the regimental commander. "I find he is quite a surgeon," admitted Mattocks, though the colonel didn't have a bit of medical training.[11]

It had been a hard day of fighting and marching. Blood had been spilled to the west and south of Harrisburg and five miles to the north at Old Town Creek. The men on both sides were punch-drunk with fatigue. The Federals

on the south side of the creek had no fires in their camps, so that their numbers and location wouldn't be revealed to the enemy. "It grew quite cold in
the night," complained Ben Thomas of the 14th Iowa, "or at least seemed so
to the men with wet clothes, so we had to exercise to keep warm." Some men
slept in the road, but most stayed in the line of battle and slept wherever they
happened to find themselves, like Pvt. Louis Hucke of the 117th Illinois, who
"had to lie in the line of battle throughout the night in a green corn field."[12]

Reveille came early for both sides on July 16. At 1:00 A.M. the Federal bugles called the men to their feet, and within a few minutes "the rebel camp
fully sounded their morning call. The clear notes of their bugle followed by
the shrill fife and drum seemed just on the other side of the hill from us." The
Union advance, Coon's cavalry brigade, set out at 2:00, and gradually the regiments and brigades formed up and fell into the column.

Most of the men had hours to wait before they began to march, and those
with food enjoyed their breakfast. Rations were getting scarce. The 122nd
Illinois was one of the regiments that passed out the last of their stores that
morning: "We have issued to us three ½ crackers to last us three days & a piece
of meat 1 inch sq. & this is all we have to last us back to LaGrange." Capt.
Ted Carter of the 7th Minnesota saw to it that his men received their one-
third ration of hardtack, though they were somewhat cheered with full rations
of coffee and sugar. "The hard tack was full of worms which the boys shook
out before eating by rapping the hard tack against something hard so as to jar
it." The men laughed and called them "worm sandwiches." The 178th New
York was out of supplies, and the men satisfied their hunger with green corn
and green apples from the fields, a diet they would pay for later in the day. By
dawn, the last of Moore's Third Division pulled back from the far side of Old
Town Creek, and the 7th Kansas Cavalry took the rear guard.[13]

The hours of rest had done nothing toward restoring Buford's division. Mc-
Culloch's brigade was also too worn out from the fight to be of much use that
morning, and the men stayed close to camp. Chalmers would have to pursue
the enemy with troops that had done little or no fighting the day before. But
using Lyon's dismounted cavalry and infantry was out of the question; the men
had already shown themselves slow on the march and prone to heatstroke. Besides, with Smith's column leaving the area and the threat to the Black Prairie
region diminished, Lyon's men were needed elsewhere. Within twenty-four
hours the heavy artillerists and infantry were on their way to Alabama.[14]

Chalmers called up Roddey's Division as well as Rucker's brigade from his
own command. Roddey's men were as fresh as any in Lee's army and had seen
little to no fighting thus far in the campaign, and their horses were well-fed

and rested. These three brigades arrived before dawn to relieve McCulloch's weary men on the picket line. When the Federals pulled out across the creek, the Confederates began a light and continuous skirmish with their rear guard, never really attacking in strength but still denying the enemy an easy march.[15]

The bulk of the Confederate army remained in the vicinity of Tupelo and Harrisburg and for the first time took stock of its condition. Roll call was held, weapons and horses counted and cared for, and the numbers of dead and wounded tallied. One of the tallies displayed how disastrous the last three days had been to Forrest's Corps: there were so many horses without riders that all of the dismounted men would soon be given new mounts and sent back to their regiments.[16]

The casualty lists made their way from the individual regiments up through the brigade and division commanders and eventually to Forrest. Staff officers compiled the totals from the pages of names (forty-six pages from Buford's command alone). Most of the entries were merely names with a check mark in the appropriate column for killed or wounded, but others were more revealing: "H.B. Knight, knee, severe; F.M. Ragland, arm, dangerously; R.H. Kilgore, lung, dangerously." The final list, as expected, was bad: 215 Confederate soldiers were dead and another 1,116 wounded. At least 51 were held by the enemy. The dismounted division under Lyon came through virtually unscathed with just 25 battle casualties, though hundreds had fallen out from the heat. Thanks to the small part they had played in the drama, Roddey's Division avoided the butcher's bill with only a handful of wounded. Chalmers's men were not so lucky: 57 men had been killed outright with an additional 253 wounded. But in Buford's division the losses were nothing short of catastrophic: 1,000 saddles had been emptied, with 153 officers and men killed, 798 wounded, and 48 missing. The overall casualty rate in this division was a staggering 31 percent, though individual regiments were even higher. For example, the 3rd Kentucky Mounted Infantry started the fight with 145 men and lost 92 of them—a 63 percent casualty rate. The hospitals overflowed with Buford's wounded, and detachments worked long into the night burying his dead.[17]

In his after-action report Forrest stated, "The battle of Harrisburg will furnish the historian a bloody record, but it will also stamp with immortality the gallant dead and the living heroes it has made." The cold numbers he was compelled to account for could not accurately reflect the stunning loss among his corps' leadership. "Three of my brigade commanders (Rucker, McCulloch, and Crossland) were severely wounded," and though all three would eventually recover, their talents would be sorely missed in the coming weeks. Of twelve regimental commanders in Buford's division, only one, Lt. Col.

Absalom Shacklett, was still on his feet. Of the others, four were killed, five wounded, and one struck down by the heat. Seven of Buford's regiments were deprived of every one of their field officers, leaving many of them under the command of captains. In all, Buford lost 130 irreplaceable officers.[18]

Mabry's command got off the lightest of Buford's brigades, though the colonel reported, "All of my regimental and nearly all of my company commanders of three regiments having been killed or wounded." Most of his casualties had occurred during the charge on the morning of July 14, when in a matter of minutes his four regiments had been decimated: forty officers killed or wounded along with 231 enlisted men. One of the officers, Maj. Robert McCay, had died in Mabry's arms, and it was his unhappy task to notify the man's wife.

> With feelings of deepest sorrow I announce to you the death of your husband—Maj. Robert C. McCay 38th Miss. (Mounted Infty). He was killed in the battle at Harrisburg Miss. On the 14th Inst. while gallantly leading his regiment.
>
> While nothing can atone to you and your children for his loss, it will be a consolation to know that he died nobly at his post. He was shot through the head and fell in my arms and expired without a struggle. None excelled him in devotion to his family, fidelity to his country and gallantry as a champion in the glorious struggle for freedom.
>
> As his commander, as his associate, as his friend I mourn with you his loss.
>
> May that faith in Him who does all things right, soften the sorrows of your sad bereavement.[19]

But mourning the dead would have to wait; the first priority was to alleviate the suffering of the wounded. The field hospitals at Dr. Calhoun's and Mrs. Samples's were filled with men, as was the captured Federal hospital in Tupelo. The Union surgeons and volunteer nurses were doing their best and were praised by Maj. Thomas Tate of the 12th Kentucky, "All my wounded who fell into the hands of the enemy were left at Tupelo and had been very kindly treated." Despite the best efforts of the surgeons, the conditions in the hospital—exacerbated by the extreme heat—were appalling. There was simply no way to keep out the clouds of flies, and the insects crawled freely across the blood-stained bandages.[20]

In comparison to the tragic casualties of the Confederates, the Union troops came away in far better condition. Only 7 officers and 62 enlisted men were killed, including brigade commander Col. Alexander Wilkin, the highest-ranking northern officer to die in the fighting. Including the 40 desperately wounded men left behind in Tupelo, there were a total of 501 wounded and another 32 missing. Smith had suffered 602 total casualties compared to Lee's 1,382.[21]

Pvt. John Hubbard of the 7th Tennessee returned to the battlefield around Harrisburg, searching for the spot where his Company E had fought: "The ground was literally strewn with the bodies of our precious slain. It was impossible to identify them except by their clothing and other articles." He found several of his friends and comrades and took particular note of Privates John Field and William McKinney, who had died while trying to find shelter behind a small tree. He counted twenty-one bullets and a round of canister in that one small tree.[22] He and a few others made their way across the slope to the road when, as he remembered it, "along came General Forrest, wounded and riding in an open buggy. Just from the battlefield and suffering with a wound, he was somewhat excited. I remember well the sentiment he uttered. It was expressed by the words: 'Boys, this is not my fight, and I take no responsibility for it,' or words tantamount to these. I knew what he meant."[23]

Such words, following so closely on a major defeat could only have a negative impact on troop morale and further erode the soldiers' confidence in General Lee. When taken together with his disparaging remarks the night before about Lee's capabilities as a West Pointer, it is obvious that Forrest was trying to shift all blame for the loss onto Lee. What makes the statement so extraordinary is that it was made in the presence of enlisted men. The dig about West Pointers was made among the senior leadership of the army, and, though still insubordinate, it was heard only by fellow officers. John Hubbard had known Forrest for thirteen years, so perhaps the general felt comfortable enough around him to vent his own frustration. But Hubbard was still just a private, and it was against all military decorum for Forrest to make such a volatile statement in front of, or that could be heard and passed on by, enlisted men.[24]

But the comments, though out of line, served a purpose. Many of Forrest's Tennessee soldiers were new to his force, recruited the previous winter behind the Union lines. Many of these men were deserters from the infantry, disillusioned with the progress of the war, and had reenlisted into what they believed to be an elite band, one that didn't know defeat. So in order to keep his newest recruits from deserting once again and to still be able to entice others to sign on, Forrest had to maintain the impression of being unbeatable. And the only way he could do so following this devastating defeat was to blame someone else: Stephen D. Lee.[25]

The burial of the Confederate dead continued throughout the day. Out at the Calhoun place the dead were buried in a small grove of trees to the west of the house. There were no coffins available, but there was an abundance of empty flour barrels that served as good substitutes. Henry Hord of the 3rd Kentucky was on one of the burial squads. "It was a very disagreeable job," he wrote. "The poor fellows had been lying out in the hot sun for forty-eight hours. We had no stretchers and had to pack them all by hand to the trench, working in pairs."[26]

The hospital facilities at Tupelo and the surrounding farms could not handle the great number of men needing attention. Wagons carried the stricken men to Okolona, where they were transferred to more established hospitals or put on trains for transport to Columbus. Belle Edmondson and a number of ladies boarded the trains shuttling the wounded southward: "Oh! My heart ached to see so much suffering; we soothed and gave them everything they wanted."[27]

* * *

Smith's column, shadowed by Chalmers, marched twelve miles the first day and went into bivouac just north of Ellistown. The heat was as bad as ever, but few men complained about it, and not a single one of them dropped out from sunstroke. They were used to it by now, though Chaplain Edwards claimed it was "warm to the limit of endurance." The road itself was rough going—dusty and deeply rutted. The wounded in the springless wagons were subjected to hours of merciless torture. Fletcher Pomeroy of the 7th Kansas Cavalry surmised, "People in this vicinity must go to mill on a mule, for they could never get there with a wagon."[28]

The rear guard came up at three o'clock in the afternoon, tired from a long day of skirmishing with the enemy. The 7th Kansas Cavalry was more than willing to pass off its duties to Company A of the 3rd Iowa Cavalry, which was ordered by Colonel Noble to establish a picket line for the night. The Iowans arrived just in time to receive the final attack by the skirmishers of Rucker's brigade. The fight was more than the company could handle by themselves, and the 7th Kansas was ordered back to straighten things out. It was swampy ground, tough to maneuver in, so, just to be on the safe side, Moore ordered a section of Battery G, 1st Illinois Light Artillery, to lob a few shells toward the enemy. Unfortunately, the first shots were too low and fell among the 7th Kansas, killing one of their own. The action was over quickly, recorded Louis Hucke of the 117th Illinois, "and then everything was quiet again."[29]

The hungry men of Smith's column spread out and foraged as best they could. There was little to find around the remains of Ellistown, which was "a name but no town," according to Brewer Mattocks of the 7th Minnesota. Luther Frost of the 119th Illinois was digging in a potato patch with some of his comrades when a group of officers approached them and ordered them away, obviously wanting the food for themselves. "About this time Genl. Smith came along," Frost wrote. "He told the officers to let them alone and tend to their own business. He said they needed the potatoes and should have them." One group of foragers from the 114th Illinois was accosted by "bushwhackers" who fired into the group, wounding one of the men with a load of buckshot before disappearing into the woods. The offenders then ran into men from the 4th Iowa Cavalry, who put an end to that nonsense. It wasn't much of a fight, recorded Private Jacob Gantz, "not to amount to anything. We got some prisiners & some horses but they was gurillies. We slipped up on them."[30]

Eventually the camp quieted down and the men fell asleep. One of the men keeping watch was Jacob Gantz of the 4th Iowa Cavalry. At ten o'clock his company and another from the 3rd Iowa was ordered out on picket. They dismounted, sent back their horses, and kept a vigilant watch throughout the night. "There had been a small band of rebs saw cloce their but they did not bother us any all night but one or two shots was fired on another road."[31]

Indeed, there was a small band of Confederate guerrillas in the area, men who were operating outside of General Chalmers's command. Capt. Clinton "Clubfoot" Fort led a small band of irregular cavalry that operated in northern Mississippi. Virtually everything known about the group is contained in a series of letters written by Fort at the end of the war in which he makes a number of outlandish claims. Fort wrote how on the evening of July 16, while the Federal army lay sleeping about Ellistown, he and his entire company "went cautiously into their camps." For three hours the men made their way about the camps, never observed, as they attempted to divine Federal intentions for the next day. "We figured it was probably to New Albany, Miss. It turned out we were correct." Fort went on to explain how over the next few days his gallant band put an end to all Federal foraging, defeated three squads of the 7th Kansas Cavalry, made another raid into the camps the next night, and so harassed the Union column that "it was almost impossible for them to guard against our unexpected and sudden attacks." In fact, he was so successful, he bragged, that "our little company must have killed or wounded three or four times the number of our enemy as compared to the size of our whole company." But none of the ubiquitous Captain Ford's story even remotely approached the truth. From the closing of the fight with Rucker's brigade near Ellistown, there was only an occasional shot or two fired for the rest of the march back to LaGrange. There were no further casualties.[32]

One thing Fort did get right was Smith's intention of leaving the road north to Ripley and instead striking out northwest toward New Albany. This was in response to Chalmers's decision to try one last time to break the Union column. In the early-morning hours of July 17, Chalmers sent Roddey's Division on a looping ride to the northeast. Roddey's orders were to take a position near

Kelly's Ford on the Little Hatchie River and strike the Federals in the flank as they were making the difficult crossing. Chalmers would remain behind with Rucker's brigade and a section of artillery and keep up a warm fire on the Union rear guard. The plan went awry, though, when cavalry scouts from Grierson's division discovered the enemy and made their presence known to General Smith. In response, Grierson recommended following the road to New Albany, which had the added benefit of moving over territory as yet untouched during this raid, a move that might offer more forage for the hungry animals and men. At 4:00 A.M. the army set out for New Albany.[33]

Repeatedly during the campaign Smith had done the opposite of what the Confederates had planned or expected him to do. The march toward New Albany would prove the final surprise. Roddey waited in vain throughout the day at Kelly's Ford for the Federals. Chalmers had had enough and called off the pursuit. The Confederates returned to Tupelo, and Smith continued his march back to Tennessee.[34]

The final days of the campaign were taxing for the Federals. With food at a premium, Smith stepped up the pace, marching the men fifteen to twenty miles a day in the blistering heat. Some men were able to find some pigs and potatoes, but the bulk of the army went without food other than their moldy hardtack. Chaplain Edwards mused that the enemy was no longer General Lee or General Forrest but "General Starvation." Riders had been sent ahead to LaGrange with orders for wagons of provisions to head out and meet the returning column in Salem. And indeed the relief train met the column in Salem on July 18, and the men were issued a full ration of hardtack, the most some of them had had since leaving LaGrange two weeks earlier.

The cavalry arrived in LaGrange on the 20th, followed the next morning by the infantry. They were not destined to stay, however, and began the move to Memphis that afternoon. On foot, horse, wagon, and rail, the expedition made its way westward and by July 24 was back in Memphis.[35]

Victory or Defeat?

On July 16, 1864, Gen. Ulysses S. Grant was working in his headquarters at City Point, Virginia, when an aide handed him a copy of that day's *Richmond Enquirer* and pointed out a dispatch from Stephen D. Lee to Braxton Bragg of July 14: "We attacked a column of the enemy under Smith yesterday on the march from Pontotoc. We attacked him in his position at Tupelo this morning but could not force his position. The battle was a drawn one and lasted three hours." Grant read the message and forwarded the information on to Gen. Henry Halleck in Washington without comment. It was the first news anyone had on Gen. A. J. Smith and his Sixteenth Corps in eleven days. When Smith had departed LaGrange on July 5, he had cut off his communications with Tennessee and for all purposes disappeared. In Memphis, Washburn was getting anxious. The previous two expeditions against Forrest had been failures. And though he spoke optimistically about Smith's raid, he couldn't help but wonder and worry as day after day passed with no word from Mississippi. He knew the general direction Smith had taken, but until he heard something definite he was in the dark. A query to Brig. Gen. Edward Hatch in LaGrange brought no useful information; the last Hatch had heard, Smith was somewhere between New Albany and Pontotoc, and that intelligence was a week old.[1]

Finally, on July 18, General Smith's chief of scouts, a man identified only as Jerry, rode into LaGrange and presented to Hatch a dispatch from Smith written the day before in New Albany: "We met Lee and Walker at Tupelo and whipped them badly on three different days. Our loss is small when compared with the rebel loss. I bring back everything in good order; nothing lost." Details of the victory could wait; Smith wanted to reassure an anxious Washburn that all was well and that there had been no reversals. A relieved Washburn immediately telegraphed Generals Sherman and McPherson and Secretary of War Stanton with the good news; "The expedition of Maj. Gen Smith has been a complete success."[2]

The following day Grant took a few moments to inform Sherman he had seen another piece in the Richmond papers, this one claiming Smith had left Tupelo and was in retreat toward Ripley. Grant was not overly concerned: "I judge from S.D. Lee's dispatch that Forrest has been badly whipped. Smith, however, ought to be instructed to keep a close watch on Forrest, and not permit him to gather strength and move into Middle Tennessee." Sherman concurred and sent off a telegram to Washburn on the evening of July 20: "Order Smith to pursue and keep after Forrest all the time. The papers announce his moving from Tupelo for Ripley, but I suppose he went to replenish his supplies. Even the Atlanta papers do not claim for Lee and Forrest a victory, although they report Smith as retreating badly whipped."[3]

Smith arrived in LaGrange on the 21st fully prepared to resupply his troops and continue with his orders to prevent Forrest from entering middle Tennessee. A letter of congratulations from Washburn was waiting for him, but Smith received it too late to share with his troops, some of whom were already making the trip by rail and horse into Memphis. Oddly, despite holding telegrams from both Grant and Sherman to keep Smith in the field, Washburn directed Smith to return to Memphis "as rapidly as transportation can be provided." Without the consent of his superiors, Washburn planned to use the Sixteenth Corps for a campaign of his own design.

When Smith arrived at Washburn's headquarters in Memphis on the 23rd, he read the dispatches sent by Sherman, and he was immediately concerned. By all outward appearances, Smith had disregarded the general's orders to remain in the field and continue active operations against Forrest. He voiced his unease with his superior. Washburn responded not to Smith but with a telegram to Sherman that failed to acknowledge it was Washburn who had disobeyed his orders by directing Smith to return to Memphis: "Yours of the 20th received. General Smith has returned. He thinks you have a wrong impression in regard to his fight. He returned for lack of supplies. That he whipped the enemy very badly there is no doubt. I have ordered General Smith to put his command in order to again move after Forrest. He will so move as soon as he can get ready, unless you should think he had better go to Mobile." Sherman replied: "It was by General Grant's special order that General Smith was required after his fight to pursue and continue to follow Forrest. He must keep after him till recalled by me or General Grant, and if Forrest goes toward Tennessee General Smith must follow him."

If Sherman and Grant were unhappy with the campaign, it was certainly not with Smith's conduct or results but with his return to Memphis and his disregard of the order to resupply and continue on with the mission. Washburn never informed the generals that it was he who had ordered Smith's return to Memphis.[4]

In his narrative of the battle, Stephen D. Lee claimed that "these telegrams tell the tale, and show Gen. Smith's superiors were greatly disappointed in the results, and reflected on him." On the contrary, Grant and Sherman were pleased with Smith's results and wanted him to go out and do more of the same. After three and a half years of warfare, it was an accepted fact in the Union army that if the "iron dice of battle" went against a commander, it was assured he would be removed from his post and either sent to the frontier or "home awaiting orders." The only exemption from this rule was extended to those with political clout. Smith had no political power or benefactors and relied solely on his own abilities. Unlike General Sturgis, Smith was sent back into the field to once again take on Forrest. If there is any doubt about Sherman's confidence in Smith, it can be laid to rest by a September 12 telegram from Sherman in Atlanta:

> I have been trying for three months to get you and Mower to me, but am headed off at every turn. Halleck asks for you to clear out [Maj. Gen. Sterling] Price. Can't you make a quick job of it and then get to me? Your command belongs to me, and is only loaned to help our neighbors, but I fear they make you do the lion's share. However, do as General Halleck orders, and as soon as possible come to me.[5]

There is no question that Harrisburg was a tactical victory for the Union. From the first engagement at Whitten Branch on July 7 to Roddey's failed ambush at Kelly's Ford on the 17th, Smith outwitted and outfought his enemies at every turn. The only engagements that could be even remotely considered Confederate victories were the cavalry fights on the Okolona and Tupelo roads on July 12. Both of these engagements were part of a Union diversion to confuse Lee and Forrest about Federal intentions. So since the enemy did precisely what Smith wanted—move their force en masse against Pontotoc and unmask the road to Tupelo—neither Duff's nor Lyon's action can be considered a southern victory.

As for a strategic victory, both sides made compelling arguments about their success relative to their individual goals. Smith had three goals when he set out from LaGrange: prevent Forrest from attacking Sherman's supply line in middle Tennessee, destroy a portion of the Mobile & Ohio Railroad, and defeat Forrest in battle. The bold statements in Sherman's letters to President Lincoln and Secretary Stanton—"follow Forrest to the death" and "pursue and kill Forrest"—were never in the orders McPherson sent to Smith. His actual orders stated, "Forrest should be followed until brought to bay somewhere and then whipped." Smith was successful in all three of his strategic goals, and though he had not destroyed Forrest's command, he had certainly "whipped" it.[6]

The claims for a southern strategic victory hinge on one accepted fact: Smith, though victorious, gave up the field and retreated to Tennessee. It is an old military maxim that whichever side possesses the field after a battle is the victor. Usually this means the foe has been defeated in the conflict and driven from the field. Rather than flee the field, however, Smith waited twenty-four hours before he ordered his army to turn north and return to Tennessee. In the intervening hours he built fortifications, cared for his wounded and those of the enemy, and buried his dead. He was not forced from his position but chose the time and manner of his departure.

James Chalmers went the furthest in claiming success for southern arms—not by defeating Smith on the field but by denying him what he believed to be Smith's main goal: the destruction of the Black Prairie.

> Although our loss in killed and wounded was severe, we nevertheless succeeded in driving the enemy back. He may have destroyed much valuable property and produced great suffering and hardship in the immediate line of march, yet the great, grand, and leading object of his raid—the destruction of these rich valleys and prairies, with their untold agricultural wealth—was signally defeated, and this region is again, comparatively, saved. In short, with our heavy losses we yet can claim to have won for our country another decided triumph.

John Wyeth not only echoed this claim but expounded on it, reasoning that when

> General Smith retreated from the field, it was an acknowledgement of his inability to hold his position and an abandonment of the object of the expedition, and therefore a Confederate victory. He had been sent out to destroy Forrest's command, and if possible to kill the Confederate leader, and incidentally to tear up the Mobile & Ohio Railroad and invade the prairie country. With the exception of about four miles of the track torn up at Tupelo, not a single object of the expedition was accomplished.

Thomas Jordan wrote, "Indeed, in view of General Smith's mere military movements, it is difficult to comprehend with what objective the campaign was undertaken."[7]

The southerners may have claimed the victory, but they admitted that it was not gained through military prowess but due to the failed nerve of the enemy. Chalmers wrote that it was "the stubborn valor" of the Confederates that "struck terror to the hearts of the superior numbers." Jordan and Pryor described the "demoralized" condition of the victorious Union generals that compelled them to flee the field without even attending to their wounded. "Between the lines," wrote Wyeth, "it is not difficult for the careful student to read the real cause of General Smith's retreat. He had never seen men fight with such desperate (if misdirected) valor. After this exhibition he did not dare to advance upon his antagonist, in compact line and behind defenses, nor could he safely remain where he was."[8]

Such claims ring hollow once it is understood that Smith never intended to move into the Black Prairie region or occupy the country he traversed. His success throughout the campaign can be attributed to his unpredictability; he never did what Lee and Forrest expected of him. He seized the initiative, made his adversaries react to his movements, and never really gave them the opportunity to do anything other than attack under unfavorable conditions.

Most of the postwar accounts agree that if Smith had counterattacked after the assaults of the 14th, he would have crushed Forrest's and Lee's force. Each becomes its own tale of missed opportunities by the Federals, while little attention is given to what Smith actually accomplished: Sherman's supply line remained intact, and the Confederates in Mississippi had been dealt a harsh defeat. As historian Edwin Bearss summarized, "The combat effectiveness of Forrest's corps was destroyed in the period of July 13–15. While Forrest would rally his force and make a number of daring raids, never again would his corps be able to stand and fight Union infantry."[9]

Tactically and strategically, the campaign was a Union victory. From July 5 until his return to LaGrange on the 20th, A. J. Smith moved at will through north Mississippi. His enemy was never sure where he was going, could not defeat him when he stopped to fight, could not drive him away till he was ready to leave, and could not detain him when he chose to depart.

TWENTY-ONE

A Second Battle

Theodore G. Carter, a former captain in Company K, 7th Minnesota Infantry Volunteers, remained active in veteran affairs after the war. It was not an easy thing to do from his home in Deadwood, South Dakota, but he attended as many functions as he could, including the gatherings of former Confederates. In 1897 he made the trek to Nashville to attend the Confederate Veteran Reunion. He delighted in talking over the battles with his former adversaries, all the old bitterness long since a thing of the past: "I met-up with one old veteran who was in Mabry's Brigade at Harrisburg, and we talked for about an hour of what we saw there; and when we shook hands at parting, he said: 'But we whipped you well, anyhow.' Evidently he believed it, and it seemed to do him so much good that I did not have the heart to try to undeceive him."[1]

Carter's anecdote was part of a reply he had written for *Confederate Veteran Magazine* in response to a letter submitted by Henry E. Hord, late private of the 3rd Kentucky Mounted Infantry, which detailed his experiences at the Battle of Tupelo. Many of Hord's claims were so outlandish that Carter felt compelled to respond.

What is in print is usually taken for history. There is a great deal in the "War Records," published by our government, that is exaggerated, and neither side has a monopoly of that kind of reports. It looks as if the idea was that it was a poor officer who could not make a good report with a very little foundation in the shape of facts. "Yaller Glory" for officers and men was a great incentive. I was present at the battle of Harrisburg, and have a vivid recollection of what took place on the whole campaign, so far as came under the observation of myself and friends. I also kept a diary.[2]

Carter filled two pages of the magazine with facts refuting Hord's outrageous recollections, but he was doing more than challenging the claims of a single man; he was attempting to call a halt to the pattern of misinformation that had flowed unchecked since the closing hours of the battle. In the thirty-three years that had passed and in the years that would follow, much was written about the battle. And though most of it is a true and compelling story, a good deal of the writing was patently false. Carter was so bothered by the exaggerations and half-truths that in 1909 he published an article with the Mississippi Historical Society to once again set the record straight. The subsequent histories of the battle have rarely succeeded in telling the truth of the battle and campaign as he desired; Carter would be sorely disappointed.[3]

The story of the Tupelo campaign is told through a great many sources, first and foremost *The War of the Rebellion: Official Records of the Union and Confederate Armies.* The after-action reports of fifty-five of the senior participants, forty-two Union and thirteen Confederate, are included in Part 1 of Volume 39; Part 2 contains dozens of supporting telegrams and letters, and though other volumes contain correspondence relevant to the campaign, the bulk of the information is found in these two books. This monumental series is the natural starting point for any study of the battle, but, as most scholars of the conflict have discovered, and as Carter alluded to, inclusion of a report does not necessarily guarantee accuracy.[4]

Stephen D. Lee did not write a report about the Harrisburg fight during the war, and so his version of the events is missing from the record. He claimed that his new duties as a corps commander in John Bell Hood's Army of Tennessee kept him too busy to file the account. He did eventually write a report of sorts, and it was published in 1902 by the Mississippi Historical Society. In his own way, Lee was trying to clear up what he considered to be misconceptions of the battle, and his efforts sadly resulted in a further muddying of the waters. He also touched off a firestorm of recriminations by suggesting that Forrest should shoulder some of the blame for the Confederate defeat.[5]

And there lies the crux of the problem with the battle accounts, whether they are biographies, articles, or even official reports: southern veterans, or those writers with a Confederate bias, have gone to great lengths to expunge the taint of defeat from Forrest in particular and Lee's army in general. As Leslie Anders claimed, "Confederates labored long after to correct an impression that their hero had been defeated." This has been done in a number of ways. Exaggerating the disparity in the size of the two opposing forces is a common theme, as is the refusal of the Federals to come out from behind their "impregnable" earthworks. Another example is the postwar accounts from southern sources, which nearly all agree that the presence of Lee on the battlefield at Harrisburg liberated Forrest from all responsibility during the fight. As George Kilmer observed, "The Confederates made every argument to take the sting out of their defeat."[6]

The *Official Records* was the point of origin for a great deal of the misconceptions about the fight. Statements that disagree with the facts were taken up by subsequent writers and either repeated or expanded on so often that the error became the truth. This is also true in a number of biographies and unit histories. Jordan and Pryor's book about Forrest, the first written and actually read by the general, is an excellent biography, but it contains serious errors. Even today, authors embrace these inaccuracies to the point where the true accounts written by the participants are frequently dismissed or even scoffed at.

There are ten issues that have been debated heatedly by the participants of the battle and subsequent writers of the battle. By no means are these the only points of disagreement in the history of the battle; the list of disputes is endless. These ten issues just happen to be the most frequently disputed when the battle is discussed in print or other forums.

- Smith's "timid" advance from Tennessee
- The Union flank march from Pontotoc on July 13
- The presence of earthworks on the battlefield
- The actual number of men in each army
- The number of casualties and the care given to them
- The reasons for A. J. Smith's withdrawal and whether it was a retreat
- The extent of Union foraging and depredations
- Forrest's refusal to command his corps
- Stephen D. Lee's account and the resulting furor
- Sherman and Grant's reactions to the results of the campaign

These are the essential elements used to illustrate the battle through the accepted tenets of the Lost Cause movement. When these individual elements are combined, the resulting history is essentially revisionist:

A timid General Smith advances into Mississippi with his army committing numerous depredations along the way. But he runs away to Tupelo when confronted by the ill-equipped and undermanned southern army. Despite overwhelming numbers, the Federals cower behind earthworks, refusing to come out and fight like men. The resulting battle frightens the northerners so badly they retreat to Memphis using feeble excuses of low rations and ammunition as justification. The Federals leave Tupelo in such a rush they abandon their wounded and are drive headlong back to Tennessee, where Smith learns that Grant and Sherman are furious because he failed to kill Forrest. The high casualties among the Confederates are regrettable but cannot be blamed on Forrest, who was not in command. After Forrest's death, Lee attempts to shift all blame from himself and lay it at the feet of the great cavalryman.

Such a scenario, as fantastic as it may seem, can actually be pieced together using the accounts found in a number of widely accepted and well-respected sources. Authors have, and continue to use, material that is flagrantly incorrect in order to advance preconceived notions and agendas. What follows is a discussion of each of the ten issues and examples of the attendant historiography.

Smith's Advance

The distance from Lagrange, Tennessee, to Pontotoc, Mississippi, following Smith's route is about seventy-five miles. Today, in a car, it takes less than two hours; but in July 1864 it took the Federals six days. At that point in the war, most of the armies had become accustomed to marching twenty to twenty-five miles a day, so much so that it was hardly worthy of mention in diaries, letters, and reports. But Smith advanced into Mississippi at a rate of about twelve miles a day. The reason for this was the heat. The Confederates felt the effects of the blistering temperatures as well, as evident in the complete breakdown of Lyon's dismounted division. But while Forrest and Buford took notice of the heat, they never considered it a factor in Smith's slow advance.[7]

In his report of the campaign, James Chalmers related how he first came into contact with the enemy on July 10. "The enemy was moving very slowly, and usually with a line of battle and skirmishers about one mile of length." Smith did deploy in a line of battle on July 10, but up to that point he had not done so. Chalmers was echoed in Lee's 1902 account when he described the approach as "very slow, and with the utmost caution to prevent surprise." In 1908 Lee amplified his reasoning in another article for the Mississippi Historical Society: "The Federal General moved very slowly and cautiously . . . and moved almost in a continuous line of battle."[8]

Thomas Jordan advanced the theory that Smith was not only moving slowly from a cautious nature but a lack of aggression as well: "The Federal Commander assuredly displayed much watchfulness in his movements, but the least possible vigor or enterprise. He appears to have restricted his movements after crossing the Tallahatchie, to the defensive against an enemy very much inferior in numbers." Other authors have referred to the advance as "careful," "deliberate," and "wary."[9] Frank A. Dennis even resisted calling the move an advance, saying, "It strains definition to call this movement a march; it was more like a tiptoe. Roll was called three times daily, allegedly to prevent stragglers, but more likely to prevent desertion." What evidence there was to support such a hypothesis is unknown, and this is the sole account that raises the possibility of desertion as a factor in the speed of the march.[10]

Henry Hord abandoned any pretense of the truth when, in his account, he described Smith's movement from Tennessee.

> We met them south of La Grange, and immediately commenced a kind of guerrilla warfare—capturing pickets, ambushing, night attacks, rushing in while they were on the march, killing the wagon guards, burning wagons, and out again before they could get a whack at us. Constantly annoyed in this way, Smith's Corps could not march more than six or seven miles a day on the route. He had to be ready to fight at all hours, day or night. The road in his rear was strewn with dead mules, burnt wagons and fresh made graves. All the way from La Grange to Harrisburg we acted as an invisible escort to Gen. Smith. He could not water his horses without taking his army to the creek with him, and he camped every night in line of battle, with heavy skirmish lines thrown about him.[11]

It was this version that prompted George Carter to respond:

> It is a very interesting account, and certainly Mr. Hord is a good writer. I do not question his veracity, as he evidently believes what he writes to be the facts; but I cannot help thinking he has confused with it some of the other hard fights of Gen. Forrest's and merged them into one . . .
>
> The guerilla warfare mentioned . . . was unknown to the main body of our army which was with the train. We were never disturbed, never camped in line of battle, made as long marches as the men could endure in that hot climate, until on the afternoon of July 10 we camped in line of battle, and remained in that position all night, but neither saw nor heard any Confederates. We lost neither wagons nor mules prior to July 13, and the graves we left along the road were filled by the victims of heat, not war. The term "invisible escort" is correctly used if the Confederates *did* escort us, for we neither saw nor heard them or of them.[12]

Hord was not alone in his contention that the southern skirmishing was a factor in slowing the advancing Federals. Claude Gentry went so far as to claim that "the Confederates contested every foot of the way." The truth lay somewhere between Hord's and Gentry's accounts and that of Carter. There was indeed skirmishing on the road to Pontotoc, but not too much. Carter himself was never in a position to see any of the enemy in the first days of the march because all of the skirmishing was done by the cavalry. Men from the 3rd and 4th Iowa and the 9th Illinois Cavalry wrote in their diaries about skirmishes on nearly every day of the approach to Pontotoc, but as John Leach of the 3rd Iowa cavalry said, "[We] followed them always but to no purpose."[13]

There is no doubt that the reason for the slow advance was Smith's response to the excessive heat. There are dozens of accounts describing the harsh weather. Diary entries abound with "Hot day, men straggling badly," "Very hot, too hot," and "Terribly hot, sunstrokes common." Frederick Humphrey, chaplain of the 12th Iowa, wrote, "The men suffered greatly from the intensity of the heat. A July sun shot down his burning rays; the men seemed to [be] broiled in the sun, and buried in the clouds of dust. I have seen hundreds of strong, athletic men lying in the shadow of fences, bushes, and trees, exhausted and fainting from the effects of the heat." Sidney Robinson of the 117th Illinois saw similar sights: "Awful to see the men falling sun struck around you, some dead, some dying & others from pure exhaustion." It is significant that while so many Federal accounts refer to the unrelenting high temperature and the numerous deaths from sunstroke, not a single southern source considered the heat as a primary factor in Smith's slow advance.[14]

The Union Flank March

A. J. Smith's decision to outflank the Confederate position at Pinson's Hill and, unintentionally, the defensive works at Prairie Mound came from his observation of those works south of Chiwapa Creek: "I did not deem it prudent to attack the position from the front if it could be flanked." Smith was able to anticipate the ambush that Forrest and Lee had laid for him and simply refused to walk into the trap.

Once he made the decision, Smith did not share it with the rank and file; operational security, then and now, dictates that the fewer people who are in the know the better. Aside from his division commanders and a handful of staffers who knew, Smith's plan remained a secret. Of course, as each man made the turn to the east at Pontotoc the next morning, the plan became evident. The most interesting and honest observations of unfolding events were those recorded into diaries and journals or in letters written immediately following the campaign. These sources were untainted by subsequent articles and books and reveal the men's thoughts as the events were occurring. Also, these men were not in the inner circle and, as such, not privy to the plans and stratagems unfolding around them.[15]

There was no bigger novice in martial matters than Elijah Edwards, chaplain of the 7th Minnesota Infantry, but even he was able to grasp the significance of the move: "It has been a matter of strategy to keep Forrest in doubt as to which point we were aiming." Edwards was able to gather from the men about him that they were headed for Tupelo, though the spontaneous cheers up and down the column may have at first confused him. The soldiers knew that Tupelo lay to the east, but, more importantly, they understood the advantage they were to gain by a rapid move to the left. "The rebels are fooled," recorded Charles Tiedman of the 178th New York. Otto Wolf of the 117th Illinois wrote, "Gen. Smith outgeneraled Forrest at Pontotoc for he thought we would go to Okolona," the same conclusion derived by Johnson Paisley of the 117th Illinois: "General Smith out generaled the rebs as they were expecting us to attack."[16]

James D. Porter, a Confederate staff officer during the war, agreed with other postwar southern authors when he stated that Smith "seemed doubtful as to his movements" during the advance, but he did concede that the Federal general "boldly turned toward Tupelo." Another Tennessean, John Hubbard of the 7th Tennessee, acknowledged Smith's movement by writing, "A tactician thoroughly acquainted with the topography of the country could not have made a more judicious move." These two authors were in the minority, however, as most southern accounts gave decidedly different reasons for the Union movement away from Pontotoc.[17]

Bedford Forrest was loath to suggest that Smith had stolen a march, and in his account he states, "The delay of the enemy at Pontotoc produced the impression that he designed to fall back towards Memphis." When he discovered that the enemy was on the move, he claimed they were "retiring in the direction of Tupelo."

In his official report James Chalmers never actually admitted that the enemy had stolen a march but did concede that they had a ten-mile head start on him before he moved in pursuit. In an account written in 1879 he stated that the enemy "moved rapidly towards Tupelo as if alarmed." The *Richmond Daily Dispatch* agreed with this assessment and deemed Smith "afraid to come further south" and "unwilling to risk an open fight, [he] moved off during the night in the direction of Tupelo." Each of these accounts gives the impression that Smith was attempting to break off contact with the Confederates with designs to either avoid battle or return to Memphis. The significance of the march was not lost on Green B. Raum in a 1901 article he wrote for the *National Tribune:* "They had mistaken Gen. Smith's splendid tactical movement for position as a precipitate retreat."[18]

Once the flank march had been discovered the Confederates pursued and attempted to break Smith's column. Claude Gentry wrote "It was here that the natural ability of Gen. Forrest was exhibited as at Brice's Crossroads one month earlier." Many authors, beginning with Forrest in his report, claimed that the Federals were pressed or pushed so hard they were forced in the direction of Tupelo. Forrest reported, "I had now driven the enemy ten miles, and as his flanks had not been attacked I was fearful that he was driven too rapidly." But Forrest was not driving his enemy, nor did he enjoy the same success he had won at Brice's Crossroads. The pace of Smith's march was not set by the pressure exerted by Forrest but by the speed of his own cavalry, which arrived in Tupelo at noon. Thomas Hawley of the 11th Missouri proudly told his family, "Did not drive us far. No not at all."[19]

As for the fighting at Bartram's Shop and Camargo Crossroads, both camps were quite accurate in their accounts, save for a few exaggerations. Chalmers reported that the enemy was "forced to abandon and burn 7 wagons, 1 caisson, and 2 ambulances." This claim has been taken at face value and repeated so many times it has become the accepted version and is so close to the truth as to hardly warrant mention. Forrest even repeated the numbers in his own report but increased "1 caisson" to "caissons." The seven wagons were certainly burned and possibly so were the two ambulances. The caisson(s), however, is another story. As Joseph Reed of the 2nd Iowa Battery correctly observed in a postwar article, "there was no artillery in that part of the column." Reed was quick to correct the error in his 1898 account and then made an outlandish and ungenerous claim about his unit's performance at Camargo Crossroads. Reed gave sole credit to himself and his men—"I have always claimed for the Second Iowa Battery that it put up the only fight that was made on our side"—when seven Union regiments as well as Reed's battery and a section of Battery E, 1st Illinois Light Artillery were really involved in the fight.[20]

Earthworks

Without doubt, the accounts of earthworks, or breastworks, at Harrisburg are the most repeated myths in the history of the battle. To be sure, there were earthworks on the field, and they were built and occupied by both sides. Where truth becomes myth is when discussing the Union works, particularly when they

were built and how they were used. Of the thirteen Confederate reports in the
Official Records, ten describe some form of enemy breastworks or fortifications.
Interestingly, the three reports that do not mention any works were written by
commanders not involved in the Confederate attacks on July 14.[21]

Forrest was the first to describe the defenses Smith was believed to have
built: "During the night [of July 13] he had constructed fortifications, and his
position being naturally strong it was now almost impregnable." Forrest did
not, however, indicate any of this activity in the observations he made during
his midnight ride with Sam Donelson, aside from a mention that the enemy
was "strongly posted." Surely if he had seen impregnable works on the ridge,
he would have insisted on alternative tactics, which he did not.[22]

By no means was Forrest alone in these observations. Chalmers, Buford,
Crossland, Bell, and Mabry all describe some form of "works," "fortifications,"
or "fortified positions." The regimental commanders of the Kentucky brigade,
who came closest to the Union line during the assaults, repeated these findings
in their own reports. Joel Cochran of the 7th Kentucky reported finding the
enemy "behind breastworks they had thrown up during the night," and Paine
Ridgeway, commander of the 3rd Kentucky, reported fighting "the enemy in
his works." Officers and enlisted men of the brigade also claimed that the
enemy had been busy during the evening hours. James McNeely of the 7th
Kentucky wrote how "the Yanks were in town and dug ditches in all night to
fight in next morning."[23]

But there were no earthworks or fortifications, at least not on the scale described by the southerners. The only fortifications constructed prior to the assault were "temporary works" thrown up the morning of the 14th by the soldiers
of the 9th Illinois Cavalry. These particular works were on the extreme left of
Smith's line and were in a sector that saw no fighting the morning of the 14th.
Just prior to the Confederate assault, the 12th Iowa Infantry broke down a rail
fence and made a barricade no higher than eighteen inches. This small barricade, subsequently used by men of the 7th Minnesota, was north of the Pontotoc–Tupelo Road and not part of the line that faced the Kentuckians. It was
Charles Murray's First Brigade that took the brunt of Crossland's assault, and
of his defenses Murray wrote, "The whole line of infantry was placed so as to
be concealed from the view of the enemy by the nature of the ground, growing corn, and bushes." Thomas Kinney of the 119th Illinois concurred: "My
men were sheltered by an elevation of ground in front, completely concealing us
from the view of the rebels." Risdor Moore of the 117th Illinois explained how
"the regiment was protected by the ridge." Adolphus Wolf of the 117th Illinois
told his parents, "Our line was right on top of the hill in plain view," and Charles

Tiedman of the 178th New York recorded in his diary that he was "concealed from the enemy by dwarf oaks." But there were no breastworks for shelter.[24]

Why is there such disparity in these eyewitness accounts? The answer lies in timing. During the assaults of July 14 no southerner approached the Union line closer than thirty yards, and at the time the line was shrouded in heavy battle smoke. Despite the claims, no Confederate actually saw any works or fortifications until *after* the Federals had abandoned the morning of the 14th. In the intervening twenty-four hours, between the assaults and their departure, the Federals had built substantial works out of logs, earth, and cotton bales, and these were the works the Confederates saw when Smith's army pulled out of Harrisburg. Given the ferocity of the fighting on the afternoon of the 15th and the high number of Confederate casualties compared to the relatively few for the Federals, it was a logical assumption that the works had been present during the fighting on the 14th.[25]

The eyewitness accounts of Forrest and his men are forgivable. These men were not privy to the Federal reports and did not know when the fortifications were constructed. What is not forgivable, however, are the books, articles, and speeches written after the *Official Records* were published that ignore or reject the fact, as made clear in the Federal reports, that there were no works during the assaults of July 14. Jordan and Pryor's biography of Forrest was published before the *Official Records*, but the authors read copies of the reports. But rather than relying on the participants' accounts, they added a few embellishments. They wrote that the ground "was well chosen for defense; and those strong, natural advantages, Major-General A. J. Smith immediately set his troops to improving, as far as practicable, during the night, by breastworks made of rails, logs, and the materials of cabins and outhouses, torn down for that purpose and covered with earth." They also incorrectly claimed, despite the evidence, that these substantial works were "discovered" by Forrest and Donelson during their nocturnal reconnaissance.[26]

Published in 1868, Jordan and Pryor's biography was widely read by veterans who were preparing to write their accounts of the war; in turn, they "borrowed" much of the material and used it to tell their own stories. R. R. Hancock of the 2nd Tennessee used the entire paragraph in the biography, word for word, that described the works made from "cabins and outhouses." John Hubbard was a bit more circumspect and only paraphrased Jordan when he wrote, "They literally tore up the town by tearing down the houses and using the lumber for breast-works." A troubling aspect of this plagiarism is that while Hubbard and Hancock were both participants and eyewitnesses, Jordan, a Confederate general, and Pryor, a professional journalist, were not. But the

Jordan and Pryor account gave these men what they considered to be a satisfactory explanation of the origins of the Federal works, and so they included
it in their own texts. The exaggerated use of Federal earthworks became an
irritant to at least one former Union soldier who knew better: "The term fortifications is made the most of in Forrest's official report of the battle. Smith's
men had no fortifications."[27]

Accounts of the Federal earthworks at Harrisburg filled biographies and
unit histories. Stephen D. Lee, John Morton, John Wyeth, and James Dinkins,
all former soldiers, claimed that there were Union earthworks present during
the July 14 assault. Twentieth-century writers continued to add to the confusion with entries. Ron Stinson claimed that the Union troops "worked all
night [July 13] reinforcing their barricades with timbers and cotton bales," and
Davison and Fox wrote, "Tired or not every [Union] regiment dug trenches
and built breastworks." John Slanaker even went so far as to write about how
houses were torn down "timber by timber" to construct the works. Refresh-
ingly, the works of Edwin C. Bearss and Jeff Giambrone stand apart for making no such claims.[28] One of the more perplexing accounts came from the pen
of James Chalmers, who maintained that "Smith entrenched himself at Harrisburg" and "the enemy would not come out of his entrenchments."

This perspective defies military logic and begs the question, Why would an
army build "impregnable" earthworks and then be expected to venture forth
and offer battle in the open? In disputing this claim, George Kilmer stated, "It
was a fair stand up fight. Forrest was not used to that sort of battle. His biographer said he found it impossible to entice the enemy from cover or assume
the offensive. In other words, his enemy would not do what he wanted him
to—play into his hands as the enemy has so often done."[29]

Numbers of the Opposing Forces

As George Carter stated, "it was a poor officer who could not make a good report with a very little foundation." The *Official Records* can be a minefield of misinformation when it comes to the number of men in a given battle, whether the
report comes from Manassas, Shiloh, Gettysburg, or any of the other Civil War
engagements. Exaggerating the numbers of the enemy or downplaying your
own numbers was a ploy to depict greater odds faced on the battlefield. A former Union soldier spoke to this commonplace: "A few more years, a few more
books, and it will appear that Lee and Longstreet, and a one armed orderly, and
a casual with a shotgun, fought all the battles of the rebellion and killed all the

Union soldiers except those who ran away." Exaggerating numbers could be used to explain away a defeat or rationalize demands for reinforcements.[30]

The vast majority of authors and participants were pretty much in agreement on the overall numbers of Union soldiers involved in the Tupelo campaign. Smith reported "about 14,000 men," and most historians accept that number, give or take a few hundred. Of course, there were different numbers. Humphreys of the 12th Iowa was so uncertain of the exact number he placed it somewhere between 10,000 and 17,000, while *Minnesota in the Civil and Indian Wars* estimated a range from a mere 10 to 12,000. Someone who should have been in the know was William Burns, Smith's acting assistant inspector general, who in his book claimed only 12,000 Federals, though later, in an article in *Battle and Leaders of the Civil War*, he bumped his figure up to 14,000.[31]

Burns wasn't the only one to change his estimate of the size of the Union force. In their biography of Forrest, Jordan and Pryor initially claimed 13,000 Federals, but only eight pages later they asserted that Smith had 16,000 men on the field. Stephen D. Lee at first placed the enemy's figures at 14,200 but gave them a modest boost to 15,000 later in the same account. These two reports are typical of Confederate writers or historians, who had a tendency toward inflating the number of Federals. Some estimates climbed to a high of 20,000.[32]

A great deal of research has gone into determining the exact number of Confederates as well. Jordan and Pryor created a remarkably accurate table that detailed the number of men present in each of the brigades and divisions, though they neglected to include the men in the five batteries of artillery. Their claim of 9,100 Confederates is on the low side but not too far off the mark, though later in the manuscript they dropped the total down to "less than 8,000." Actual Confederates on the field numbered between 9,400 and 9,600, but creative accounting by some writers makes understanding the figure a challenge.[33] What makes these numbers suspect is the habit of determining not the number of men in the field but the number of "effectives" and, in some instances, just the men engaged. John Wyeth and J. Harvey Mathes both claim a reasonable number of 9,460 men but further qualify that figure by stating that only 7,500 were "available." Lee's accounting is particularly confusing; he gives a total of 7,500 men on the field, of which only 6,600 were "effectives," while later in the same text states his numbers as somewhere between 6,000 and 6,500. The single widest margin of difference in the two armies was claimed by none other than Bedford Forrest, who stated in his report that his numbers "did not exceed 5,000" while his enemy mustered no fewer than 18,000–20,000—a ratio of better than 4:1.[34]

The fluctuating numbers represent attempts to account for the men engaged in holding horses and therefore unable to participate in the fighting. Other than

Lyon's Division, the southern army was made up exclusively of mounted caval-rymen. Because all of the fighting was conducted dismounted, every fourth man held the horses, reducing even the best regiments by 25 percent of their effective fighting force. Moreover, troops that were not engaged, or only lightly, were not counted either. For this reason Lyon's and Roddey's divisions were not included in the tallies of "effectives." The fault in this way of counting is obvious: able-bodied men who were present were not counted—not because of any deficiency on their part but because the army's leadership did not call them into action.

Such accounting could be tolerated if it had been used for the Federal figures as well, but it was not. Grierson's division also utilized horse holders, but in no case were his figures rounded down to reflect such activity. In the same light, several Union brigades stood idle during each day's fighting, but southern ac-counts nearly always place all 14,000 men as engaged and on the front lines.

Another issue is the counting of teamsters and quartermasters. In Smith's army each of the individual regiments had four wagons assigned to carry ra-tions and officer's baggage. Men from the regiments were detailed to serve as wagon drivers and care for the animals, thus detracting from the overall readi-ness of the regiment. The army used civilian teamsters for the reserve artillery and ammunition trains, but their numbers were also included in the overall total. On the Confederate side, the teamsters and wagon drivers were most often impressed slaves and, as such, not included in the total numbers.

Casualties and the Care Given to Them

The total number of casualties each of the armies suffered was reported fairly accurately by Smith and Forrest, but both fell prey to the temptation to over-estimate the opponent's figures. Forrest reported 1,326 Confederates killed, wounded, or captured, a very accurate figure backed up by detailed casualty lists. Smith's total of 674 Federals killed, wounded, or captured, broken down by regiment, is also considered to be a correct number. Forrest did not place a specific number on his foe's losses but did state that the "enemy's loss was equal to my own." Similarly, Smith did a poor job calculating the southern casualties and more than doubled the true figure up to 3,000. Accurately esti-mating the enemy's losses was difficult, if not impossible, because many dead and wounded were removed from the scene by their comrades, leaving the opponents to only guess at the losses.[35]

The soldiers on the field wrote in their diaries and letters and without fail estimated losses too high for the enemy and too low for themselves. It's un-derstandable how anyone reading the descriptions of the Tupelo/Harrisburg

battlefield, about the human wreckage scattered across the slope, could easily overestimate the actual casualties. Union diarists recorded the numbers of
Confederates as anywhere between 1,500 and 4,000. There were newspaper
correspondents on the field, and they, too, were wide of the mark on casualty
numbers. *Harper's Weekly* informed its readers of 2,000 Confederates taken
prisoner, including the entire 7th Tennessee Cavalry. The *Philadelphia Press*
reported 2,500 enemy casualties, with Forrest shot in the back. Predictably,
these papers reported fewer than 300 Union casualties. The *Richmond Times
Dispatch* was just as inaccurate as its northern counterparts, reporting only
1,000 Confederate casualties but claiming 1,700 Federals fell from "deaths,
disease & desertion."[36]

In his report of the battle, Smith described how he moved the wounded
Confederates into Tupelo along with "forty of the worst wounded cases of my
own command." Forrest made no mention of these wounded in his report,
though Thomas Tate of the 12th Kentucky did report that his wounded had
been "kindly treated by the enemy." Jordan and Pryor included an excerpt
from Forrest's notes concerning the events at Harrisburg in which he mentions the wounded, saying that due to poor conditions "and the extreme heat
of the weather, many of the wounds, both of the Confederates and Federals found in Tupelo, were fly-blown and already in a putrid, maggoted condition, from which the men suffered fearfully."[37] But the biographers went
beyond Forrest's note saying that *all* of the men in the hospital were Union
soldiers and described "250 Federals, too severely hurt to be removed, and
few of whose wounds had been dressed." Later in the text the pair asserts that
Smith's army was "so demoralized they could not attend the wounded." John
Morton added his own embellishments, claiming the Confederates "found
two hundred and fifty Federal prisoners, who had been abandoned," but they
were in such poor condition "nothing could be done for them except to bury
them when their awful sufferings came to an end." Henry Hord charged, "The
Yanks had never given their wounded any attention, and the poor fellows suffered fearfully. Their wounds were flyblown, and many of them died under the
surgeon's knife."[38] And so Forrest's simple statement on the condition of the
wounds changed with each telling.

Of the twentieth-century authors, Gentry copied the embellished Jordan
account word for word, while Davison and Fox took their exaggeration one
step further: "[Smith] was in such a hurry to disengage and return to Memphis
that he left his seriously wounded behind in order to facilitate his withdrawal";
"Forrest was *horrified* to find many of the men had wounds that were 'fly-
blown and filled with maggots.'" Brian Steel Wills stayed true to the known

facts when he wrote, "Because he lacked sufficient wagons and ambulances, Smith had to leave forty of his most severely wounded men in Tupelo."[39]

The Reasons for A. J. Smith's Withdrawal and Whether It Was a Retreat

"The word withdrawal sounds a little better than retreat," explained Elijah Edwards. "The last carried with it the idea of defeat, which on this field none are willing to admit, since in every separate engagement of the three days preceding our troops had been successful either in holding our own position or driving the enemy from theirs."[40]

No one could convince the Federal soldiers they were retreating. They had prevailed on the battlefield, their morale was sky high, and they believed they had pulled off the job they set out to do. Cornelius Corwin of the 89th Indiana refused to call it a retreat in his diary, instead noting, "Commenced our backward march after giving the rebels a sound thrashing." Reed of the 12th Iowa and Bartlett of the 33rd Missouri also wrote of having "accomplished the mission." Smith never did claim the job was finished, though he did report that his corps had "whipped them badly on three different days."

Smith's reason for departing the field at Harrisburg was based on the critical rations situation and the depletion of the artillery ammunition. Most, if not all, of the Federals had been on reduced rations for days, and they understood what was behind the general's order. "We commenced our return, obliged on account of rations," wrote one man. Another stated, "Started back to Memphis, had not rations to press the enemy." There was also a problem of food for the animals. George Carter of the 33rd Wisconsin wrote to his brother that though "the mission was accomplished . . . our rations were getting short and had been out of forage for two days." And William Scott, adjutant of the 4th Iowa Cavalry, wrote how Smith's "men were on half rations, and the animals on yet scantier forage."[41]

One of the few northerners who broke ranks with those supporting Smith's decision was Benjamin Grierson, who left his personal opinions out of his official report but spoke his mind in his memoirs. Smith may have felt it prudent to return to Tennessee due to the "want of supplies," but not his cavalry commander, who stated, "In my judgment, it would have been better to have gone on and taken the chances of obtaining supplies from the enemy, or to have lived on corn and other products, or even sent back for supplies to be forwarded from LaGrange." Yet, support for Smith came from an unlikely quarter, the pages of *Confederate Military History*, where Charles Hooker conceded,

"The object of the expedition led by General Smith had been accomplished. He had won a victory."[42]

Few southern writers agreed with Hooker, however. Forrest reported Smith as "retreating," but he never speculated as to his opponent's reasons. Chalmers agreed that the Federals were moving "as if in retreat" despite the fact "we were badly defeated," but he, too, declined to give a reason. In 1908 John Wyeth attributed Smith's retreat to fear, saying, "He had never seen men fight with such desperate (if misdirected) valor. After this exhibition he did not dare to advance upon his antagonist . . . nor could he safely remain where he was." This was the same reason the *Edgefield Advertiser* gave just days after the battle: "The enemy fought stubbornly when compelled to do so, but was evidently afraid of a set fight."[43]

Over the years Smith's reasons for withdrawal have continued to be routinely dismissed and the rationale for it deemed "lame," "weak," and "feeble." Michael Ballard questions whether Smith "lost his nerve," and Davison and Fox disregard the explanation of low rations, stating, "Smith seemed more concerned with getting the hell out of the Black Prairie and becoming the first commander to engage Forrest and escape with his hair." As for the claim that rations were the reason, John Slonaker insisted that "no one reported hunger in his unit." But impossible to disregard are the fifty individual Federal accounts, diaries, reports, and letters inspected for this chapter, in which every soldier, without fail, described the want of food on the return march to LaGrange.[44]

Federal Foraging and Depredations

A common practice when writing about a defeat is to explain how the better armed, better fed, and more numerous enemy lacked in mercy and morals. Both sides wrote extensively about the heavy-handed Union campaign.

On July 23, 1864, James Chalmers finished his account of the campaign:

I cannot close this report without mentioning the robbery and desolation which attended the march of the invading army. Every species of vandalism was committed. Not only were non-combatant citizens maltreated, their houses were rifled of clothing, money, and other valuables, besides the theft of every pound of bacon and every ounce of meal, but the same course of rapine and cruelty was shown toward unprotected widows and orphans, who were stripped of their all, and in many cases turned out of doors, with nothing left them save the wearing apparel on their persons. Cows and calves were killed from wantonness, and left in private yards and on the public thoroughfare.

As appalling as his account appears, Chalmers understated the situation.[45] The excessive foraging, pillaging, and destruction were well documented by the Federals themselves.

The most thorough recording of the depredations was by Elijah Edwards of the 7th Minnesota. As Edwards pointed out, there were strict orders in place about foraging. George Brockway, 35th Iowa, wrote how the men were cautioned that they would be shot or hanged if caught destroying property, a warning repeated by Ezra Fish of the 114th Illinois in his diary—"Strict orders against wanton pillaging"—though he admitted it was easy enough to forage by evading the pickets. But Thomas Hawley of the 11th Missouri stated that there were "no orders against foraging."[46]

The *Richmond Daily Dispatch* reported, "The destruction of property in the enemy's line of march far exceeds that of all other raids in North Mississippi. Families were left entirely destitute of provisions." The *Montgomery Weekly Advertiser*, however, might have disagreed that depredations came only at the hands of the Union. As Smith was marching toward LaGrange a division of the Confederate force moved east into Alabama and the paper reported:

> We have had a party of Roddey's command in the neighborhood for several days, and a more rude, ungentlemanly, thieving set, no people were ever cursed with. They have marauded the entire country for miles, destroying watermelon patches, peach and apple orchards, not only taking what they wanted but destroying all that was green. They may be friends to our country but one may well exclaim, "the good Lord deliver us from our friends."[47]

The worst example of arson during the campaign was in Ripley. Ripley resident Judge Orlando Davis recorded in his diary, "Thirty-five stores, dwellings and churches, including the courthouse were burned." Andrew Brown carefully researched the burning of Ripley and noted, "In destroying the business and public buildings at Ripley, Smith was following Sherman's instructions to devastate the country over which Forrest passed. The destruction of three dwellings seems to have been accidental, as usually the federals did not destroy private homes. There are persistent rumors that a brisk wind was blowing at the time, which would explain the spread of the flames."

In his lengthy account of the campaign, Ted Carter grudgingly admitted that the burnings took place but wrote, "Far be it from me to attempt to justify them in such wanton acts, but there was a cause for it which does not seem to be generally known," attempting to justify the burning with the accounts of the murders of Sturgis's men as they retreated through the village after their defeat at Brice's Crossroads. Earlier in his account he attempted to distance

himself from the depredations and claimed to have seen only a single building enveloped in flames during the entire campaign.[48] And even Edwards was
only too willing to accept the burning of Ripley as justified retribution for the
attacks on retreating soldiers following the fight at Brice's Crossroads. His
claim—"the firing [of Ripley] was not done by special order"—is just one of
several attempts by northern authors to distance A. J. Smith from the responsibility for several such incidents.[49] But whether or not Smith gave the orders
for the Union depredations against the civilians—or what his personal feelings
were about such actions—is irrelevant; as commanding officer, he bears sole
responsibility for the conduct of his troops.

Forrest's Refusal to Command His Corps

Perhaps no other aspect of the Battle of Tupelo/Harrisburg produces such
passion as the controversy over Forrest's responsibilities and leadership during
the battle and their effect on its outcome. The accounts that form the basis for
the controversy come almost exclusively from southern participants and Forrest's biographers, though the northern press and unit historians initiated the
controversy by claiming that Forrest had been defeated by Smith.

Forrest never admitted to having been bested, but according to most of
the accounts, the battle was never his to lose. In 1908 John Wyeth raised the
standard that others rallied around when he stated:

> Even if the result at Harrisburg had been a victory for the Federal commander,
> it could not in fairness be considered a defeat for Forrest. While it was true
> fully three-fourths of the troops on the field, and all those who took part in
> the encounter, belonged to Forrest's command, he positively refused to take
> charge of the battle and, as General Lee states, left him to assume the respon-
> sibility of the engagement.[50]

In his description of the battle, Wyeth quotes Lee as saying:

> I said to General Forrest that a large proportion of the troops now on the
> ground belonged to his immediate command, had served under him in his re-
> cent campaigns, had just won the splendid victory at Brice's Crossroads, having
> beaten some of the troops that they would have to encounter to-day, and that,
> knowing Forrest better than myself, they would have more implicit confidence
> in his leadership. General Forrest however, positively declined to take the com-
> mand, saying that I was his senior, and that I should take the responsibility.[51]

Stephen D. Lee, however, never said this on the field or in his 1902 report. Lee's report, excepting the introduction, was written entirely in the third person and invariably refers to himself as "General Lee" and refrains from using the word "I." For his own reasons, Wyeth rephrased two separate sections of Lee's manuscript and passed them off as a single quote. The difference is remarkable. Lee actually wrote:

> On the Confederate side blunders and mistakes complicated matters. The troops were all of Forrest's command, and he should have had supreme command, but he insisted on Gen. Lee's, the department commander, assuming the responsibility and being present. Forrest had just won his splendid victory at Brice's Crossroads over Gen. Sturgis, and his troops had confidence in him. Gen. Lee used this argument to insist on his commanding on the field, but he said no; that the responsibility was too great, and that his superior in rank should assume and exercise the command; that he considered the Confederate troops inadequate to defeat Smith. He also said his health was not good and Gen. Lee must take charge.

The difference in the two accounts is that in his actual report Lee infers that Forrest refused to command not only due to Lee's rank but also out of a belief that the battle was doomed to failure.[52]

As with Smith as commanding officer, there is no question that the ultimate responsibility lay with Lee. Article 62 of the Confederate *Articles of War* made it implicitly clear that the senior officer on the field was in command. Because Lee stated Forrest should have the "supreme command," Lee was in violation of the order. However, neither Article 62 nor any other article, relieves a subordinate of the responsibilities of his own command if a senior officer is present. To put it in the simplest terms, a corps commander remains a corps commander, just as division commander remains a division commander in the presence of his superior officer. Lee's presence made Forrest subject to his orders but did not relieve him of his personal responsibilities as a senior officer on the field of battle.[53]

Why did Forrest refuse to lead his own men in battle? Ballard suggests that Forrest was "uncomfortable" with Lee's presence. Davison and Foxx assert that "others have suggested that Forrest's heart was not in the coming battle because of alleged feeling of jealousy toward Lee due to his promotion to lieutenant general. This theory is based on the possibility that the Tennessee general believed that Lee had been receiving credit for victories that Forrest had actually won." Another of Forrest's biographers, Jack Hurst, contends, "Forrest was too much of an individual tactician and too accustomed to making instantaneous decisions under fire to be able to operate very effectively under anybody else's hands-on-command, especially that of someone as unimaginative as Lee was that day." But, as Ballard notes, "Lee's mistakes do not absolve Forrest of a poor performance. Whether due to boils or jealousy of Lee, Forrest seemed passive during much of the battle."[54]

Whatever his reasons, Forrest declined a leading role in the fight other than directing Roddey's Division on the Confederate right flank. Right or wrong, his decision to call off the attack Lee had ordered him to conduct on the right prompted Herman Hattaway to charge Forrest "guilty of disobedience to Lee's orders."[55]

Stephen D. Lee's Account and the Resulting Furor

When Lee finally wrote his own version of events in 1902, he began with a short preface to explain why he never made an official report: "I left the battlefield of Harrisburg to go to the great battles around Atlanta, and amid those scenes I had no time to dwell on my campaigns in Mississippi." This statement, however, does not agree with a letter he wrote in 1878 to J. F. H. Claiborne in which he answered Claiborne's query of why there had not been an official report. Lee claimed that if he had written a report during the war it would have initiated an investigation as to why Roddey's Division had not attacked as ordered. Such an investigation would have implicated Forrest—but to what gain? As Lee explained, such a course of action would have "paralyzed him and his command which was much attached to him—and they were the only troops I had to defend the State."[56]

Lee remained silent on the matter of Harrisburg for eight years, until he responded to a letter written by Francis Wolff, a response he requested not be used for publication. He revealed to Wolff, "There is an inside history of the battle of Harrisburg, fought July 14th and 15th, 1864, which is not generally known to the public." The inside story was Lee's attempt to justify why he had not filed an official report. "My reason for not mailing the report was that Gen. Forrest failed to carry out the plan of battle as agreed on between us." The letter, filled with technical errors, goes on to explain the battle and how Forrest's refusal to follow orders resulted in the Confederate attack being repulsed and how, if he filed a report at the time, an investigation would have ensued, which would have benefited no one. "I felt that he did what he thought best. I thought he made a great mistake not carrying out my orders on the field. I certainly did what I thought best."[57]

Wolff disregarded Lee's request, and the letter was printed in the *Clarion*, a Jackson, Mississippi, newspaper. Little note was taken of the article at the time other than a pair of letters from two old soldiers of the 38th Mississippi Mounted Infantry. James Jones wrote a letter to the *Woodville Republican* (which was later reprinted in the *Clarion*) that told of how, after the battle, all of the men blamed Lee for the defeat: "It was the common report in camp that Gen. Lee had caused it against Gen. Forrest's earnest protest. In his letter Gen. Lee does but tardy justice to himself and I hasten to acknowledge, on behalf of my regiment, that we have all been wrong in the matter."[58] William Crisler also wrote to the *Clarion* with his account of the battle, which ended with, "I must say I am grateful that Gen. Lee made the statement he did—that he has been vindicated and no blame attached to his grand name."[59]

It wasn't until 1902 and the publication by the Mississippi Historical Society of Lee's full account of the Battle of Harrisburg that sentiment began to swing in the other direction. The problem with Lee's account is that it is an exceptionally poor description of the events. His facts are too often in error, and he made statements that could not be backed up by documentation or other witnesses. He frequently took parts of letters and statements from the *Official Records* out of context and sequence to build his case against Smith and Forrest. If he had stuck to criticizing just Smith, it is doubtful there would have been any negative response to his account. But Lee's "report" was soon after its release discussed and debated in the columns of the *Clarion* and other southern papers.[60]

Forrest died in 1877 and was unable to reply to the accusations that he had shirked his responsibilities during the fight. This was simply unacceptable to a core group of men who had served under Forrest, men who were willing to respond on his behalf. The first to reply was David C. Kelley, "Forrest's Fighting Parson," who penned a long letter after conferring with John Morton, Charles Anderson, Tyree Bell, and James Cowan, the general's surgeon as well as his wife's first cousin. The letter, printed in the pages of the *Memphis Commercial Appeal*, picked apart the numerous mistakes in Lee's account and outright rejected any hint that Forrest should share the blame for the defeat. Kelley treated Lee with a modicum of respect but hinted that he was in his dotage: "General Lee's veracity is beyond question, but he is growing—as most of us are—to be an old man. He has brooded over these questions evidently for years."[61]

A few weeks later a compilation of letters from Edmund Rucker, Hylan Lyon, and Tyree Bell was published in the *Times-Picayune*. These individual rebuttals were not spontaneous responses to Lee's publication but were written at the behest of John Morton, the late captain of artillery who made it his personal quest to contest Lee's article and eradicate any tarnish connected to his mentor. His work culminated in 1909 with the publication of *The Artillery of Nathan Bedford Forrest's Cavalry: The Wizard of the Saddle*.[62] Chapter 15 of his book focuses on the Battle of Harrisburg, and Morton took particular care to lay the blame for the defeat squarely on the shoulders of Lee. He underscored numerous passages just in case the reader missed his intended point. In many ways, Morton's account is an excellent resource, as it provides fascinating details of the artillery not found in other books. However, in pointing out all of the mistakes in Lee's account, Morton fell into the morass of myth and misinformation that became a hallmark of the battle's history. His account might have carried more weight were it not for the significant numbers of errors it either repeated or created.[63]

Sherman's and Grant's Reactions to the Results of the Campaign

Different writers have varying accounts of Sherman's and Grant's responses to Smith's raid. Statements that the two generals were "furious," "disappointed," "frustrated," "not satisfied," etc., abound in the different accounts. Lee's biographer, Dabney Lipscomb, even went so far as to say that Grant and Sherman "rebuked" Smith for his performance.[64]

The basis for these remarks and evaluations is a series of telegrams written by Smith, Washburn, Sherman, and Grant. If the messages are read in the order they were written and received, it is immediately apparent that the two senior Union commanders were in no way disappointed with Smith. If anything, they were upset with Washburn, who, in turn, attempted to cast any guilt and negative comments onto Smith. And if the messages are taken out of order, or if any are left out, their purpose can be, and has been, distorted. In order to appreciate the comments made by historians an understanding of the telegraphed correspondence is necessary.

On July 18 Washburn, in Memphis, received the following message from Smith: "We met Lee and Walker at Tupelo, and whipped them badly on three different days. Our loss is small when compared with the rebel loss. I bring back everything in good order; nothing lost." Still feeling the repercussions of the Sturgis defeat, a delighted Washburn sent telegrams to Stanton and Sherman to relay the welcome news, and then he sent an identical dispatch to McPherson with an added paragraph not included in those to Sherman and Stanton.

It will be one week before General Smith with his troops will arrive here. I shall put them in complete marching order with the least possible delay. What with the Sturgis disaster, and the past twenty day's hard service with Smith, my cavalry must be very run down. As soon as they recuperate a little I shall pay my respects to General Shelby, who is north of White River, in Arkansas, with 2,500 mounted men.

The orders that had sent Smith into Mississippi had originated with Grant and Sherman and were still in effect. Washburn's telegram to McPherson gave notice of his intent to rescind the order, recall Smith to Memphis, and send Grierson's cavalry across the Mississippi River to Arkansas.[65]

Grant's dispatch to Sherman on July 19 exhibited no particular concern with Smith's move north from Tupelo, but it did ask for assurance that Smith would continue on with his orders. He had yet to see a copy of Washburn's letter to McPherson: "I see by the Richmond papers of yesterday that Smith had left Tupelo, and is moving toward Ripley. Although they call it a retreat I judge from S.D. Lee's dispatch that Forrest has been badly whipped. Smith, however, ought to be instructed to keep a close watch on Forrest, and not permit him to gather strength and move into Middle Tennessee."[66] Later that same evening, Smith arrived in LaGrange and informed Washburn, "Will go into camp and await further orders." There were no plans at that time to return the column to Memphis. Smith intended to replenish his rations and ammunition, check with Washburn for any new orders, and continue on with his expedition. The following day, July 20, Sherman learned from McPherson about Washburn's new plans for Smith's troops. Sherman's response was immediate: "Order Smith to pursue and keep after Forrest all the time. The papers announce his moving from Tupelo for Ripley, but I suppose he went to replenish his supplies. Even the Atlanta papers do not claim for Lee and Forrest a victory." In just two lines Sherman revealed his understanding of Smith's movement and squashed Washburn's Arkansas plan. However, two and a half days passed before the message arrived in Memphis.[67]

The afternoon of the 20th brought another telegram to Washburn from Smith in LaGrange: "I have just arrived with my supply train and colored brigade. My two divisions encamp to-night at Davis' Mills, six miles from here, and will be in early in the morning. I wait your further instructions." Washburn received Smith's message almost immediately, and, since there had been no communications from Sherman or McPherson, he went ahead with his Arkansas plan. He sent a return telegram to Smith: "You will remove your infantry by rail to Memphis as rapidly as transportation can be furnished, and your artillery and wagon train in, with an escort of cavalry, by easy marches." Smith made the necessary plans to comply with his new orders.[68]

At nine o'clock that evening, not long before retiring for the night, Sherman wired Halleck in Washington with an update of the fighting around Atlanta. The message also requested that Halleck send a telegram to Grant to assure him that A. J. Smith "has the very orders he suggests, viz, to hang on Forrest and prevent his coming to Tennessee. I will, however, renew the orders."[69]

By July 23 Smith's infantry was back in its Memphis camps and the artillery and supply trains were beginning to roll in. The 23rd also brought Sherman's dispatch from the evening of July 20 directing Smith to stay in the field. It's unknown whether Washburn ever informed Smith about the plan to take away his cavalry and send them across the river. At any rate, when Washburn passed the message along to Smith, the late telegram made it seem that Smith had disregarded Sherman's and Grant's orders to keep after Forrest, which naturally caused him some consternation.

Later that day Washburn wrote to Sherman: "Yours of the 20th received. General Smith has returned. He thinks you have a wrong impression in regard to his fight. He returned for lack of supplies. That he whipped the enemy very badly there is no doubt. I have ordered General Smith to put his command in order to again move against Forrest. He will so move as soon as he can get ready, unless you should think he should go to Mobile." Washburn's letter was truthful but subtly deceptive. When he wrote that Smith had returned for supplies, he neglected to mention that it was he who had ordered him in from LaGrange to Memphis. He also clumsily attempted to shift the attention to Smith, inferring that Smith was upset by the July 20 message. And finally, his statement about sending Smith's column into Alabama was a final shot at salvaging his Arkansas gambit.[70]

Washburn's attempt to dictate strategy came to an end once and for all when Sherman sent a final wire on July 25:

> It was General Grant's special order that General Smith was required after his fight to pursue and continue to follow Forrest. He must keep after him till recalled by me or General Grant, and if Forrest goes toward Tennessee General Smith must follow him. General Smith must keep well out after Forrest, but rather watch him closely than attempt to pursue him, but when he does fight he should keep an advantage. The railroad could supply him out as far as Grand Junction. It is of vital importance that Forrest does not go to Tennessee.

This mild chastisement was sufficient to let Washburn know that he should have never moved Smith to Memphis and that his plans for Alabama and Arkansas were vetoed. These messages make it quite clear that neither Sherman nor Grant was disappointed with Smith's performance but that they were put out by Washburn's recall of the army from LaGrange.[71]

Stephen D. Lee's 1902 report took snippets of quotes out of both context and chronological order and used them to build a misleading chain of events. "These telegrams tell the tale," Lee wrote, "and show Gen. Smith's superiors were greatly disappointed in the results, and reflected on him." Lee's report, as well as the out-of-order and -context correspondence, fueled the authors who would follow his lead. Andrew Lytle wrote, "Grant and Sherman were not entirely pleased with Smith's conduct." Robert Selph Henry claimed that "that redheaded realist of war [Sherman] was not so much impressed with the victory as Washburn and Smith thought he ought to have been. This business of marching back to Memphis, even if it was 'in good order; nothing lost' and for the replenishing of supplies, was not what he had sent Smith out to do . . . Harrisburg, then, was a battle satisfactory to no one in results."[72]

Byron Stinson noted how while Washburn and Smith were "jubilant," Grant and Sherman were "less than enthusiastic." Slonaker claimed that Sherman "did not accept Smith's 'alibis' and immediately ordered a return to the offensive." In his notes, he tried to explain the sequence of the individual telegrams, but he, too, was guilty of taking fragmentary quotes and using them in a rambling assessment of the chain of command. Davison and Foxx theorize that "Smith's campaign had failed to achieve total success," and, as a consequence, "Sherman was not satisfied." Even Shelby Foote explained how "Sherman was downright critical." Ballard goes one step further and states that Sherman was "pleased at first when word spread that Forrest had died from lockjaw as a result of his wound at Old Town Creek, grew angry when he learned the truth. Forrest still lived and would recover. Sherman immediately ordered another expedition by Smith into Mississippi."

As for Sherman himself, in his memoir he expresses no disappointment with Smith's action in July 1864: "I ordered General Smith to go out from Memphis and renew the offensive [started by Sturgis], so as to keep Forrest off our roads. This he did finally, defeating Forrest at Tupelo, on the 13th, 14th and 15th days of July; and he so stirred up matters in North Mississippi that Forrest could not leave for Tennessee."[73]

* * *

An aged Ulysses S. Grant, wracked with cancer and fighting to complete his memoir, wrote about the great Battle of Shiloh:

The Battle of Shiloh, or Pittsburg Landing, has been perhaps less understood, or, to state the case more accurately, more persistently misunderstood, than any other engagement between National and Confederate troops during the entire rebellion. Correct reports of the battle have been published . . . but all of these appeared long subsequent to the close of the rebellion and after public opinion had been most erroneously formed.

He could have been referring to Tupelo/Harrisburg.[74]

The facts about the Tupelo campaign have been alternately stretched, exaggerated, fabricated, minimized, and even outright ignored. It is easy to be misled when reading about the Harrisburg fight, for it is a natural expectation when reading an eyewitness account to assume that the writer, whether he is a general or a private, is telling the truth. Likewise, a reader expects an author of a book or an article to approach the subject with a desire to present the unvarnished truth. With Harrisburg, this is rarely the case.

In the case of Harrisburg, there have simply been too many writers willing to distance themselves from the truth in order to promote and maintain the legend and myth of Nathan Bedford Forrest. He was—and still is—a polarizing figure, alternately loved and reviled. In the decades after the war, his character and record were held high, and he became a rallying point for the Lost Cause movement. For a great many, he epitomized the southern fighting man: a soldier who was never defeated in battle and who only surrendered when overcome by superior numbers.

There is no question that Forrest was the best at what he did; North or South, he had no peers when it came to raiding and fighting with mounted infantry. However, the embellishments and exaggerations of his character and record do him no credit; in fact, they do him a disservice. He was not Mars on the field of battle. He was fallible and he made mistakes, as all humans do. He made errors during the Tupelo campaign, and he and Lee suffered a major defeat—a defeat that neither he nor many of his followers could or would admit. Years after the fight author and veteran George L. Kilmer wrote, "Next to knowing he is whipped a good general should candidly admit it." This observation was taken a step further by James Chalmers, a great admirer of Forrest's, who, when writing about Harrisburg, said, "Forrest was a great general; but he never rose to that greatness of dignity of soul which enabled Robert E. Lee at Gettysburg to assume the responsibility of a failure."[75]

Public opinion within the Civil War community does not change easily or quickly, and many are resistant to the claim that Harrisburg was a Confederate defeat, that A. J. Smith out-generalled his opponents, or that Forrest performed well below what was expected of him and what he was capable of achieving. New ideas that challenge these notions are labeled "revisionist history." Long-buried or long-suppressed details are treated in a similar fashion, when, in truth, these accounts reveal the revision of the truth that actually began in the days following the battle. It is up to the diligent researcher to pursue the facts, reject the lies, and hold fast to the truth.

Order of Battle

Confederate Forces

Lt. Gen. Stephen D. Lee

Cavalry Corps

MAJ. GEN. NATHAN B. FORREST (W)

Escort: Forrest's Escort, Tennessee Cavalry, Capt. John C. Jackson

Chalmers's Division

BRIG. GEN. JAMES R. CHALMERS

Escort: Company M, 3rd Kentucky Mounted Infantry, Capt. Clay Horne

Second Brigade: Col. Robert "Black Bob" McCulloch (w); Col. David C. Kelly

2nd Missouri Cavalry, Lt. Col. Robert A. "Red Bob" McCulloch

1st Mississippi Partisan Rangers (7th Mississippi Cavalry), Lt. Col. Samuel M. Hyams Jr.

5th Mississippi Cavalry, Lt. Col. Nathaniel Wickliffe

McDonald's Battalion (3rd Tennessee), Col. David C. Kelly/ Lt. Col. James M. Crews[1]

Willis's Battalion (Texas Cavalry), Capt. Thomas M. Harwood

(k) killed, (w) wounded, (mw) mortally wounded

1. McDonalds Battalion: a.k.a. Crew's Battalion, Balch's Battalion, Forrest's Old Regiment, 3rd Tennessee Cavalry. This battalion sized unit had recently been ordered back to regimental size and was awaiting the return of four companies from Alabama. Though Crews commanded the battalion, Kelly had been ordered to take command of the regiment. Both men were present during the campaign.

Sixth Brigade: Col. Edmund W. Rucker (w); Col. William L. Duckworth
   7th Tennessee Cavalry, Col. William L. Duckworth; Lt. Col. William F. Taylor
   8th Mississippi Cavalry, Col. William L. Duff (w); Captain Charles W. Johnston (w)
   18th Mississippi Battalion, Col. Alexander H. Chalmers
   Saunders's Scouts, Capt. B. F. Saunders

Second Division
BRIG. GEN. ABRAHAM BUFORD

Third Brigade: Col. Edward Crossland (w); Lt. Col. Absalom R. Shacklett
   3rd Kentucky Mounted Infantry, Col. Gustaves A. C. Holt (incapacitated); Capt. S. Paine Ridgeway
   7th Kentucky Mounted Infantry, Lt. Col. L. J. Sherrill (k); Maj. Henry S. Hale (w); Capt. Joel T. Cochran
   8th Kentucky Mounted Infantry, Col. Absalom R. Shacklett
   Morgan's Cavalry (detachment), Capt. William Campbell
   12th Kentucky Cavalry (Faulkner's Cavalry), Col. William W. Faulkner (w); Maj. Thomas S. Tate Jr.
Fourth Brigade: Col. Tyree Bell
   2nd Tennessee Cavalry, Col. Clark R. Barteau (w)
     Lt. Col. George Morton (incapacitated); Lt. George E. Seay
   15th Tennessee (20th Tennessee) Cavalry, Col. Robert M. Russell (w)
   16th Tennessee Cavalry, Col. Andrew N. Wilson (w)
   19th Tennessee Cavalry, Col. John F. Newsom (w)
Mabry's Brigade: Col. Hinchie P. Mabry
   14th Confederate Cavalry, Lt. Col. John B. Gage (mw)
   4th Mississippi Cavalry, Lt. Col. Thomas R. Stockdale (w)
   6th Mississippi Cavalry, Col. Isham Harrison (k); Lt. Col. Thomas Nelson (k)
   38th Mississippi Mounted Infantry, Maj. Robert C. McCay (k)

Roddey's Division
COL. PHILIP D. RODDEY

Patterson's Brigade: Col. Josiah Patterson
   5th Alabama Cavalry, Lt. Col. James M. Warren
   10th Alabama Cavalry, Col. Richard O. Pickett
   Stuart's Alabama Cavalry Battalion, Maj. James H. Stuart
Johnson's Brigade: Col. William A. Johnson
   4th Alabama Cavalry, Lt. Col. Francis M. Windes

Moreland's Battalion Alabama Cavalry, Maj. J. N. George
Williams's Alabama Cavalry Battalion: Capt. John F. Doan

LYON'S DIVISION

BRIG. GEN. HYLAN B. LYON

Gholson's Brigade, dismounted men
  Ashcroft's (Mississippi) Regiment, detachment
  Ham's (Mississippi) Regiment, detachment
  Lowry's (Mississippi) Regiment, detachment
  McGuirk's (Mississippi) Regiment, detachment
Beltzhover's Battalion: Col. Charles Fuller
  1st Louisiana Heavy Artillery, Col. Charles Fuller
  1st Mississippi Light Artillery, Maj. Henry A. Clinch
Neely's First Brigade, Chalmers's Division, dismounted men
  12th Tennessee Cavalry, detachment
  14th Tennessee Cavalry, detachment
  15th Tennessee Cavalry, detachment
  Higgs's (Tennessee) Company, detachment
Regiment dismounted cavalry, formed from dismounted men from Crossland's brigade: Lt. Col. Thomas T. Barnett, 3rd Kentucky Mounted Infantry
1st Mississippi Infantry: Lt. Col. Marshall Polk
  Reynolds Battalion

ARTILLERY BATTALION

CAPT. JOHN W. MORTON JR.

Pettus Flying Artillery (Mississippi): Lt. E. S. Walton
Morton's Battery (Tennessee): Lt. T. S. Sale
Ferrell's Battery (Georgia): Capt. C. B. Ferrell
Rice's Battery (Tennessee): Capt. Thomas W. Rice
Thrall's Battery (Arkansas): Capt. James C. Thrall

Union Forces
SIXTEENTH ARMY CORPS (RIGHT WING)
MAJ. GEN. ANDREW JACKSON SMITH

FIRST DIVISION
BRIG. GEN. JOSEPH A. MOWER
  First Brigade: Col. William L. McMillen
    114th Illinois Infantry, Capt. Benjamin C. Berry (w); Capt. S. W. Shoup
    93rd Indiana Infantry, Capt. Charles A. Hubbard
    10th Minnesota Infantry, Lt. Col. Samuel P. Jennison
    72nd Ohio Infantry, Maj. Eugene A. Rawson (k); Capt. S. A. J. Snyder
    95th Ohio Infantry, Lt. Col. Jefferson Brumback
    1st Illinois Light Artillery, Battery E (first section), Lt. Orrin W. Cram
  Second Brigade: Col. Alexander Wilkin (k); Col. John D. McClure
    47th Illinois Infantry, Col. John D. McClure
    5th Minnesota Infantry (detachment), Capt. Timothy J. Sheehan
    9th Minnesota Infantry, Lt. Col. Josiah F. Marsh
    11th Missouri Infantry, Col. William L. Barnum
  8th Wisconsin, Capt. Benjamin S. Williams
    2nd Iowa Light Artillery, Lt. Joseph R. Reed
  Third Brigade: Col. Joseph J. Woods
    12th Iowa Infantry, Lt. Col. John H. Stibbs
    35th Iowa Infantry, Col. Sylvester G. Hill
    7th Minnesota Infantry, Col. William R. Marshall
    33rd Missouri Infantry, Lt. Col. William H. Heath
  Fourth Brigade: Col. Lyman M. Ward
    41st Illinois Infantry (detachment), Lt. James A. Wilson
    14th Wisconsin Infantry, Lt. Col. James W. Polleys
    33rd Wisconsin Infantry, Col. Frederick S. Lovell
    6th Indiana Light Artillery, Capt. Michael Mueller (using the four guns
       of the 1st Missouri Light Artillery, Battery M)

THIRD DIVISION
COL. DAVID MOORE
  First Brigade: Col. Charles D. Murray
    58th Illinois Infantry, Capt. Phillip R. Heelan
    119th Illinois Infantry, Col. Thomas J. Kinney
    122nd Illinois Infantry, Col. John I. Rinaker
    89th Indiana Infantry, Lt. Col. Hervey Craven

21st Missouri Infantry, Lt. Col. Edwin Moore
9th Indiana Light Artillery, Lt. Wallace Hight
Second Brigade: Col. James I. Gilbert
14th Iowa Infantry, Capt. William J. Campbell
27th Iowa Infantry, Capt. Amos M. Haslip
32nd Iowa Infantry, Maj. Jonathan Hutchison
24th Missouri Infantry, Maj. Robert W. Fyan
3rd Indiana Light Artillery, Lt. Richard Burns
Third Brigade: Col. Edward H. Wolfe
49th Illinois Infantry, Capt. John A. Logan
117th Illinois Infantry, Col. Risdon M. Moore
52nd Indiana Infantry, Lt. Col. Zalmon S. Main
178th New York Infantry, Capt. George F. Young
2nd Illinois Light Artillery, Battery G, Lt. John W. Lowell
14th Indiana Light Artillery, Lt. F. W. Morse

COLORED BRIGADE
COL. EDWARD BOUTON
59th U.S. Colored Troops, Maj. James C. Foster
61st U.S. Colored Troops, Col. Frank A. Kendrick
68th U.S. Colored Troops, Col. J. Blackburn Jones
2nd U.S. Colored Light Artillery, Battery I,
    Capt. Louis B. Smith

CAVALRY DIVISION
BRIG. GEN. BENJAMIN H. GRIERSON
Second Brigade: Col. Edward F. Winslow
3rd Iowa Cavalry, Col. John W. Noble
4th Iowa Cavalry, Lt. Col. John H. Peters
10th Missouri Cavalry, Maj. Martin H. Williamson
1st Illinois Light Artillery, Battery K, Capt. Jason B. Smith
Third Brigade: Col. Datus E. Coon
3rd Illinois Cavalry (detachment), Maj. James H. O'Conner
7th Illinois Cavalry (detachment), unknown
9th Illinois Cavalry, Lt. Col. Henry B. Burgh
2nd Iowa Cavalry, Maj. Charles C. Horton
Unassigned
7th Kansas Cavalry, Col. Thomas P. Herrick

Notes

1. The Gorillas

1. Gerling, *The One Hundred and Seventeenth Illinois Infantry*, 76–77; June 8, 1864, James Frederick Krafft Diary, Dean B. Krafft Private Collection; Gibson, *Assault and Logistics*, 329; Gibson, *Dictionary of Transports and Combatant Vessels*, 198.

2. *War of the Rebellion: A Compilation of the Official Records of the Union and Confederate Armies* (hereafter cited as *OR*), vol. 34, pt. 2:494, 514–15, 610.

3. Ibid., pt. 2:180; pt. 3:715; pt. 4:16, 73, 212, 240.

4. Joiner, *Through the Howling Wilderness*, 51.

5. Chestnut, *Mary Chestnut's Civil War*, 268.

6. Warner, *Generals in Blue*, 454–64, 592–93; Warner, *Generals in Gray*, 279–86. The only known reference to Whisky Smith I've found in wartime writings is in *History of the Second Iowa Cavalry*, in which the author, Pierce, claims the nickname was given to Smith by the "rebels" (101). A search of *Confederate Veteran Magazine* and the *Southern Historical Society Papers* finds Smith was mentioned in sixty-four separate articles, but not once is the name "Whisky" used in reference to him. More often than not he is characterized respectfully by his former adversaries.

7. Faust, *Historical Times Illustrated Encyclopedia of the Civil War*, 694; Perry, "Major General Andrew Jackson Smith."

8. Williams, *Chicago's Battery Boys*, 304; Grant, *The Papers of Ulysses S. Grant*, 17:180.

9. Wiley, *The Civil War Diary of a Common Soldier*, 69–70, 99.

10. Orton, *Records of California Men in the War of the Rebellion 1861 to 1867*, 168; Grant, *Personal Memoirs of U.S. Grant*, 291–92; Joiner, *One Damn Blunder from the Beginning to End*, 115, 167; Shepley, *Movers and Shakers, Scalawags and Suffragettes*, 221; *OR*, vol. 34, pt. 3:153–54.

11. *OR*, vol. 34, pt. 1:309; Forsyth, *The Red River Campaign of 1864 and the Loss by the Confederacy of the Civil War*, 82, 84; Joiner, One *Damn Blunder from Beginning to End*, 115–16.

12. Perry, "Major General Andrew Jackson Smith"; Elijah Edwards Journal, Minnesota Historical Society, p. 5; Warner, *Generals in Blue*, 454; *OR*, vol. 49, pt. 1:669. On February 8, 1865, Smith wrote, "I am now without a heading or identity for my command. Unless I receive a number or a name for my command, I must style myself the Wandering Tribe of Israel." Halleck replied, "Continue on in your exodus as the Wandering Tribe of Israel. On reaching the land of Canby you will have a number and a name."

13. Elijah Edwards Journal, p. 33; Scott, *Story of the Thirty Second Iowa Infantry Volunteers*, 289; June 11, 1864, Albert Underwood Diary, Richard Johnson Private Collection; letter to parents, June 17, 1864, in Wolf, "Letters from an Illinois Drummer Boy"; Thomas and McCann, *Soldier Life*, 93; June 10, 1864, Benjamin R. Hieronymous Diary, Abraham Lincoln Presidential Library and Museum.

14. June 28, 1864, Ibbetson, "William H. H. Ibbetson Diary."

15. Burdette, *The Drums of the 47th*, 172–74.

16. Pierce, *History of the Second Iowa Cavalry*, 97; Tucker, *The Fourteenth Wisconsin Veterans Volunteer Infantry*, 4; Newton, *A Wisconsin Boy in Dixie*, 113; Burdette, *The Drums of the 47th*, 174.

17. *OR*, vol. 39, pt. 2:79.

18. Ibid., 80.

2. A Pair of Raids

1. *OR*, vol. 32, pt. 1:173–74; Sherman, *Memoirs*, 414–17.

2. *OR*, vol. 32, pt. 1:181–82; Ballard *The Civil War in Mississippi*, 174–75.

3. Sherman, *Memoirs*, 418; *OR*, vol. 32, pt. 1:181–82.

4. Reid, *Ohio in the War*, 884–86.

5. Wills, *The Confederacy's Greatest Cavalryman*, 8.

6. Ibid., 26, 29, 35.

7. Ibid., 26, 46.

8. Lytle, *Bedford Forrest and His Critter Company*, 181.

9. Wills, *The Confederacy's Greatest Cavalryman*, 144.

10. Ibid., 148–50; Lytle, *Bedford Forrest and His Critter Company*, 243.

11. Hattaway, *General Stephen D. Lee*, 3–5; Lipscomb "General Stephen D. Lee," 15.

12. William Dorsey Pender was mortally wounded on the field at Gettysburg and never saw his infant son, Stephen Lee Pender.

13. Hattaway, *General Stephen D. Lee*, 6, 10; Faust, *Historical Times Illustrated Encyclopedia of the Civil War*, 430, 31; Lipscomb, "General Stephen D. Lee," 15.

14. Hattaway, *General Stephen D. Lee*, 14, 15.

15. Ibid., 16, 17.

16. Ibid., 28–29, 33. Wade Hampton and Nathan B. Forrest were the only officers to rise to the rank of lieutenant general in the Confederate States Army who were not trained at West Point.

17. Sifakis, *Who Was Who in the Civil War*, 382; Hattaway, *General Stephen D. Lee*, 41, 50, 55.

18. Sifakis, *Who Was Who in the Civil War*, 382; Hattaway, *General Stephen D. Lee*, 75, 98–99; Lipscomb, "General Stephen D. Lee," 20.

19. Wills, *The Confederacy's Greatest Cavalryman*, 144; *OR*, vol. 31, pt. 3:646.

20. Hattaway, *General Stephen D. Lee*, ix.

21. Wills, *The Confederacy's Greatest Cavalryman*, 150, 156.

22. *OR*, vol. 32, pt. 1:176.

23. Ibid., 173.

24. Smith, "The Mississippi Raid," 383–84; Sherman, *Memoirs*, 423.

25. *OR*, vol. 32, pt. 1:255; Ballard, *The Civil War in Mississippi*, 189.

26. Ballard, *The Civil War in Mississippi*, 189.

27. Chalmers, "Forrest and His Campaigns," 465.

28. *OR*, vol. 32, pt. 1:354.

29. Bearss, "Forrest Puts the Skeer on the Yankees," 9–10; Wills, *The Confederacy's Greatest Cavalryman*, 169.

30. Bearss, *Forrest at Brice's Crossroads and in North Mississippi in 1864*, 331; Sifakis, *Who Was Who in the Civil War*, 632–33.

31. This excursion into north Mississippi is often referred to as a raid unto itself, which would make for a total of three raids rather than two. In this case, Sturgis was following Forrest in an effort to drive him from Tennessee and would have followed him no matter where he went. It was not a planned raid into Mississippi.

32. *OR*, vol. 32, pt. 1:698.

33. Ballard, *The Civil War in Mississippi*, 196.

34. *OR*, vol. 39, pt. 1:85.

35. Ibid., vol. 92, pt. 1:89–90.

36. Bearss, "Forrest Puts the Skeer on the Yankees," 19; Ballard, *The Civil War in Mississippi*, 199–200.

37. *OR*, vol. 39, pt. 1:86.

38. Ibid., 87; Ballard, *The Civil War in Mississippi*, 203–4.

39. Wyeth, *That Devil Forrest*, 350; Bearss, "Forrest Puts the Skeer on the Yankees," 19; Ballard, *The Civil War in Mississippi*, 206.

40. Ballard, *The Civil War in Mississippi*, 210–11.

41. *OR*, vol. 39, pt. 1:231; Bearss, "Forrest Puts the Skeer on the Yankees," 50.

3. A Third Raid

1. *OR*, vol. 39, pt. 2:106–7.

2. The two brothers spelled their last names differently, Elihu choosing to add an *e* to the end of his.

3. Warner, *Generals in Blue*, 542–43; letter, Cadwallader Washburn to Elihu B. Washburne, March 28, 1863, in McPherson, *Battle Cry of Freedom*, 588.

4. Tucker, *The Fourteenth Wisconsin Vet. Vol. Infantry*, 6; Burns, "A. J. Smith's Defeat of Forrest at Tupelo," 421.

5. *OR*, vol. 39, pt. 2:107, 109.

6. Ibid., 109.

7. June 10, 1864, Benjamin R. Hieronymous Diary, Abraham Lincoln Presidential Library and Museum.

8. *OR*, vol. 39, pt. 2:109; Black, *A Civil War Diary*, 215.

9. *OR*, vol. 39, pt. 2:118–19.

10. Ibid., 115, 118; vol. 38, pt. 5:123.

11. Ibid., vol. 39, pt. 2:119.

12. Ibid., 122.

13. Wiley, *The Life of Billy Yank*, 342–43.

14. *OR*, vol. 39, pt. 1:259; Minnesota Board of Commissioners, *Minnesota in the Civil and Indian Wars 1861–1865*, 426.

15. June 23, 1864, Harrison T. Chandler Diary, Abraham Lincoln Presidential Library and Museum.

16. Reed, *Campaigns and Battles of the Twelfth Regiment Iowa Veteran Volunteer Infantry*, 149; Pierce, *History of the Second Iowa Cavalry*, 97; Martin, *Transactions of the Kansas State Historical Society*, 1903–1904, 43; Grierson, *A Just and Righteous Cause*, 258; *OR*, vol. 39, pt. 2:276.

17. *OR*, vol. 39, pt. 2:121.

18. Ibid., 122.

19. Scott, *Story of the Thirty-Second Iowa Infantry Volunteers*, 290; *OR*, vol. 39, pt. 2:109, 119, 122.

20. *OR*, vol. 39, pt. 2:124.

21. Ibid., 123.

22. Ibid., 124–25.

23. Ibid., 123.

24. McCall, *Three Years in the Service*, 37; *OR*, vol. 39, pt. 2:126.

25. *OR*, vol. 39, pt. 2:142.

26. Minnesota Board of Commissioners, *Minnesota in the Civil and Indian Wars 1861–1865*, 356; June 26, 1864, Bailey O. Bowden Diary, U.S. Army Heritage and Education Center.

27. June 21–22, 1864, Charles H. Tiedman Diary, U.S. Army Heritage and Education Center; June 22–23, 1864, Lot Abraham Diary, University of Iowa Libraries; Newton, *A Wisconsin Boy in Dixie*, 112–13; June 10–14, 1864, Jacob A. Melick Diary, Abraham Lincoln Presidential Library and Museum.

28. June 19, 1864, Hieronymous Diary.

29. Hugh Bay to Wife, June 20 and July 2, 1864, Civil War Letters of Hugh Bay, Indiana Historical Society; *War of the Rebellion: A Compilation of the Official Records of the Union and Confederate Navies* (hereafter cited as *ORN*), vol. 26:377.

30. Bir, "Remenecence of My Army Life," 39–40.

31. Thomas and McCann, *Soldier Life*, 97.

32. Henry McConnell to "Dear wife," June 21, 1864, Civil War Times Illustrated Collection, U.S. Army Heritage and Education Center; Thomas and McCann, *Soldier Life*, 97.

33. Thomas and McCann, *Soldier Life*, 97.

34. Carter, "The Tupelo Campaign," 91–92.

35. June 22, 1864, William Truman Diary, U.S. Army Heritage and Education Center; Williams, *"The Eagle Regiment,"* 8th Wis. Inf'ty Vols., 28; June 22, 1864, Fletcher Pomeroy Diary, David Habura Private Collection

36. June 23, 1864, Pomeroy Diary; *OR*, vol. 39, pt. 1:295; June 23, 1864, Chandler Diary; June 23–24, 1864, Erastus W. Bennett Diary, Boone County Historical Society.

37. Talbert, *Civil War Letters*, 45; June 23, 1864, Chandler Diary; *OR*, vol. 39, pt. 2:139.

38. *OR*, vol. 39, pt. 2:142; June 24–25, 1864, John W. Noble Diary, Iowa Historical Society.

39. *OR*, vol. 39, pt. 2:131.

4. Stretched to the Limit

1. Truth be told, the addition of Gholson's brigade was of little help to Adams. Gholson's command was a collection of ill-disciplined and poorly organized partisan rangers, militia, and detached companies organized into state regiments and transferred into Confederate service. Before sending the brigade to Adams, state authorities stripped it of serviceable equipment and horses. *OR*, vol. 39, pt. 2:650.

2. Ibid., 625.

3. Ibid., 652.

4. Ibid., 633, 663.

5. Ibid., 652.

6. Wise, *Lifeline of the Confederacy*, 177; June 7, 1864, William T. Mumford Diary, Museum of Mobile.

7. *OR*, vol. 39, pt. 2:657.

8. Bearss, *The Tupelo Campaign*, 26.

9. Chap. 47, William Pirtle Memoirs, Filson Historical Society; Jordan and Pryor, *The Campaigns of Lieut.-Gen. N. B. Forrest* 496.

10. *OR*, vol. 39, pt. 2: 655.

11. Symonds, *Joseph E. Johnston*, 304.

12. Johnston, *Narrative of Military Operations, Directed, During the Late War Between the States*, 359–60.

13. *OR*, vol. 38, pt. 4:774.

14. Ibid., vol. 39, pt. 2:658.

15. Ibid., vol. 52, pt. 2:680–81.

16. Ibid., vol. 38, pt. 2:805; pt. 5:876.

17. Ibid., vol. 38, pt. 5:858.

18. Ibid., vol. 39, pt. 2:688.

19. Ibid., vol. 52, pt. 2:687.

20. Ibid., vol. 38, pt. 5:875–76.

21. Hurst, *Nathan Bedford Forrest*, 198.

22. *OR*, vol. 39, pt. 2:657–58.

5. A Gathering Army

1. Carter, "The Tupelo Campaign," 92; Faust, *Historical Times Illustrated Encyclopedia of the Civil War*, 86; June 26, 1864, James F. Krafft Diary, Dean B. Krafft Private Collection; Henry S. McConnell to "Dearest Wife," June 26, 1864, Henry S. McConnell Letters, U.S. Army Heritage and Education Center.

2. Tucker, *The Fourteenth Wisconsin Vet. Vol. Infantry*, 8.

3. "Vivid War Experiences at Ripley, Miss.," 262–63; June 13, 1863, *Diary of Judge Orlando Davis; OR*, vol. 39, pt. 2:125.

4. *OR*, vol. 39, pt. 2:148; June 26, 1864, William P. Mallonee Diary, Indiana Historical Society; June 26, 1864, Erastus W. Bennett Diary, Boone County Historical Society.

5. Thomas and McCann, *Soldier Life*, 97.

6. Carter, "The Tupelo Campaign," 93.

7. Hunt, *Colonels in Blue*, 299; June 27, 1864, Charles H. Tiedman Diary, U.S. Army Heritage and Education Center; Nehemiah Starr to "My Dear Ettie," July 1, 1864, Nehemiah Davis Starr Letters, U.S. Army Heritage and Education Center.

8. Scott, *Story of the Thirty Second Iowa Infantry Volunteers*, 290.

9. *OR*, vol. 17, pt. 1:49.

10. June 26–27, 1864, Ibbetson, "William H. H. Ibbetson Diary."

11. June 26–27, 1864, Bailey O. Bowden Diary, U.S. Army Heritage and Education Center; June 26–27, 1864, Ibbetson, "William H. H. Ibbetson Diary."

12. *OR*, vol. 39, pt. 1:251; pt. 2:147; Dyer, *Compendium of the Civil War*, 1733–34.

13. *OR*, vol. 32, pt. 2:586–87; Jordan and Pryor, *The Campaigns of Lieut.-Gen. N. B. Forrest*, 485–86.

14. *OR*, vol. 32, pt. 2:588–89.

15. Jordan and Pryor, *The Campaigns of Lt. Gen. N. B. Forrest*, 491.

16. *OR*, vol. 39, pt. 2:155.

17. Ibid., 162.

18. Grierson had three brigades in camp, but the Second Brigade under Col. George Waring was slated to be sent back to Memphis before the expedition commenced.

19. June 26–27, 1864, Bowden Diary.

20. *OR*, vol. 39, pt. 2:121; Stuart, *Iowa Colonels and Regiments*, 250; June 27, 1864, Charles Ewringmann Diary, University of Iowa Libraries.

21. Faust, *Historical Times Illustrated Encyclopedia of the Civil War*, 609.

22. *OR*, vol. 38, pt. 5:123.

23. *OR*, vol. 39, pt. 2:121, 124, 142.

24. Reed, "Guntown and Tupelo," 311; *OR*, vol. 39, pt. 2:666–67.

25. *OR*, vol. 30, pt. 2:123; Parson, *Bear Flag and Bay State in the Civil War*, 93; Temple, *East Tennessee in the Civil War*, 391–92; Burchard, *One Gallant Rush*, 108–9.

26. Burns, *Recollections of the 4th Missouri Cavalry*, 65–67.

27. Ibid., 67, 74.

28. June 28, 1864, James F. Krafft Diary; Nehemiah Starr to "My Dear Ettie," July 1, 1864, Starr Letters; June 27, 1864, Harrison T. Chandler Diary, Abraham Lincoln Presidential Library and Museum; Virgil Downing to "Uncle," July 1, 1864, Abraham Lincoln Presidential Library and Museum; Thomas and McCann, *Soldier Life*, 97.

29. Driggs, *Opening of the Mississippi*, 23, 146.

30. "Reminiscences of Aurelius T. Bartlett," Missouri History Museum, 25.

31. July 27, 1864, Fletcher Pomeroy Diary, David Habura Private Collection; Thomas and McCann, *Soldier Life*, 98.

32. June 28, 1864, Thomas B. Allin Diary, U.S. Army Heritage and Education Center; June 28, 1864, Lot Abraham Diary, University of Iowa Libraries; July 5, 1864, William H. Rogers Diary, Iowa Historical Society.

33. *OR*, vol. 39, pt. 2: 149.

34. Ibid., 307–8; Scott, *The Story of a Cavalry Regiment*, 282.

35. July 4, 1864, Fletcher Pomeroy Diary; July 4, 1864, Lot Abraham Diary.

36. July 4, 1864, James F. Krafft Diary; Reed, *Campaigns and Battles of the Twelfth Regiment Iowa Veteran Volunteer Infantry*, 151; Elijah Edwards Journal, Minnesota Historical Society, 8; Thomas and McCann, *Soldier Life*, 98.

37. July 4, 1864, Ibbetson, "William H. H. Ibbetson Diary."

38. Scott, *The Story of a Cavalry Regiment*, 282–83; July 4, 1864, Lot Abraham Diary; July 4, 1864, Simon P. Duck Diary, U.S. Army Heritage and Education Center.

39. *OR*, vol. 39 pt. 2:163; Gantz, *Such Are the Trials*, 62.

40. Burns, *Recollections of the 4th Missouri Cavalry*, 130–31.

41. Ibid.

42. *OR*, vol. 39, pt. 2:162.

43. Ibid., 162.

44. Adolphus Wolf to "Dear Parents," June 25, 1864, Adolphus P. Wolf Letters, Civil War Times Illustrated Collection, U.S. Army Heritage and Education Center; *National Tribune*, March 11, 1886.

6. Watching and Waiting

1. *OR*, vol. 39, pt. 2:656–57. Red-haired and -bearded, Red Bob McCulloch was the cousin of his brigade commander, Robert "Black Bob" McCulloch, who presumably had black hair and a black beard.

2. Ibid., 657, 663; A. D. Clifton to "Dear Wife, Mother, Sisters and Children," June 23, 1864, Gilder Lehrman Institute of American History; John A. Cato to "My Dear Wife," June 15, 1864, John A. Cato Letters, Anders Collection, U.S. Army Heritage and Education Center.

3. Reid, "Morton's Battery," 853; Morton, *The Artillery of Nathan Bedford Forrest's Cavalry*, 173–74; Montague, "My Experiences as a Confederate Soldier," University of Memphis, University Libraries.

4. Montague, "My Experiences as a Confederate Soldier," 9–10.

5. Hubbard, *Notes of a Private*, 110; Morton, *The Artillery of Nathan Bedford Forrest's Cavalry*, 201.

6. *OR*, vol. 39, pt. 2:659–60.

7. Ibid., 660.

8. Ibid., 671.

9. Hurst, *Nathan Bedford Forrest*, 199.

10. Jordan and Pryor, *The Campaigns of Lieut.-Gen. N. B. Forrest*, 497; Hancock, *Hancock's Diary*, 410.

11. OR, vol. 39, pt. 2:666.

12. Ibid., 666–67.

13. Ibid., vol. 38, pt. 5:82.

14. Jordan and Pryor, *The Campaigns of Lieut.-Gen. N. B. Forrest*, 497.

15. *OR*, vol. 39, pt. 2:682.

16. Hollis, "Notes and Documents," 103.

17. June 1864, William T. Mumford Diary, Museum of Mobile.

18. Robert C. McCay to his wife, July 5, 1864, McCay (R. C.) Papers, Mississippi Department of Archives and History; John A. Cato to "My Dear Wife," July 1, 1864, Cato Letters.

19. Samuel M. Rennick to "Dear Brother," June 29, 1864, Abraham Lincoln Bookshop.

20. Galbraith and Galbraith, *A Lost Heroine of the Confederacy*, xiv, xxii, xxiii, xxvi; Record Group 109, roll 0067, National Archives and Record Administration; July 5, 8, 1864, Diary of Belle Edmonson, January–November 1864, University of North Carolina.

21. June–July 1864, Belle Edmondson Diary; William Elder to "Sis Susie," July 4, 1864, William Elder Letters, Mississippi Department of Archives and History.

7. Marching South

1. *OR*, vol. 39, pt. 2:166.

2. Ibid., 165; July 5, 1864, Lot Abraham Diary, University of Iowa Libraries; Gantz, *Such Are the Trials*, 62; July 5, 1864, Erastus W. Bennett Diary, Boone County Historical Society.

3. *OR*, vol. 39, pt. 2:165; Bearss, *The Tupelo Campaign*, 21.

4. *OR*, vol. 39, pt. 2:165; vol. 39 pt. 1:317; Elijah Edwards Journal, p. 8, Minnesota Historical Society.

5. Edwards Journal, 9.

6. Parson, "Thwarting Grant's First Drive on Vicksburg," 42–46.

7. Edwards Journal, 9.

8. Pierce, *History of the Second Iowa Cavalry*, 98; Carter, "The Tupelo Campaign," 93; Reed, *Campaigns and Battles of the Twelfth Regiment Iowa Veteran Volunteer Infantry*, 151; Edwards Journal, 9.

9. Ballard, *The Battle of Tupelo*, 8.

10. Burdette, *The Drums of the 47th*, 11–12.

11. July 21, 1864, Benjamin R. Hieronymous Diary, Abraham Lincoln Presidential Library and Museum.

12. Braun, "Inventory of Effects," http://www.33wis.com/articles/pdf/effects.pdf, 2002.

13. Hucke, *The Civil War Diary of Louis Huch/Hucke*, 7.

14. *OR*, vol. 39, pt. 1:315.

15. Thomas and McCann, *Soldier Life*, 98; July 7, 1864, John W. Noble Diary, Iowa Historical Society.

16. Hord, "Personal Experiences at Harrisburg, Miss.," 361; Carter, "Reply to 'Experiences at Harrisburg,'" 310.

17. July 7, 1864, Abraham Diary; Talbert, *Civil War Letters*, 45.

18. *OR*, vol. 39, pt. 1:317; Pierce, *History of the Second Iowa Cavalry*, 98.

19. July 7, 1864, Fletcher Pomeroy Diary, David Habura Private Collection.

20. Pierce, *History of the Second Iowa Cavalry*, 98–99.

21. *OR*, vol. 39, pt. 1:315–18. A slightly romanticized version of the engagement was told by an unnamed Confederate soldier. When the 1st Mississippi Partisan Rangers

rode through Ripley, the soldier, who was home recovering from a wound he'd received in Virginia, learned that this was his father's regiment and received permission to take his father's place in the ranks. The regiment rode out and soon fell into the skirmish with the 2nd Iowa, leaving the brave young soldier behind, buried in a roadside grave. *Southern Sentinel*, July 5, 1894. There is an unknown soldier buried under a Confederate-style government headstone on County Road 419 on a hill above North Tippah Creek, the modern name for Whitten Branch. The text of the headstone claims that the soldier was from the 7th Mississippi Cavalry, an alternate name for the 1st Mississippi Partisan Rangers. It is believed by the local Sons of Confederate Veterans and United Daughters of the Confederacy that this is the grave of the Virginia soldier.

22. July 7, 1864, Pomeroy Diary.

23. Carter, "The Tupelo Campaign," 94; July 7, 1864, Harrison T. Chandler Diary, Abraham Lincoln Presidential Library and Museum.

24. Edwards Journal, 9–11.

25. *OR*, vol. 34, pt. 2:573; vol. 39, pt. 2:123; July 6, 1864, George Brockway Diary, Iowa Historical Society.

26. *OR*, vol. 39, pt. 1:308.

27. Carter, "The Tupelo Campaign," 94.

28. Edwards Journal, 11; July 8, 1864, Pomeroy Diary; July 8, 1864, Noble Diary.

29. *OR*, vol. 39, pt. 1:304; Edwards Journal, 11.

30. There are several references to Kelly's Ford on the Tallahatchie River, but these are erroneous. The headwaters of the Tallahatchie River are in Tippah County, south of Ripley. Kelly's Ford was on the Little Hatchie, a tributary of the Hatchie River. The two rivers rise within ten miles of each other.

31. *OR*, vol. 39, pt. 1:308.

32. Ibid.; July 8, 1864, Noble Diary.

33. *OR*, vol. 39, pt. 1:308.

34. Carter, "The Tupelo Campaign," 94; Edwards Journal, 11.William "Buffalo Bill" Cody of the 7th Kansas Cavalry related a similar story in his autobiography, but the tale is too contrived to be credible.

35. Carter, "The Tupelo Campaign," 95; Edwards Journal, 12.

36. July 8, 1864, John Danielson Diary, Minnesota Historical Society; Carter, "The Tupelo Campaign," 95.

37. July 8, 1864, Danielson Diary; Thomas and McCann, *Soldier Life*, 99; July 8, 1864, David King Diary, Indiana Historical Society.

38. Edwards Journal, 9–10; Aughey, *Tupelo*, 526.

39. July 7–8, 1864, Chandler Diary; "Reminiscences of Aurelius T. Bartlett," Missouri History Museum, 26; July 7, 1864, Cornelius Corwin Diary, Indiana Historical Society;Thomas Hawley to "Dearest Parents, Brothers and Sisters," July 21, 1864, Thomas Hawley Letters, Missouri History Museum.

40. July 8, 1864, Abraham Diary; July 8, 1864, Bailey O. Bowden Diary, U.S. Army Heritage and Education Center; July 8, 1864, James F. Krafft Diary, Dean B. Krafft Private Collection; July 8, 1864, Pomeroy Diary; July 8, 1864, Charles H. Tiedman Diary, U.S. Army Heritage and Education Center.

41. "Reminiscences of Aurelius T. Bartlett," 26.

42. July 8, 1864, Chandler Diary.

43. Riley, "Extinct Towns and Villages of Mississippi," 372–73; July 8, 1864, Noble Diary.

44. July 8, 1864, Ibbetson, "William H. H. Ibbetson Diary."

45. Bearss, *The Tupelo Campaign*, 41; July 9, 1864, Ibbetson, "William H. H. Ibbetson Diary"; July 9, 1864, Chandler Diary; Thomas and McCann, *Soldier Life*, 99.

46. Carter, "The Tupelo Campaign," 96; July 9, 1864, Krafft Diary; July 9, 1864, Ibbetson, "William H. H. Ibbetson Diary."

47. July, 9, 1864, Ibbetson, "William H. H. Ibbetson Diary."

48. July 6–9, 1864, John M. Keltner Diary, Anders Collection, U.S. Army Heritage and Education Center; July 9, 1864, William Truman Diary, U.S. Army Heritage and Education Center; Edwards Journal, 12.

49. *OR*, vol. 39, pt. 2:160; Faust, *Historical Times Illustrated Encyclopedia of the Civil War*, 615–16.

50. Thomas and McCann, *Soldier Life*, 99.

8. Pontotoc

1. *OR*, vol. 39, pt. 1:306, 308, 320, 329, 346; Hancock, *Hancock's Diary*, 411.

2. *OR*, vol. 39, pt. 1:320, 329, 346; Hancock, *Hancock's Diary*, 411.

3. *OR*, vol. 39, pt. 1:320, 329; Hancock, *Hancock's Diary*, 411.

4. *OR*, vol. 39, pt. 1:329; Hancock, *Hancock's Diary*, 412.

5. Lindsley, *Military Annals of Tennessee*, 612; Hancock, *Hancock's Diary*, 412; *OR*, vol. 39, pt. 1:329.

6. July 10, 1864, Talbert, *Civil War Letters*, 45; July 10, 1864, Harrison T. Chandler Diary, Abraham Lincoln Presidential Library and Museum.

7. July 10, 1864, Fletcher Pomeroy Diary, David Habura Private Collection; July 10, 1864, Lot Abraham Diary, University of Iowa Libraries.

8. Elijah Edwards Journal, pp. 12–13, Minnesota Historical Society. A "snowy tidy" is a diaper.

9. Edwards Journal, 12–13.

10. *OR*, vol. 39, pt. 1:308; July 10, 1864, Abraham Diary.

11. *OR*, vol. 39, pt. 1:308, 312.

12. Hancock, *Hancock's Diary*, 412.

13. Mathes, *The Old Guard in Gray*, 34–35.

14. Hancock, *Hancock's Diary*, 413; July 10, 1864, Pomeroy Diary.

15. July 10, 1864, Pomeroy Diary; Hancock, *Hancock's Diary*, 413; Fox, *The Early History of the Seventh Kansas Cavalry*, 43.

16. July 10, 1864, Pomeroy Diary.

17. *OR*, vol. 39, pt. 1:329, 342.

18. Ibid., 329, 342, 344.

19. Ibid., 320, 324–25; pt. 2:696.

20. Jones, "James Ronald Chalmers," 168–70.

21. *OR*, vol. 10, pt. 1:533; vol. 20:689; Bearss, *Forrest at Brice's Crossroads and in North Mississippi in 1864*, 338.

22. Wills, *The Confederacy's Greatest Cavalryman*, 170–71; Jones, "James Ronald Chalmers," 168–70; *OR*, vol. 32, pt. 3:610.

23. Dyer, *The Tennessee Civil War Veterans Questionnaires*, 1799; *OR*, vol. 39, pt. 2:700; Lee, draft manuscript, "The Battle of Tupelo, or Harrisburg, July 14th, 1864," p. 5, Mississippi Department of Archives and History; Jordan and Pryor, *The Campaigns of Lieut.-Gen. N. B. Forrest*, 500.

24. July 9, 1864, Diary of Belle Edmondson, Southern Historical Collection, University of North Carolina, Chapel Hill.

25. *OR*, vol. 39, pt. 1:325.

26. Ibid., 325.

27. Hancock, *Hancock's Diary*, 413.

28. July 10, 1864, Pomeroy Diary.

29. Edwards Journal, 13; Carter, "The Tupelo Campaign," 96.

30. Carter, "The Tupelo Campaign," 96.

31. July 10, 1864, George Brockway Diary, Iowa Historical Society.

32. *OR*, vol. 39, pt. 1:329.

33. Ibid., 250; chap. 48, William Pirtle Memoirs, Filson Historical Society.

34. *OR*, vol. 39, pt. 1:325.

35. Ibid., 321, 325.

36. Bearss, "Forrest Puts the Skeer on the Yankees," 13; Brown, *Lamb's Biographical Dictionary of the United States*, 297. McMillen's spotty reputation was sealed at the Battle of Nashville. He accepted the sword of Confederate general Thomas Benton Smith in surrender and then beat his captive savagely with the flat of the weapon, causing irreversible brain damage.

37. July 11, 1864, Pomeroy Diary.

38. Pierce, *History of the Second Iowa Cavalry*, 100.

39. Ibid.

40. July 11, 1864, Pomeroy Diary; Edwards Journal, 15; Pierce, *History of the Second Iowa Cavalry*, 100.

41. July 11, 1864, Thomas B. Allin Diary, U.S. Army Heritage and Education Center.

42. *OR*, vol. 39, pt. 1:344; Lindsley, *Military Annals of Tennessee*, 779.

43. *OR*, vol. 39, pt. 1:344.

44. Ibid., 321; Pierce, *History of the Second Iowa Cavalry*, 101.

45. *OR*, vol. 39, pt. 1:321; Grierson, *A Just and Righteous Cause*, 261.

9. Pinson's Hill

1. July 12, 1864, Ibbetson, "William H. H. Ibbettson Diary"; July 12, 1864, Erastus W. Bennett Dairy, Boone County Historical Society.

2. Elijah Edwards Journal, p. 15, Minnesota Historical Society; *National Tribune*, January 28, 1886.

3. *OR*, vol. 39, pt. 1:250; Grierson, *A Just and Righteous Cause*, 261.

4. *OR*, vol. 39, pt 1:250; Grierson, *A Just and Righteous Cause*, 261.

5. Grierson, *A Just and Righteous Cause*, 261; Scott, *The Story of a Cavalry Regiment*, 118.

6. *OR*, vol. 39, pt. 1:308.

7. July 12, 1864, John W. Noble Diary, Iowa Historical Society; *OR*, vol. 39, pt. 1:309.

8. Scott, *The Story of a Cavalry Regiment*, 118.

9. Grierson, *A Just and Righteous Cause*, 262; Scott, *The Story of a Cavalry Regiment*, 119.

10. Grierson, *A Just and Righteous Cause*, 26; *OR*, vol. 39, pt. 1:304.

11. Grierson, *A Just and Righteous Cause*, 262; *OR*, vol. 39, pt. 1:321; Rowland, *Military History of Mississippi*, 81–87.

12. *OR*, vol. 39, pt. 1:317.

13. Ibid., 250–51.

14. Grierson, *A Just and Righteous Cause*, 263: July 12, 1864, Noble Diary.

15. Grierson, *A Just and Righteous Cause*, 263; Burns, *Recollections of the 4th Missouri Cavalry*, 131.

16. Jordan and Pryor, *The Campaigns of Lieut.-Gen. N. B. Forrest*, 501.

17. *OR*, vol. 39, pt. 1:325–26; Young, *The Seventh Tennessee Cavalry*, 96.

18. *OR*, vol. 39, pt. 2:700, 702.

19. *OR*, vol. 39, pt. 1:320–21; Jordan and Pryor, *The Campaigns of Lieut.-Gen. N. B. Forrest*, 401.

20. *OR*, vol. 39, pt. 1:321, 326, 346; Jordan and Pryor, *The Campaigns of Lieut.-Gen. N. B. Forrest*, 501.

21. Jordan and Pryor, *The Campaigns of Lieut.-Gen. N. B. Forrest*, 501; Rowland, *Military History of Mississippi*, 142–43.

22. Marshall Polk to "My Dearest Wife," July 12, 1864, Tennessee State Library and Archives.

23. *OR*, vol. 39, pt. 1:330, 335–36.

24. Edwards Journal, 16.

25. Edwards Journal, 15.

26. Edwards Journal, 15; Thomas and McCann, *Soldier Life*, 100; July 12, 1864, Ibbetson, "William H. H. Ibbetson Diary"; July 12, 1864, Ezra Fish Diary, Abraham Lincoln Presidential Library and Museum.

27. *OR*, vol. 39, pt. 1:301, 345.

28. Lee, draft manuscript of "The Battle of Tupelo, or Harrisburg, July 14th, 1864," p. 6, Mississippi Department of Archives and History.

29. *OR*, vol. 39, pt. 1:325; Hancock, *Hancock's Diary*, 414–15.

30. *OR*, vol. 39, pt. 1:321, 325, 330; Hollis, "Notes and Documents," 104.

10. The Road to Tupelo

1. Elijah Edwards Journal, p. 17, Minnesota Historical Society; Scott, *Story of the Thirty Second Iowa Infantry Volunteers*, 291.

2. *OR*, vol. 39, pt. 1:251; Ward et al., *The Civil War*, 272.

3. *OR*, vol. 39, pt. 1:251, 276, 301, 306, 319.

4. Ibid., 301, 309; July 13, 1864, Lot Abraham Diary, University of Iowa Libraries.

5. *OR*, vol. 39, pt. 1:326, 345.

6. Ibid., 345.

7. Ibid., 349.

8. Chap. 49, William Pirtle Memoirs, Filson Historical Society.

9. *OR*, vol. 39, pt. 1:326.

10. Jordan and Pryor, *The Campaigns of Lieut.-Gen. N. B. Forrest*, 502; *OR*, vol. 39, pt. 1:321; Lee, draft manuscript, "The Battle of Tupelo, or Harrisburg, July 14th, 1864," p. 6, Mississippi Department of Archives and History.

11. *OR*, vol. 39, pt. 1:326.

12. Ibid., 330.

13. Ibid., 301, 319.

14. Ibid., 309.

15. Holloway, "Incidental to the Battle of Harrisburg," 526.

16. Thomas and McCann, *Soldier Life*, 100; Wolf, "Letters from an Illinois Drummer Boy," 154; July 13, 1864, Johnson Paisley Diary, John M. Paisley Papers, Newberry Library; Adolphus Wolfe to parents, July 25, 1864, Adolphus P. Wolf Letters, Civil War Times Illustrated Collection, U.S. Army Heritage and Education Center; July 13, 1864, Charles H. Tiedman Diary, U.S. Army Heritage and Education Center; Hubbard, *Notes of a Private*, 111.

17. *OR*, vol. 39, pt. 1:349; July 13, 1864, Fletcher Pomeroy Diary, David Habura Private Collection.

18. Fox, *The Early History of the Seventh Kansas Cavalry*, 43; July 13, 1864, Pomeroy Diary.

19. *OR*, vol. 39, pt. 1:301.

20. Ibid., 301; Fox, *The Early History of the Seventh Kansas Cavalry*, 43.

21. *OR*, vol. 39, pt. 1:301; Cowden, *A Brief Sketch of the Organization and Services of the Fifty-Ninth Regiment of United States Colored Infantry*, 127; July 13, 1864, Pomeroy Diary.

22. *OR*, vol. 39, pt 1:301.

23. Letter from Major James Foster, undated, Ross County Historical Society.

24. Fox, *The Early History of the Seventh Kansas Cavalry*, 42.

25. Cowden, *A Brief Sketch of the Organization and Services of the Fifty-Ninth Regiment of United States Colored Infantry*, 128–29; *OR*, vol. 39, pt. 1:301–2.

26. *OR*, vol. 39, pt. 1:321.

27. Ibid., 304, 309, 345. Tyler later reported that the morning skirmishes cost him one man killed, though Noble claimed that six Confederates had died in the fighting. General Grierson reported seeing seven enemy dead, and numerous Union infantrymen noted dead southerners along the route of march.

28. *OR*, vol. 39, pt. 1:313–14.

29. Ibid., 345.

30. Ibid., 305, 306, 312, 316, 317.

11. Bertram's Shop and the Camargo Crossroads

1. *OR*, vol. 39, pt. 1: 24–25.

2. John Johnson, "To My Son," p. 11, Abraham Lincoln Book Shop; Henry, *First with the Most*, 319.

3. Johnson, "To My Son," 111–13; *OR*, vol. 39, pt. 1:341.

4. *OR*, vol. 39, pt. 1:326, 330.

5. Ibid., 276.

6. Ibid.

7. Ibid., 257, 272; Elijah Edwards Journal, p. 18, Minnesota Historical Society.

8. Ellis, "Major General Joseph Anthony Mower, U.S.A.," 401; *New York Times*, June 4, 1883; Bryner, *Bugle Echoes*, 61; Cozzens, *The Darkest Days of the War*, 62, 236; Edwards Journal, 5.

9. Edwards Journal, 17–18; Carter, "The Tupelo Campaign," 97.

10. Reminiscences of Aurelius T. Bartlett, p. 26, Missouri History Museum; Edwards Journal, 18.

11. Young, *From These Hills*, 151.

12. Bryner, *Bugle Echoes*, 127; Tucker, *The Fourteenth Wisconsin Vet. Vol. Infantry*, 9.

13. Tucker, *The Fourteenth Wisconsin Vet. Vol. Infantry*, 9; *OR*, vol. 39, pt. 1:257, 276.

14. Reminiscences of Aurelius Bartlett, 26; *OR*, vol. 39, pt. 1:270.

15. *OR*, vol. 39, pt. 1:272; Edwards Journal, 19.

16. Tucker, *The Fourteenth Wisconsin Vet. Vol. Infantry*, 10; *OR*, vol. 39, pt. 1:276.

17. *OR*, vol. 39, pt. 1:276.

18. Jordan and Pryor, *The Campaigns of Lieut.-Gen. N. B. Forrest*, 503–4; *OR*, vol. 39, pt. 1:276–77; Braun, "Where Is Camargo Crossroads?"; Record Group [RG] 109, roll 0031, National Records and Records Administration.

19. Braun, Robert A., "Where Is Camargo Crossroads?"; *OR*, vol. 39, pt. 1:270, 272, 277.

20. Hancock, *Hancock's Diary*, 97; Jordan and Pryor, *The Campaigns of Lieut.-Gen. N. B. Forrest*, 504; *OR*, vol. 39, pt. 1:270, 272, 277.

21. Young, *From These Hills*, 151; Carter, "Reply to 'Experiences at Harrisburg,'" 310; *OR*, vol. 39, pt. 1:277.

22. *Tupelo Lee County Tribune*, Jan. 16, 1953; Lytle, *Bedford Forrest and His Critter Company*, 35.

23. *OR*, vol. 39, pt. 1:257.

24. Otey, "Story of our Great War," *Confederate Veteran Magazine* 9 (1901): 110; McNeilly, "With the Rear Guard," ibid., 26 (1918): 338.

25. "Abram Buford," *Confederate Veteran Magazine* 2 (1894): 326; Davis, *The Confederate General*, 145–46; Allardice and Hewitt, *Kentuckians in Gray*, 49–55; Johnston, *Narrative of Military Operations*, 228–30.

26. Hancock, *Hancock's Diary*, 417.

27. Reed, *Campaigns and Battles of the Twelfth Regiment Iowa Veteran Volunteer Infantry*, 314; *National Tribune*, Jan. 28, 1886.

28. *OR*, vol. 39, pt. 1:330, 347.

29. *Roster and Record of Iowa Soldiers*, 1728; Reed, *Campaigns and Battles of the Twelfth Regiment Iowa Veteran Volunteer Infantry*, 314–15; Satterlee, *The Journal and the 114th*, 257, 265.

30. *OR*, vol. 39, pt. 1:259, 262; Reed, *Campaigns and Battles of the Twelfth Regiment Iowa Veteran Volunteer Infantry*, 315.

31. *OR*, vol. 39, pt. 1:278; Reed, *Campaigns and Battles of the Twelfth Regiment Iowa Veteran Volunteer Infantry*, 315; Phillips, *Some Things Our Boy Saw During the War*, 45; *Roster and Record of Iowa Soldiers*, 1728.

32. Reed, *Campaigns and Battles of the Twelfth Regiment Iowa Veteran Volunteer Infantry*, 315–16; Phillips, *Some Things Our Boy Saw During the War*, 45.

33. *OR*, vol. 39, pt. 1:265; Williams, *"The Eagle Regiment,"* 28.

34. *OR*, vol. 39, pt. 1:265–67, 347; Hancock, *Hancock's Diary*, 418.

35. *OR*, vol. 39, pt. 1: 265–67.

36. Hancock, *Hancock's Diary*, 418.

37. *OR*, vol. 39, pt. 1:330; Phillips, *Some Things Our Boy Saw During the War*, 46; Reed, *Campaigns and Battles of the Twelfth Regiment Iowa Veteran Volunteer Infantry*, 316.

38. Carter, "The Tupelo Campaign," 98; Edwards Journal, 20.

39. Hancock, *Hancock's Diary*, 419; "Capt. Moses Waddell McKnight," *Confederate Veteran Magazine* 18 (1910): 37; RG 109, roll 0078.

40. *OR*, vol. 39, pt. 1:330, 347; Hancock, *Hancock's Diary*, 418–19; Jordan and Pryor, *The Campaigns of Lieut.-Gen. N. B. Forrest*, 504.

41. Pou, "How Young Tupelo Got an Old Battle," *Tupelo Daily Journal*, Centennial Issue, 1971.

42. Ibid.

43. Phillips, *Some Things Our Boy Saw During the War*, 46.

44. *OR*, vol. 39, pt. 1:259; July 13, 1864, Harrison T. Chandler Diary, Abraham Lincoln Presidential Library and Museum; Bryner, *Bugle Echoes*, 128; Reed, *Campaigns and Battles of the Twelfth Regiment Iowa Veteran Volunteer Infantry*, 316; *Roster and Record of Iowa Soldiers*, 1728.

12. Harrisburg

1. Rowland, *Mississippi, Comprising Sketches of Counties, Towns, Events, Institutions, and Persons*, 830; Chalmers, "Forrest and His Campaigns," 476.

2. July 13, 1864, John W. Noble Diary, Iowa Historical Society.

3. *OR*, vol. 39, pt. 1:330, 336, 342.

4. Ibid., 350.

5. Jordan and Pryor, *The Campaigns of Lieut.-Gen. N. B. Forrest*, 507; *OR*, vol. 39, pt. 1:251.

6. *OR*, vol. 39, pt. 1:279, 282; Davis, *The Official Military Atlas of the Civil War*, plate 63, map 2.

7. Thomas and McCann, *Soldier Life*, 100; Talbert, *Civil War Letters*, 45; *OR*, vol. 39, pt. 1:279; Davis, *The Official Military Atlas of the Civil War*, plate 63, map 2; William Donnan to "My Ever dear Wife," July 24, 1864, William Donnan Letters, Iowa Historical Society.

8. July 13, 1864, James F. Krafft Diary, Dean Krafft Private Collection; *OR*, vol. 39, pt. 1:295; Hucke, *The Civil War Diary of Louis Hucke*, 8.

9. Henry McConnel to wife, July 23, 1864, Henry S. McConnel Letters, Civil War Times Illustrated Collection, U.S. Army Heritage and Education Center.

10. Hubbs, "The Civil War and Alexander Wilkin,"174–87.

11. Tucker, *The Fourteenth Wisconsin, Vet. Vol. Infantry*, 12; Newton, *A Wisconsin Boy in Dixie*, 114.

12. Cowden, *A Brief Sketch of the Organization and Service of the Fifty-Ninth Regiment of United States Colored Infantry*, 129; Davis, *The Official Military Atlas of the Civil War*, plate 63, map 2.

13. July 13, 1864, Fletcher Pomeroy Diary, David Habura Private Collection; *OR*, vol. 39, pt. 1:312.

14. *OR*, vol. 39, pt. 1:312, 316, 317; Gantz, *Such Are the Trials*, 64.

15. Reminiscences of Aurelius Bartlett, p. 27, Missouri History Museum; July 13, 1864, Ebenezer B. Mattocks Diary, Ebenezer Brewer Mattocks and Family Papers, Minnesota Historical Society.

16. Wyeth, *That Devil Forrest*, 384.

17. *OR*, vol. 39, pt. 1:322; Morton, *The Artillery of Nathan Bedford Forrest's Cavalry*, 204; Jordan and Pryor, *The Campaigns of Lieut.-Gen. N. B. Forrest*, 505.

18. Bearss, "Forrest Puts the Skeer on the Yankees,"20.

19. Wyeth, *That Devil Forrest*, 384; Morton, *The Artillery of Nathan Bedford Forrest's Cavalry*, 204.

20. Morton, *The Artillery of Nathan Bedford Forrest's Cavalry*, 204–5.

21. Jordan and Pryor, *The Campaigns of Lieut.-Gen. N. B. Forrest*, 505; *OR*, vol. 39, pt. 1:322–23; Morton, *The Artillery of Nathan Bedford Forrest's Cavalry*, 204; Henry, *"First with the Most,"*. 316.

22. Jordan and Pryor, *The Campaigns of Lieut.-Gen. N. B. Forrest*, 505.

23. Hord, "Personal Experiences at Harrisburg, Miss.," 361.

24. Ibid.

25. Chap. 49, William Pirtle Memoirs, Filson Historical Society.

26. Chap. 49, Pirtle Memoirs.

13. Opening Moves

1. *OR*, vol. 39, pt. 1:309, 277; July 14, 1864, Simon P. Duck Diary, Harrisburg Civil War Round Table Collection, U.S. Army Heritage and Education Center.

2. *OR*, vol. 39, pt. 1:309; July 14, 1864, Duck Diary; Gantz, *Such Are the Trials*, 64; Scott, *The Story of a Cavalry Regiment*, 286.

3. Lee, draft manuscript, "The Battle of Tupelo, or Harrisburg, July 14th, 1864," p. 4, Mississippi Department of Archives and History.

4. Lee, "The Battle of Tupelo, or Harrisburg, July 14th, 1864," 8.

5. Henry, *First with the Most*, 317.

6. Chalmers, "Forest and His Campaigns," 476; Lee, "Battle of Tupelo, or Harrisburg, July 14th, 1864," 5; Jordan and Pryor, *The Campaigns of Lieut-Gen. N. B. Forrest*, 507.

7. *OR*, vol. 39, pt. 1:322.

8. Lee, "The Battle of Tupelo, or Harrisburg, July 14th, 1864," 7.

9. Wyeth, *That Devil Forrest*, 386.

10. Porter, "Tennessee," 240; Hancock, *Hancock's Diary*, 422.

11. Puryear, "No Man's Battle," 510.

12. *OR*, vol. 39, pt. 1:330, 336; John Johnson, "To My Son," p. 117, Abraham Lincoln Bookshop.

13. "Col. Thomas Ringland Stockdale," *Confederate Veteran Magazine* 7 (1899): 176; Gardner, "About the Fight at Harrisburg, Miss.," 166.

14. Smith, "Hard Fighting at Harrisburg," 34; Robert McCay to "Dear Wife," July 8, 1864, McCay (R.C.) Papers, Mississippi Department of Archives and History; *OR*, vol. 39, pt. 1:322.

15. *OR*, vol. 39, pt. 1:330–31; Chalmers, "Forrest and His Campaigns," 476–77.

16. Owen, *History of Alabama and Dictionary of Alabama Biography*, 1454; Alabama State Historical marker, Moulton, AL; Sifakis, *Who Was Who in the Civil War*, 550.

17. *OR*, vol. 39, pt. 1:323, 326; Lee, "The Battle of Tupelo, or Harrisburg, July 14th, 1864," 7.

18. Morton, *The Artillery of Nathan Bedford Forrest's Cavalry*, 22, 207.

19. Ibid., 207.

20. Ibid., 208; Sifakis, *Who Was Who in the Civil War*, 382.

21. Lindsley, *Military Annals of Tennessee*, 864–65.

22. Hancock, *Hancock's Diary*, 423; Lee, "The Battle of Tupelo, or Harrisburg, July 14th, 1864," 7.

23. Hattaway, *Stephen Dill Lee*, 188; Lee, "The Battle of Tupelo, or Harrisburg, July 14th, 1864," 7; Jordan and Pryor, *The Campaigns of Lieut.-Gen. N. B. Forrest*, 507–8.

24. *OR*, vol. 39, pt. 1:345.

25. Ibid., 257; July 14, 1864, William Truman Diary, J. Riggs Collection, U.S. Army Heritage and Education Center; Reed, *Campaigns and Battles of the Twelfth Regiment Iowa Veteran Volunteer Infantry*, 154; Elijah Edwards Journal, p. 21, Minnesota Historical Society.

26. Carter, "The Tupelo Campaign," 99; *OR*, vol. 39, pt. 1:257, 262, 265, 270, 271, 272, 274, 277.

27. *OR*, vol. 39, pt. 1:270; Carter, "The Tupelo Campaign," 99; Reed, *Campaigns and Battles of the Twelfth Regiment Iowa Veteran Volunteer Infantry*, 154.

28. Phillips, *Some Things Our Boy Saw During the War*, 45.

29. *OR*, vol. 39, pt. 1:257, 277.

30. Ibid., 262.

31. Ibid., 280, 282, 285.

32. Ibid., 251.

33. Ibid., 345.

34. Ibid., 297–98; June 27, 1864, Charles H. Tiedman Diary, U.S. Army Heritage and Education Center; Wolf, "Letters from an Illinois Drummer Boy," 154.

35. *OR*, vol. 39, pt. 1:299; Churchill, *Genealogy and Biography of the Churchill Family in America*, 75.

36. *OR*, vol. 39, pt. 1: 345.

37. Ibid., 302; Cowden, *A Brief Sketch of the Organization and Service of the Fifty-Ninth Regiment of United States Colored Infantry*, 129.

38. Davis, *Official Military Atlas of the Civil War*, plate 63; *OR*, vol. 39, pt. 1:334; Bearss, *The Tupelo Campaign*, plate 3.

39. *OR*, vol. 39, pt. 1:317; Carter, "Reply to 'Experiences at Harrisburg,'" 310.

40. Davenport, *History of the Ninth Regiment Illinois Cavalry Volunteers*, 120.

14. "A Medley of Blunders"

1. *OR*, vol. 39, pt 1:309; Jordan and Pryor, *The Campaigns of Lieut.-Gen. N. B. Forrest*, 508; Morton, *The Artillery of Nathan Bedford Forrest's Cavalry*, 208; Phillips, *Some Things Our Boy Saw During the War*, 45; Wyeth, *That Devil Forrest*, 387–88.

2. Genoways, *A Perfect Picture of Hell*, 227.

3. Lee, draft manuscript, "The Battle of Tupelo, or Harrisburg, July 14th, 1864," p. 7, Mississippi Department of Archives and History; Morton, *The Artillery of Nathan Bedford Forrest's Cavalry*, 208.

4. Lee, "The Battle of Tupelo, or Harrisburg, July 14th, 1864," 7.

5. Henry, *First with the Most*, 317.

6. *OR*, vol. 39, pt. 1:322; Jordan and Pryor, *The Campaigns of Lieut.-Gen. N. B. Forrest*, 508.

7. *OR*, vol. 39, pt. 1:322.

8. Ibid., 331; Bearss, *The Tupelo Campaign*, 101.

9. Lee, "The Battle of Tupelo, or Harrisburg, July 14th, 1864," 7.

10. George, *History of the 3d, 7th, 8th and 12th Kentucky C.S.A.*, 100, 101.

11. Chap. 49, William Pirtle Memoirs, Filson Historical Society.

12. John Johnson, "To My Son," p. 118, Abraham Lincoln Bookshop; Wright, "Twelfth Kentucky Cavalry," 780.

13. July 14, 1864, Simon P. Duck Diary, United States Army Heritage and Educations Center; Phillips, *Some Things Our Boy Saw During the War*, 45; Gantz, *Such are the Trials*, 64.

14. *OR*, vol. 39, pt. 1:280, 294, 331, 336; Jordan and Pryor, *The Campaigns of Lieut.-Gen. N. B. Forrest*, 509.

15. A 6-pounder rifle was actually a smooth-bore cannon that had been altered by rifling the bore. This allowed the piece to fire a 12-pound James shell, thus making it a more formidable weapon.

16. *OR*, vol. 39, pt. 1:282; Luther Frost to "Dear Parents," July 21, 1864, Luther and Orville Frost Papers, Abraham Lincoln Presidential Library and Museum.

17. *OR*, vol. 39, pt. 1:294, 295, 299.

18. Johnson, "To My Son," 118; Hord, "Personal Experiences at Harrisburg, Miss.," 362.

19. Though Rice's guns were advanced by hand, to save the time lost in hitching and unhitching the pieces to their limbers, the limbers and their ammunition chests were still drawn by teams of six horses.

20. Puryear, "No Man's Battle," 510; Wyeth, *That Devil Forrest*, 390; Haller, "Rice's Battery," 867; Morton, *The Artillery of Nathan Bedford Forrest's Cavalry*, 209.

21. Johnson, "To My Son," 118.

22. *OR*, vol. 39, pt. 1:282; Johnson, "To My Son," 119.

23. *OR*, vol. 39, pt. 1:343; Bearss, *The Tupelo Campaign*, 104.

24. Johnson, "To My Son," 119–20.

25. *OR*, vol. 39, pt. 1:343.

26. Ibid., 280–82.

27. July 14, 1864, Bailey O. Bowden Diary, Civil War Times Illustrated Collection,

U.S. Army Heritage and Education Center; Luther Frost to "Dear Parents," July 21, 1864, Frost Papers.

28. Johnson, "To My Son," 120.

29. *OR*, vol. 39, pt. 1:283.

30. Ibid., 280–83.

31. Ibid., 336.

32. Sidney Z. Robinson to "Dear Mother," July 26, 2864, Abraham Lincoln Presidential Library and Museum.

33. Chap. 49, William Pirtle Memoirs, Filson Historical Society; Wyeth, *That Devil Forrest*, 394; *OR*, vol. 39, pt. 1:327.

34. *OR*, vol. 39, pt. 1:327.

35. Ibid., 285–86.

36. Thomas and McCann, *Soldier Life*, 100–101; William Donnan to "My Dear Wife," July 24, 1864, William Donnan Letters, Iowa Historical Society.

37. *OR*, vol. 39, pt. 1:287, 290, 292.

38. Reed, *Campaigns and Battles of the Twelfth Regiment Iowa Veteran Volunteer Infantry*, 154; *OR*, vol. 39, pt. 1:265, 270.

39. Reminiscences of Aurelius T. Bartlett, p. 28, Missouri History Museum; Reed, *Campaigns and Battles of the Twelfth Regiment Iowa Veteran Volunteer Infantry*, 158; Elijah Edwards Journal, p. 24, Minnesota Historical Society.

40. Wyeth, *That Devil Forrest*, 331; *OR*, vol. 39, pt. 1:390–91.

41. Wyeth, *That Devil Forrest*, 389; *OR*, vol. 39, pt. 1:349, 389.

42. *OR*, vol. 39, pt. 1:349.

43. The cannons frequently referred to as Rodmans were actually 3-inch iron ordnance rifles. Their distinctive black color and bottle shape were similar to the design of the much larger Rodman rifles.

44. Reed, *Campaigns and Battles of the Twelfth Regiment Iowa Veteran Volunteer Infantry*, 154; Carter, "The Tupelo Campaign," 79; *OR*, vol. 39, pt. 1:272, 294.

45. *OR*, vol. 39, pt. 1:277; Bearss, *The Tupelo Campaign*, plate 3.

46. Gardner, "About the Fight at Harrisburg, Miss.," 166. It is unclear if Gardner's use of the word "crape" refers to a traditional black mourning badge or the green chevrons worn by members of the Ambulance Corps, the stretcher bearers who collected the wounded from the field while the battle was in progress.

47. *OR*, vol. 39, pt. 1:252.

48. Ibid., 349–50.

49. H. P. Mabry to Mrs. McCay, July 20, 1864, McCay (R.C.) Papers, Mississippi Department of Archives and History; "Col. Thomas Ringland Stockdale," *Confederate Veteran Magazine* 7 (1899): 176; "Richard Abner Jarvis," ibid., 27 (1919): 28; *OR*, vol. 39, pt. 1:350.

50. Phillips, *Some Things Our Boy Saw During the War*, 48.

51. Ibid., 50.

52. Philips, *Some Things Our Boy Saw During the War*, 45–47.

53. Alexander Gray to "Dear Mother," July 28, 1864, Alexander Gray Letters, Wisconsin Historical Society.

54. *OR*, vol. 39, pt. 1:268, 272; Reed, *Campaigns and Battles of the Twelfth Regiment Iowa Veteran Volunteer Infantry*, 156.

55. *OR*, vol. 39, pt. 1:265–66.

56. *OR*, vol. 39, pt. 1:266–67; Hubbs, "The Civil War and Alexander Wilkin," 190; *National Tribune*, Mar. 11, 1886.

57. *OR*, vol. 39, pt. 1:252; Genoways, *A Perfect Picture of Hell*, 227.

58. *OR*, vol. 39, pt. 1:270, 272; Carter, "The Tupelo Campaign," 99.

59. Agnew, "Battle of Tishomingo Creek," 131; Smith, "Hard Fighting at Harrisburg," 34; *OR*, vol. 39, pt. 1:350; Giambrone, *Beneath Torn and Tattered Flag*, 97.

60. "John A. Snell," *Confederate Veteran Magazine* 24 (1916): 32.

61. Carter, "The Tupelo Campaign," 99.

62. Ibid., 99–100.

63. *OR*, vol. 39, pt. 1:272; Carter, "The Tupelo Campaign," 100.

64. *OR*, vol. 39, pt. 1:272.

15. "Endurance Had Reached a Limit"

1. *OR*, vol. 39, pt. 1:331, 334, 347; Wyeth, *That Devil Forrest*, 391.

2. *OR*, vol. 39, pt. 1:347; Morton, *The Artillery of Nathan Bedford Forrest's Cavalry*, 209.

3. Hancock, *Hancock's Diary*, 424. The eloquence of Hancock's memoirs, written twenty-two years after the war, still managed to convey his own terror and anxiety as he heard someone next to him scream out his name. "I found my brother, W. C. Hancock, with his right leg shivered to pieces between the knee and ankle by a cannon ball." Hancock put a tourniquet on his brother, took him to the field hospital, and sat with him under the trees while waiting for a surgeon.

4. Hager, "Second Tennessee Cavalry," 618–19; *OR*, vol. 39, pt. 1:335.

5. Morton, *The Artillery of Nathan Bedford Forrest's Cavalry*, 209; Henry, *First with the Most*, 323; Reid, "Morton's Battery," 854.

6. Jordan and Pryor, *The Campaigns of Lieut.-Gen. N. B. Forrest*, 510; Henry, *First with the Most*, 323; Stinson, "Hot Work in Mississippi," 6.

7. *OR*, vol. 39, pt. 1:270; Carter, "The Tupelo Campaign," 100; Genoways, *A Perfect Picture of Hell*, 227; Reed, *Campaigns and Battles of the Twelfth Regiment Iowa Veteran Volunteer Infantry*, 156.

8. *OR*, vol. 39, pt. 1:326; George, *History of the 3d, 7th, 8th and 12th Kentucky C.S.A.*, 100.

9. *OR*, vol. 39, pt. 1:326.

10. This last reply of Forrest's appears in the hand-annotated draft written by Lee found in the Mississippi Department of Archives and History, but it was edited out of the final draft released in the *Publications of the Mississippi Historical Society*.

11. Lee, draft manuscript, "The Battle of Tupelo, or Harrisburg, July 14th, 1864," pp. 8–9, Mississippi Department of Archives and History; *OR*, vol. 39, pt. 1:322.

12. Lee, "The Battle of Tupelo, or Harrisburg, July 14th, 1864," 10.

13. *OR*, vol. 39, pt. 1:257, 326; Young, *The Seventh Tennessee Cavalry*, 115; Mississippi, Pontotoc County, p. 174, U.S. Federal Census, 1860, National Archives and Record Administration.

14. John Somerville to Mrs. Augustine Claiborne, July 20, 1864, *Records of East Tennessee*; Wyeth, *That Devil Forrest*, 395; Jordan and Pryor, *The Campaigns of Lieut.-Gen. N. B. Forrest*, 511.

15. *OR*, vol. 39, pt. 1:326; Jordan and Pryor, *The Campaigns of Lieut.-Gen. N. B. Forrest*, 511; Young, *The Seventh Tennessee Cavalry*, 98.

16. Jordan and Pryor, *The Campaigns of Lieut.-Gen. N. B. Forrest*, 511.

17. *OR*, vol. 39, pt. 1:326.

18. *OR*, vol. 39, pt. 1:252, 257, 259, 264, 326; Jordan and Pryor, *The Campaigns of Lieut.-Gen. N. B. Forrest*, 511, Young, *The Seventh Tennessee Cavalry*, 98; Mattie Morrow to "Billie & Jimmie," July 14 [15], 1864, Mississippi State University Libraries; Record Group 109, roll 0037, National Archives and Record Administration.

19. *OR*, vol. 39, pt. 1:259, 264; Minnesota Board of Commissioners, *Minnesota in the Civil and Indian Wars* 1861–1865, 463–64.

20. Minnesota Board of Commissioners, *Minnesota in the Civil and Indian Wars* 1861–1865, 464; *OR*, vol. 39, pt. 1:264; Henry McConnel to "My Dear Wife," July 23, 1864, Henry S. McConnel Letters, Civil War Times Illustrated Collection, U.S. Army Heritage and Education Center; George Carter to "My Dear Brother Bill," July 23, 1864, George B. Carter Letters, Wisconsin Historical Society.

21. Young, *The Seventh Tennessee Cavalry*, 98; John Somerville to Mrs. Augustine Claiborne, July 20, 1864, *Records of East Tennessee*.

22. Hubbard, *Notes of a Private*, 115; Jordan and Pryor, *The Campaigns of Lieut.-Gen. N. B. Forrest*, 511; Young, *The Seventh Tennessee Cavalry*, 90; John Somerville to Mrs. Augustine Claiborne, July 20, 1864, *Records of East Tennessee*; Hager, "Second Tennessee Cavalry," 650.

23. *OR*, vol. 39, pt. 1:322, 326; Hubbard, *Notes of a Private*, 115, 117; Jordan and Pryor, *The Campaigns of Lieut.-Gen. N. B. Forrest*, 511.

24. *OR*, vol. 39, pt. 1:252, 270; Carter, "The Tupelo Campaign," 100; July 14, 1864, John Danielson Diary, Minnesota Historical Society; George Carter to "My Dear Brother Bill," July 23, 1864.

25. *OR*, vol. 39, pt. 1:268, 272, 274.

26. Ibid., 266; July 14, 1864, John M. Williams Diary, Wisconsin Historical Society.

27. "Richard Abner Jarvis," *Confederate Veteran Magazine* 27 (1919): 28; *OR*, vol. 39, pt. 1:274.

28. *OR*, vol. 39, pt. 1:267.

29. Ibid., 257; Genoways, *A Perfect Picture of Hell*, 227.

30. *OR*, vol. 39, pt. 1:257–58, 273; Reed, *Campaigns and Battles of the Twelfth Regiment Iowa Veteran Volunteer Infantry*, 156.

31. *OR*, vol. 39, pt. 1:322; Jordan and Pryor, *The Campaigns of Lieut.-Gen. N. B. Forrest*, 512; Hancock, *Hancock's Diary*, 428.

32. *OR*, vol. 39, pt. 1:322–23; Jordan and Pryor, *The Campaigns of Lieut.-Gen. N. B. Forrest*, 512; Lee, "The Battle of Tupelo, or Harrisburg, July 14th, 1864," 11.

33. *OR*, vol. 39, pt. 1:351.

34. Ibid., 336, 340, 343.

35. Ibid., 252–53, 271; Reed, *Campaigns and Battles of the Twelfth Regiment Iowa Veteran Volunteer Infantry*, 320.

36. Tucker, *The Fourteenth Wisconsin Vet. Vol. Infantry*, 14; Elijah Edwards Journal, p. 23, Minnesota Historical Society; *Los Angeles Herald*, May 31, 1909.

37. July 14, 1864, Ezra Fish Diary, Abraham Lincoln Presidential Library and Museum; James Harrison to "Dear Bro. Vane," July 28, 1864, Wisconsin Historical Society;

Phillips, *Some Things Our Boy Saw During the War*, 46; July 14, 1864, Harrison T. Chandler Diary, Abraham Lincoln Presidential Library and Museum; *OR*, vol. 39, pt. 2:666. This misperception that Smith's army was made up of inferior troops originated with Forrest himself in late June when he wrote, "Most of their force consists of 100-days men—at any rate a large number of that character have arrived at Memphis."

38. Carter, "The Tupelo Campaign," 101.

39. *OR*, vol. 39, pt. 1:271, 273, 277.

40. Ibid., 284.

41. Sidney Robinson to "Dear Mother," July 26, 1864, Abraham Lincoln Presidential Library and Museum.

42. July 14, 1864, Stephen H. Smith Diary, Anders Collection, U.S. Army Heritage and Education Center; July 14, 1864, Allen Higgins Diary, Door County Library; July 14, 1864, Ibbetson, "William H. H. Ibbetson Diary"; July 14, 1864, William P. Mallonee Diary, William P. Mallonee Family Materials, Indiana Historical Society; July 14, 1864, Charles H. Tiedman Diary, U.S. Army Heritage and Education Center; *OR*, vol. 39, pt. 1:253; M319, Record Group 109, roll 0062.

43. Edwards Journal, 23.

44. Edwards Journal, 24; Otto Wolf to "Dear Parents," July 26, 1864, in Wolf, "Letters from an Illinois Drummer Boy."

45. Reminiscences of Aurelius T. Bartlett, p. 28, Missouri History Museum.

46. Edwards Journal, 23.

16. "Who Will Care for Mother Now?"

1. Henry, *First with the Most*, 324; Hancock, *Hancock's Diary*, 428; Gentry, *The Battle of Harrisburg (Tupelo)*, 15; Slonaker, *The Battle of Tupelo*, 27; Jordan and Pryor, *The Campaigns of Lieut.-Gen. N. B. Forrest*, 512; Wyeth, *That Devil Forrest*, 396.

2. Jordan and Pryor, *The Campaigns of Lieut.-Gen. N. B. Forrest*, 506; July 6–12, 1864, William T. Mumford Diary, Museum of Mobile; Marshall Polk to "My Dearest Wife," July 12, 1864, Marshall Tate Polk Family Papers, Tennessee State Library and Archives; *OR*, vol. 39, pt. 1:350–51.

3. Wills, "Brig. Gen. Hylan Benton Lyon," 180–83.

4. Jordan and Pryor, *The Campaigns of Lieut.-Gen. N. B. Forrest*, 506; Hancock, *Hancock's Diary*, 421.

5. Jordan and Pryor, *The Campaigns of Lieut.-Gen. N. B. Forrest*, 572; Lytle, *Bedford Forrest and His Critter Company*, 314; Gentry, *The Battle of Harrisburg (Tupelo)*, 19; *Tupelo–Lee County Tribune*, Jan. 16, 1953. Willie was serving as the general's aide, and while the staff officers were busy rallying the men, a shell burst directly over his head, the concussion throwing him from his horse.

6. *OR*, vol. 39, pt. 1:322–23, 331.

7. Hancock, *Hancock's Diary*, 424–25.

8. John Somerville to Mrs. Augustine Claiborne, July 20, 1864, *Records of East Tennessee*.

9. Daniel Farrar to Mrs. Cato, July 17, 1864, John A. Cato Letters, Anders Collection, U.S. Army Heritage and Education Center.

10. Hancock, *Hancock's Diary*, 592; Pou, "How Young Tupelo Got an Old Battle."

11. *OR*, vol. 39, pt. 1:283. Another structure consigned to the flames was the Gardner home on the north side of the road across from the church. The Gardner family, one of the few still living in Harrisburg, had fled south in an oxcart before the battle. As it turned out, Edwin Gardner of the 4th Mississippi, Mabry's Brigade, had charged and retreated within sight of his father's home; later he passed by and saw the house had been reduced to ashes. Near the end of the morning's fighting, McCulloch's brigade advanced in support of Buford's retreating troops and crossed over the Gardner farm. Pvt. Franklin P. Gardner of the 1st Mississippi Partisan Rangers was moving past a large tree just as it was struck by a shell. The round buried itself deep in the three-foot-diameter trunk and showered Gardner with bark. He was luckier than his comrades on either side, who were knocked off their feet by the impact. Years later, at a Confederate reunion, Gardner posed for a picture next to that scarred tree.

12. *OR*, vol. 39, pt. 1:327; Gardner, "Autobiography," Davidson-Giles-Shelby County Archives. Gardner photograph, box 267, folder 2, Menhel Collection, Mississippi Department of Archives and History.

13. *OR*, vol. 39, pt. 1:310, 327.

14. Ibid., 323.

15. Ibid.; chap. 49, William Pirtle Memoirs, Filson Historical Society.

16. *OR*, vol. 39, pt. 1:309; July 14, 1864, Erastus W. Bennett Diary, Boone County Historical Society.

17. *OR*, vol. 39, pt. 1:304, 317.

18. Ibid., 345.

19. Ibid., 306.

20. Ibid.

21. Ibid., 345.

22. Ibid., 252, 306; July 14, 1864, Lot Abraham Diary, University of Iowa Libraries; Grierson, *A Just and Righteous Cause*, 266.

23. *OR*, vol. 39, pt. 1:306, 310; July 14, 1864, John W. Noble Diary, Iowa Historical Society.

24. July 14, 1864, Simon P. Duck Diary, Harrisburg Civil War Round Table Collection, U.S. Army Heritage and Education Center; July 14, 1864, J. C. Leach Diary, Davis County Iowa Genweb.

25. *OR*, vol. 39, pt. 1:310; Gantz, *Such Are the Trials*, 65.

26. *OR*, vol. 39, pt. 1:286; Thomas and McCann, *Soldier Life*, 101.

27. *OR*, vol. 39, pt. 1:252.

28. July 14, 1864, John M. Keltner Diary, U.S. Army Heritage and Education Center; *OR*, vol. 39, pt. 1:286, 289, 291–92.

29. *OR*, vol. 39, pt. 1:323.

30. Ibid., 323; Bearss, *The Tupelo Campaign*, 123; July 14, 1864, Stephen H. Smith Diary, U.S, Army Heritage and Education Center; July 14, 1864, Charles H. Tiedman Diary, U.S. Army Heritage and Education Center.

31. Church and Chappel, *History of Buchanan County Iowa*, 205, 206; Young, *The Seventh Tennessee Cavalry*, 99.

32. *OR*, vol. 39, pt. 1:295, 297; Gerling, *The One Hundred Seventeenth Illinois Infantry Volunteers*, 80; Thomas and McCann, *Soldier Life*, 101. The 117th Illinois was known

as the McKendree Regiment, since a great number of the rank and file were alumni of McKendree University in Lebanon, IL. The commanding officer of the unit, thirty-seven-year-old Col. Risdon Moore, was a professor of mathematics and astronomy. Why Sergeant Saunders referred to the 117th as the "Sunday School Regiment" is unknown.

33. Otto Wolfe to parents, July 26, 1864, in Wolfe, "Letters from an Illinois Drummer Boy," 155; *OR*, vol. 39, pt. 1:323.

34. Sidney Robinson to "Dear Mother," July 26, 1864, Abraham Lincoln Presidential Library and Museum; Thomas and McCann, *Soldier Life*, 101.

35. Jordan and Pryor, *The Campaigns of Lieut.-Gen. N. B. Forrest*, 513.

36. Elijah Edwards Journal, p. 24, Minnesota Historical Society.

37. Lytle, *Bedford Forrest and His Critter Company*, 315; Hurst, *Nathan Bedford Forrest*, 207; Davison and Foxx *Nathan Bedford Forrest*, 297; *Tupelo–Lee County Tribune*, Jan. 16, 1953.

38. *OR*, vol. 39, pt. 1:323, 331; Lee, draft manuscript, "The Battle of Tupelo, or Harrisburg, July 14th, 1864," p. 11, Mississippi Department of Archives and History.

39. *OR*, vol. 39, pt. 1:252.

17. The Federal Withdrawal

1. *OR*, vol. 34, pt. 3:154.

2. *OR*, vol. 39, pt. 1:252.

3. Wyeth, *That Devil Forrest*, 399; Jordan and Pryor, *The Campaigns of Lieut.-Gen. N. B. Forrest*, 518.

4. Slonaker, *The Battle of Tupelo*, 30. In response to Mr. Slonaker's query, "What would Forrest have done with such a paltry supply? Invade Ohio?": Forrest had captured all of Sturgis's ready and reserve ammunition at Brice's Crossroads. Combined with his own supply of ammunition, he most likely had a larger reserve of artillery ammunition than did his Federal counterpart.

5. *OR*, vol. 39, pt. 2:160; French et al., *Instruction for Field Artillery*, 5. As an example of the amount of artillery ammunition consumed during the battle, Lt. Richard Burns's 3rd Indiana Battery fired "near 500 rounds" of ammunition during the battle. If his four-gun battery was down to 100 rounds for each weapon after using 125 rounds per gun, it is obvious that he did not start the campaign with the required 400 rounds. *OR*, vol. 39, pt. 1:294.

6. *OR*, vol. 39, pt. 1:252; Reed, *Campaigns and Battles of the Twelfth Regiment Iowa Veteran Volunteer Infantry*, 159; Reminiscences of Aurelius T. Bartlett, p. 29, Missouri History Museum.

7. July 14 [15], 1864, John Danielson Diary, Minnesota Historical Society.

8. Reminiscences of Aurelius T. Bartlett, 29; *OR*, vol. 39, pt. 1:253.

9. *OR*, vol. 39, pt. 1:252–53; Lee, draft manuscript, "The Battle of Tupelo, or Harrisburg, July 14th, 1864," p. 11, Mississippi Department of Archives and History; Thomas and McCann, *Soldier Life*, 101.

10. *OR*, vol. 39, pt. 1:306; Gantz, *Such Are the Trials*, 76; July 15, 1864, Lot Abraham Diary, University of Iowa Libraries; July 15, 1864, Simon P. Duck Diary, Harrisburg

Civil War Round Table Collection, U.S. Army Heritage and Education Center; Carter, "The Tupelo Campaign," 102.

11. *OR*, vol. 39, pt. 1:281, 316.

12. Ibid., 262–64, 266, 267, 269, 270.

13. Ibid., 331, 347, 350.

14. Ibid., 331, 350, 351.

15. Ibid., 327, 351.

16. Ibid., 253; July 15, 1864, Fletcher Pomeroy, David Habura Private Collection.

17. *OR*, vol. 39, pt. 1:306, 310, 314; *Roster and Record of Iowa Soldiers in the War of the Rebellion*, 651; July 15, 1864, Abraham Diary; Scott, *The Story of a Cavalry Regiment*, 289; July 15, 1864, John W. Noble Diary, Iowa Historical Society.

18. *OR*, vol. 39, pt. 1:351.

19. Ibid., 306, 310, 314.

20. Ibid., 258, 269.

21. Carter, "Reply to 'Experiences at Harrisburg,'" 310; *OR*, vol. 39, pt. 1:266, 270.

22. *OR*, vol. 39, pt. 1:269; Carter, "The Tupelo Campaign," 102–3; introductory notes by Theodore Carter, Elijah Edwards Journal, p. 2, Minnesota Historical Society.

23. Edwards Journal, 26.

24. Edwards Journal, 5n, 26; Carter, "The Tupelo Campaign," 104.

25. *OR*, vol. 39, pt. 1:263, 271, 351.

26. Ibid., 275; Philips, *Some Things Our Boy Saw During the War*, 47.

27. *OR*, vol. 39, pt. 1:263; Record Group 94, roll 472, National Archives and Records Administration; McCall, *Three Years in the Service*, 39; Treadway, "The Letters of Charles Wesley Treadway," 144.

28. *OR*, vol. 39, pt. 1:275, 351.

29. Edwards Journal, 26.

30. *OR*, vol. 39, pt. 1:266, 267, 269, 273, 275.

31. Ibid., 271; Henry McConnel to "My Dear Wife," July 23, 1864, Henry S. McConnel Letters, Civil War Times Illustrated Collection, U.S. Army Heritage and Education Center.

32. *OR*, vol. 39, pt. 1:331; chap. 50, William Pirtle Memoirs, Filson Historical Society.

33. *OR*, vol. 39, pt. 1:337; chap. 50, Pirtle Memoirs; Wyeth, *That Devil Forrest*, 397.

34. *OR*, vol. 39, pt. 1:262, 203, 316–17.

35. Ibid., 262; chap. 50, Pirtle Memoirs.

36. There were no Union earthworks on this part of the field, other than a small breastwork constructed the previous day by the 9th Illinois Cavalry, which was farther to the east and not used in the engagement.

37. *OR*, vol. 39, pt. 1:303; Cowden, *A Brief Sketch of the Organization and Services of the Fifty-Ninth Regiment of United States Colored Infantry*, 130.

38. *OR*, vol. 39, pt. 1:262, 303, 316, 317.

39. Ibid., 253, 303; Burns, *Recollections of the 4th Missouri Cavalry*, 136.

40. Chap. 50, Pirtle Memoirs.

41. *OR*, vol. 39, pt. 1:323, 331, 332, 338; chap. 50, Pirtle Memoirs.

42. *OR*, vol. 39, pt. 1:317.

43. Ibid., 316–17.

44. Ibid., 317; Davenport, *History of the Ninth Regiment Illinois Cavalry Volunteers*, 121.

45. Davenport, *History of the Ninth Regiment Illinois Cavalry Volunteers*, 122.

46. Ibid., 122.

47. *OR*, vol. 39, pt. 1:261, 263, 278.

18. Old Town Creek

1. *OR*, vol. 39, pt. 1:258, 327; Lee, draft manuscript, "The Battle of Tupelo, or Harrisburg, July 14th, 1864," p. 11, Mississippi Department of Archives and History.

2. *OR*, vol. 39, pt. 1:323, 327.

3. Ibid., 323.

4. Ibid., 317, 329.

5. Lee, "The Battle of Tupelo, or Harrisburg, July 14th, 1864," 11; *OR*, vol. 39, pt. 1:323; Henry, *First with the Most*, 317; Hurst, *Nathan Bedford Forrest*, 203.

6. *OR*, vol. 39, pt. 1:323, 327, 332; Lee, "The Battle of Tupelo, or Harrisburg, July 14th, 1864," 11.

7. *OR*, vol. 39, pt. 1:348; Jordan and Pryor, *The Campaigns of Lieut.-Gen. N. B. Forrest*, 515; Hancock, *Hancock's Diary*, 432; Hager, "Second Tennessee Cavalry," 867.

8. *OR*, vol. 39, pt. 1:323; Jordan and Pryor, *The Campaigns of Lieut.-Gen. N. B. Forrest*, 506, 515.

9. *Southern Sentinel*, May 7, 1941; Record Group 109, rolls 0035 and 0120, National Archives and Records Administration; United States Census, 1860.

10. *OR*, vol. 39, pt. 1:287; Scott, *Story of the Thirty Second Iowa Infantry Volunteers*, 293; Thomas and McCann, *Soldier Life*, 101.

11. *OR*, vol. 39, pt. 1:304; Grierson, *A Just and Righteous Cause*, 269; Thomas and McCann, *Soldier Life*, 101.

12. Thomas and McCann, *Soldier Life*, 101.

13. Scott, *Story of the Thirty Second Iowa Infantry Volunteers*, 293; Thomas and McCann, *Soldier Life*, 101; Gerald Creely, interview with the author, Jan. 14, 2011.

14. *OR*, vol. 39, pt. 1:263, 304.

15. Ibid., 306, 310, 314.

16. Ibid., 332; July 15, 1864, Simon P. Duck Diary, Harrisburg Civil War Round Table Collection, U.S. Army Heritage and Education Center,.

17. July 15, 1864, Duck Diary; Grierson, *A Just and Righteous Cause*, 269.

18. Jordan and Pryor, *The Campaigns of Lieut.-Gen. N. B. Forrest*, 515.

19. *OR*, vol. 39, pt. 1:304–5, 310; Grierson, *A Just and Righteous Cause*, 269.

20. *OR*, vol. 39, pt. 1:253, 258, 305, 310; Burns, *Recollections of the 4th Missouri Cavalry*, 136.

21. *OR*, vol. 39, pt. 1:348; July 15, 1864, Duck Diary.

22. Hubbard, *Notes of a Private*, 117.

23. July 15, 1864, Harrison T. Chandler Diary, Abraham Lincoln Presidential Library and Museum; July 15, 1864, Stephen H. Smith Diary, U.S. Army Heritage and Education Center.

24. Rolfe, *A Civil War Soldier Describes His Army Life*, 17–18, 119.

25. George Carter to "My Dear Brother Bill," July 23, 1864, George B. Carter Letters, Wisconsin Historical Society; Genoways, *A Perfect Picture of Hell*, 228.

26. *OR*, vol. 39, pt. 1:310.

27. Ibid., 260, 263.

28. Ibid., 277; George Carter to "My Dear Brother Bill," July 23, 1864.

29. *OR*, vol. 39, pt. 1:277, 287; Rolfe, *A Civil War Soldier Describes His Army Life*, 119.

30. Thomas and McCann, *Soldier Life*, 101–2.

31. *OR*, vol. 39, pt. 1: 279; Jordan and Pryor, *The Campaigns of Lieut.-Gen. N. B. Forrest*, 515; Haller, "Rice's Battery," 868; Hord, "Personal Experiences at Harrisburg, Miss.," 363.

32. *OR*, vol. 39, pt. 1:332, 337.

33. Ibid., 287, 289, 290.

34. Ibid., 261, 332; Jordan and Pryor, *The Campaigns of Lieut.-Gen. N. B. Forrest*, 515; Hancock, *Hancock's Diary*, 432–33.

35. *OR*, vol. 39, pt. 1:340; Jordan and Pryor, *The Campaigns of Lieut.-Gen. N. B. Forrest*, 515; Hancock, *Hancock's Diary*, 432–33; Haller, "Rice's Battery," 868.

36. Thomas and McCann, *Soldier Life*, 102; William Donnan to "My Dear Wife," July 21, 1864, William Donnan Letters, Iowa Historical Society; Church and Chappel, *History of Buchanan County Iowa*, 205–6.

37. *OR*, vol. 39, pt. 1:287; Thomas and McCann, *Soldier Life*, 102; *Southern Sentinel*, May 7, 1941.

38. *OR*, vol. 39, pt. 1:287, 332, 338; Thomas and McCann, *Soldier Life*, 102.

39. *OR*, vol. 39, pt. 1:337, 338, 341.

40. Ibid., 323, 327.

41. Ibid., 327; Wyeth, *That Devil Forrest*, 327.

42. Mathes, *General Forrest*, 261.

43. *Tennesseans in the Civil War*, 55.

44. *Southern Sentinel*, May 7, 1941.

45. Hord, "Personal Experiences at Harrisburg, Miss," 363.

46. *OR*, vol. 39, pt. 1:286, 296.

47. Ibid., 323–24, 327.

48. *Southern Sentinel*, May 7, 1941.

49. *OR*, vol. 39, pt. 1:324. Hurst, *Nathan Bedford Forrest*, 208; Davison and Fox, *Nathan Bedford Forrest, In Search of the Enigma*, 300; George Carter to "My Dear Brother Bill," July 23, 1864; Hancock, *Hancock's Diary*, 433; "James B. McNeely, Company E, 7th Kentucky," in Fulton County Genealogical Society, *Fulton Genealogical Journal*.

50. *OR*, vol. 39, pt. 1:327.

51. Ibid., 261, 263, 311; July 15, 1864, John W. Noble Diary, Iowa Historical Society; Scott, *Story of the Thirty Second Iowa Infantry Volunteers*, 290; Gantz, *Such Are the Trials*, 65.

52. *OR*, vol. 39, pt. 1:327.

19. Return to Memphis

1. *OR*, vol. 39, pt. 1:327; Jordan and Pryor, *The Campaigns of Lieut.-Gen. N. B. Forrest*, 327.

2. Davison and Foxx, *Nathan Bedford Forrest*, 300; Wyeth, *That Devil Forrest*, 398; Compiled Service Records of Confederates Who Served in Organizations from the State of Tennessee, Record Group 109, National Archives and Record Administration.

3. *OR*, vol. 39, pt. 1:324, 327.

4. Ibid., 324, 327, 328; Lee, draft manuscript, "The Battle of Tupelo, or Harrisburg, July 14th, 1864," p. 12, Mississippi Department of Archives and History.

5. *OR*, vol. 39, pt. 1:329, 335; Dinkins, *Personal Recollections and Experiences in the Confederate Army* 169; Hancock, *Hancock's Diary*, 435.

6. *OR*, vol. 39, pt. 1:281, 287, 289.

7. Ibid., 258, 263, 281, 287; July 15, 1864, Stephen H. Smith Diary, U.S. Army Heritage and Education Center.

8. Sweeny, "Nursing a Wounded Brother."

9. *Southern Sentinel*, May 7, 1914.

10. July 15, 1864, Harrison T. Chandler Diary, Abraham Lincoln Presidential Library and Museum.

11. July 15, 1864, Ebenezer B. Mattock Diary, Minnesota Historical Society; Ebenezer Mattock to "My Dear Sister," July 26, 1864, Ebenezer Brewer Mattocks and Family Papers, Minnesota Historical Society.

12. Hucke, *The Civil War Diary of Louis Huch/Hucke*, 8; Thomas and McCann, *Soldier Life*, 102.

13. Thomas and McCann, *Soldier Life*, 102; Talbert, *Civil War Letters*, 47; Carter, "The Tupelo Campaign," 104; July 16, 1864, Fletcher Pomeroy Diary, David Habura Private Collection; July 16, 1864, William Truman Diary, J. Riggs Collection, U.S. Army Heritage and Education Center; July 16, 1864, Charles H. Tiedman Diary, U.S. Army Heritage and Education Center; Carter, "Reply to 'Experiences at Harrisburg,'" 310.

14. *OR*, vol. 39, pt. 2:717–19; July 17, 1864, Belle Edmondson Diary, Southern Historical Collection, University of North Carolina, Chapel Hill.

15. *OR*, vol. 39, pt. 1:328; Jordan and Pryor, *The Campaigns of Lieut.-Gen. N. B. Forrest*, 517.

16. *OR*, vol. 39, pt. 2:715.

17. Ibid., pt. 1:339, 351; newspaper article, J. L. Power Scrapbook, Mississippi Department of Archives and History; Casualty report, Second Division, M836, Record Group 109.

18. *OR*, vol. 39, pt. 1:324, 332, 335.

19. Ibid., 350; Mabry to Mrs. McCay, July 20, 1864, McCay (R.C.) Papers, Mississippi Department of Archives and History.

20. *OR*, vol. 39, pt. 1:344; Carter, "The Tupelo Campaign," 107; Jordan and Pryor, *The Campaigns of Lieut.-Gen. N. B. Forrest*, 514.

21. *OR*, vol. 39, pt. 1:254–55.

22. Hubbard, *Notes of a Private*, 120.

23. Ibid.; Lytle, *Bedford Forrest and His Critter Company*, 316.

24. Hubbard, *Notes of a Private*, 120.

25. Lytle, *Bedford Forrest and His Critter Company*, 257; Wills, *The Confederacy's Greatest Cavalryman*, 158, 201–2; Henry, *First with the Most*, 215.

26. Chap. 51, William Pirtle Memoirs, Filson Historical Society; Pou, "How Young Tupelo Got an Old Battle"; Hancock, *Hancock's Diary*, 434; Hord, "Her Little Flag," 474; July 18, 1864, Edmondson Diary; "Calhoun Place, p. 33, Historical Research Project, Assignment No. 3, Lee County Library.

27. July 18, 1864, Edmondson Diary; "Calhoun Place," p. 33.

28. July 16, 1864, Harrison T. Chandler Diary, Abraham Lincoln Presidential Library and Museum; Gantz, *Such Are the Trials*, 65; Hucke, *The Civil War Diary of Louis Huch/Hucke*, 9; July 18, 1864, Pomeroy Diary; July 16, 1864, William H. Rogers Diary, Iowa Historical Society; Elijah Edwards Journal, p. 30, Minnesota Historical Society.

29. *OR*, vol. 39, pt. 1:296; *The Union Army*, 380; July 16, 1864, Pomeroy Diary; Hucke, *The Civil War Diary of Louis Huch/Hucke*, 9; July 16, 1864, David King Diary, Indiana Historical Society.

30. July 16, 1864, Ebenezer B. Mattocks Diary, Minnesota Historical Society; July 16, 1864, Ibbetson, "William H. H. Ibbetson Diary"; Edwards Journal, 30; Luther Frost to "Dear Parents," July 22, 1864, Luther and Orville Frost Papers, Abraham Lincoln Presidential Library and Museum; Gantz, *Such Are the Trials*, 65; July 16, 1864, Chandler Diary.

31. Thomas and McCann, *Soldier Life*, 102; Gantz, *Such Are the Trials*, 65–66.

32. Letter No. 9, Fort, 14 *Letters to a Friend*.

33. Jordan and Pryor, *The Campaigns of Lieut.-Gen. N. B. Forrest*, 517; *OR*, vol. 39, pt. 1:270, 328: Grierson, *A Just and Righteous Cause*, 270.

34. *OR*, vol. 39, pt. 1:328.

35. Edwards Journal, 31; July 18, 1864, Tiedman Diary; Thomas and McCann, *Soldier Life*, 103–4; July 20–24, 1864, Chandler Diary; Talbert, *Civil War Letters*, 9; July 20–24, 1864, Ibbetson, "William H. H. Ibbetson Diary."

20. Victory or Defeat?

1. *OR*, vol. 39, pt. 2:172, 178.

2. Ibid., 179, 180.

3. Ibid., 182, 184.

4. Ibid., 185, 197, 204, 205.

5. Lee, draft manuscript, "The Battle of Tupelo, or Harrisburg, July 14th, 1864," p. 13, Mississippi Department of Archives and History; *OR*, vol. 39, pt. 2:370.

6. *OR*, vol. 39, pt. 2:121, 124, 142.

7. Ibid., pt. 1:328–29; Wyeth, *That Devil Forrest*, 399; Jordan and Pryor, *The Campaigns of Lieut.-Gen. N. B. Forrest*, 518.

8. *OR*, vol. 39, pt. 1:328; Jordan and Pryor, *The Campaigns of Lieut.-Gen. N. B. Forrest*, 518; Wyeth, *That Devil Forrest*, 401.

9. Bearss, *The Tupelo Campaign*, 151.

21. A Second Battle

1. Carter, "Reply to 'Experiences at Harrisburg,'" 309.

2. Hord, "Personal Experiences at Harrisburg Miss.," 361–63; Carter, "Reply to 'Experiences at Harrisburg,'" 309.

3. Carter, "Reply to 'Experiences at Harrisburg,'" 309.

4. Ibid.

5. Lee, "The Battle of Tupelo, or Harrisburg, July 14th, 1863," 40; Hattaway, *Stephen Dill Lee*, 191.

6. Anders, *The Twenty-First Missouri* 180; *North Platte Semi-Weekly Tribune*, Oct. 26, 1897.

7. *OR*, vol. 39, pt. 1:323, 331.

8. Ibid., 325; Lee, draft manuscript, "The Battle of Tupelo, or Harrisburg, July 14th, 1864," p. 6, Mississippi Department of Archives and History; Lee, "The War in Mississippi after the Fall of Vicksburg, July 4, 1863," 59.

9. Jordan and Pryor, *The Campaigns of Lieut.-Gen. N. B. Forrest*, 518; Wills, *The Confederacy's Greatest Cavalryman*, 220; Henry, *First with the Most*, 314; Slonaker, *The Battle of Tupelo*, 23.

10. Dennis, "Tupelo," 196.

11. Hord, "Personal Experiences at Harrisburg, Miss.," 361.

12. Carter, "Reply to 'Personal Experiences at Harrisburg, Miss.,'" 309–10.

13. Gentry, *The Battle of Harrisburg (Tupelo)*, 6; July 6–10, 1864, J. C. Leach Diary, Davis County Iowa Gen Web; July 7–10, 1864, William H. Rogers Diary, Iowa Historical Society; Davenport, *History of the Ninth Regiment Illinois Cavalry Volunteers*, 117.

14. Genoways, *A Perfect Picture of Hell*, 226; Sidney Z. Robinson to "Mother," July 26, 1864, Abraham Lincoln Presidential Library and Museum.

15. *OR*, vol. 39, pt. 1:251.

16. Elijah Edwards Journal, p. 17, Minnesota Historical Society; July 13, 1864, Charles H. Tiedman Diary, U.S. Army Heritage and Education Center; July 13, 1864, Johnson M. Paisley Diary, John M. Paisley Papers, Newberry Library; Thomas and McCann, *Soldier Life*, 100; Reed, *Campaigns and Battles of the Twelfth Regiment Iowa Veteran Volunteer Infantry*, 316; Wolf, "Letters from an Illinois Drummer Boy," 154.

17. Porter, "Tennessee," 239.

18. *OR*, vol. 39, pt. 1:321, 326; Chalmers, "Forrest and His Campaigns," 476; *Richmond Times Dispatch*, Aug. 11, 1864; *National Tribune*, Jan. 15, 1903.

19. Gentry, *The Battle of Harrisburg (Tupelo)*, 8; *OR*, vol. 39, pt. 1:321; Wyeth, *That Devil Forrest*, 382; Lytle, *Bedford Forrest and His Critter Company*, 309; Thomas Hawley to "Parents, Brother and Sisters," July 21, 1864, Missouri History Museum.

20. *OR*, vol. 39, pt. 1:321, 326; Reed, "Guntown and Tupelo," 316.

21. *OR*, vol. 39, pt. 1:322–50.

22. Ibid., 322.

23. Ibid., 328, 331, 339–41, 346, 347, 349; "James B. McNeely, Company E, 7th Kentucky," in Fulton County Genealogical Society, *Fulton Genealogical Journal*; *Washington Herald*, July 14, 1914.

24. Reed, *Campaigns and Battles of the Twelfth Iowa Veteran Volunteer Infantry*, 154; Carter, "The Tupelo Campaign," 99; *OR*, vol. 39, pt. 1:270, 282, 296; Adolphus Wolf to parents, July 25, 1864, Adolphus P. Wolf Letters, Civil War Times Illustrated Collection, U.S. Army Heritage and Education Center; July 14, 1864, Tiedman Diary.

25. Henry Hord's fanciful account does claim that the Confederates briefly pierced the Federal line, and there was hand-to-hand fighting within the earthworks: "We planted our flag on Gen. Smith's breastworks, while twenty thousand infantrymen and

eighteen guns fired on our one brigade." Hord, "Personal Experiences at Harrisburg, Miss.," 361–63.

26. Jordan and Pryor, *The Campaigns of Lieut.-Gen. N. B. Forrest*, 505.

27. Hancock, *Hancock's Diary*, 421; Hubbard, *Notes of a Private*, 112; *North Platte Semi-Weekly Tribune*, Oct. 26, 1897.

28. Stinson, "Hot Work in Mississippi," 8; Davison and Foxx, *Nathan Bedford Forrest*, 289; Wills, *The Confederacy's Greatest Cavalryman*, 222; Slonaker, *The Battle of Tupelo*, 17.

29. Chalmers, "Forrest and His Campaigns," 477; *North Platte Semi-Weekly Tribune*, Oct. 26, 1897.

30. Carter, "Reply to 'Experiences at Harrisburg,'" 309–10; Palfrey, *The Antietam and Fredericksburg*, 64–65.

31. *OR*, vol. 39, pt. 1:250; Genoways, *A Perfect Picture of Hell*, 226; *Minnesota in the Civil and Indian Wars*, 356; Burns, *Recollections of the 4th Missouri Cavalry*, 130; Burns, "A. J. Smith's Defeat of Forrest at Tupelo (July 14th, 1864)," 421.

32. Lee, "The Battle of Tupelo, or Harrisburg, July 14th, 1864," 40, 44; Jordan and Pryor, *The Campaigns of Lieut.-Gen. N. B. Forrest*, 498, 506; letter no. 1, in Fulton County Genealogical Society, *Fulton Genealogical Journal*; *OR*, vol. 39, pt. 1:324.

33. Jordan and Pryor, *The Campaigns of Lieut.-Gen. N. B. Forrest*, 506.

34. Wyeth, *That Devil Forrest*, 387; Mathes, *General Forrest*, 257; Lee, "The Battle of Tupelo," 42, 44; Jordan and Pryor, *The Campaigns of Lieut.-Gen. N. B. Forrest*, 506; *OR*, vol. 39, pt. 1:324.

35. *OR*, vol. 39, pt. 1:253–56, 324–25.

36. Thomas Hawley to parents, July 21, 1864; Genoways, *A Perfect Picture of Hell*, 228–29; *Harper's Weekly*, Aug. 6, 1864; *The Press* (Philadelphia), July 25, 1864; *Richmond Times Dispatch*, Aug. 11, 1864.

37. *OR*, vol. 39, pt. 1:253, 344; Jordan and Pryor, *The Campaigns of Lieut.-Gen. N. B. Forrest*, 514.

38. Morton, *The Artillery of Nathan Bedford Forrest's Cavalry*, 212; Hord, "Personal Experiences at Harrisburg, Miss.," 363.

39. Gentry, *The Battle of Harrisburg*, 19; Davison and Foxx, *Nathan Bedford Forrest*, 298, 299; Wills, *The Confederacy's Greatest Cavalryman*, 228.

40. Edwards Journal, 27.

41. Reed, *Campaigns and Battles of the Twelfth Regiment Iowa Veteran Volunteer Infantry*, 159; Reminiscences of Aurelius T. Bartlett, p. 28, Missouri History Museum; *OR*, vol. 39, pt. 2:179; Henry S. McConnell to wife, July 23, 1864, McConnel Letters; July 15, 1864, Bailey O. Bowden Diary, Civil War Times Illustrated Collection, U.S. Army Heritage and Education Center; George Carter to "Brother Bill," July 23, 1864, George B. Carter Letters, Wisconsin Historical Society; Scott, *The Story of a Cavalry Regiment*, 289.

42. Grierson, *A Just and Righteous Cause*, 267; Hooker, "Mississippi," 240.

43. *OR*, vol. 39, pt. 1:323; Chalmers, "Forrest and His Campaigns," 476; Wyeth, *That Devil Forrest*, 401; *Edgefield Advertiser*, July 20, 1864.

44. Hurst, *Nathan Bedford Forrest*, 237; Hattaway, *Stephen Dill Lee*, 194; Slonaker, *The Battle of Tupelo*, 30; Ballard, *The Civil War in Mississippi* 240; Davison and Foxx, *Nathan Bedford Forrest*, 298.

45. *OR*, vol. 39, pt. 1:328.

46. July 19, 1864, John M. Williams Diary, Wisconsin Historical Society.

47. *Richmond Daily Dispatch*, Aug. 11, 1864; *Montgomery Weekly Advertiser*, Aug. 17, 1864.

48. July 9, 1864, *Diary of Judge Orlando Davis*; Carter, "The Tupelo Campaign," 95, 111.

49. Edwards Journal, 10–12.

50. Wyeth, *That Devil Forrest*, 399.

51. Ibid., 386.

52. Lee, "The Battle of Tupelo," 51.

53. Confederate States of America, *Articles of War*, 12–13.

54. Ballard, *The Civil War in Mississippi*, 232, 242; Davison and Foxx, *Nathan Bedford Forrest*, 90–91; Hurst, *Nathan Bedford Forrest*, 209–10.

55. Hattaway, *Stephen Dill Lee*, 189.

56. Lee, "The Battle of Tupelo," 40; Lee to J. F. H. Claiborne, April 22, 1878, J. F. H. Claiborne Papers, Southern Historical Collection, University of North Carolina, Chapel Hill.

57. *Clarion*, Mar. 31, 1886. The errors in Lee's letter include: "Our artillery [drove] off the artillery of the enemy; "Not a gun was fired on the right wing"; "Only one brigade of Buford (Crossland's Kentuckians) was repulsed. The other three were close up to the enemy and doing as gallant fighting as I saw during the war, when ordered to fall back. The enemy were so badly punished by these three brigades, that not a man followed in pursuit, and they leisurely formed in rear of the second line of battle. The next day, the enemy retreated toward Ripley, leaving their wounded and the field in my possession, and was vigorously pursued."

58. Ibid., 1886.

59. Ibid.

60. Lee, "The Battle of Tupelo," 39–52. The errors in Lee's account include: "[Smith's] orders were to find and 'follow Forrest to the death if it cost 10,000 lives and breaks the treasury'" (41); Lee's force consisted of only 7,500, of whom only 6,600 were effectives (42); Smith's advance from Tennessee was slow due to "the utmost caution to prevent surprise" (42); Smith was "driven back" by Confederate forces south of Pontotoc on July 12 (43); on July 13 Rucker "had possession of [Smith's] train," and "destroyed some wagons" (43); on reaching Harrisburg, Smith turned and formed a "double line of battle" (43); on the morning of July 14, the "dismounted men had not yet arrived on the field" (44); Chalmers's Division included Neely's brigade (44, 46, 52); the Confederate force on the field "did not exceed 6,000 or 6,500 men, as against 15,000 of the enemy" (44); the Union concentrated the fire of both divisions on Crossland's brigade (46); the Federal artillery had been "silenced or driven off" during the assault on the 14th (46); the Union "left wing," Moore's division, was not engaged in any fighting in its front (46); there was no Union advance on the 14th, and "he did not move out of his chosen position" (48); at Old Town Creek Buford "stampeded the enemy's cavalry and train" (49); the "enemy left the field and his wounded behind him" (50); Smith's only idea after Pontotoc was "to stand on the defensive and get away from [Lee]" (50); "He never left his lines, but was always on the defensive" (50); "Gen. Smith's superiors were greatly disappointed in the results, and reflected on him" (51).

61. *Commercial Appeal*, Feb. 16, 1902.

62. *Times-Picayune*, Mar. 16, 1902.

63. Morton, *The Artillery of Nathan Bedford Forrest's Cavalry*, 201–15. Examples of Morton's errors include: "[Smith] was told to 'keep after him till recalled' by General Sherman or General Grant" (202); Smith's force was destined for the Black Prairie region (202); Lyon's Division "detained" Smith in Pontotoc (203); General Smith "determined to abandon his attempt to reach Okolona" because of swampy ground and Confederate resistance (203); Forrest and a lieutenant scouted inside the Federal lines at Harrisburg (204); General Forrest learned the position and resources of the enemy in his scout (205); "The morning of July 14 found the enemy strongly intrenched behind breastworks" (205); "They were strongly fortified" (206); "General Forrest, from his knowledge of the enemy's position, deemed an attack unwise and declined the command" (206); "On the 13th of July the Federals had constructed strong works" (206); "Two hundred and fifty Federal prisoners had been abandoned" (212); Morton agrees with Wyeth that Smith "did not dare to advance against his antagonist" (213); Smith did not give reasons for failing to follow up his victory by occupying the Black Prairie region (213); Smith had never actually engaged Forrest because the portion of the line commanded by Forrest "had not fired a single volley" (213).

64. Lipscomb, "General Stephen D. Lee," 21.

65. *OR*, vol. 39, pt. 2:179.

66. Ibid., 182.

67. Ibid., 184.

68. Ibid., 185.

69. Ibid., pt. 5: 194–95.

70. Ibid., pt. 2: 201.

71. Ibid., 204.

72. Lee, "Battle of Tupelo," 50–51; Lytle, *Bedford Forrest and His Critter Company*, 316; Henry, *First with the Most*, 326.

73. Stinson, "Hot Work in Mississippi," 48; Slonaker, *The Battle of Tupelo*, 30; Davison and Foxx, *Nathan Bedford Forrest*, 301; Foote, *The Civil War*, 513; Ballard, *The Civil War in Mississippi*, 242; Sherman, *Memoirs*, 523.

74. Grant, *Personal Memoirs*, 140.

75. *North Platte Semi-Weekly Tribune*, Oct. 26, 1897; Chalmers, "Forrest and His Campaigns," 477.

Bibliography

Manuscript Collections

Abraham Lincoln Bookshop. Chicago
Abraham Lincoln Presidential Library. Springfield, IL
Boone County Historical Society. Boone, IA
Davis County Iowa GenWeb. Bloomfield, IA
Door County Library, Sturgeon Bay, WI
Duke University, Durham, NC
Filson Historical Society, Louisville, KY
Gilder Lehrman Institute of American History, New York, NY
David Habura Private Collection
Indiana Historical Society, Indianapolis
Iowa Historical Society, Des Moines
Dean B. Krafft Private Collection
Lee County Library, Tupelo, MS
Minnesota Historical Society, St. Paul
    Elijah Edwards Journal, with permission of DePauw University Archives
Mississippi Department of Archives and History, Jackson
Mississippi State University Libraries, Starkville
Missouri History Museum, St. Louis
Museum of Mobile, Mobile, AL
National Archives and Record Administration, Washington, DC
Newberry Library, Chicago
Ross County Historical Society, Chillicothe, OH
Tennessee State Library and Archives, Nashville
U.S. Army Heritage and Education Center, Carlisle, PA
    Anders Collection
    Civil War Times Illustrated Collection
    Harrisburg Civil War Round Table Collection

J. Riggs Collection
Vreeland-Warden Collection
U.S. Army War College, Washington, DC
University of Iowa Libraries, Iowa City
University Libraries, University of Memphis
University of North Carolina, Chapel Hill
    Southern Historical Collection
Wisconsin Historical Society, Madison

Newspapers & Magazines

American Presbyterian (Philadelphia)
Brownsville Democrat (Brownsville, TN)
Clarion (Jackson, MS)
Cleveland Morning Leader (Cleveland)
Daily Evening Bulletin (Philadelphia)
Edgefield Advertiser (Edgefield, SC)
Harper's Weekly
Los Angeles Herald
Montgomery Weekly Advertiser (Montgomery, AL)
National Tribune (Washington, DC)
New Albany Gazette (New Albany, MS)
New York Times
North Platte Semi-Weekly Tribune (North Platte, NE)
Pennsylvania Daily Telegraph (Harrisburg)
Press (Philadelphia)
Richmond Daily Dispatch (Richmond, VA)
Southern Sentinel (Ripley, MS)
Sun (New York)
Times-Picayune (New Orleans)
Tomahawk (White Earth, MN)
Tupelo Daily Journal (Tupelo, MS)
Tupelo–Lee County Tribune (Tupelo, MS)
Washington Herald (Washington, DC)
Woodville Republican (Woodville, MS)

Published Sources

"Abram Buford." *Confederate Veteran Magazine* 2 (1894).
Agnew, Samuel A. "Battle of Tishomingo Creek." *Confederate Veteran Magazine* 8 (1900).
Allardice, Bruce S., and Lawrence Lee Hewitt, eds. *Kentuckians in Gray: Confederate Generals and Field Officers of the Bluegrass State*. Lexington: University Press of Kentucky, 2008.

Anders, Leslie. *The Twenty-First Missouri: From Home Guard to Union Regiment.* West-
port, CT: Greenwood Press, 1975.

Aughey, John H. *Tupelo.* Lincoln, NE: State Journal Co., 1888.

Ballard, Michael B. *The Battle of Tupelo, Mississippi, July 14 and 15, 1864.* Danville, VA:
Blue and Gray Education Society, 1996.

———. *The Civil War in Mississippi: Major Campaigns and Battles.* Jackson: University
Press of Mississippi for the Mississippi Historical Society and the Mississippi Department of Archives and History, 2011.

Barnitz, Albert, and Jennie Barnitz. *Life in Custer's Cavalry: Diaries and Letters of Albert
and Jennie Barnitz, 1867–1868.* Ed. Robert M. Utley. Lincoln: University of Ne-
braska Press, 1987.

Bearss, Edwin C. *Forrest at Brice's Crossroads and in North Mississippi in 1864.* Dayton,
OH: Morningside Bookshop, 1979.

———. "Forrest Puts the Skeer on the Yankees." *Blue and Gray Magazine* 16, no. 6 (1999).

———. *Protecting Sherman's Lifeline: The Battles of Brice's Cross Roads and Tupelo.* Washington, DC: National Park Service Publications, 1972.

———. *The Tupelo Campaign, June 22–July 23, 1864: A Documented Narrative and Troop
Movement Maps.* Washington, DC: Department of the Interior, 1969.

Bir, Louis. "Remenecence of My Army Life." Ed. George P. Clark. *Indiana Magazine of
History* 101 (March 2005): 15–56.

Black, James A. *A Civil War Diary: January 1, 1862–December 31, 1865.* Bloomington, IN:
Author House, 2008.

Bradley, Michael R. *Nathan Bedford Forrest's Escort and Staff,* Gretna, LA: Pelican, 2006.

Braun, Robert A. "Inventory of Effects: A Brief Examination of the Effects of Deceased
Soldiers from the Thirty-third Wisconsin Volunteer Infantry Regiment." Available
at http://www.33wis.com/articles/pdf/effects.pdf.

———. "Where Is Camargo Crossroads?" Available at http://www.33wis.com/articles/
pdf/xroad.pdf.

Brown, Andrew. *History of Tippah County, Mississippi: The First Century.* Ripley, MS: Tippah County Historical and Genealogical Society, 1998.

Brown, John H, ed. *Lamb's Biographical Dictionary of the United States.* Vol. 5. Boston:
James H. Lamb, 1903.

Bryner, Cloyd. *Bugle Echoes: The Story of Illinois 47th.* Springfield, IL: Cloyd Bryner, 1905.

Burchard, Peter. *One Gallant Rush.* New York: St. Martin's Press, 1965.

Burdette, Robert J. *The Drums of the 47th.* Indianapolis: Bobbs-Merrill, 1914.

Burns, William S. "A. J. Smith's Defeat of Forrest at Tupelo (July 14th, 1864)." In
Battles and Leaders of the Civil War. Vol. 4. Ed. Robert U. Johnson. New York: Castle
Books, 1956.

———. *Recollections of the 4th Missouri Cavalry.* Ed. Frank A. Dennis. Dayton, OH:
Morningside Books, 1988.

Buttolph, John R. *A War Story: Memoirs of the Civil War.* N.p.: Loren D. Buttolph, 1962.

Byers, S. H. M. *Iowa in War Times.* Des Moines, IA: W. D. Condit, 1888.

"Capt. Moses Waddell McKnight." *Confederate Veteran Magazine* 18 (1910).

Carter, Theodore G. "Reply to 'Experiences at Harrisburg.'" *Confederate Veteran Magazine* 14 (1906).

———. "The Tupelo Campaign as Noted by a Line Officer in the Union Army." In

Publications of the Mississippi Historical Society. Vol. 10. Jackson: Mississippi Historical Society, 1909.

Castleberry, D. B. "Lyon's Brigade at Brice's Crossroads." *Confederate Veteran Magazine* 34 (1926).

Chalmers, James R. "Forrest and His Campaigns." In *Southern Historical Society Papers*, Vol. 7: *January to December, 1879*. Wilmington, NC: Broadfoot, 1990.

Chestnut, Mary B. *Mary Chestnut's Civil War.* Ed. C. Vann Woodward. New Haven, CT: Yale University Press, 1981.

Church, Harry, and Joella Chappel. *History of Buchanan County, Iowa, and Its Peoples.* Vol. 1. Chicago: S. J. Clark, 1914.

Churchill, Samuel J. *Genealogy and Biography of the Connecticut Branch of the Churchill Family in America.* Lawrence, KS: Journal Publishing, 1901.

Claiborne, John F. H. *Mississippi as a Province, Territory and State with Biographical Notices of Eminent Citizens.* Jackson, MS: Power & Barksdale, 1880.

Cody, William F. *An Autobiography of Buffalo Bill.* New York: Cosmopolitan, 1920.

"Col. Thomas Ringland Stockdale." *Confederate Veteran Magazine* 7 (1899).

Confederate States of America. *Articles of War for the Government of the Army of the Confederate States.* Montgomery, AL: Barrett, Wimbish, 1861.

Coppock, Paul R., "The Memphis and Charleston Depot." *West Tennessee Historical Society Papers* 21 (1967): 48–59.

Cowan, George I. "Forrest's Escort." In *Military Annals of Tennessee.* Ed. John Berrien Lindsley. Wilmington, NC: Broadfoot, 1995.

Cowden, Robert. *A Brief Sketch of the Organization and Services of the Fifty-Ninth Regiment of United States Colored Infantry, and Biographical Sketches.* Dayton, OH: United Brethren, 1883.

Cozzens, Peter. *The Darkest Days of the War: The Battles of Iuka and Corinth.* Chapel Hill: University of North Carolina Press, 2006.

Cullum, George W. *Biographical Register of the Officers and Graduates of the U.S. Military Academy at West Point, N.Y.* New York: Houghton, Mifflin, 1891.

Davenport, Edward, ed. *History of the Ninth Regiment Illinois Cavalry Volunteers,* Chicago, 1888.

Davis, George B. *The Official Military Atlas of the Civil War.* Fairfax, VA: Fairfax Press, 1993.

Davis, William C., ed. *The Confederate General.* Vol. 1. Washington, DC: National Historical Society, 1992.

Davison, Eddy W., and Daniel Foxx. *Nathan Bedford Forrest: In Search of the Enigma.* Gretna, LA: Pelican, 2007.

Dennis, Frank A. "Tupelo." *The Civil War Battlefield Guide.* Ed. Frances H. Kennedy. Boston: Houghton Mifflin, 1990.

Diary of Judge Orlando Davis. Available at http://www.rootsweb.ancestry.com/~mscivilw/davis.htm.

Dimitry, John. "Louisiana." *Confederate Military History.* Atlanta: Confederate Publishing, 1899.

Dinkins, James. *Personal Recollections and Experiences in the Confederate Army, 1861 to 1865, by an Old Johnnie.* Cincinnati: Robert Clark, 1897.

Driggs, George W. *Opening of the Mississippi: or, Two Years' Campaigning in the Southwest.* Whitefish, MT: Kessinger, 2009.

Duncan, Thomas D. *Recollections of Thomas D. Duncan, a Confederate Soldier.* Nashville: McQuiddy, 1922.

Dyer, Frederick. *Compendium of the Civil War.* Dayton, OH: Morningside Bookshop, 1978.

Dyer, Gustaves W., and John Trotwood Moored, comps. *The Tennessee Civil War Veterans Questionnaires.* Vol. 5. Greenville, SC: Southern Historical Press, 1985.

Dyer, William. *The Civil War Diary of William R. Dyer, a Member of Forrest's Escort.* Ed. Wayne Bradshaw. N.p.: Wayne Bradshaw, 2009.

Ellis, William A. "Major General Joseph Anthony Mower, U.S.A." In *Norwich University 1819–1911: Her History, Her Graduates, Her Roll of Honor.* Vol. 2. Ann Arbor: University of Michigan Library, 1911.

Eng, Robert F., and Corey M. Brooks, eds. *Their Patriotic Duty: The Civil War Letters of the Evans Family of Brown County, Ohio.* New York: Fordham University Press, 2007.

Faust, Patricia, ed. *Historical Times Illustrated Encyclopedia of the Civil War.* New York: Harper & Row, 1986.

Foote, Shelby. *The Civil War: A Narrative.* New York: Vintage Books, 1986.

Forsyth, Michael J. *The Red River Campaign of 1864 and the Loss of the Confederacy of the Civil War.* Jefferson, NC: McFarland, 2002.

Fort, Clinton D. *14 Letters to a Friend.* Edinberg, TX: Laurier B. McDonald, 2007.

Foster, Buck T. *Sherman's Mississippi Campaign.* Tuscaloosa: University of Alabama Press, 2006.

Foster, James. "My Experiences at Guntown and on the Retreat to Memphis in June, 1864." In *The West Tennessee Historical Society Papers.* Vol. 60. Memphis: West Tennessee Historical Society, 2007.

Fowlkes, John A. "Inquiry About Seventh Kansas Cavalry." *Confederate Veteran Magazine* 21 (1913).

Fox, Simeon. *The Early History of the Seventh Kansas Cavalry.* Topeka: Kansas State Historical Society, 1910.

Fulton County Genealogical Society. *Fulton Genealogical Journal.* Fulton, KY: Fulton County Genealogical Society, 1988.

Galbraith, William, and Loretta Galbraith, eds. *A Lost Heroine of the Confederacy: The Diaries and Letters of Belle Edmondson.* Jackson: University Press of Mississippi, 1991.

Gantz, Jacob. *Such Are the Trials: The Civil War Diaries of Jacob Gantz.* Ed. Kathleen Davis. Ames: Iowa State University Press, 1991.

Gardner, A. E. "About the Fight at Harrisburg, Miss." *Confederate Veteran Magazine* 17 (1909).

Gardner, Edwin M. "Autobiography." In *Davidson-Giles-Shelby County, Tennessee Archives, Biographies.* Comp. Joy Fisher. Available at http://files.usgwarchives.net/tn/davidson/bios/gardner265nbs.txt.

Genoways, Ted, and Hugh Genoways, eds. *A Perfect Picture of Hell: Eyewitness Accounts by Civil War Prisoners from the 12th Iowa.* Iowa City: University of Iowa Press, 2001.

Gentry, Claude. *The Battle of Brice's Crossroads.* Baldwyn, MS: Magnolia, 1981.

———. *The Battle of Harrisburg (Tupelo).* Baldwyn, MS: Magnolia, 1981.

George, Henry. *History of the 3d, 7th, 8th and 12th Kentucky C.S.A.* Louisville, KY: Dearing, 1911.

Gerling, Edwin G. *The One Hundred Seventeenth Illinois Infantry Volunteers (The McKendree Regiment) 1862–1865.* Highland, IL: Edward G. Gerling, 1992.

Giambrone, Jeff T. *Beneath Torn and Tattered Flag: A History of the 38th Mississippi Infantry C.S.A.* Bolton, MS: Smokey Row Press, 1998.

Gibson, Charles D. *The Army's Navy Series*, Vol. 2: *Assault and Logistics, Union Army Coastal and River Operations, 1861–1866.* Camden, ME: Ensign Press, 1995.

———. *The Army's Navy Series: Dictionary of Transports and Combatant Vessels, Steam and Sail, Employed by the Union Army, 1861–1868.* Camden, ME: Ensign Press, 1996.

Grant, Ulysses S. *The Papers of Ulysses S. Grant.* 31 vols. Starkville, MS: Ulysses S. Grant Association, 1985.

———. *Personal Memoirs of U. S. Grant.* New York: DaCapo Press, 1982.

Greene, J. H. *Letters to My Wife: A Civil War Diary from the Western Front.* Ed. Sharon L.D. Kraynek. Apollo, PA: Closson Press, 1995.

———. *Reminiscences of the War: Bivouacs, Marches, Skirmishes and Battles.* Medina, OH: Gazette Print, 1886.

Grierson, Benjamin H. *A Just and Righteous Cause: Benjamin H. Grierson's Civil War Memoir.* Ed. Bruce J. Dinges and Shirley A. Leckie. Carbondale: Southern Illinois University Press, 2008.

Hager, George F. "Second Tennessee Cavalry." In *Military Annals of Tennessee.* Ed. John Berrien Lindsley. Wilmington, NC: Broadfoot, 1995.

Haller, B. F. "Rice's Battery." *Military Annals of Tennessee.* Ed. John Berrien Lindsley. Wilmington, NC: Broadfoot, 1995.

Hancock, Harold, ed. *Our Ancestors of the Westerville Area: A Genealogical History.* Westerville, OH: Otterbein College Print Shop/Westerville Historical Society, 1981.

Hancock, Richard R. *Hancock's Diary: or, A History of the Second Tennessee Confederate Cavalry, with Sketches of First and Seventh Battalions; also, Portraits and Biographical Sketches.* Nashville: Brandon, 1887.

Hattaway, Herman M. *General Stephen D. Lee.* Jackson: University Press of Mississippi, 1976.

———. "Stephen Dill Lee: A Biography." Ph.D. dissertation, Louisiana State University and Mechanical College, 1969.

Henry, Robert S. *"First with the Most": Forrest.* Wilmington, NC: Broadfoot, 1987.

History of Lewis, Clark, Knox and Scotland Counties, Missouri. St. Louis: Goodspeed, 1887.

Hollis, Elisha T. "Notes and Documents: The Diary of Captain Elisha Tompkin Hollis, CSA." Ed. William W. Chester. In *West Tennessee Historical Society Papers.* Vol. 39. Memphis: West Tennessee Historical Society, 1985.

Holloway, F. H. "Incidental to the Battle of Harrisburg." *Confederate Veteran Magazine* 18 (1910).

Hooker, Charles E. "Mississippi." *Confederate Military History.* Atlanta: Confederate Publishing, 1899.

Hord, Henry E. "Her Little Flag," *Confederate Veteran Magazine* 23 (1915).

———. "Personal Experiences at Harrisburg, Miss." *Confederate Veteran Magazine* 13 (1905).

Houp, J. Randall. *The 24th Missouri Volunteer Infantry "Lyon Legion."* Little Rock, AR: J & B Quality Book Bindery, 1997.

Howell, Elmo, *Mississippi Home Places: Notes on Literature and History.* Memphis, TN: Howell, 1988.

Hubbard, John M. *Notes of a Private.* Memphis, TN: E. H. Clarke, 1909.

Hubbs, Ronald M. "The Civil War and Alexander Wilkin." *Minnesota History Magazine* 39 (Spring 1965): 173–90.

Hucke, Louis. *The Civil War Diary of Louis Huch/Hucke: A Private in the 117th Regiment of the Illinois Infantry, Captain Robert A. Halbert, February 1864 to July 1865*. Trans. Karl Mandi. Ed. Janet Flynn. Monroe County, IL: Monroe County Genealogical Society, 2001.

Hughes, Nathaniel C. *Brigadier General Tyree H. Bell, C.S.A.: Forrest's Fighting Lieutenant*. Knoxville: University of Tennessee Press, 2004.

Hunt, Roger. *Colonels in Blue: Union Colonels of the Civil War—New York*. Mechanicsburg, PA: Stackpole Books, 2007.

Hurst, Jack. *Nathan Bedford Forrest: A Biography*. New York: Vintage Books, 1994.

Ibbetson, William H. H. "William H. H. Ibbetson Diary." In *Transactions of the Illinois State Historical Society for the Year 1930*. Springfield: Illinois State Historical Society, 1930.

"John A. Snell." *Confederate Veteran Magazine* 24 (1916).

Johnson, Albert S. "Northern Men in the Confederate Army." *Confederate Veteran Magazine* 36 (1928).

Johnson, Bradley E. *A Memoir of the Life and Public Service of Joseph E. Johnston*. Baltimore: R. H. Woodward, 1891.

Johnston, Joseph E. *Narrative of Military Operations, Directed, During the Late War Between the States*. New York: D. Appleton, 1874.

Joiner, Gary D. *One Damn Blunder from Beginning to End: The Red River Campaign of 1864*. Wilmington, DE: Scholarly Resources, 2003.

———. *Through the Howling Wilderness: The 1864 Red River Campaign and Union Failure in the West*. Knoxville: University of Tennessee Press, 2006.

Jordan, Thomas, and J. P. Pryor. *The Campaigns of Lieut.-Gen. N. B. Forrest, and of Forrest's Cavalry, with Portraits, Maps and Illustrations*. New Orleans: Bedlock, 1868.

Kansas Historical Society. *Transactions of the Kansas State Historical Society*. Topeka, KS: W. Y. Morgan, 1902.

Kelley, D. C. "Forrest's (Old) Regiment, Cavalry." In *Military Annals of Tennessee*. Ed. John Berrien Lindsley. Wilmington, NC: Broadfoot, 1995.

Lee, Stephen D. "The Battle of Tupelo, or Harrisburg, July 14th, 1864." In *Publications of the Mississippi Historical Society*. Jackson: Mississippi Historical Society, 1902.

———. "The War in Mississippi after the Fall of Vicksburg, July 4, 1863." In *Publications of the Mississippi Historical Society*. Jackson: Mississippi Historical Society, 1908.

Leftwich, William G. "The Battle of Brice's Cross Roads." *West Tennessee Historical Society Papers* 20 (1966): 5–19.

Lindsley, John Berrien, ed. *The Military Annals of Tennessee: Confederate*. Vol. 2. Wilmington, NC: Broadfoot, 1995.

Lipscomb, Dabney. "General Stephen D. Lee: His Life, Character, and Services." In *Publications of the Mississippi Historical Society*. Jackson: Mississippi Historical Society, 1909.

Logwood, Thomas H. "Fifteenth Tennessee Cavalry." *Military Annals of Tennessee*. Ed. John Berrien Lindsley. Wilmington, NC: Broadfoot, 1995.

Lyon, Hylan B. "Memoirs of Hylan B. Lyon, Brigadier General C.S.A." *Tennessee Historical Quarterly* 38 (March 1959): 35–51.

Lytle, Andrew N. *Bedford Forrest and His Critter Company*. Nashville: J. S. Sanders, 1931.

Martin, George, ed. *Transactions of the Kansas State Historical Society, 1903–1904: Together with Addresses at Annual Meetings, Miscellaneous Papers, and a Roster of Kansas for Fifty Years.* Topeka, KS: George A. Clark, 1904.

Mathes, J. Harvey. *General Forrest.* New York: D. Appleton, 1902.

———. *The Old Guard in Gray.* Memphis, TN: S. C. Toof, 1897.

Maury, Dabney. "Forrest and His Campaigns." In *Southern Historical Society Papers.* Vol. 7. Wilmington, NC: Broadfoot, 1990.

McCall, D. *Three Years in the Service. A Record of the Doings of the 11th Reg. Missouri Vols.* Springfield, MO: Baker & Phillips, 1864.

McNeilly, James H. "With the Rear Guard." *Confederate Veteran Magazine* 26 (1918).

McPherson, James M. *Battle Cry of Freedom: The Civil War Era.* New York: Oxford University Press, 2003.

Miller, John. "From Mount Saint Mary's College Professor to Civil War Hero: Confederate Lt. Colonel Daniel Beltzhhover."Available at http://www.emmitsburg.net/archive_list/articles/history/civil_war/daniel_beltzhoover.htm.

Minnesota Board of Commissioners. *Minnesota in the Civil and Indian Wars 1861–1865.* St. Paul, MN: Pioneer Press, 1890.

Moore, Frank, ed. *The Rebellion Record: A Diary of American Events, with Documents, Narratives, Illustrative Incidents, Poetry, etc.* New York: G. P. Putnam, 1864.

Morton, John W. *The Artillery of Nathan Bedford Forrest's Cavalry: "The Wizard of the Saddle."* Nashville: M. E. Church, South, 1909.

Newton, James K. *A Wisconsin Boy in Dixie: The Selected Letters of James K. Newton.* Ed. Stephen E. Ambrose. Madison: University of Wisconsin Press, 1961.

Newton, Steven H. *Lost for the Cause: The Confederate Army in 1864.* El Dorado Hills, CA: Savas, 2000.

Orton, Richard H. *Records of California Men in the War of the Rebellion 1861 to 1867.* Sacramento, CA: State Printing Office, 1890.

Otey, Mercer. "Story of our Great War." *Confederate Veteran Magazine* 9 (1901).

Owen, Thomas A. *History of Alabama and Dictionary of Alabama Biography.* Chicago: S. J. Clark, 1921.

Palfrey, Francis W. *The Antietam and Fredericksburg,* New York: Scribner's, 1912.

Parson, Thomas E. *Bear Flag and Bay State: The Californians of the Second Massachusetts Cavalry.* Jefferson, NC: McFarland, 2001.

———. "Thwarting Grant's First Drive on Vicksburg: Van Dorn's Holly Springs Raid." *Blue and Gray Magazine* 27, no. 3 (2010).

Perry, Leslie. "Major General Andrew Jackson Smith." *Twenty Seventh Annual Reunion of the Association of Graduates of the United States Military Academy at West Point.* Saginaw, MI: Seeman & Peters, 1896.

Phelps, H. W. "Soldiers Brave in the Civil War." *Our Ancestors of the Westerville Area: A Genealogical History.* Ed. Harold Hancock. Westerville, OH: Otterbein College/Westerville Historical Society, 1981.

Phillips, Lewis. *Some Things Our Boy Saw During the War.* Gravity, IA: L. F. Phillips, 1911.

Pierce, Lyman B. *History of the Second Iowa Cavalry: Containing a Detailed Account of its Organization, Marches, and the Battles in Which It has Participated; Also, a Complete Roster of Each Company.* Burlington, IA: Hawk-Eye, 1865.

Porter, James D. "Tennessee." In *Confederate Military History*. Vol. 8. Atlanta: Confederate Publishing, 1899.

Puryear, G. J. "No Man's Battle." *Confederate Veteran Magazine* 22 (1914).

Records of East Tennessee: Civil War Records. Vol. 2. Nashville, TN: Historical Records Survey, 1939.

Reece, J. N. *Report of the Adjutant General of the State of Illinois*, Vol. 3: *Containing Reports for the Years 1861–66*. Springfield, IL: Phillips Bros., 1901.

Reed, David W. *Campaigns and Battles of the Twelfth Regiment Iowa Veteran Volunteer Infantry, from Organization, September, 1861, to Muster-Out, January 20, 1866*. Salem, MA: Higginson, 1903.

Reed, Joseph R. "Guntown and Tupelo." *War Sketches and Incidents as Related by the Companions of the Iowa Commandery, Military Order of the Loyal Legion of the United States*. Vol. 2. Wilmington, NC: Broadfoot, 1994.

Reid, Frank T. "Morton's Battery." In *Military Annals of Tennessee*. Ed. John Berrien Lindsley. Wilmington, NC: Broadfoot, 1995.

Reid, Whitlaw. *Ohio in the War: Her Statesmen, Generals and Soldiers*. Vol. 1. Cincinnati: Moore, Wilstach & Baldwin, 1868.

Report of the Adjutant General of the State of Indiana. Vol. 3. Indianapolis: State Printing Office, 1866.

"Richard Abner Jarvis." *Confederate Veteran Magazine* 27 (1919).

Richardson, T. M. "Soldiering in Mississippi." *Confederate Veteran Magazine* 23 (1915).

Riley, Franklin L. "Extinct Towns and Villages of Mississippi." *Publications of the Mississippi Historical Society*. Vol. 5. Jackson: Mississippi Historical Society, 1902

Rolfe, Edward. *A Civil War Soldier Describes His Army Life as Three Years of "Hard Marches, Hard Crackers, and Hard Beds, and Pickett Guard in Desolate Country": The Edward Rolfe Civil War Letters and Diaries; The Three Year Adventure of an Iowa Farmer as a Union Soldier in Company F of the 27th Regiment Iowa Infantry Volunteers, August 1862–August 1865; Transcribed and Compiled with Additional Text by Edward Rolfe's Great Grandson Laurance F. Lillibridge*. Prescott Valley, IA: Prescott Valley, 1993.

Roster and Record of Iowa Soldiers in the War of the Rebellion Together with Historical Sketches of Volunteer Organizations 1861–1866. Vol. 5. Des Moines, IA: State Printing Office, 1911.

Rowland, Dunbar. *Military History of Mississippi, 1803–1898: Including a List of All Known Mississippi Confederate Military Units*. Madison, WI: Chickasaw Bayou Press, 2003.

———. *Mississippi, Comprising Sketches of Counties, Towns, Events, Institutions, and Persons, Arranged in Cyclopedic Form*. Atlanta: Southern Historical Publishing Association, 1907.

Satterlee, John L. *The Journal and the 114th*. Springfield, IL: Phillips Brothers, 1979.

Scott, John. *Story of the Thirty Second Iowa Infantry Volunteers*. Nevada, IA: John Scott, 1896.

Scott, William F. *The Story of a Cavalry Regiment: The Career of the Fourth Iowa Veteran Volunteers, from Kansas to Georgia 1861–1865*. New York: G. P. Putnam's Sons, 1893.

Segelquist, Dennis. "Civilian and Military Surname Searcher." Available at http://www. civilwarthosesurnames.blogspot.com.

Shepley, Carol F. *Movers and Shakers, Scalawags and Suffragettes: Tales from Bellefontaine*. St. Louis: Missouri History Museum Press, 2008.

Sherman, William T. *Memoirs of William T. Sherman*. New York: Literary Classics of the United States, 1990.

Sickles, John. "The Second Missouri Cavalry, C.S.A." *Military Images Magazine*, March/ April 2006, 15–17.

Sifakis, Stewart. *Who Was Who in the Civil War*. New York: Facts on File, 1988.

Singletary, Don. "The Battle of Brice's Crossroads." *Confederate Veteran Magazine* 34 (1926).

Slonaker, John J. *The Battle of Tupelo, July 13–15, 1864*. Tupelo, MS: Natchez Trace Parkway, 1968.

Smith, Joel. "The Tupelo Sideshow." Unpublished manuscript. 2011.

Smith, T. W. "Hard Fighting at Harrisburg." *Confederate Veteran Magazine* 19 (1911).

Smith, William Sooy. "The Mississippi Raid." *Military Order of the Loyal Legion of the United States: Illinois*. Vol. 4. Wilmington, NC: Broadfoot, 1907.

Starr, N. D., and T. W. Holman. *The 21st Missouri Regiment Infantry Veteran Volunteers: Historical Memoranda*. Fort Madison, IA: Roberts & Roberts, 1899.

Starr, Stephen Z. *Jennison's Jayhawker's: A Civil War Cavalry Regiment and Its Commander*. Baton Rouge: Louisiana State University Press, 1974.

Stinson, Byron. "Hot Work in Mississippi: The Battle of Tupelo." *Civil War Times Illustrated* (July 1972): 4–48.

Stuart, A. A. *Iowa Colonels and Regiments: Being a History of Iowa Regiments in the War of the Rebellion; and Contains a Description of the Battles in Which They Have Fought*. Des Moines, IA: Mills, 1865.

Sweeny, Joseph H. "Nursed a Wounded Brother." *Annals of Iowa* 3, no. 31 (1952).

Symonds, Craig L. *Joseph E. Johnston: A Civil War Biography*. New York: W. W. Norton, 1992.

Talbert, Harrison. *Civil War Letters*. Ed. Jack C. Hulquist. Lone Jack, MO: Jack C. Hulquist, 1999.

Temple, Oliver P. *East Tennessee in the Civil War*. Johnson City, TN: Overmountain Press, 1995.

Tennesseans in the Civil War: A Military History of Confederate and Union Units with Available Rosters of Personnel. Part 1. Nashville: Civil War Centennial Commission, 1964.

Thomas, Benjamin F., and J. A. McCann, eds. *Soldier Life*. Iowa City, IA: Camp Pope Bookshop, 2008.

Treadway, Charles W. "The Letters of Charles Wesley Treadway." *Quarterly of the Richland County Genealogical and Historical Society* 9 (Summer & Fall 1986).

Tucker, W. H. *The Fourteenth Wisconsin Veterans Volunteer Infantry (General A. J. Smith's Command) in the Expedition and Battle of Tupelo: also, Wanderings Through the Wilds of Missouri and Arkansas in Pursuit of Price*. Indianapolis: W. H. Tucker, 1892.

The Union Army: A History of the Military Affairs in the Loyal States 1861–1865: Records of the Regiments in the Union; Cyclopedia of Battles; Memoirs of Commanders and Soldiers. Madison, WI: Federal, 1908.

U.S. Surgeon General's Office. *The Medical and Surgical History of the Civil War*. Washington, DC: Government Printing Office, 1870.

U.S. War Department. William Henry French, William Farquhar Barry, and Henry Jackson Hunt. *Instruction for Field Artillery*. Philadelphia: J. B. Lippincott, 1860.

War of the Rebellion: A Compilation of the Official Records of the Union and Confederate Armies [*OR*]. 128 vols. Series 1. Washington, DC: Government Printing Office, 1880–1901.

War of the Rebellion: A Compilation of the Official Records of the Union and Confederate Navies [*ORN*]. 30 vols. Series 1. Washington, DC: Government Printing Office, 1897.

Ward, Geoffrey C., Ken Burns, and Ric Burns. *The Civil War: An Illustrated History*. New York: Knopf Doubleday, 1990.

Warner, Ezra. *Generals in Blue: Lives of the Union Commanders*. Baton Rouge: Louisiana State University Press, 2006.

———. *Generals in Gray: Lives of the Confederate Commanders*. Baton Rouge: Louisiana State University Press, 1989.

Weigand, Marie. *The 119th Illinois Infantry Volunteers: A Contribution Toward Its History*. Notre Dame, IN: University of Notre Dame, 1936.

Wheeler, Joseph. "Alabama." *Confederate Military History*. Vol. 7. Atlanta: Confederate Publishing, 1899.

White, Helen M. *Tale of a Comet and Other Stories*. St. Paul: Minnesota Historical Society Press, 1984.

White, John H. "Forgotten Cavalrymen: General Edward Francis Winslow, U.S. Volunteers." *Journal of the United States Cavalry Association* 25 (January 1915): 375–89.

Wiley, Bell. *"This Infernal War": The Confederate Letters of Sgt. Edwin H. Fay*. Austin: University of Texas Press, 1958.

———. *The Life of Billy Yank: The Common Soldier of the Union*. Baton Rouge: Louisiana State University Press, 1979.

Wiley, William. *The Civil War Diary of a Common Soldier: William Wiley of the 77th Illinois Infantry*. Ed. Terrence J. Winschel. Baton Rouge: Louisiana State University Press, 2001.

Williams, John M. *"The Eagle Regiment," 8th Wis. Inf'ty Vols.: A Sketch of Its Marches, Battles and Campaigns from 1861 to 1865*. Belleville, WI: Recorder Print, 1890.

Williams, Richard. *Chicago's Battery Boys: The Chicago Mercantile Battery in the Civil War's Western Theatre*. New York: Savas Beatie, 2005.

Williams, S. E. "The Many Lives of A. J. Smith." Available at http://www.48ovvi.org/oh48ajsmith.html.

Wills, Brian S. *The Confederacy's Greatest Cavalryman: Nathan Bedford Forrest*. Lawrence: University Press of Kansas, 1992.

Wise, Stephen R. *Lifeline of the Confederacy: Blockade Running During the Civil War*. Columbia: University of South Carolina Press, 1989.

Wolf, Otto E. "Letters from an Illinois Drummer Boy." Ed. Robert R. Madden. *Journal of Mississippi History* 26, no. 2 (1964): 152–57.

Wright, Z. N. "Twelfth Kentucky Cavalry." In *The Military Annals of Tennessee: Confederate*. Wyeth, John Allen. *That Devil Forrest: Life of General Nathan Bedford Forrest*. Baton Rouge: Louisiana State University Press, 1908.

Young, Callie B., ed. *From These Hills: A History of Pontotoc County*. Fulton, MS: Itawamba County Times, 1976.

Young, J. P. *The Seventh Tennessee Cavalry (Confederate): A History*. Nashville: House of the M. E. Church, 1890.

Index